TRADITIONS

A Taste of the Good Life

*"How to save the old that's worth saving, whether
in landscapes, houses, manners, institutions or
human types, is one of our greatest problems, and
one that we bother the least about. . ."*

John Galsworthy

Underwritten in part by

Presented By

The Junior League of Little Rock, Incorporated

Publisher of
LITTLE ROCK COOKS
and
APRON STRINGS: Ties to the Southern Tradition of Cooking

Any Inquiries or Orders for Additional Copies should be directed to:
The Junior League of Little Rock, Incorporated
3600 Cantrell Road, Suite 102
Little Rock, Arkansas 72202
P.O. Box 7453
Little Rock, Arkansas 72217
Telephone (501) 666-0658 or FAX (501) 666-0589
www.jllr.org

Proceeds from the sale of *Little Rock Cooks*, *Traditions*, and *Apron Strings* support
the projects and programs of the Junior League of Little Rock, Incorporated.

*The Junior League of Little Rock, Incorporated, is an organization of women committed to
promoting voluntarism, developing the potential of women, and improving the community
through the effective action and leadership of trained volunteers. Its purpose is exclusively
educational and charitable.*

Manufactured in the United States by
Favorite Recipes® Press
an imprint of

FRP

2451 Atrium Way
Nashville, Tennessee 37214

F · O · R · E · W · O · R · D

Cookbooks are history books. They tell us something important about the age and place that produced them. What might we have learned from a detailed cookbook from the time of Aristotle, or Julius Caesar, or Henry VIII? This book is not only a sharing of culinary ideas that have become traditions in our homes in these last days of the 20th Century, it will one day be a valuable source book for historians who want to know something about us in Little Rock. If we are what we eat, as the old adage says, this book should give a good sketch of us. On a more practical level, this book will give to us who are here to use it many pleasant days in the kitchen and at table. That's a great gift.

Richard Allin

ACKNOWLEDGEMENTS

TRADITIONS, A Taste of The Good Life, is a collection of 737 very special recipes that have been tested three times and carefully evaluated. The Cookbook Committee wishes to thank all of the many contributors and testers who have been so supportive during the production of this cookbook.

CHAIRMAN
Ellen Golden

RECIPE CO-CHAIRMAN
Helen Sloan

FORMAT CO-CHAIRMAN
Julie Haught

FINANCE AND MARKETING CHAIRMAN
Cynthia Weber

EDITOR
Cindy Miller

MARKETING ASSISTANTS
Ben Hussman
Loris Mayersohn

ASSOCIATE EDITORS
Nancy Couch
Robin Smith

ADMINISTRATIVE ASSISTANT
Janie Lowe

INDEX EDITOR
Diane Lord

RECIPE COMMITTEE

Julie Allen
Martha Carle
Debbie Coates
Ellon Cockrill
Nancy Couch

Jo Ann Drew
Ben Hussman
Beth Jackson
Diane Lord
Loris Mayersohn
Carole Meyer

Cindy Miller
Beverly Moore
Carol Rasco
Robin Smith
Cynthia Weber

WINE CONSULTANTS
R. E. Hardberger
Tom Baxley

COVER DESIGN AND GRAPHICS
Bruce Wesson, The Art Department, Inc.
COVER PHOTOGRAPH
Willie Allen
Sandy Roberts
Architectural Antiques, Ltd.

FOREWORD
Richard Allin
DIVISION PAGE QUOTATIONS
Paul Thomas
PREFACE TO MENUS
Mary Dee Terry

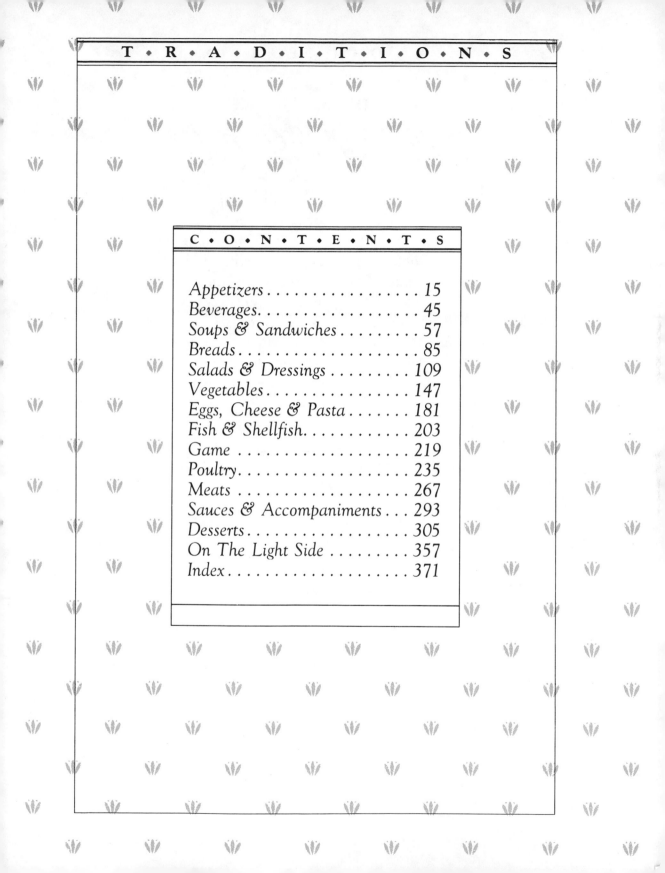

T·R·A·D·I·T·I·O·N·S

C·O·N·T·E·N·T·S

A Taste of the Good Life

There is magic in a successful blend of flavors, flowers and favorite companions. The perfect combination repeated once is a gift, more often than that a tradition. We are a collection of people for whom certain traditions stretch back into time immemorial. But at the same time, we are an upstart nation young enough to create entirely new concepts worthy of becoming traditions. Regardless of category, the carefully planned menus which follow were chosen to help create that magic we all seek to enrich our lives as we enjoy our daily bread. We invite you to share with us "A Taste of the Good Life."

Spring

EASTER BUFFET

Milk Punch
Marion's Cheese Crackers
Roasted Leg of Lamb
Plantation Green Beans
Carrot Soufflé
Cointreau Fruit
Mary's Homemade Rolls

California Cabernet Sauvignon

Coconut Cake

A VERY SPECIAL DINNER

Jacques and Suzanne Escargots
French Bread
Easy Onion Soup
Fresh Mushroom Salad
Brandy Cornish Hens
Easy Raisin Rice

California Fumé Blanc
Robert Mondavi Winery

Hot Lemon Soufflé

DINNER AT EIGHT

Fresh Asparagus Vinaigrette
a la Crème
Souffléed Sole

Pouilly Fuissé

Les Mignons de Veau Au Citron
Basil Cherry Tomatoes
Spinach and Mushroom Roll
French Bread

French Red Bordeaux

*Assorted Cheeses

Tawny Port Wine

Pears with Red Wine Sauce

AFTERNOON TEA AND SHERRY PARTY

Garden Sandwiches
Special Pimiento Cheese Sandwiches
Spinach Sandwiches
Scotch Shortbread
Pecan Cups
Oatmeal Lace Cookies
Lemon Crumb Squares
My Mother's Sour Cream Sugared Nuts
Cream Cheese Mints
Russian Tea

Dry Sack Sherry

BIRTHDAY LUNCHEON

Refreshing Wine Daiquiri
Boursin Cheese
Fresh Mushroom Soup
Salad Niçoise
Very Special Lemon Muffins

*California Sauvignon Blanc
Sterling Vineyards*

Maple Mousse

FIESTA

Frozen Margaritas Supreme

or Carta Blanca Beer

Spicy Cheese Mold
Tortilla Soup
Crunchy Guacamole Salad
Chicken Olé
Colache
Microwave Pralines

APRIL 15TH TAX PARTY

Bohemian Beer

Chunky Cheese Spread
*Green Salad
Best Oil and Vinegar Dressing
Sally's Red Beans and Rice
Favorite Monkey Bread

*California Burgundy
Beaulieu Vineyard*

Chocolate Deadly Delights

DERBY DAY BRUNCH

Beverly's Quiche
*Fruit Salad
Strawberry Dressing
Cinnamon Nut Ring

*California Chenin Blanc
Burgess Cellars*

* Recipe is not included in book.

Summer

FATHER'S DAY BRUNCH

George Morgan's Bloody Mary Mix
Bacon-Oyster Bites
Charcoal Grilled Trout
Daddy's Eggs
Fruit Salad with Nuts
Poppy Seed Bread

*California Gewürztraminer
Joseph Phelps Vineyard*

DINNER ON THE PATIO

Black Olive Soup
Anchovy Biscuits
Cobb Salad
Picatta Chicken
Fettuccini with Mushrooms
and Zucchini

Italian Classico Chianti

Cold Orange Soufflé

SUMMER LUNCHEON

Squash Soup
Scallop and Shrimp Pasta Salad
Cheese Muffins

*California Chardonnay
Sebastiani Vineyards*

Melon Madness

FOURTH OF JULY BARBECUE

Holiday Punch
Cheese Pie
*Sliced Tomatoes
Blender Basil Mayonnaise
Cauliflower Slaw
Brisket Barbecue
Potatoes au Gratin
La Petite Tea Room Lucious Loaf
Our Homemade Ice Cream
Fabulous Fudgecake

SUMMER SUPPER

White Sangria
Twelfth Night Shrimp
Barbecued Herb Chicken
Fresh Broccoli Salad
Fresh Corn and Bacon Casserole

*California Chardonnay or
French White Burgundy*

Blueberry Cream Pie

* Recipe is not included in book.

CHRISTENING BRUNCH

Kir Champagne Punch
Tennessee Crab Crescents
Spicy Egg Casserole
*Fruit Cradle
Celery Seed Dressing
Orange Muffins

California Chenin Blanc

Little Rock Cheesecake

(Create fruit cradle with
a watermelon shell
filled with assorted fruits)

ANNIVERSARY DINNER

Fried Pasta

*California Champagne
Domaine Chandon*

Hearts of Palm with Salmon
Scalloppine of Pork Marsala
Simply Elegant Potatoes
Broiled Tomatoes with Dill Sauce

*California Cabernet Sauvignon
or French Red Bordeaux*

Flan

LIGHT LUNCH

Fresh Zucchini Soup
Veal with Pasta Salad
*Melba Toast
*Fruit Platter
Yogurt Dressing For Fruit

DIETER'S DELIGHT

Low-Calorie Vichyssoise
Sole Stuffed With Shrimp
and Mushrooms
Citrus Carrots
Sesame Broccoli
*Fresh Pineapple Fingers with
Puréed Strawberries

LABOR DAY FISH FRY

Spinach Dip
Onion Lover's Salad
Tomato-Bean Salad
*French Fries
Mustard Fish
Skipper's Hush Puppies
Butter Pecan Ice Cream

* Recipe is not included in book.

Fall

WINE TASTERS' DINNER

Caviar Mousse

French Brut Champagne
Dom Perignon

Vegetable Pâté
Coquilles Saint-Jacques

French White Burgundy
Beaune Clos des Mouches

Strawberry Sorbet
Imperial Tenderloin
Roast Potatoes
Baked Asparagus
Refrigerator Rolls

French Red Bordeaux
Chateau Latour

*Fresh Spinach
Tarragon Dressing for Fresh
Spinach Salad
Tart Tatin
Fried Walnuts

Tawny Port Wine

BREAKFAST FOR COMPANY

Orange Jubilee
Sausage and Egg Casserole
Night Before Coffee Cake
*Seasonal Fruit

TRADITIONAL THANKSGIVING DINNER

Artichoke Oyster Bisque
Molded Cranberry and Orange Salad

California Sauvignon Blanc
or Chardonnay

Baked Turkey and Giblet Gravy
Cornbread Turkey Dressing
Golden Sweet Potatoes
Broccoli Casserole
Mary's Homemade Rolls

California Johannisberg Riesling

Frozen Pumpkin Pie
Best Ever Carrot Cake
Our Traditional Apple Pie

California Moscato d' Oro
Robert Mondavi Winery

SAILING PICNIC

Almond, Bacon and Cheddar
Sandwich
Whole Wheat Bread
Gazpacho
Chilled Duck Salad
*Fresh Fruit

Robert Mondavi Vintage
Table White Wine or Rosé

German Chocolate Caramel Bars

* Recipe is not included in book.

TAILGATE PICNIC

Ice Breaker
Coppa Zione
Marinated Vegetable Salad
Butterscotch Brownies with
Caramel Icing

AFTER THE SYMPHONY SUPPER

Spinach Soup
Crab and Wild Rice Salad
Cheese Bread

French Graves

Mud Pie

AUTUMN LUNCH

Hot Chicken Salad
Spinach Soufflé
Pineapple Apricot Muffins

California Chenin Blanc

Rum Cream Pie

Winter

DUCK HUNTERS' DINNER

Artichoke Squares
Red Currant Duck
*Wild Rice
Broccoli Stuffed Tomatoes
Duck Hunters' Cabbage
Sidney Nisbet's Buttery Rolls

*California Petit Sirah
Caymus Vineyards*

Fresh Applecake with
Hot Buttered Rum Sauce

TREE TRIMMING PARTY

Wassail
Holiday Cheese Ball
Sausage and Lentil Soup
Layered Salad
Popovers

*Bouchard Pere et Fils
"VALBON"
Red or White*

Mother's English Pecan Cake

* Recipe is not included in book.

CHRISTMAS EVE DINNER

Eggnog Deluxe
Clam-Puffed Artichokes
Holiday Soup

California Sauvignon Blanc

Crown of Pork and Plum Sauce
Wild Rice with Snow Peas
Carrots Chablis
Red Apple Inn Rolls

California Pinot Noir or
French Burgundy

Chocolate Amaretto Cheesecake
garnished with Kiwi Fruit
and Strawberries

California Champagne
Domaine Chandon
Blanc de Noirs

CHINESE NEW YEAR DINNER

Egg Rolls
Hot Mustard and Plum Sauce
Sweet and Sour Spareribs
Sour and Hot Soup
Chinese Velvet Chicken
Almond Beef with Broccoli
Fried Rice

Tsingtao Beer

Sweet Won Ton Cookies
*Sherbet

SNOWY DAY LUNCH

Frijole Soup
Jane's Hot Ham Sandwiches
Snow Ice Cream
Peanut Butter Cookies

VALENTINE COCKTAIL BUFFET

Chicken Strips
Plum Sauce
Salmon Mousse
Cheese and Bacon Stuffed Mushrooms
Antipasto Appetizer
Stuffed Snow Peas
Marinated Tenderloin
Horseradish Cream
*Biscuits
*Cheese Board with Fruit
and Crackers
Melting Moments

PASTA POTPOURRI

Salmon Bisque
*Fresh Salad Greens
Mustard Vinaigrette
Shrimp and Feta Cheese Sauce
with Pasta
Pasta Primavera
Mama Donimo's Lasagne
French Bread

Beaujolais Villages

Zabaglione
Cappuccino

ST. PATRICK'S DAY DINNER

Green Beer

Drink Mores
Pepper Jelly Mold
Spinach, Artichoke and
Hearts of Palm Salad
Reuben Casserole
Irish Soda Bread

Alsatian Gewürztraminer

Cake 'n Ale

* Recipe is not included in book.

APPETIZERS

It is a rare appetizer which does not snuff out the appetite. But the same can be said of an appetizer served sparely.

CLAM-PUFFED ARTICHOKES

Yield: 40 appetizers

2 (8 ounce) packages frozen
   artichoke hearts
1 (7 ounce) can clams, minced and
   drained (reserve juice)
1 (8 ounce) package cream cheese,
   softened

1 Tablespoon chopped chives
½ cup mayonnaise
1 teaspoon fresh lemon juice
Several dashes of Tabasco
Several dashes of Worcestershire
   sauce

Cook artichoke hearts in boiling water, briefly. Do not cook as long as instructions on package state. Drain well. If artichoke hearts are whole, cut in half, lengthwise. Blend softened cream cheese, chives, mayonnaise, lemon juice, Tabasco and Worcestershire sauce together thoroughly. Stir in clams and add clam juice until desired consistency (somewhat stiff). Arrange artichoke hearts on a cookie sheet with cut side up. Spoon clam mixture on top and broil until puffy and golden. Serve hot.

Robyn Dickey

ARTICHOKE SQUARES

Oven: 325°
Yield: 30 to 40 squares

2 (6 ounce) jars marinated artichoke
   hearts
1 small onion, finely chopped
1 clove garlic, chopped
4 eggs
¼ cup fine, dried bread crumbs
⅛ teaspoon black pepper

¼ teaspoon salt
⅛ teaspoon oregano
⅛ teaspoon Tabasco
½ pound sharp Cheddar cheese,
   grated (approximately 2 cups)
2 Tablespoons chopped parsley

Drain juice from artichoke hearts and reserve the juice from one jar. Use the reserved artichoke juice to sauté the onions and garlic. Sauté the onions and garlic until limp. Chop drained artichoke hearts into small pieces and set aside. In a medium-sized bowl, beat eggs. Add bread crumbs and seasonings and mix. Stir in cheese, parsley, sautéed onions, artichoke hearts and garlic. Put into a 7 x 11 pan. Bake at 325° for 30 minutes, uncovered. Let cool and cut into squares.

Nancy Couch Lee (Mrs. James M., Jr.)

For hot and spicy artichoke squares, add 1 (4 ounce) can green chilies, drained and chopped, and 1 (4 ounce) can jalapeño peppers, drained and chopped. Follow the same directions as written for artichoke squares.

CHEESE AND BACON STUFFED MUSHROOMS

Oven: 325°
Yield: Approximately 48 mushrooms

3 pints fresh mushrooms
10 strips bacon, cooked and
    crumbled
½ medium onion, finely chopped

¾ cup Hellmann's mayonnaise
Lawry's seasoned salt to taste
1½ cups grated Cheddar cheese

Remove stems from mushrooms. Wash in salted water, then drain on paper towels. While mushrooms are draining, cook bacon until crisp, then crumble. Chop onion and grate cheese. Mix mayonnaise, seasoned salt, onion, cheese and crumbled bacon. Place mushrooms, cup side up, in a 9 x 13 buttered pyrex dish. Fill each mushroom with cheese and bacon mixture. Cover with foil. Bake at 325⁰ for 15 to 20 minutes. Serve hot.

Liz Burks (Mrs. Larry W.)

This may be prepared ahead but must be served hot from the oven.

DILL STUFFED MUSHROOMS

Oven: 500°
Yield: 6 to 8 servings

12 to 18 fresh mushrooms,
    depending on size
3 Tablespoons unsalted butter
2 large shallots, finely minced
Salt to taste
White pepper to taste
1 (6 ounce) package cream cheese,
    softened

2 Tablespoons fresh minced dill
2 Tablespoons fresh imported,
    finely grated Parmesan cheese
Parsley or fresh chives, finely
    chopped

Trim the ends of mushroom stems. Wipe mushrooms clean with a damp paper towel. Remove the stems, finely chop the stems and set aside. In a heavy skillet, heat 3 Tablespoons butter, add the chopped mushroom stems and shallots, and cook the mixture until lightly browned. Cook until water evaporates from the mushroom stems. Season with salt and white pepper. Combine the cream cheese, dill and Parmesan cheese in a bowl, using a wooden spatula. Fold in the mushroom mixture. Taste and correct the seasonings. Chill for 30 minutes. Stuff the mushroom caps with the filling and broil in a 500⁰ oven for 3 to 5 minutes, or until lightly browned. Garnish the mushrooms with parsley or fresh chives.

Mrs. J. Paul Faulkner
Jackson, Mississippi

ROLLED MUSHROOM APPETIZER
(Must be prepared 1 day in advance)

Oven: 450°
Yield: 30 appetizers

1 (8 ounce) package cream cheese, softened

1 (4 ounce) can mushrooms, drained and chopped

1 (10¾ ounce) can cream of mushroom soup

1 (4 ounce) can chopped almonds, or 1 (6 ounce) package almonds, chopped

Dash of garlic salt

½ Tablespoon Worcestershire sauce

½ to 1 Tablespoon horseradish

1½ loaves thin sliced white bread

Butter, melted

Mix mushrooms, cream cheese, soup and seasonings together and set aside. Cut crust off of bread and flatten each piece with a rolling pin, making rolling procedure easier. Spread 1 Tablespoon mushroom mixture on bread slices, covering center of bread only, not to edges. This will prevent mixture from running out of rolls while cooking. Roll each slice and fasten with a wooden toothpick. Place in refrigerator overnight. Brush rolls with melted butter and toast at 450⁰ until brown. Serve hot.

Marjorie Thalheimer (Mrs Bruce)

PICKLED MUSHROOMS
(Must be prepared 1 day in advance)

Serves: 10 to 12

1 (12 ounce) carton fresh mushrooms

¾ cup oil

¼ cup wine vinegar

½ cup Worcestershire sauce

½ teaspoon dry mustard

5 cloves garlic

1 teaspoon salt

1 Tablespoon sugar

½ teaspoon paprika

¼ teaspoon pepper

Dash of red pepper

Dash of Tabasco

Dash of basil leaves

Clean mushrooms with damp paper towels. Mix all ingredients together in a large air-tight container or ziplock bag and marinate overnight.

Barbara Hoffman

"To invite a person to your house is to take charge of his happiness as long as he is beneath your roof."

BRILLAT-SAVARIN
1755-1826

ANCHOVY BISCUITS

Oven: 400°
Yield: 20 to 30 biscuits

1 stick butter or margarine,
  softened
1 (3 ounce) package cream cheese,
  softened

1 cup flour
¼ teaspoon garlic salt
1 tube anchovy paste

Cream butter and cheese. Add flour and garlic salt. Work dough into ball shape. Cut dough ball in half. Roll dough out on a floured surface. Dough should be the thickness of pie pastry. Cut out dough with small biscuit cutter. Squeeze a dab of anchovy paste in the center of each biscuit. Fold over dough into half-moon shape. Freeze immediately. When frozen, bake at 400° for 10 minutes or until golden brown.

Willie Braxton

JACQUES AND SUZANNE ESCARGOTS

(Escargot butter must be prepared several days in advance)

Yield: 4 servings

Escargot Butter

14 ounces (1¾ cups) unsalted
  butter
½ ounce (5 medium-sized cloves)
  garlic, finely chopped
½ ounce (1½ Tablespoons) shallots,
  finely chopped
1½ ounce (4 Tablespoons) parsley,
  finely chopped
½ piece anchovy filet, finely chopped

1 piece filbert, chopped
2½ teaspoons salt
Pinch of white pepper
Pinch of cayenne pepper
Juice of ¼ lemon
1 teaspoon Pernod liqueur
2 teaspoons dry white wine

For Service

¾ cup whipping cream
24 snail pieces

1½ cups dry white wine
½ cup whipped cream

Prepare all ingredients for escargot butter. Place garlic, shallots, parsley, anchovy filet and filbert in blender and blend thoroughly. Place butter and dry seasonings in mixing bowl and beat until butter is well incorporated with air. Add purée mixture from blender, lemon juice, Pernod and white wine and continue beating. Place snail butter in covered container and refrigerate for several days. Butter can be frozen if not for immediate use. For service, butter should be at room temperature. Heat 24 snails in dry white wine. Place the snails in escargot dishes. Reduce ¾ cup of whipping cream by half. Remove from heat and when it is tepid, using a French whip, incorporate piece by piece 1½ cups of the soft (room temperature) butter. Fold in the ½ cup of whipped cream. Pour the prepared butter-cream mixture over the snails and glaze them quickly under the broiler. Serve with crusty French bread.

Restaurant Jacques and Suzanne

CRAB FINGER OR SHRIMP MARINADE

(Must be prepared 1 day in advance)

Serves: 6

¾ cup olive oil
¼ cup vinegar
Juice of ⅓ lemon
1 teaspoon salt
4 drops Tabasco
1 Tablespoon Worcestershire sauce
½ teaspoon Dijon mustard
1 Tablespoon capers, mashed and
  drained

¼ cup finely chopped green onions
¼ cup finely chopped celery
1 Tablespoon chopped parsley
6 cloves garlic, minced
½ teaspoon thyme
1 (15 ounce) can crab fingers or 2
  (6 ounce) cans shrimp, drained

Mix all ingredients except crab fingers or shrimp. Add crab fingers or shrimp and marinate at least 24 hours in refrigerator.

Susan Freeling Carr (Mrs. Phil)
Washington, DC

TENNESSEE CRAB CRESCENTS

Oven: 375°
Yield: 8 crescents

1 (8 ounce) can crabmeat, drained
  and flaked
1 (6 ounce) can water chestnuts,
  drained and chopped
½ cup shredded Swiss cheese
1 small onion, finely chopped

1 Tablespoon lemon juice
1 Tablespoon Worcestershire sauce
¼ teaspoon salt
Curry powder to taste (Optional)
1 can Pillsbury Crescent Rolls

Combine all ingredients in a mixing bowl except rolls. Separate rolls into 8 triangles. Spoon about 2 Tablespoons crab mixture into each triangle. Roll up, starting at the shortest side and roll toward longest side. Bake at 375° for 15 to 18 minutes. Serve hot. Crescent rolls may be cut in half, lengthwise, before adding crab and before being rolled, to make smaller appetizers.

Tandy Cobb (Mrs. Bill)

"Seeing is deceiving. It's eating that's believing."
JAMES THURBER
1894-1961

SHRIMP LOUISIANA

Serves: 10

½ cup white vinegar
20 bay leaves
1 pound medium-sized shrimp,
   cooked
2 medium onions, sliced

1 teaspoon paprika
Dash of cayenne pepper
2 cups salad oil
¼ cup Worcestershire sauce
1 teaspoon salt

Heat vinegar and 10 whole bay leaves. DO NOT BOIL. Remove leaves. Let vinegar cool. In a large bowl or Tupperware container, make a layer of shrimp, onion, and a few bay leaves. (You may reuse the bay leaves you cooked in the vinegar.) Layer until all shrimp, onion and bay leaves are used up. Make dressing of heated vinegar and remaining ingredients and pour over shrimp. Allow to marinate in refrigerator for at least 8 hours. (It is better the longer it marinates.) Stir or shake occasionally. Serve in a large bowl, with cocktail forks or toothpicks. Serve with Triscuits and lots of napkins.

Debby Bransford Coates (Mrs. Wayne)

MARINATED GREEN OLIVES
(Must be prepared 1 to 3 days in advance)

Serves: 6

1 (8 ounce) jar green olives, drained
¼ cup vinegar
2 Tablespoons dried chives

¼ cup (good quality) olive oil
1 clove garlic, mashed
¼ teaspoon whole peppercorns

Combine all ingredients in a heavy duty plastic bag. Put bag of olives in a bowl in case of drips, and turn over from time to time. Let marinate at room temperature for 1 to 3 days. Drain before serving.

Dee Dowell Wright (Mrs. Richard)
Texarkana, Arkansas

BACON-OYSTER BITES

Oven: 350°
Yield: 16 appetizers

8 slices bacon
½ cup herbed seasoned stuffing

1 (5 ounce) can oysters, chopped
¼ cup water

Preheat oven to 350°. Cut bacon slices in half and cook slightly. DO NOT OVERCOOK. Bacon must be soft enough to roll easily around balls. Combine stuffing, oysters and water. Roll into bite-sized balls, approximately 16. Wrap balls in bacon. Bake at 350° for 25 minutes. Serve warm.

STUFFED SNOW PEAS

Yield: 50 snow peas

1 (8 ounce) package cream cheese,
   softened
50 snow peas
⅛ cup dried chopped chives

1 teaspoon seasoned salt
⅛ teaspoon Worcestershire sauce
⅛ teaspoon white pepper
Pastry bag or cake decorating tube

While cream cheese softens at room temperature, prepare snow peas as follows: Rinse snow peas in running water. String peas. This makes it easy to open pod later to expose peas. Place pods in boiling water for 2 minutes. Rinse immediately with cold running water. Drain and pat dry with paper towels. With a sharp knife, slice open each pod. To the softened cream cheese, add the remaining ingredients and mix well. Put cream cheese mixture into bag or tube and fill each pod. Chill at least 1 hour. Frozen snow peas may be substituted only when fresh ones are not available.

Jane Johnson

MARION'S CHEESE CRACKERS

Oven: 350°
Yield: 5 to 6 dozen

½ cup butter or margarine,
   softened
1 teaspoon white pepper
1 teaspoon salt
1 teaspoon Tabasco

½ pound sharp Cheddar cheese,
   grated
1½ cups flour
½ cup thinly sliced pecans

Whip softened butter. Add pepper, salt, Tabasco and cheese and mix again. Add flour and mix well with pastry cutter and hands. If food processor is available, use steel blade for mixing. The secret to these is to mix thoroughly! Add pecans and mix well. Make into rolls about 1½ inches in diameter. Chill on waxed paper until cold (at least 1 hour or longer). Slice thinly, approximately ⅛ to ¼ inch thick. Bake 9 to 11 minutes at 350° on cookie sheet sprayed with Pam. Bake in preheated oven. Can be sliced with a food processor using 3 mm blade and small round feed tube. This will make slices approximately 1⁄16 inch thick.

Lora Parnell (Mrs. Cliff)

"Many's the long night I've dreamed of cheese - toasted mostly."
ROBERT LOUIS STEVENSON
Treasure Island
1850-1894

ATHENIAN CHEESE PIE

Oven: 350°
Serves: 15 to 20

8 eggs
1¼ pound Greek Feta cheese, crumbled
1 pound cottage cheese
¼ cup Parmesan cheese

Salt to taste
Pepper to taste
1 pound filo pastry
¾ pound butter, melted

Beat eggs until light and creamy. Fold in crumbled Feta, cottage and Parmesan cheeses. Season with salt and pepper. Place half of pastry sheets in buttered 11 x 17 pan, brushing each pastry sheet individually with butter. DO NOT SUBSTITUTE WITH MARGARINE. Pour in cheese filling. Cover with remaining half of pastry sheets, brushing each with butter. Brush entire pie generously with butter. Bake, uncovered, at 350° for 45 minutes, or until golden. Cut into squares, while still hot, and serve warm. This may be prepared and frozen.

Helen N. Damaskos (Mrs. James)
Aurora, Colorado

Working with filo pastry is a little difficult, but this dish is very different and delicious so it's well worth the trouble.

DRINK MORES

Oven: 375°
Yield: 2 dozen

¼ pound butter, softened
1½ cups flour
⅓ pound very sharp cheese, grated
1 teaspoon salt

½ teaspoon red pepper
2 dozen dates
2 dozen pecan halves

Mix butter, flour, cheese, salt and pepper and form into a dough. Roll out and cut with a biscuit cutter. Push pecan halves inside dates, then wrap dough circles around dates, covering completely. Place on cookie sheet and bake in preheated oven at 375° for 12 to 15 minutes. Serve hot.

Libby Strawn (Mrs. Jim)

"As after cheese, nothing to be expected."
THOMAS FULLER
1608-1661

VEGETABLE PÂTÉ
(Must be prepared in advance)

Oven: 425°
Yield: 8 servings

Spinach Layer

**2 cups chopped spinach, cooked
   and squeezed dry**
2 eggs, lightly beaten

½ teaspoon salt
¼ teaspoon nutmeg
¼ teaspoon pepper

Tomato Layer

¼ cup chopped onion
¼ teaspoon minced garlic
1½ teaspoons unsalted butter
**1 pound tomatoes, peeled, seeded
   and chopped**

2 eggs, lightly beaten
½ teaspoon salt
¼ teaspoon cayenne

Leek Layer

**4 large leeks (white part only),
   minced**
Boiling salted water

½ cup whipping cream
2 eggs, lightly beaten
½ teaspoon salt

Horseradish Sauce

1 cup plain yogurt

2 Tablespoons horseradish, drained

Combine all the ingredients for the spinach layer and set aside. For the tomato layer, sauté onion and garlic in the butter for 3 minutes. Add tomatoes and cook for 45 minutes. Let cool. Add eggs, salt and cayenne and mix completely. Set tomato mixture aside while preparing leeks. Blanch leeks in salted, boiling water for 3 minutes, covered. Drain and refresh with cold water. Pat dry. Combine leeks with cream and cook 10 minutes. Let cool. Add eggs and salt. Layer the 3 mixtures in a greased 1½ quart terrine beginning with half of spinach mixture, all the tomato mixture, all the leek mixture and ending with the remaining spinach mixture. Cover the terrine and set a deep baking pan filled with enough boiling water to reach ⅓ up the sides of the terrine. Bake the pâté in a 425° oven for 1 hour or until firm. Cool in terrine for 10 minutes. Unmold and cool completely. Serve with horseradish sauce.

Horseradish sauce looks lovely served in a hollowed out cucumber section. This is a time consumming dish but well worth the trouble. May also be served as a vegetable.

"Epicure: One who gets nothing better than the cream of everything but cheerfully makes the best of it."

OLIVER HERFORD
1863-1935

OLIVE BREAD RING

Oven: 325°
Serves: 10 to 12

¾ cup warm buttermilk
1 (13¾ ounce) package Pillsbury
  Hot Roll mix
1 egg, beaten
2 Tablespoons sugar

¾ cup shredded Swiss cheese
¾ cup chopped walnuts
¾ cup thinly sliced stuffed green
  olives

Warm buttermilk in sauce pan. DO NOT BOIL. Sprinkle yeast from roll mix over warm buttermilk. Thoroughly blend in egg with fork or wire whisk, add sugar, and set aside, cooling to room temperature. In a bowl, mix together roll mix. Stir in cheese, walnuts and olives. Add buttermilk mixture and stir until dough clings together. Turn onto lightly floured board and knead 5 or 6 times. Place in buttered bowl. Cover and allow to stand in a warm place until doubled (about 1½ hours). On lightly floured board, knead dough 8 to 10 times. Shape into roll about 16 to 18 inches long and place in a well-buttered bundt pan, making certain that the ends are well sealed. Cover and let stand in a warm place until doubled (about 45 minutes). Bake in a preheated 325° oven for 35 to 40 minutes or until done. Test with a cake tester. Turn onto wire rack to cool. May be served with Bacon Cheddar Cheese Spread (See Index).

Nancy Couch Lee (Mrs. James M., Jr.)

EMPAÑADAS

Yield: 45 to 50 appetizers

3 pie crust sticks (comes 2 to a box)
  or favorite pie crust recipe
1 pound ground beef
1 Tablespoon oil
1 medium onion, finely chopped
1 green pepper, finely chopped
1 teaspoon capers

10 stuffed green olives, chopped
1 large ripe tomato, finely chopped
Pinch of oregano
Salt to taste
Pepper to taste
Hot Sauce (See Index)

Make pie crust dough according to directions on package and chill while preparing meat mixture. Brown meat in oil. Add the other ingredients (except hot sauce) and simmer for ½ hour. Roll out dough ⅛ inch thick on a slightly floured board and cut with round cookie cutter. On each round of dough, put ½ teaspoon of filling. Fold over and flute edges with a damp fork. Fry in hot grease until golden brown. Drain and serve hot with Hot Sauce.

Elenia Keyes (Mrs. Cloud)

Well worth the effort! May be made and then frozen.

PIZZA ON RYE

Yield: 75 pizzas

1 pound hot sausage, cooked and drained
1 pound ground beef, cooked and drained
1 pound Velveeta cheese

1 teaspoon basil
2 Tablespoons parsley flakes
1 teaspoon oregano
1 teaspoon garlic salt
2 loaves party rye bread

In separate pans, brown sausage and ground beef. DO NOT COOK TOGETHER. Drain meats once, and then drain again, on paper towels. Make sure meat is drained thoroughly. Cut Velveeta cheese into cubes and put meats and cheese into a large pan. Heat until cheese has melted. Add seasonings and mix until blended. Spread meat mixture on party rye and place on cookie sheet in freezer until set. Store pizzas in plastic bags in freezer until ready to cook. When cooking, put pizzas on lowest rack of oven and broil until brown.

Robin Ratley Smith (Mrs. Michael)

COPPA ZIONE

Oven: 350°
Yield: 3 loaves

Filling
½ pound bulk Italian sausage
½ pound ham, chopped
2 (6 ounce) sticks pepperoni, sliced
2½ pounds Ricotta cheese

1½ cups Parmesan cheese
3 Tablespoons minced parsley
2 eggs, beaten
1 Tablespoon black pepper

Dough
4 cups flour
1 teaspoon baking powder
1 teaspoon salt
½ cup shortening

3 eggs, beaten
½ cup milk (enough to make pliable)

Egg yolk

2 Tablespoons water

Cook Italian sausage. Chop ham and slice pepperoni, then mix all filling ingredients together and set aside. Mix dough ingredients together thoroughly. Form into 3 balls. With rolling pin, roll each ball out as long as possible, making dough approximately ¼ inch thick. Spread filling over dough within ¼ inch of edge and roll up, jellyroll style. Seam sides down and tuck edges. Brush top with egg yolk, beaten with 2 Tablespoons water. Bake at 350° in preheated oven for 20 to 30 minutes or until golden brown. When cool, slice into ½ to 1 inch slices. Freezes well.

Barbara Molinaro (Mrs. Robert)
Kansas City, Missouri

EGG ROLLS

Yield: 16 egg rolls

16 Egg Roll wrappers
½ pound fresh bean sprouts, or 1
  (16 ounce) can
½ pound raw shrimp, in their shells
3 Tablespoons oil
½ pound lean boneless pork,
  ground
2 to 3 fresh mushrooms, cut into ¼
  inch slices
1 Tablespoon soy sauce

1 Tablespoon Chinese rice wine or
  pale dry sherry
½ teaspoon sugar
4 cups finely chopped celery
1 Tablespoon salt
1 Tablespoon cornstarch, dissolved
  in 2 Tablespoons cold chicken
  stock or cold water
3 cups Wesson oil or peanut oil
1 egg, beaten

Prepare ahead. If using fresh bean sprouts, rinse in cold water and discard the husks. Shell and devein the shrimp and finely chop both ingredients.

For filling. Set a 12 inch wok or 10 inch skillet on high for 30 seconds. Pour in 1 Tablespoon of oil and swirl it about, heating for 30 seconds more. Turn the heat down and add the pork. Stir fry for 2 minutes or until pork is no longer red. Add shrimp, sliced mushrooms, soy sauce, wine and sugar and fry for another minute or until shrimp turns pink. Transfer the mixture to a bowl and set aside. Pour remaining 2 Tablespoons of oil into wok and heat for 30 seconds. Add chopped celery and stir fry for 5 minutes. Add salt and bean sprouts. Mix. Pour pork and shrimp mixture back into wok and stir until all ingredients are well combined. Cook over moderate heat, stirring constantly, until liquid starts to boil. Spoon out 2 or 3 Tablespoons of oil from mixture. Transfer to a bowl and set aside to cool to room temperature.

To assemble: Open wrappers and cover with a damp towel. Place ¼ cup of filling diagonally across center of each wrapper. Lift the lower triangular flap over the filling and tuck the point under it, leaving the upper point of wrapper exposed. Bring each of the small end flaps, one at a time, up to the top of the filling and press the points firmly down. Brush the upper and exposed triangle of wrapper with lightly beaten egg and roll the wrapper into a neat package. Place the egg rolls on a plate and cover them with a dry towel.

To cook. Set a 12 inch wok or heavy deep fryer over high heat. Add 3 cups oil and heat it until a haze forms or it reaches a temperature of 375⁰. Place 2 or 3 egg rolls in the hot oil and deep fry for 3 to 4 minutes or until they become golden brown and crisp. Transfer the egg rolls to a double thickness of paper towels and let the oil drain while you fry remaining egg rolls.

Shirley C. Juan

"It (tradition) cannot be inherited, and if you want it you must obtain it by good labour."

T.S. ELIOT
1888-1965

ORIENTAL MEAT BALLS

Serves: 10 to 12

Meat balls:

1 (8¾ ounce) can crushed
   pineapple, drained
2 pounds ground beef
1 pound ground pork
1 (8 ounce) can water chestnuts,
   drained and finely chopped
1½ teaspoons soy sauce

1 clove garlic, pressed
1 teaspoon salt
¼ teaspoon ginger
2 eggs, beaten
⅓ cup milk
1 cup uncooked oats

Sweet and Sour Sauce

3 Tablespoons cornstarch
1½ cups brown sugar
1 cup vinegar

1½ cups pineapple juice
2 Tablespoons soy sauce

Meat balls: Combine all ingredients and shape into small balls. Cook over medium heat in just enough oil to cover bottom of a large frying pan. Turn frequently until browned on all sides. Drain on paper towels.

Sweet and sour sauce: Mix cornstarch and brown sugar in a saucepan. Add remaining ingredients. Bring to a boil and simmer for 1½ minutes. Combine sauce and meat balls and serve in chafing dish. Serve hot.

Mrs. Herb Sturdivant
Springdale, Arkansas

Meat balls can be made ahead and frozen. Sauce can be cooked a day ahead and reheated for serving. Meat balls may also be served as a main dish if made larger.

SAUSAGE MEAT BALLS

Oven: 425°
Yield: 4 dozen

1 pound hot sausage
1 egg, beaten
⅓ cup bread crumbs
½ teaspoon sage
½ cup ketchup

½ cup chili sauce
2 Tablespoons brown sugar
2 Tablespoons soy sauce
1½ Tablespoons vinegar

Combine first 5 ingredients and roll into bite-sized balls. Place on an edged cookie sheet and bake at 425° for 20 minutes. While sausage balls are cooking, combine remaining ingredients in a saucepan. Add cooked sausage balls to sauce and simmer over low heat for 30 minutes. These can be frozen in sauce and served later or served immediately. Water may need to be added to sauce if sauce is too thick.

Katherine Anne Stewart (Mrs. George)
St. Paul, Minnesota

CHICKEN STRIPS
(Must be prepared 1 day in advance)

Oven: 350°
Yield: 10 to 15

6 whole chicken breasts, boned and
  skinned
1½ cups buttermilk
2 Tablespoons lemon juice
2 teaspoons Worcestershire sauce
1 teaspoon soy sauce
1 teaspoon paprika
1 Tablespoon Greek seasoning

1 teaspoon salt
1 teaspoon pepper
2 cloves garlic, minced
4 cups bread crumbs
½ cup sesame seeds
¼ cup butter
¼ cup shortening

Cut chicken into ½ inch strips. Combine buttermilk, lemon juice, sauces, and seasonings.
Add chicken to buttermilk mixture and mix until well-coated. Cover and refrigerate overnight. Drain chicken thoroughly in a colander. Combine bread crumbs and sesame seeds,
mixing well. Add chicken and toss in a ziplock bag until coated. Place chicken in 2 greased 9 x 13 baking dishes. Melt butter and shortening and brush on chicken. Bake, uncovered,
at 350⁰ for 35 to 40 minutes or until crisp. Serve with Plum Sauce (See Index).

Sunny Hawk (Mrs. Boyce)

STEAK TARTARE

Serves: 10 to 12

1½ pounds round steak, NO FAT,
  ground twice
1 raw egg
1 Tablespoon anchovy paste
½ teaspoon garlic powder
½ teaspoon onion powder
½ teaspoon cayenne pepper

1 Tablespoon Worcestershire sauce
1 Tablespoon A-1 sauce
1 teaspoon Pick-a-Peppa sauce
1 hard-boiled egg, grated
4 green onions with tops, chopped
Capers
1 loaf party rye bread

Have butcher take off fat and grind meat two times, or do your own at home. Spread
meat on large chopping board. Make a hole in center and drop raw egg inside. Add each of
the next ingredients, one at a time, chopping them into meat, completely and slowly. The
secret to great Steak Tartare is this chopping procedure. Mold in rounded bowl and
refrigerate 1 to 2 hours. Unmold and top with chopped onions, capers and grated egg,
or have toppings available in bowls for guests to add if desired. Serve with party rye bread.

Bruce Thalheimer

SWEET AND SOUR SPARERIBS

Oven: 325°
Serves: 8

**3 pounds spareribs, cracked into 2
   to 3 inch pieces**
1 teaspoon monosodium glutamate

3 Tablespoons soy sauce
½ cup prepared mustard
1 cup brown sugar

Have butcher cut ribs into small pieces. Bake ribs at 325⁰ for 1½ hours. Drain on paper towels. Make sauce with remaining ingredients, then brush on ribs. Return ribs to 300⁰ oven for 45 minutes. Baste several times while cooking.

TOASTED PUMPKIN SEEDS

Oven: 350°
Yield: Ask the Great Pumpkin!

Pumpkin seeds from 1 pumpkin
**1 teaspoon garlic salt and/or
   Lawry's seasoned salt**

**1 teaspoon Cavender's Greek
   Seasoning**
2 Tablespoons butter, melted
1 teaspoon Worcestershire sauce

Preheat oven to 350⁰. Remove large fibers from pumpkin seeds. DO NOT WASH SEEDS. Mix ingredients together and add to pumpkin seeds, coating well. Arrange seeds on a cookie sheet with edges. Bake at 350⁰ for 15 minutes or until crisp. Stir occasionally.

Lindsey Watson Allen

FRIED PASTA

Yield: 50 to 60 strips

1 package egg roll skins
2 cups oil

Salt to taste

Cut egg roll skins into ½ inch wide strips. Use a large knife and cut through the entire stack of skins. On a damp dish towel, separate skins into individual strips. Heat oil in a wok or skillet until just hot, approximately 375⁰. Drop skins into hot oil. Cook a few seconds, then turn and cook a few more seconds, browning slightly. Remove quickly and drain on paper towels. Salt to taste. Cook only a handful of skins at a time.

Marilyn Hussman Augur (Mrs. James)
Dallas, Texas

Serve as you would peanuts or chips.

ITALIAN SEA CRACKERS

Oven: 425°
Yield: 6 to 8 dozen

Crackers
1 (11 ounce) package pie crust mix
**1 envelope Italian salad dressing
    mix**

5 Tablespoons cold water

Topping
**1 (6 ounce) can cocktail shrimp,
    drained**
½ cup mayonnaise
2 Tablespoons chopped parsley

**1 teaspoon freshly squeezed lemon
    juice**
Dash of cayenne pepper
Paprika

For crackers, preheat oven to 425°. Mix pie crust and dry salad mix in a large bowl. Add water. 1 Tablespoon at a time, and mix gently with a fork. Roll out half at a time to ⅛ inch thick on a lightly floured surface. Cut into 1½ inch rounds with a biscuit cutter. Prick each round several times with a fork before cooking. Bake on cookie sheet in 425° oven until golden brown, about 8 minutes. Cool and set aside. For topping, mix all ingredients together and chill, letting flavors blend. Top each cracker with shrimp mixture and sprinkle with paprika. Crackers may be made ahead of time and stored in air-tight container. Salad can be made ahead and refrigerated. DO NOT put together until serving time.

David Dickey

CAVIAR ARTICHOKE DELIGHT

Serves: 8

**2 (8 ounce) packages cream cheese,
    softened**
**2 (8½ ounce) cans artichoke hearts,
    drained and chopped**

1 small onion, grated
1 (3½ ounce) jar caviar, drained
2 hard-boiled eggs, grated

Mix cream cheese and artichoke hearts with mixer. Add grated onion. Mold into a circle on a serving tray. Before serving, spread caviar on top of cream cheese mixture and place grated egg on top of caviar. Serve with crackers.

Georgea McKinley Greaves (Mrs. Thomas G., III)

Mold can be made in advance and caviar and egg added before serving.

BACON CHEDDAR CHEESE SPREAD

Yield: 2½ cups

5 strips crisp bacon, crumbled
2½ cups grated Cheddar cheese

**5 green onions with tops, finely
  chopped**
1 cup sour cream

Mix bacon, cheese and onion with sour cream until well blended. Serve with Olive Bread Ring (See Index). May also be served separately with crackers.

Nancy Couch Lee (Mrs. James M., Jr.)

CHEESE RING WITH STRAWBERRY JAM

(Must be prepared 1 day in advance)

Serves: 8 to 10

**1 pound sharp Cheddar cheese,
  grated**
1 cup chopped pecans
2 cups mayonnaise

1 onion, finely chopped
1 garlic clove, pressed
½ teaspoon Tabasco
1 cup strawberry jam

Mix first 6 ingredients together thoroughly. Place in a greased ring mold. Refrigerate overnight. Unmold onto serving plate and place strawberry jam in the center. Serve with crackers.

Mrs. Lucy W. Gardner

Beautiful dip for Christmas parties.

CHUNKY CHEESE SPREAD

Yield: 4 cups

**1 (1 pound) box Kraft cheese with
  jalapeño peppers, softened**
**1 (8 ounce) package cream cheese,
  softened**
3 Tablespoons chopped bell pepper
3 Tablespoons chopped onion

**1 (2 ounce) jar pimientos, drained
  and chopped**
**1 (16 ounce) can chopped
  sauerkraut, drained**
Olive slices
Paprika

Mix first 6 ingredients together thoroughly. Garnish with either black or green olive slices and paprika. Serve at room temperature with your favorite crackers.

Peggy Willbanks Jordan (Mrs. Don)

CHEESE PIE

Serves: 10 to 12

3 (8 ounce) packages cream cheese, softened

1 (4 ounce) package Bleu cheese, crumbled

4 ounces Cheddar cheese, grated

1 package Hidden Valley Ranch Original salad dressing mix

6 or 8 different condiments: chopped ripe olives, green olives, nuts, caviar, shrimp, green onion, pimiento and cooked bacon

In 3 separate bowls, mix 1 package cream cheese with Bleu cheese, 1 package with Cheddar cheese, and 1 with Ranch dressing mix. Layer cheeses in a pie plate starting with Bleu cheese mixture on bottom, Cheddar in the middle and Ranch dressing on top. Mark off 6 or 8 sections with a knife or toothpick and fill in each section with the condiment of your choice, being careful to make it colorful. The cheese part may be prepared ahead and refrigerated. Add topping before serving and serve at room temperature with crackers.

BLEU CHEESE CAKE

Oven: 300°
Serves: 20 to 30

2 Tablespoons margarine, melted

¾ cup crushed wheat crackers

2 (8 ounce) packages cream cheese, softened

2 (4 ounce) packages Bleu cheese, crumbled

1⅔ cups sour cream

3 eggs, beaten

⅛ teaspoon white pepper

Preheat oven to 300°. Stir melted margarine into cracker crumbs and press in a springform pan. Bake at 300° for 20 minutes. Combine softened cream cheese and Bleu cheese. Stir in ⅔ cup sour cream, reserving the rest for later. Stir in 3 eggs and the white pepper. Pour mixture on top of cooked crust and bake at 300° for 45 minutes. Spread remaining sour cream over top of hot cheese and return to oven for 10 more minutes.

Anne Wait Gardner (Mrs. Jack)
Searcy, Arkansas

"In the early eighteenth century little strips of salted hard cheese were sold to New York City theater audiences who could eat them or throw them at the actors. They did both."

ANONYMOUS

SPICY CHEESE MOLD

Serves: 20

1 pound Velveeta cheese
1 pound sharp Cheddar cheese
1 pound mild Cheddar cheese

1 pound HOT sausage
4 jalapeño peppers, seeded and
  finely chopped

Melt cheeses in top of double boiler. While cheeses are melting, fry sausage and drain well. Mix cheeses and sausage together. Add chopped peppers. Pour into a WELL-greased bundt pan. Put in refrigerator to harden. Unmold onto platter and serve with assorted crackers.

Marcia Johnston (Mrs. Richard S.)

For a spicier mold, add cumin, garlic powder or fresh garlic, and onion powder.

PEPPER JELLY MOLD

Yield: 3½ cup mold

2 (8 ounce) packages cream cheese,
  softened
1 cup hot pepper jelly, homemade if
  available

1 Tablespoon unflavored gelatin
¼ cup cold milk
½ cup boiling milk

Blend cream cheese until smooth. Add jelly and mix again. Soften gelatin in cold milk, then add boiling milk to completely dissolve gelatin. Add milk to cream cheese mixture and pour into 3½ cup mold. Chill until set. Unmold onto serving plate and serve with Triscuits or favorite crackers.

Linda Burrow VanHook (Mrs. Fred F.)

This dip can be prepared in food processor, if available, and can be made one day in advance.

BOURSIN CHEESE

(Better if prepared 1 day in advance)

Serves: 12

1 (8 ounce) package cream cheese,
  softened
1 stick butter, softened
½ teaspoon dill weed

½ teaspoon Fines Herbes
¼ teaspoon garlic salt
2 to 3 sprigs parsley
Lemon pepper (Optional)

Combine all ingredients in food processor bowl until well blended or use a mixer. Chill until stiff enough to form into whatever shape is desired. Refrigerate until ready to serve. May be served as is, or rolled in lemon pepper. Serve with wheat crackers.

Julie Truemper (Mrs. John J., Jr.)

Great for Christmas gifts.

PEPPER CHEESE BALL

Serves: 35 to 40

3 (8 ounce) packages cream cheese,
  softened
2 sticks margarine, softened
  DO NOT USE BUTTER

4 cloves garlic, pressed
Dash of Worcestershire sauce
Coarsely ground pepper

Mix cream cheese and margarine together until well blended. Add garlic and Worcestershire and mix again. Form into 1 large ball or 2 average size balls and cover with ground pepper. Chill in refrigerator until serving time. Serve with plain melba rounds.

Betty Jane Howell (Mrs. Gilbert)

If entire ball is not used, remold leftover and cover again with pepper. Serve again!

HOLIDAY CHEESE BALL

Yield: 12 to 15 servings

2 (8 ounce) packages cream cheese,
  softened
1 (8 ounce) package Cheddar
  cheese, grated
3 green onions with tops, chopped
½ green pepper, chopped

1 Tablespoon lemon juice
1 Tablespoon Worcestershire sauce
½ teaspoon garlic powder
Salt to taste
1 (4 ounce) jar pimientos, drained
  and chopped

Mix all ingredients with cream cheese and form into 1 large ball or 2 small balls. Chill until serving time.

Ceile Faulkner (Mrs. Jim)

CAVIAR MOUSSE

Serves: 10 to 15

5 hard-boiled eggs, grated
3 Tablespoons grated onion
1 cup mayonnaise
1½ Tablespoons Worcestershire
  sauce
2 Tablespoons lemon juice

2 dashes Tabasco
½ cup sour cream
1 (4 ounce) can Black Lump caviar,
  drained
1 package unflavored gelatin

Reserve 2 Tablespoons of grated egg and 2 teaspoons of caviar to garnish. Combine first 7 ingredients. Dissolve unflavored gelatin in ¼ cup hot water. Cool the gelatin and add it to the first 7 ingredients. Fold in caviar. Put mixture into a 3 to 4 cup oiled mold. Refrigerate until set, about 4 hours or overnight. After unmolding, decorate top with small dollops of caviar and sprinkle with grated egg. Serve with sesame or club crackers.

Mrs. Frank Farella, Jr.
Sausalito, California

SALMON MOUSSE

Serves: 20 to 25

1 envelope unflavored gelatin
¼ cup cold water
½ cup boiling beef stock
½ cup mayonnaise
1 Tablespoon lemon juice
1 teaspoon Tabasco
½ teaspoon paprika

1 teaspoon salt
1 Tablespoon chopped capers
½ cup chopped celery
½ cup chopped green onion
2 cups flaked salmon
½ cup whipping cream, whipped

Soften gelatin in cold water. Add boiling beef stock and stir. Set aside to cool. Add mayonnaise and spices. Chill to consistency of egg whites. While mayonnaise mixture is chilling, chop capers, celery and green onions. Mix this with chilled mayonnaise mixture. Add salmon and blend thoroughly. In a separate bowl, whip cream, then fold into salmon mixture. Turn into one 5½ cup mold and chill until set. Unmold onto a serving platter and serve with crackers or melba rounds.

Carol H. Rasco (Mrs. Terry)

SMOKED OYSTER ROLL

Serves: 10

2 (8 ounce) packages cream cheese,
    softened
2 or 3 Tablespoons mayonnaise
2 teaspoons Worcestershire sauce
Tabasco or Louisiana Hot Sauce to
    taste

½ small onion, finely chopped
⅛ teaspoon salt
1 or 2 garlic cloves, pressed
2 (3.66 ounce) cans smoked oysters,
    drained and chopped
Paprika

With plastic blade of food processor, or a mixer, mix cream cheese and mayonnaise. Add Worcestershire, Tabasco, chopped onion, salt and garlic. Mix well. Refrigerate until mixture hardens somewhat. Spread mixture, ½ inch thick, on waxed paper. Spread chopped oysters over cream cheese mixture and roll jellyroll style. If time allows, chill again before rolling. This will make rolling procedure much easier. Chill until ready to serve. Sprinkle with paprika and dress with parsley and cherry tomatoes. Serve with Triscuits or crackers.

Debby Bransford Coates (Mrs. Wayne)

"There is more simplicity in the man who eats caviar on impulse than in the man who eats grapenuts on principle."

G. K. CHESTERTON
1874-1936

MOCK PÂTÉ DE FOIE GRAS SPREAD

Yield: 1 cup mold

½ pound liverwurst
4 Tablespoons minced parsley

4 Tablespoons mayonnaise
1 Tablespoon minced onion

Place all ingredients in a food processor and mix; or mash liverwurst and add remaining ingredients and blend with mixer. Mold into desired shape or serve in a bowl with crackers or melba rounds.

Sandy Ledbetter (Mrs. Joel Y., Jr.)

Recipe can easily be doubled.

ROBERT'S DUCK SALAD SPREAD

Yield: 3 quarts

2 ducks
1 dozen eggs, hard-boiled
1 large bunch celery, chopped
1 (8 ounce) jar sweet relish
3 cups mayonnaise

2 ounces lemon juice
Salt to taste
Pepper to taste
1 cup chopped pecans (Optional)

Boil ducks in salted water until meat falls off the bone. Chill. Remove meat from bone and chop into bite-sized pieces. Chop eggs and celery. Mix eggs and celery with duck, relish, mayonnaise and lemon juice. Add more mayonnaise, if needed. Salt and pepper to taste. Add chopped pecans and chill until ready to serve. Serve with crisp crackers.

Robert M. Goff

HOT ARTICHOKE - SEAFOOD DIP

Oven: 325°
Serves: 12 to 14

2 (14 ounce) cans artichoke hearts,
   drained and chopped
2 cups mayonnaise
2 cups grated Parmesan cheese

2 (6 ounce) packages frozen
   crabmeat with shrimp, thawed,
   drained, and flaked
½ cup dry seasoned bread crumbs

Combine ingredients, mixing well. Spoon into a lightly greased 1½ quart casserole. Bake at 325° for 15 to 20 minutes. Serve with crackers. Can be assembled ahead.

Ellon Cockrill (Mrs. Rogers)

If the frozen crabmeat with shrimp is hard to find, use 1 (6 ounce) can crabmeat and 1 (6 ounce) can shrimp, drained.

ANTIPASTO APPETIZER
(Must be prepared 1 day in advance)

Serves: 15 to 20

¾ cup fresh broccoli flowerets
¾ cup fresh cauliflower flowerets
2 (4 ounce) cans button mushrooms,
  drained
1 (14 ounce) can artichoke hearts,
  drained and chopped
1 (4 ounce) jar pimientos, chopped

1 (4 ounce) jar stuffed green olives,
  drained and sliced
3 ribs celery, chopped
1 (8 ounce) can sliced water
  chestnuts, drained
1 onion, chopped
1 green bell pepper, chopped

Dressing
⅔ cup vinegar
⅔ cup oil
1 package Italian dressing mix
1 teaspoon salt
½ teaspoon garlic salt

1 teaspoon onion salt
1 teaspoon sugar
¼ cup minced dry onion
1 teaspoon Aćcent
½ teaspoon pepper

Combine vegetables and set aside. Combine remaining ingredients in saucepan and bring to a boil. Pour over vegetables. Refrigerate for 24 hours. Serve with crackers. Keeps for weeks. Use a food processor for a different texture.

SALSA

Serves: 8

2 (4¼ ounce) cans chopped ripe
  olives, drained
1 (7 ounce) can diced green chilies,
  drained
5 tomatoes, chopped
1 bunch green onions, chopped
1 Tablespoon chopped parsley

1 Tablespoon oil
1 Tablespoon vinegar
Salt to taste
Pepper to taste
1 (7 ounce) can Ortega Salsa
  (Optional)

Chop and combine vegetables and set aside. Mix oil, vinegar, salt and pepper and stir into chopped vegetables. Add Ortega Salsa, if desired. Chill at least 8 hours, or overnight. Food processor may be used.

Betty Biggadike Scroggin (Mrs. Carroll)
Palos Verdes, California

Delicious served on top of salads.

SPINACH DIP
(Must be prepared 1 day in advance)

Serves: 6 to 8

1 (10 ounce) package frozen
   chopped spinach, thawed and
   drained
½ cup chopped parsley
½ cup green onions
½ teaspoon dill weed

1 teaspoon Cavender's Greek
   Seasoning
1 cup sour cream
1 cup mayonnaise
Juice of ½ lemon

Combine all ingredients. Mix well and refrigerate. This dip is better made 1 day in advance so flavors will have time to blend. Serve with raw vegetables.

Cynthia Weber (Mrs. James R.)

VEGETABLE DIP

Yield: 1 cup

2 (3 ounce) packages cream cheese,
   softened
2 chicken flavored bouillon cubes
2 Tablespoons boiling water
2 Tablespoons mayonnaise
2 Tablespoons minced onions

1 teaspoon minced garlic
⅛ teaspoon garlic powder
Dash of pepper
Dash of Tabasco
Parsley flakes (Optional)

Dissolve bouillon cubes in boiling water. Mix all ingredients together and chill until serving time. Garnish with parsley flakes, if desired. Serve with raw vegetables.

Lisa Chapman (Mrs. Richard W., Jr.)

HOT SAUCE

Yield: 1 quart

½ onion
3 to 5 cloves garlic
3 to 5 jalapeño peppers, seeded
5 teaspoons ground cumin
4 tablespoons Accent

2 Tablespoons oil
2 (16 ounce) cans whole tomatoes
Freshly ground black pepper to
   taste

Blend all ingredients except tomatoes in food processor with a steel blade until a relish consistency. You may use a blender if you chop onion before blending. Add tomatoes and blend quickly so tomatoes are not liquified. Sprinkle top with freshly ground black pepper and blend once more. Pour into a saucepan and heat for 10 to 15 minutes. Stir occasionally. Serve at room temperature or chilled. Keep refrigerated. Serve with Doritos. Will keep for several weeks.

Robin and Mike Smith

TWELFTH NIGHT SHRIMP

Serves: 8 to 10

½ cup mayonnaise
½ cup sour cream
¼ teaspoon salt
½ teaspoon paprika
1 (6 ounce) can tiny shrimp, drained
   and crumbled
½ cup grated onion

1 teaspoon horseradish
Dash of Tabasco
3 teaspoons chili sauce
1 (14 ounce) can artichoke hearts,
   drained and chopped
Worcestershire sauce to taste

Combine all ingredients. Chill several hours in the refrigerator until ready to serve. Serve with crackers or melba rounds as a dip.

Melinda Morse

CRABMEAT APPETIZER

Serves: 8 to 10

12 ounces cream cheese, softened
2 Tablespoons Worcestershire
   sauce
1 Tablespoon lemon juice
2 Tablespoons mayonnaise
½ onion, grated, or 1 Tablespoon
   dried minced onion

Dash of garlic salt
6 ounces of chili sauce
1 Tablespoon horseradish
1 (6 ounce) can crabmeat, drained
   and flaked

Mix cream cheese with Worcestershire sauce, lemon juice, mayonnaise, onion and garlic salt. Press into a pie pan. Mix chili sauce and horseradish and spread on top of cream cheese mixture. Top with flaked crabmeat. Serve with melba rounds or Triscuits.

Mrs. Ron Hardin

CRABMEAT CHEESE DIP

Serves: 10

½ pound Velveeta cheese
2 (6 ounce) cans crabmeat, well
   drained

5 to 6 green onions (tops and
   bottoms), chopped
2 cups Hellmann's mayonnaise

Melt cheese in top of double boiler. Add crabmeat, green onions and mayonnaise to melted cheese. Serve hot with melba rounds or chips.

Linda Humphries (Mrs. Steve)

MMM'S SEAFOOD PIZZA DIP

Serves: 15 to 20

1 (8 ounce) package cream cheese, softened
1 Tablespoon mayonnaise
¼ teaspoon Worcestershire sauce
Juice of 1 lemon
½ teaspoon seasoned salt
½ teaspoon lemon pepper
1 (12 ounce) jar cocktail sauce
1 (6 ounce) can crabmeat, drained and flaked

1 (4 ounce) package Monterey Jack cheese, grated
1 (4 ounce) package Mozzarella cheese, grated
6 green onions (tops and bottoms), chopped
½ bell pepper, chopped
½ cup chopped ripe olives
1 tomato, chopped

Mix cream cheese until smooth. Add mayonnaise, Worcestershire, lemon juice and seasonings. Spread on the bottom of a 9 x 13 pyrex dish or serving platter. Refrigerate while preparing other toppings. Drain and flake crabmeat. (Shrimp may be substituted for crabmeat.) Chop onions, bell pepper, olives and tomato. Layer ingredients on top of cream cheese as follows: cocktail sauce, crabmeat, Monterey Jack cheese, Mozzarella cheese, green onions, bell pepper, olives and tomatoes. Serve with melba rounds or crackers.

Melinda Morse

CHEESE DIP

Serves: 8

¼ cup olive oil
1 medium onion, chopped
½ green pepper, chopped
½ pound fresh mushrooms, sliced
1 (10 ounce) can Ro-Tel tomatoes
1 (2¼ ounce) can sliced black olives, drained
1½ pounds Velveeta cheese, cubed

4 Tablespoons chopped parsley
4 teaspoons garlic salt
¼ cup Worcestershire sauce
10 to 12 drops Tabasco
4 Tablespoons chili powder
½ teaspoon Italian Seasonings
4 Tablespoons cornstarch (Optional)

Sauté onion, green pepper and mushrooms in olive oil. Add Ro-Tel and olives. Heat until hot. Transfer to top of double boiler and add remaining ingredients except cornstarch. Heat cheese mixture until melted and well blended. Add cornstarch and water paste if dip needs thickening. Serve hot with Fritos or Doritos. Jalapeño peppers and/or artichoke hearts may be included in dip, if desired.

Jim Wilson

MEXICAN CHEESE DIP

Serves: 10 to 15

1 pound American cheese
1 (5.3 ounce) can Pet evaporated milk
¼ teaspoon garlic powder

1 teaspoon cumin
1 Tablespoon chili powder
1 (10 ounce) can Ro-Tel tomatoes

Cut up and melt cheese in a double boiler. Mix together Pet milk, garlic powder, cumin, chili powder and Ro-Tel in blender. Blend well. Add liquid from blender to cheese and mix. Serve hot with chips.

Cindy Miller (Mrs. Patrick)

Recipe can easily be doubled but you must do the blender ingredients separately, one recipe at a time, before mixing all together.

LAYERED TACO DIP

Serves: 10 to 15

1 (15 ounce) can refried beans
3 ripe avocados
2 Tablespoons lemon juice
¼ teaspoon salt
¼ teaspoon pepper
¼ teaspoon garlic powder
1 (8 ounce) carton sour cream
2 Tablespoons mayonnaise
1 (1¼ ounce) package taco
    seasoning mix

2 tomatoes, chopped
1 bunch green onions (tops and
    bottoms), chopped
1 (8 ounce) package Cheddar
    cheese, grated
1 (4¼ ounce) can chopped black
    olives, drained
Picanté sauce (Optional)
Jalapeño peppers (Optional)
Tortilla chips

Spread refried beans on the bottom of a 9 x 13 pyrex dish and set aside. Mash avocados. Mix with lemon juice, salt, pepper and garlic powder. (You may use a 16 ounce container Calavo avocado dip instead of avocado mixture.) In another bowl, combine sour cream, mayonnaise and taco seasoning mix. Spread avocado mixture over refried beans. Spread the sour cream mixture over the avocado mixture. Sprinkle with tomatoes, onions, cheese and olives, making each a separate layer. You should have 7 layers when completed. Serve cold with tortilla chips. Picanté sauce may be spooned over tomato layer, if desired, and jalapeño peppers may be added to the top.

Nancy Couch Lee (Mrs. James M., Jr.)
Kenan Keyes (Mrs. Griff)
Alta Jean Good

For a special occasion, make a crust of 1½ to 2 cups corn chips and ¼ cup melted butter. Place in bottom and sides of a springform pan and bake for 8 to 10 minutes at 350⁰. Layer the taco dip ingredients in the pan. Refrigerate for several hours and unmold at serving time.

GUACAMOLE

Yield: 2 to 3 cups

2 large avocados
1 (6 ounce) container Calavo
  avocado dip, thawed
1 (8 ounce) package cream cheese,
  softened
1 teaspoon garlic salt
¼ teaspoon Tabasco

½ teaspoon Worcestershire sauce
½ teaspoon seasoned salt
½ teaspoon onion salt
1 medium onion, finely chopped
1 medium firm tomato, finely
  chopped
1 Tablespoon lemon juice

Peel and mash avocados with a fork, not a blender. Mix in avocado dip and cream cheese. Consistency of dip may be left a little lumpy, if desired. Add seasonings and mix again. Chop onion and tomato and mix once more. Mix carefully so as not to mash tomatoes. Squeeze lemon juice on top and cover with plastic wrap.

Julie Byars
Janet Hartman

This dip can be made ahead and refrigerated until serving time.

MEXICAN APPETIZER PLATTER

Oven: 400°
Serves: 16 to 18

1 pound LEAN ground beef
1 large onion, chopped
Salt to taste
1 pound refried beans
1 (4 ounce) can chopped chilies,
  drained
1½ cups grated Monterey Jack
  cheese

1½ cups grated mild Cheddar
  cheese
¾ cup taco sauce
3 green onions, chopped
1 (2¼ ounce) can sliced ripe olives,
  drained
1 medium avocado, mashed
1 cup sour cream
Tortilla chips

Brown beef and onion. DRAIN THOROUGHLY. Season with salt. Spread refried beans in a 10 x 15 ovenproof dish. Top with meat and onion mixture. Sprinkle with chopped chilies, then cheeses. Drizzle taco sauce over all. Bake, uncovered, at 400 degrees for 20 minutes. Garnish with green onions and olives. Mound avocado in center. Top with sour cream. Tuck tortilla chips around the outside edge of dish. Serve immediately.

Ellon Cockrill (Mrs. Rogers)
Ann Truemper

First 5 layers, meat through taco sauce, can be prepared in advance and chilled until cooking time.

BEVERAGES

Wet your whistle! Wet it again! Again and again! For the sake of appearances, taste the soup.

AMARETTO SPECIAL

Yield: 1 drink

1 ounce Amaretto
½ ounce dark crème de cacao

1 ounce chocolate syrup
2 scoops vanilla ice cream

Using blender, combine all ingredients. Mix well.

Beverly Moore (Mrs. Richard N., Jr.)

MELON MADNESS

Yield: 4 servings

1½ ounces Midori melon liqueur
1 ounce white crème de cacao
3 cups vanilla ice cream

Honeydew melon slices (Optional)
Fresh strawberry (Optional)

Combine liqueurs and ice cream in blender. Blend until thickness of drinkable ice cream. Serve in stemmed glasses. Garnish each glass with a skewered slice of honeydew melon and a fresh strawberry.

Chester Regan Cummins

UNCLE BUD'S HUMMERS

Yield: 2 servings

1 ounce Kahlua
2 ounces light rum

1 pint vanilla ice cream or ice milk
Ice cubes, crushed

Place Kahlua, rum and ice cream in the blender. Blend and slowly add crushed ice cubes.

Mary Lehnhard (Mrs. Skip)

VELVET HAMMER

Yield: 4 to 6 servings

1½ ounces brandy
1½ ounces Triple Sec
1½ ounces crème de cacao

4 ice cubes
1 quart vanilla ice cream

Blend brandy, Triple Sec, crème de cocao and ice. Add ice cream and blend until smooth and thick. Serve in stemmed glasses.

Marti Thomas (Mrs. A. Henry)

May be stored in the freezer for a few hours or days. Mix again before serving.

GEORGE MORGAN'S BLOODY MARY MIX
(Must be prepared 1 day in advance)

Yield: 10 to 12 servings

2 (48 ounce) cans tomato juice
1 (16 ounce) can tomato juice
3 teaspoons salt
3 Tablespoons cracked pepper

Juice of 3 lemons
2 teaspoons Tabasco
2 teaspoons horseradish
1 onion

Mix first 7 ingredients. Cut onion in half and soak in mixture overnight. Remove onion and serve chilled over ice.

Marcia Johnston (Mrs. Richard S.)

ICE BREAKER

Yield: 4 servings

1 (10¾ ounce) can tomato soup, undiluted
1 (10¾ ounce) can beef broth, undiluted

1 cup water
⅓ cup vodka
1 teaspoon Worcestershire sauce
Tabasco to taste

Combine all ingredients in a saucepan and heat just to boiling, stirring occasionally. Serve in mugs.

MILK PUNCH

Yield: 1 drink

1½ ounces brandy, bourbon or scotch
1 cup milk or cream

1 teaspoon sugar
Ground nutmeg (Optional)

Mix all ingredients together. Serve over ice.

Cloud Keyes

HARBOUR ISLAND RUM PUNCH

Yield: 1 drink

1½ ounces dark rum
1 ounce orange juice
1 ounce pineapple juice

1 ounce grapefruit juice
¼ lime, freshly squeezed
Ice

Combine all ingredients. Pour over ice. May easily be made in quantity by doubling, tripling, etc. all ingredients.

Anne Hickman (Mrs. Robert C.)

STRAWBERRY DAIQUIRI

Yield: 2 (8 ounce) servings

1 (5 ounce) package frozen
   strawberries, sweetened
½ cup white rum
2 Tablespoons cream of coconut

2 teaspoons lemon juice
1 teaspoon Grenadine
Crushed ice

Chill 2 stemmed 8 ounce glasses. In a blender, combine all ingredients but crushed ice for 5 seconds. Divide the mixture between glasses half-filled with crushed ice.

Mrs. V. H. Guymon

May be made into a frozen daiquiri by adding crushed ice to blender.

REFRESHING WINE DAIQUIRI

Yield: 4 to 6 servings

1 (6 ounce) can frozen lemonade
1 (10 ounce) package frozen
   strawberries, slightly thawed

12 ounces white wine
Ice cubes

Place lemonade, strawberries and wine in blender. Blend slightly. Add ice cubes and continue to blend to desired consistency.

Ellon Cockrill (Mrs. Rogers)

Great on a hot summer day. Light and refreshing!

ORANGE JUBILEE

Yield: 6 to 8 servings

1 (12 ounce) can frozen orange
   juice
1½ cups milk
1½ cups water
¼ to ½ cup sugar to taste

1½ teaspoons vanilla extract
15 to 20 ice cubes
Orange slices and mint leaves for
   garnish

Place all ingredients in blender except ice cubes for 15 to 20 seconds. Slowly add ice cubes, a few at a time, until slushy. Refrigerate until ready to serve.

Marylee Robinson (Mrs. Dan)

Good for morning meetings or before a brunch.

FROZEN MARGARITAS SUPREME

Yield: 4 servings

Lime wedge
Salt
1 (6 ounce) can frozen limeade
   concentrate, thawed

¾ cup Tequila
¼ cup Triple Sec or other orange
   flavored liqueur
Crushed ice

Rub rim of 4 glasses with wedge of lime. Place salt in saucer and spin rim of each glass in salt. Set glasses aside. Combine limeade, Tequila and Triple Sec in blender and blend well. Add crushed ice to fill blender ¾ full. Blend well. Pour beverage into prepared glasses. Garnish with a slice of lime.

Roxanne Vowell

SANGRIA SOUTHERN

Yield: 6 to 8 servings

1 lemon, thinly sliced
1 orange, thinly sliced
1 lime, thinly sliced
1 to 2 Tablespoons sugar

1 (1½ ounce) jigger Triple Sec
1 (⅘ quart) bottle dry red wine
½ cup club soda, chilled
Additional lime slices

Remove seeds from sliced fruit. Place slices in glass pitcher and add 1 to 2 Tablespoons sugar. Allow to stand for a few minutes. Add Triple Sec to sliced fruit. Stir with a wooden spoon, bruising fruit to extract juices. Add wine. More sugar may be added if desired. Chill. Just before serving, add club soda. Serve over ice and garnish with additional lime slices.

Tish Nisbet (Mrs. Wyck)

Refreshing summer drink.

WHITE SANGRIA

Yield: 6 servings

1 (750 ml) bottle dry white wine
½ cup Curacao
¼ cup sugar
1 orange, thinly sliced
1 lemon, thinly sliced

1 lime, thinly sliced
4 to 5 large strawberries, thinly
   sliced
1 (10 ounce) bottle club soda

Combine wine, Curacao and sugar in pitcher and stir until sugar is dissolved. Add fruits. Cover and chill in refrigerator for at least 1 hour to let flavors blend. Before serving, add soda and ice cubes and stir gently to mix. Serve in wine glasses or champagne flutes.

Linda Deloney (Mrs. Phil)

SPICED WINE

Yield: 6 servings

Spiced Wine Packet

½ teaspoon whole allspice
6 whole cloves
½ teaspoon dried ground orange
   peel

2 (1½ inch) sticks cinnamon
Dash of nutmeg
3 inch square cheesecloth and
   string

Spiced Wine

1 (750 ml) bottle red wine
½ cup sugar

Spice packet

To make spiced wine packet, place spices and peel on cheesecloth and tie into bag with string. Combine wine, sugar and spice packet in saucepan and simmer for 20 minutes. DO NOT BOIL. Remove packet before serving.

Linda Deloney (Mrs. Phil)

For a wonderful gift, tie a spice packet to a bottle of wine with instructions for use.

HOT SPICED WINE

Yield: 12 to 16 servings

4 cups water
1 cup sugar
12 whole cloves
6 whole allspice
4 (1 inch) sticks cinnamon
½ teaspoon powdered ginger

Rind of 1 orange
Rind of 1 lemon
2 cups strained orange juice
1 cup strained lemon juice
1 (750 ml) bottle Burgundy or claret
   wine

In a saucepan combine water, sugar, spices and citrus rinds. Bring to a boil, stirring to dissolve sugar. Simmer for 10 to 15 minutes, remove from heat and let stand for 1 hour. Strain and add fruit juices and wine.

Alice Lynn Overbey (Mrs. Thomas L.)

CAPPUCCINO

Yield: 6 to 8 servings

3 cups coffee
3 cups Half and Half
4 ounces crème de cacao

2 ounces rum
2 ounces brandy

Combine all ingredients in a saucepan. Heat. Serve immediately.

Wyck Nisbet

KEOKI COFFEE

Yield: 1 serving

1 ounce Kahlua
1 ounce brandy

Coffee
Whipping cream, whipped

Pour Kahlua and brandy into warmed mug or stemmed glass. Fill with hot coffee and mix well. Top with whipped cream.

Julie Headstream Haught (Mrs. William D.)

KAHLUA

(Must be prepared in advance)

Yield: 1 gallon

4 cups sugar
4 cups water
¾ cup instant coffee granules
2 Tablespoons vanilla extract

2 Tablespoons chocolate syrup
1 liter vodka
1 gallon glass container with tight
  lid

Boil sugar and water for 10 minutes. When cool, add coffee, vanilla and chocolate syrup. Stir well. Add vodka and pour into gallon container. Shake every other day for 14 to 16 weeks. Flavor improves with age.

Jeffrey Baskin
Susan Weinstein

HOT CHOCOLATE

Yield: 6 cups

6 ounces bittersweet chocolate,
  broken into pieces
2 Tablespoons sugar
2 cups boiling water
2 cups milk

1 cup Half and Half
⅔ cup Kahlua or Tia Maria
  (Optional)
½ cup whipping cream, whipped

Place chocolate and sugar in a heavy saucepan. Pour in boiling water. Stir with whisk until chocolate is melted. Cook, stirring occasionally, over low heat to simmering point, 10 to 15 minutes. Remove from heat. Heat milk and Half and Half in a saucepan over low heat, just until bubbles form around edges. Slowly pour milk mixture into chocolate mixture, whisking until smooth. Simmer 5 minutes, then add liqueur. Beat cream until stiff. Ladle chocolate into mugs and top each with whipped cream.

Anne Fryer

MOCHA MIX
(Must be prepared 1 week in advance)

Yield: 6½ cups

1 vanilla bean, cut in fourths
1 cup unsweetened cocoa
2 cups sugar

2 cups non-fat dry milk powder
2 cups non-dairy creamer
¼ cup instant coffee granules

Combine ingredients and refrigerate for 1 week in an air-tight container. Use 3 Tablespoons per 6 ounces of hot water. Top with whipped cream or marshmallows.

Donna Bressinck (Mrs. Rene)

A perfect Christmas gift.

HOT BUTTERED RUM

Yield: 24 cups

1 pound butter, softened
1 pound light brown sugar
1 pound powdered sugar
2 teaspoons ground cinnamon
2 teaspoons ground nutmeg

1 quart vanilla ice cream, softened
Light rum
Whipped cream
Cinnamon sticks

Combine butter, sugars and spices. Beat until fluffy. Add ice cream, stirring until well blended. Spoon mixture into a 2 quart freezer container. Freeze. Place 3 Tablespoons of slightly thawed butter mixture and 1½ ounces rum in a large mug. Fill with boiling water. Stir well. Top with whipped cream and serve with a cinnamon stick.

Lynn Monk (Mrs. James W.)

Any unused butter mixture may be refrozen and used later!

MINTED ORANGE TEA

Yield: 6 drinks

3 cups very strong tea (use 5
  Tablespoons orange pekoe tea
  and 3 cups boiling water - let
  steep 10 minutes)
½ cup orange juice

⅓ cup lemon juice
1 teaspoon sugar
2 cups ginger ale
Mint
Orange slices

Combine tea, orange juice, lemon juice and sugar. Chill. Add 2 cups ginger ale. Pour over ice. Garnish with mint and orange slices.

KIR CHAMPAGNE PUNCH

Yield: 30 (4 ounce) servings

2 (10 ounce) packages frozen
   raspberries, thawed
1 (32 ounce) bottle club soda,
   chilled

1 cup crème de cassis, chilled
3 (750 ml) bottles champagne,
   chilled

Place one package of raspberries in a blender. Process until smooth. Strain. Pour raspberry puree into punch bowl with club soda and cassis. Stir gently. Break up remaining package of raspberries and add to punch bowl. Pour slowly, resting champagne bottles on the edge of punch bowl. Stir gently with an up and down motion. Serve at once.

Martha H. Carle (Mrs. Kenneth)
Stuttgart, Arkansas

DELICIOUS COFFEE PUNCH

Yield: 50 servings

4 quarts strong coffee
5 teaspoons vanilla
5 Tablespoons sugar

1 quart whipping cream, whipped
   and chilled
2 quarts (or more) vanilla ice cream

Prepare coffee. Add vanilla and sugar. Chill. Before serving, spoon ice cream into punch bowl. Add coffee mixture and fold in whipped cream. Mix well. Taste before serving and add more sugar, if needed.

May be halved.

WASSAIL

Yield: 8 to 12 servings

7 cinnamon sticks
18 cloves, whole
1½ teaspoons allspice, whole
2 cups cranberry juice
2 cups orange juice
¼ cup lemon juice

1½ quarts apple cider
¼ cup sugar
Lemon slices
Orange slices
2 cups vodka or rum (Optional)

Tie cinnamon sticks, cloves and allspice together in cheesecloth. Combine juices and sugar. Simmer 15 minutes with spices. Float fruit slices on top. Remove bag of spices. Add vodka or rum, if desired. Serve hot.

Polly Brewer (Mrs. Larry)

Wassail may be prepared and served from a large electric percolator.

RUSSIAN TEA

Yield: 75 punch cups

3 sticks cinnamon
3 teaspoons whole cloves
3 quarts water
4 tea bags
1 cup sugar
1 (16 ounce) can jellied cranberry
   sauce

1 (8 to 10 ounce) package red hots
4 (6 ounce) cans frozen orange juice
8 (6 ounce) cans water
2 (6 ounce) cans frozen lemonade
1 (46 ounce) can pineapple juice

Prepare cloth bag containing cinnamon and cloves. Bring 3 quarts water to boil, add spice bag and simmer for 1 hour. Add tea bags. Let stand for 5 minutes and remove tea bags. Add sugar, cranberry sauce and red hots. Stir over low heat. Add orange juice, water, lemonade, and pineapple juice. Stir and continue to heat but do not boil. Serve hot. A dash of vodka may be added to the cup before tea is poured!

Sally Davis

Can be made and served in a very large coffee pot.

EGGNOG DELUXE

(Must be prepared 1 day in advance)

Yield: 2½ quarts

6 egg yolks
¾ cup plus 2 Tablespoons sugar
½ teaspoon vanilla extract
¼ teaspoon ground nutmeg
¼ cup plus 2 Tablespoons rum
¾ cup brandy

3 cups whipping cream
2 cups milk
6 egg whites
3 Tablespoons sugar
Ground nutmeg

Beat egg yolks until thick and lemon-colored (about 10 minutes). Gradually add ¾ cup plus 2 Tablespoons sugar, vanilla and nutmeg, beating well. Slowly stir in rum and brandy. Cover the container and store in refrigerator overnight. Place chilled mixture in a punch bowl. Gradually stir in cream and milk. Beat egg whites in large mixing bowl until soft peaks form. Gradually add 3 Tablespoons sugar and beat until stiff. Fold whites into chilled mixture. Sprinkle with nutmeg.

Alice Gazette (Mrs. Gary)

If you never liked eggnog because of the bourbon flavor, you will love this recipe because the liquor flavor is very light!

"I am willing to taste any drink once."
JAMES BRANCH CABELL
1879-1958

HOLIDAY PUNCH

Yield: 30 punch cup servings

2 (16 ounce) cans jellied cranberry
   sauce
1 cup lemon juice

4 Tablespoons almond extract
1 quart white wine
1 quart ginger ale, chilled

Blend cranberry sauce, lemon juice and almond extract in electric blender or mixer. Add wine. Pour over ice in a punch bowl. Immediately before serving, add ginger ale.

Nancy Couch (Mrs. James)

TROPICAL PUNCH

Yield: 75 punch cups

3 (46 ounce) cans pineapple juice
2 (12 ounce) cans frozen orange
   juice
3 (12 ounce) cans frozen lemonade

3½ quarts water
½ cup sugar
1 quart ginger ale
Orange slices, cherries and
   strawberries for garnish

Mix all ingredients but ginger ale. Refrigerate. Add ginger ale to punch bowl before serving.

Ruby Hampton (Mrs. F. Barnes)
DeWitt, Arkansas

A very good yellow punch base. Vodka or rum may be added.

CHRISTMAS AROMA
(Not for consumption)

Yield: 3 quarts

1 quart pineapple juice
1 quart water
1 quart apple cider
4 pieces ginger

3 cinnamon sticks
16 cloves, whole
1 teaspoon allspice
1 or 2 teaspoons pickling spice

Place all ingredients in a large kettle and bring to a boil for several minutes. Turn down to a simmer and allow house to fill with a wonderful Christmas aroma. Keep mixture for days adding water and stirring as needed.

Ben Hussman (Mrs. Walter, Jr.)
Carol Sitlington (Mrs. Mike)

SOUPS · SANDWICHES

There is something to be said for being left
after certain meals with a desire for more.

CREAM OF ARTICHOKE SOUP

Yield: 4 to 6 servings

½ to ¾ cup chopped shallots and
   onions (green or white)
2 medium carrots, sliced
2 medium ribs celery, sliced
3 to 4 Tablespoons butter
1 bay leaf
½ teaspoon thyme

4 cups chicken broth
1 (14 ounce) can artichoke hearts,
   drained and sliced
Salt to taste
Pepper to taste
2 egg yolks
1 cup whipping cream

Sauté chopped onion-shallot mixture, carrots and celery in butter. Add bay leaf, thyme, chicken broth and artichoke hearts. Simmer 10 to 15 minutes. Remove bay leaf and season with salt and pepper. Stir two egg yolks into cream. Add a small amount of warm soup mixture to egg-cream mixture. Stir well and add to warm soup mixture, blending well. Heat, stirring constantly, but do not boil.

Melinda Morse

ARTICHOKE OYSTER BISQUE

Yield: 6 to 8 servings

½ cup butter
2 cups chopped onion
1 (14 ounce) can artichoke hearts,
   drained and chopped
2 cups fresh sliced mushrooms
1 cup chopped celery
3 Tablespoons chopped fresh
   parsley
½ cup chopped green onion tops
2 teaspoons garlic salt
2 teaspoons coarsely ground black
   pepper

½ teaspoon Tony's All Season salt
   and pepper
1 (10¾ ounce) can cream of
   mushroom soup
1 pint Half and Half
1 (14 ounce) can artichoke hearts,
   drained and quartered
2 (8 ounce) jars fresh oysters,
   drained and halved
½ teaspoon gumbo filé

In the butter, sauté onion, 1 can of chopped artichoke hearts, mushrooms, celery, parsley, green onion tops and seasonings for 10 minutes, stirring often. In a large pan, combine mushroom soup and Half and Half. Add onion-artichoke mixture and simmer over low heat for 30 minutes. Add quartered artichoke hearts, oysters and gumbo filé and continue to heat for 10 more minutes.

Mary Lorraine Wyatt (Mrs. George Cox)

EASY ASPARAGUS SOUP

Yield: 4 servings

1 (10¾ ounce) can cream of
   asparagus soup
1 cup sour cream
3 dashes Tabasco
½ teaspoon celery salt

1 cup milk
Asparagus tips (Optional)
4 teaspoons finely chopped green
   onions

Combine first 5 ingredients and mix well. Add chopped asparagus tips, if desired. Chill for at least 4 hours before serving. Garnish each serving with 1 teaspoon of finely chopped green onions.

Jo Ann Drew (Mrs. Tommy, Jr.)

RUTH AGAR'S AVOCADO SOUP

Yield: 4 servings

1 cup puréed avocado
1 cup sour cream
1 (10¾ ounce) can chicken broth
1 Tablespoon lemon juice
2 Tablespoons Orange Curacao

⅛ to ¼ teaspoon nutmeg
Salt to taste
Pepper to taste
Lime slices for garnish

Combine avocado, sour cream and chicken broth. Mix in blender until smooth. Add remaining ingredients. Serve cold. Garnish with lime slices.

Kristin Agar
Cynthia East (Mrs. Robert C.)

SPICY BROCCOLI SOUP

Yield: 6 to 8 servings

1 medium onion, chopped
2 Tablespoons butter
2 (10 ounce) packages frozen
   chopped broccoli
2 (10¾ ounce) cans cream of
   mushroom soup

4 cups milk
1 (6 ounce) roll Kraft Jalapeño
   cheese, use only 3 ounces
1 teaspoon Accent (Optional)

Sauté chopped onion in butter. Cook broccoli according to directions on package. Drain broccoli. Place onion, broccoli and rest of ingredients in saucepan on top of stove. Cook over moderate heat, stirring often, until cheese melts. Serve hot.

Judy Grundfest (Mrs. Dave, Jr.)

CREAM OF BROCCOLI SOUP

Yield: 4 servings

1 (10 ounce) package frozen
  chopped broccoli
½ cup chopped onion
1 (10¾ ounce) can chicken broth
2 Tablespoons butter
2 Tablespoons flour

2 cups Half and Half
1 teaspoon salt
1 teaspoon finely crumbled basil
½ teaspoon pepper
3 ounces of sliced almonds

Combine broccoli, onions and broth in a saucepan. Heat to boiling and simmer for 5 minutes. Pour into a blender and blend until smooth. Melt butter and blend in flour. Stir in broccoli mixture, Half and Half, salt, basil and pepper. Heat slowly, just to boiling. Simmer 1 minute, stirring. Top each serving with sliced almonds.

Julie Fulgham (Mrs. Edward)

BROCCOLI NOODLE SOUP

Yield: 8 to 10 servings

2 Tablespoons salad oil
¾ cup chopped onion
6 cups water
6 chicken bouillon cubes
8 ounces medium egg noodles
1 teaspoon salt

2 (10 ounce) packages frozen
  chopped broccoli
⅛ teaspoon garlic powder
6 cups milk
1 pound Velveeta cheese
Pepper to taste

Heat oil in a large Dutch oven. Sauté onion over medium heat in oil for 3 minutes. Add water and bouillon cubes. Heat to boiling, stirring occasionally, until cubes are dissolved. Gradually add noodles and salt, making certain bouillon mixture continues to boil. Cook, uncovered, for 3 minutes, stirring occasionally. Stir in broccoli and garlic powder. Cook 4 minutes more. Lower heat and add milk, cheese, and pepper. Continue cooking until cheese melts.

Mrs. Lucy W. Gardner

CANTALOUPE SOUP

Yield: 6 servings

4 ripe cantaloupes, cut in chunks
6 ounces orange juice
¼ to ⅓ cup honey

½ to 1 teaspoon cinnamon
½ pint whipping cream
½ cup Calvados (Optional)

Purée cantaloupe in food processor or blender. Add orange juice, honey, cinnamon, whipping cream and Calvados. Chill. May be served in cantaloupe halves with mint sprigs for garnish.

Gayle Leonard (Mrs. Donald)

BEAN SOUP

Yield: 8 to 10 servings

1½ cups bean mixture (see below)
1 teaspoon salt
2 quarts water
Ham bone, or 1 pound of ham,
    diced
1 (10 ounce) can Ro-Tel tomatoes
1 large onion, diced

1 clove garlic, minced
Juice of 1 lemon
1 long red or green chili pepper, or
    cayenne pepper to taste
½ to 1 pound sliced Polish sausage,
    cooked and drained (Optional)

Wash bean mixture. Cover with water, add salt and soak overnight, or bring to a boil for 5 minutes, remove from heat, and soak 1 hour. Drain. Place beans in water, add ham bone or ham and simmer for 3 hours. Add Ro-Tel, onion, garlic, lemon juice, red or green chili pepper, and simmer for 2 hours. If using sausage, add and simmer for 1 more hour.

Bean Mixture: The base mixture for this soup is 8 assorted packages of dried peas and beans. For example: lentils, split peas, baby limas, black beans, red beans, black-eyed peas, navy beans and barley.

Susan Diffey Johnson

Suggestion: 1½ cup amounts can be packaged in a plastic bag and tied with a plaid ribbon with recipe enclosed for a Christmas remembrance.

CUBAN BLACK BEAN SOUP

Yield: 6 servings

1 pound black beans
2 quarts water
2 Tablespoons salt
5 ounces oil
½ pound onions, chopped
½ pound green pepper, chopped
5 cloves garlic, crushed

½ Tablespoon cumin
½ Tablespoon oregano
1 ounce white vinegar
1½ cups cooked rice
Oil
Vinegar
1 cup finely chopped onion

Soak beans in water overnight. Add salt and boil beans until soft. Heat oil in a pan, adding onions and green pepper. Sauté until the onions are browned. Add the garlic, cumin, oregano and vinegar, cooking slowly. Drain some of the water off the beans before adding them to the pan and cook slowly until ready to serve. Marinate cooked rice in a mixture of oil and vinegar. Do the same with the cup of onions. Spoon rice and onions into each serving of soup.

Julie Allen (Mrs. Wally)

STRAWBERRY SOUP

Yield: 6 servings

1 cup fresh strawberries, washed
   and drained
1 cup orange juice

¼ cup honey
¼ cup sour cream
½ cup sweet white wine (Optional)

Combine all ingredients in container of blender. Process until strawberries are puréed. Remove from blender container and chill thoroughly. Stir before serving.

Reita Miller (Mrs. Bill)

CREAMY CAULIFLOWER SOUP

Yield: 8 to 10 servings

1 medium head cauliflower, cut in
   bite-sized pieces
¼ cup butter or margarine
⅔ cup chopped onion
2 Tablespoons flour
2 cups chicken broth

2 cups Half and Half
½ teaspoon Worcestershire sauce
Salt to taste
1 cup grated Cheddar cheese
Chopped parsley

Cook cauliflower in boiling salted water. Drain, reserving water. Melt butter, add onion and cook until soft. Blend in flour, add broth and stir constantly until mixture comes to a boil. Stir in 1 cup liquid drained from cauliflower (add water if necessary to make 1 cup), Half and Half, Worcestershire sauce and salt. Add cauliflower. Heat to boiling. Stir in cheese. Serve sprinkled with parsley.

Mrs. Allen Weintraub

CHEDDAR BISQUE WITH WALNUTS

Yield: 6 servings

2 cups milk
2 cups Half and Half
8 ounces sharp Cheddar cheese,
   grated
1 Tablespoon Worcestershire sauce

1 teaspoon salt
6 Tablespoons butter
¾ cup flour
6 ounces dry white wine
6 Tablespoons chopped walnuts

In top of a double boiler, heat milk, Half and Half and cheese until cheese is melted. Stir well. Add Worcestershire sauce and salt. In another pan, melt butter, stir in flour and cook until smooth. Stir well, add flour-butter mixture to cheese mixture and simmer 2 to 3 minutes until well blended. Add wine, simmer 10 minutes. Pour into serving bowls and sprinkle 1 Tablespoon of walnuts over each serving.

Robert M. Eubanks

CHEESE CHOWDER

Yield: 4 to 6 servings

3 Tablespoons butter
1½ cups sliced celery
1 cup finely chopped carrots
¼ cup finely chopped green onions
2 (10¾ ounce) cans cream of potato soup
1 (14½ ounce) can chicken broth

Few dashes of Tabasco
2 Tablespoons snipped parsley
8 ounces Cheddar cheese, shredded
1 (13 ounce) can evaporated milk
3 Tablespoons sherry
Parsley or green onions for garnish

In a soup pot melt butter and sauté celery, carrots and onion until tender. Add soup, broth, Tabasco and parsley. Heat until hot. Add cheese, milk and sherry, cooking until thoroughly mixed. DO NOT BOIL. Garnish with parsley or onion if desired.

Donna Bressinck (Mrs. Rene)

CHICKEN-SAUSAGE GUMBO

Yield: 12 to 16 servings

3 quarts water
1 (4 to 5 pound) chicken
2 ribs celery with leaves
1 carrot, cut in fourths
1 onion, cut in fourths
2 bay leaves
1 teaspoon salt
⅓ cup oil
½ cup flour
1 pound frozen sliced okra
1 cup chopped onion
¾ cup chopped celery
½ cup chopped green pepper
½ cup chopped green onions
2 cloves garlic, chopped

2 bay leaves
1 teaspoon thyme
1 teaspoon marjoram
1 teaspoon basil
1 (14½ ounce) can tomatoes, undrained
½ pound ham, cubed
1 pound smoked sausage, sliced
2 Tablespoons Worcestershire sauce
1 Tablespoon salt
1 teaspoon pepper
Tabasco to taste
Steamed rice

In a stock pot bring water to a boil. Add chicken, celery, carrot, onion, bay leaves and salt, and simmer for 25 minutes. Remove chicken and take meat from bones. Set meat aside and return bones to broth, continuing to simmer. In another 4 quart pan, heat oil and flour. Cook this roux until a nice brown color (30 minutes), stirring constantly. Add okra, onions, celery, green pepper, and cook about 5 to 10 minutes. Add green onions, garlic, bay leaves, thyme, marjoram, basil, tomatoes, ham and cooked chicken meat. Strain stock and add to gumbo. Fry sausage, drain well, and add to gumbo. Simmer 1½ hours. Add Worcestershire sauce, salt and pepper. Add Tabasco to taste. Serve over steamed rice in a bowl.

Courtney Jackson (Mrs. J. Presley)

CORN CHOWDER

Yield: 6 servings

5 slices bacon, cut in 1 inch pieces
1 medium white onion, thinly sliced
2 cups potatoes, cut in ½ inch
　cubes
½ teaspoon salt
Water to barely cover

1 (10¾ ounce) can cream of
　chicken soup
½ soup can of milk
1 (12 ounce) can vacuum-packed
　whole kernel corn
Pepper to taste

Sauté bacon pieces until crisp in a Dutch oven. Remove bacon and reserve. Sauté onion slices in bacon drippings. Add potatoes and salt. Barely cover with water and simmer until potatoes are tender. Add soup and stir until blended. Add milk and corn. Stir well. Heat through. Add pepper to taste and serve. Top with crumbled bacon.

Kathy Wilkins (Mrs. James H., Jr.)

CRAB BISQUE

Yield: 6 servings

1 (10¾ ounce) can cream of celery
　soup
1 (10½ ounce) can pepper pot soup

1 pint Half and Half
1 (6½ ounce) can crabmeat, drained
¼ cup sherry

Mix soups and Half and Half. Shred crabmeat and add. Heat. Just before serving, add sherry.

Julie Headstream Haught (Mrs. William D.)

COLD CUCUMBER SOUP

Yield: 4 servings

1 large cucumber, peeled and
　seeded
12 ounces cream cheese
3 or 4 green onions with 3 inch
　green tops
1 bunch fresh parsley, stems
　removed

3 Tablespoons sour cream
¾ teaspoon salt
Heavy or light cream according to
　preference
Freshly ground white pepper

Cut cucumber, cream cheese and green onions into 1 inch pieces and place with parsley, sour cream and salt in food processor. Whirl for 6 seconds. Scrape down container's sides and whirl for 1 or 2 seconds more to achieve a fairly smooth texture. Refrigerate for at least 4 hours. Thin with cream to desired consistency. Pour into chilled bowls and sprinkle with white pepper.

Diane A. Larrison (Mrs. James H., Jr.)

FRIJOLE SOUP

Yield: 6 to 8 servings

2 quarts water
1 pound pinto beans
½ pound salt pork
1 clove garlic, minced
1 medium onion, chopped
6 Tablespoons olive oil

1 (16 ounce) can tomatoes,
   undrained
2 (10¾ ounce) cans chicken broth
Salt to taste
Pepper to taste
Muenster cheese
Sour cream

Place water, beans and salt pork in a soup pot. Cook beans until tender. Drain beans, reserving water. Purée beans in blender, adding reserved water as needed. Sauté garlic and onion in olive oil. Add tomatoes and cook for 10 minutes. Add beans and chicken broth and simmer for 20 minutes. Place a slice of cheese in each soup bowl. Pour soup over cheese and top with sour cream.

Norma C. Rauch

GAZPACHO

Yield: 4 servings

½ cup soft bread crumbs
½ cup water
1 teaspoon salt
2 Tablespoons olive oil
3 Tablespoons red wine vinegar
1 small clove garlic, minced
1 Tablespoon chopped onion

2 Tablespoons diced pimiento
2 cups peeled, diced tomatoes
⅓ cup finely chopped celery
⅓ cup finely chopped green pepper
Several dashes of Tabasco
2 cups tomato juice

Purée all ingredients except tomato juice in blender. Add juice and mix until well blended.

Marcia Johnston (Mrs. Richard S.)

Much better made a day ahead.

"Beautiful soup! Who cares for fish, game, or any other dish? Who would not give all else for two pennyworth only of beautiful soup?"

LEWIS CARROLL
Alice in Wonderland
1832-1898

WILD DUCK GUMBO

Yield: 8 to 10 servings

2 dressed ducks
½ cup butter
1 cup sifted flour
1 heaping soup plate chopped onion
  (about 3 cups)
1 heaping soup plate chopped
  celery (about 3 cups)
3 cloves garlic, finely chopped
1 (6 ounce) can tomato paste
1 (20 ounce) can tomatoes,
  undrained
2 teaspoons Accent

1 heaping soup plate chopped green
  peppers (about 3 cups)
1 bunch green onions, chopped
1 bunch parsley, finely chopped
  (remove ½ cup for garnish)
1 teaspoon oregano
1 teaspoon thyme
1 Tablespoon salt
1 Tablespoon pepper
½ Tablespoon red pepper
2 pounds shrimp, cooked and
  peeled
Wild and white rice, cooked

Boil dressed ducks until tender (2 hours or so) in slightly salted water to cover. Drain, reserving stock. Melt butter in a heavy iron pot and add flour to make roux the color of an Indian squaw. Stir constantly over medium heat. When roux is ready, add onions and celery. Cook with reduced heat until onions and celery brown. Add garlic, tomato paste, tomatoes, Accent, green peppers, green onions, parsley and seasonings. Add 2 quarts of reserved duck stock and boil rapidly for ½ hour. Remove meat from duck carcasses and cut into bite-sized pieces. Add meat to pot. More stock may be added to make a rich gumbo. Add cooked and peeled shrimp. To serve, pour gumbo over cooked rice in soup plates. Sprinkle chopped parsley on top.

Mary Kumpuris (Mrs. Dean)

EGG NOODLE - CHEESE - SPINACH SOUP

Yield: 6 to 8 servings

1 Tablespoon oil
½ cup chopped onion
1 clove garlic, crushed
3 cups water
3 chicken bouillon cubes
4 ounces very fine egg noodles
½ teaspoon salt

3 cups milk
1 (10 ounce) package frozen
  chopped spinach, thawed and
  drained
¼ pound Cheddar cheese, shredded
¼ pound Swiss cheese, shredded

Heat oil and sauté onion and garlic. Add water and bouillon cubes. Heat to boiling. Add noodles and salt. Cook, uncovered, for 6 minutes. Stir occasionally. Add milk, spinach and cheeses. Heat until cheese melts. Do not boil.

Lora Parnell (Mrs. Cliff)

RICHARD ALLIN'S GUMBO

Yield: 3 quarts

2 wild ducks
⅔ cup vegetable oil
⅔ cup flour
2 cups chopped onions
⅔ cup chopped green pepper
½ cup chopped green onion tops
2 Tablespoons minced parsley
6 to 10 garlic cloves, minced
3½ teaspoons salt
1½ teaspoons black pepper
Pinch of cayenne pepper

1 teaspoon dried thyme
3 bay leaves, crushed
3 Tablespoons gumbo filé
¼ pound ham, cut in bite-sized
   pieces
¼ pound cured sausage, thinly
   sliced
2 pounds raw, peeled shrimp
½ to 1 pound crabmeat
Cooked rice

Simmer ducks in water to cover until done and tender. Reserve 2 quarts of the stock. Make a roux with the oil and flour, stirring until it becomes a milk chocolate color. Add onion, green pepper, onion tops, parsley and garlic. Continue cooking over low heat for 10 minutes. Add reserved stock to vegetable mixture, then add all seasonings. Cut duck meat into bite-sized pieces. Add duck meat, ham and sausage. Mix thoroughly. Bring slowly to a boil, reduce heat, and simmer 30 minutes. Add shrimp and simmer a few minutes, add crabmeat and bring to simmer. Remove from heat and add gumbo filé. Serve in bowls over rice.

Richard Allin

This gumbo is good even if you are missing one of the prime ingredients (duck, shrimp or crabmeat). Make it anyway!

FRESH HERB SUMMER SOUP

Yield: 8 to 10 servings

6 cups chicken broth or stock
⅔ cup snipped fresh chives
⅔ cup minced fresh basil
1½ cups finely minced fresh
   parsley

4 Tablespoons minced fresh mint
   leaves
4 egg yolks, room temperature
3 cups whipping cream
White pepper to taste

Pour chicken broth into a large saucepan. Add the fresh herbs. Bring to a boil, lower heat, and simmer for 20 minutes. In a separate bowl, beat the egg yolks lightly with the cream. Slowly whisk 1 cup of the hot broth mixture into the cream-yolk mixture. Pour this mixture into the pan in a stream, whisking constantly. Cook for 6 to 8 minutes or until thickened. Do not boil. Cool completely. Chill, covered, for at least 3 hours, better if chilled overnight. Season with white pepper. Garnish with minced fresh herbs.

Ben Hussman (Mrs. Walter, Jr.)

HOLIDAY SOUP

Yield: 6 to 8 servings

3 (10½ ounce) cans tomato
  madrilène
3 ripe avocados
3 Tablespoons sour cream
3 Tablespoons mayonnaise

1½ teaspoons minced onion
Salt to taste
Pepper to taste
2½ Tablespoons lemon juice
Sour cream for garnish

Divide 1 can of the madrilene among 6 to 8 clear sherbet glasses to make a first layer. Place in refrigerator to set. Mash avocados with sour cream, mayonnaise, onion, salt, pepper and lemon juice. Gently spoon half the avocado mixture on the tomato layer, dividing equally among the glasses. Divide another can of madrilène, pouring it over the avocado making the third layer. Chill until set. Use the second half of the avocado mixture as the next layer. Finish the layers using the third can of tomato madrilène. Chill until set. Garnish with some leftover avocado mixture or dollop of sour cream.

Helen Sloan (Mrs. John C.)

SOUR AND HOT SOUP

Yield: 4 to 6 servings

4 dried Chinese mushrooms
½ cup canned bamboo shoots
2 squares (3 inches each) fresh soy
  bean cake, Tofu
¼ pound boneless pork
1 quart chicken stock, fresh or
  canned
1 teaspoon salt
1 Tablespoon soy sauce

¼ teaspoon ground white pepper
2 Tablespoons white vinegar
2 Tablespoons cornstarch mixed
  with 2 Tablespoons cold water
1 egg, lightly beaten
2 teaspoons sesame seed oil
  (Optional)
1 scallion, including the green top,
  finely chopped

Prepare ahead: In a small bowl, cover the mushrooms with ⅔ cup of warm water and let them soak for at least 30 minutes. Discard the water. Cut away and discard the tough stems of the mushrooms. Cut the caps into thin slices. Drain the pieces of bamboo shoots and bean cake. Rinse in cold water and finely slice. Trim the pork of all fat, then slice as thinly as possible into narrow strips, about 1½ to 2 inches long.

To cook: Combine in a heavy 3 quart saucepan the stock, salt, soy sauce, mushrooms, bamboo shoots and pork. Bring to a boil over high heat, then immediately reduce heat to low. Cover and simmer for 3 to 5 minutes. Add the bean cake, pepper and vinegar. Bring to a boil again. Stir the cornstarch and pour it into the soup. Stir for a few seconds until the soup thickens, then slowly pour in the beaten egg. Stir gently. Remove the soup from the heat. Stir in the sesame seed oil and sprinkle the top with scallions. Serve at once.

Shirley C. Juan

FRESH MUSHROOM SOUP

Yield: 8 servings

1 bunch green onions (including green tops), finely chopped
¾ cup butter
½ cup flour
Salt to taste
White pepper to taste
5 (10¾ ounce) cans chicken broth
1½ pounds fresh mushrooms, washed and sliced
2 cups Half and Half

Sauté onions in butter until clear. Add flour, salt and white pepper to taste. Cook for 10 minutes, stirring constantly. Slowly add heated chicken broth and bring to a boil. Add mushrooms (reserve some for garnish) and cook for 10 minutes. Blend until smooth in blender or food processor. Return to stove, add Half and Half. Heat thoroughly, do not boil. Garnish each serving with fresh mushroom slices.

Donna Kay McLarty (Mrs. Thomas F.)

CURRIED MUSHROOM SOUP

Yield: 5 servings

12 ounces fresh mushrooms
5 Tablespoons butter or margarine
1 teaspoon curry powder
2 Tablespoons flour
1 (10½ ounce) can consommé
2 cups Half and Half
1 cup milk
Salt to taste
Pepper to taste

Clean mushrooms and slice in halves or thirds. Sauté in 4 Tablespoons of butter and sprinkle with curry powder. After 3 to 5 minutes, remove from skillet and add 1 Tablespoon of butter. Then add 2 Tablespoons flour and stir thoroughly. Add 1 can undiluted consommé and simmer, stirring frequently. When slightly thickened, add Half and Half and milk. Simmer about 8 minutes. Do not boil. Return mushrooms to soup and season. When mushrooms are heated, serve immediately. For a thicker soup, more flour may be used.

Mrs. Ned Stewart
Texarkana, Arkansas

"No gentleman has soup at luncheon."
LORD CURZON OF KEDLESTON
1859-1925

MUSHROOM CUCUMBER SOUP

Yield: 4 to 6 servings

3 medium cucumbers
3 Tablespoons butter
1 small white onion, finely sliced
1 pound fresh mushrooms, sliced
1 heaping Tablespoon flour

1 (10¾ ounce) can chicken broth
1 pint sour cream
Salt to taste
Pepper to taste

Peel cucumbers and slice very thin. Melt butter and sauté onion until clear. Add mushrooms and sauté. Cover and simmer until mushrooms are slightly tender. Sprinkle flour over onions and mushrooms, stir to thicken. Slowly add chicken broth, then add cucumber slices. Simmer until cucumber slices are barely transparent. Add sour cream and heat. Season to taste. If prepared early, reheat and add sour cream just before serving.

Robyn Dickey

EASY ONION SOUP

Yield: 6 servings

5 large yellow onions, thinly sliced
½ cup butter
2 (10½ ounce) cans beef broth
1 soup can water

1 soup can white or sauterne wine
Salt to taste
Pepper to taste

Topping
French bread, sliced 1 inch thick
½ pound Gruyère cheese

6 Tablespoons Parmesan cheese

Sauté onions in butter until brown in a large soup pot. Add remaining ingredients and simmer for 1 hour. Before serving, place soup in individual crocks and top with bread and cheeses. Broil until cheese melts.

Cindy Miller (Mrs. Patrick)

"Part of the secret of success in life is to eat what you like."
MARK TWAIN
1835-1910

BLACK OLIVE SOUP

Yield: 10 servings

6 cups chicken stock
3 cups chopped pitted black olives
2 Tablespoons grated onion
2 cloves garlic, minced
⅔ cup flour
3 cups Half and Half

4 Tablespoons Worcestershire
  sauce
Salt to taste
Pepper to taste
Lemon slices (Optional)
Chopped parsley (Optional)

Combine the chicken stock, olives, onion and garlic in a large saucepan. Simmer for 15 minutes. Blend together flour and cream and add to hot mixture. Stir constantly until mixture thickens and reaches the boiling point. Boil for 1 minute. Stir in Worcestershire sauce. Season with salt and pepper. Purée in blender and refrigerate. Garnish with lemon slices and parsley if desired. Serve cold.

Helen Sloan (Mrs. John C.)

PARSLEY SOUP

Yield: 6 to 8 servings

6 Tablespoons butter
6 Tablespoons flour
3 cups hot chicken stock
1 teaspoon dried summer savory or
   thyme

3 cups Half and Half
2 cups minced fresh parsley
Pinch of nutmeg
Pinch of salt
Croutons (Optional)

Melt 6 Tablespoons butter. Add 6 Tablespoons flour. Cook and stir for 3 minutes. Take pot from heat and add hot chicken stock. Whisk until thick but DO NOT boil. Add 1 teaspoon dried summer savory or thyme. Simmer for 5 minutes. Add Half and Half and parsley. Add a pinch of nutmeg and salt. Cook over low heat until ready to serve. Top with croutons, if desired.

Ann Morrison (Mrs. Pat)

"Only the pure of heart can make a good soup."
LUDWIG VAN BEETHOVEN
1770-1827

PORK AND CABBAGE SOUP

Yield: 6 servings

1 to 1½ pounds lean boneless pork, cut into half inch cubes
1 Tablespoon cooking oil
1 (10¾ ounce) can tomato soup
1 (10½ ounce) can beef broth
2⅔ cups water
4 cups shredded cabbage

½ cup chopped onion
¼ cup dry sherry
1 teaspoon salt
Dash of pepper
½ teaspoon paprika
1 bay leaf
Sour cream

In a large Dutch oven, brown pork in hot oil. Drain off excess fat. Add tomato soup, beef broth, water, cabbage, onion, sherry, salt, pepper, paprika and bay leaf. Bring to boiling. Reduce heat, cover and simmer for 40 minutes. Season with salt and pepper to taste. Garnish with dollop of sour cream.

Diane Lord (Mrs. E. Fletcher, Jr.)

POTATO CLAM SOUP

Yield: 4 servings

4 leeks, chopped
4 carrots, sliced
2 to 4 ribs celery, sliced
¼ cup butter
2 (10¾ ounce) cans chicken broth
3 large potatoes, thinly sliced

Salt to taste
White pepper to taste
16 ounces Half and Half
Bay leaf (Optional)
1 (7 ounce) can minced clams, undrained

In a large heavy saucepan, sauté leeks, carrots and celery in butter. Add broth and potatoes, cook until tender. Add salt and white pepper to taste. Mash through a sieve. Pour back into saucepan and add Half and Half. Check seasonings. Add bay leaf and can of minced clams with juice. Heat and serve. Better made the day before.

Elinor Stallworth Saxton (Mrs. Jim)

"The day has the color and the sound of winter.
Thoughts turn to chowder...Chowder breathes reassurance.
It steams consolation."

CLEMENTINE PADDLEFORD

GREEK RICE SOUP

Yield: 4 to 6 servings

½ cup chopped onion
2 Tablespoons butter
2 (10¾ ounce) cans chicken broth
1 cup milk
2 eggs, beaten

2 Tablespoons dill
3 Tablespoons uncooked rice
2 small cans chicken meat, drained,
  or 2 cooked chicken breasts
1 cup sour cream

Sauté onion in butter until golden. Heat chicken broth to boiling point. Do not boil. Combine 1 cup milk, eggs and dill in a separate bowl. Add a small amount of warm chicken broth to milk-egg mixture. Slowly add warmed milk-egg mixture to chicken broth, stirring constantly. Add onion and rice. Stir until thick, about 15 minutes. Add chicken meat and simmer for 10 minutes. Before serving, stir in sour cream.

Patrick D. Miller

SALMON BISQUE

Yield: 4 servings

1 Tablespoon minced onion
6 Tablespoons melted butter or
  margarine
5 Tablespoons flour
1 bay leaf
1¾ cups chicken broth
½ cup dry white wine

1 Tablespoon tomato paste
1 (7¾ ounce) can pink salmon,
  undrained
1 cup Half and Half
Salt to taste
Pepper to taste
Croutons (Optional)

Sauté onion in butter in a saucepan for about 5 minutes or until onion is transparent. Blend in flour, stirring constantly. Add bay leaf. Gradually stir in broth. Cook, stirring constantly, until thick and smooth. Stir wine into sauce and cook over low heat for 10 minutes. Discard bay leaf. Add tomato paste and salmon. Blend until smooth. Return to saucepan and add Half and Half. Season with salt and pepper. Heat and serve. Garnish with croutons, if desired.

Gail W. Davis (Mrs. Bill)
Batesville, Arkansas

"Of soup and love, the first is best."
SPANISH PROVERB

SPINACH SOUP

Yield: 6 to 8 servings

½ onion, chopped
2 Tablespoons butter
2 (10 ounce) packages frozen
  spinach
6 Tablespoons butter
6 Tablespoons flour
2 cups milk

3 cups chicken broth
½ to 1 teaspoon salt
Freshly ground pepper to taste
1 teaspoon curry powder
Several drops of Tabasco (Optional)
Lemon slices
Parmesan cheese

Sauté onion in butter until clear. Follow directions for cooking spinach on package, but just cook it long enough to separate. Drain the spinach well, squeezing out all excess liquid. Make a white sauce using the butter, flour and milk. The white sauce will be thick. Put half of the spinach, broth and onions in a blender and blend. Repeat with the remaining spinach, broth and onions. Combine spinach mixture and white sauce. Add salt, pepper, curry and Tabasco. Heat. Top each serving with a slice of lemon and Parmesan cheese.

Linda S. Mehlburger

SQUASH SOUP

Yield: 6 servings

1 medium onion, finely chopped
¼ cup butter or margarine
2 Tablespoons all-purpose flour
¾ teaspoon salt
Dash of pepper
⅓ teaspoon ground nutmeg
14 ounces homemade chicken stock

1 cup milk
1½ cups cooked, cubed yellow
  squash
2 teaspoons Worcestershire sauce
1 egg yolk, slightly-beaten
½ cup light or heavy cream

Sauté the onion in butter until soft, about 5 minutes, in Dutch oven. Add the flour, salt, pepper and nutmeg. Stir until blended and bubbly. Remove from heat and gradually stir in the chicken stock and milk. Return to heat, bring to a boil, and cook, stirring until thickened. Add the squash and Worcestershire sauce. Reduce heat to low and cook, stirring often, until heated through. Blend together the egg yolk and cream. Stir in some of the hot soup, then stir back into the hot soup. Cook until soup is heated through and the egg has thickened. May be served as a cold soup.

Mrs. Jack L. Graham

SAUSAGE AND LENTIL SOUP

Yield: 2½ quarts

1 pound lentils
8 cups water
2 (16 ounce) cans tomatoes,
   undrained
2 bay leaves
1 Tablespoon salt
1 teaspoon pepper

8 slices bacon, diced
1 cup diced or thinly sliced carrots
1 medium onion, diced
1 cup chopped celery
2 pounds sausage, browned and
   drained

Wash lentils and combine with water, tomatoes and seasonings. Bring to a boil and reduce heat. Fry bacon until limp, then add carrots, onions and celery. Sauté over medium heat for 15 minutes, stirring constantly. Add bacon mixture and browned sausage to lentils. Simmer for 1 hour.

A Very Special Tearoom

STEAK SOUP

Yield: 1 gallon

½ cup margarine
1 cup flour
8 cups water or stock
1 to 2 pounds ground beef
1 large onion, chopped
1 cup sliced carrots
1 cup sliced celery
1 (28 ounce) can tomatoes,
   undrained

1 to 2 (10 ounce) packages frozen
   vegetables (any style)
1 Tablespoon Aćcent
2 Tablespoons bouillon crystals or 6
   bouillon cubes
1 teaspoon pepper
¼ teaspoon basil
¼ teaspoon thyme
1 bay leaf

Melt margarine and gradually stir in flour. Add 8 cups water or stock, stirring as water is slowly added. Sauté ground beef in a separate pan. Drain thoroughly. Add drained beef to above mixture. Add remaining ingredients. Bring to a boil, then lower heat and simmer about 2 hours.

Nancy Mitcham (Mrs. Robert)

The more vegetables and meat you add, the thicker and better the soup. It's better the next day.

" 'It's a comforting sort of thing to have,' said Christopher Robin."
A.A. MILNE
House at Pooh Corner
1882-1956

TOMATO CHEESE SOUP

Yield: 2 quarts

1 medium onion, chopped
⅓ cup butter
1 (29 ounce) can tomato purée
2½ cups water

10 ounces extra sharp Cheddar
   cheese, shredded
½ teaspoon salt
1 cup sour cream

Sauté onion in butter in a large saucepan until onion is soft. Stir in tomato purée, water, cheese and salt. Heat until cheese melts, stirring constantly. Do not allow to boil. Remove from heat. Let cool for 10 minutes. Stir 1 cup of warm soup into the sour cream in a small bowl. Gradually stir back into remaining soup. Gently warm to serve.

Tommye A. Davis (Mrs. William A., Jr.)

TORTILLA SOUP

Yield: 8 to 10 servings

1½ (3.2 ounce) jars Spice Island
   chicken seasoned stock base
1 teaspoon ground coriander
4 ribs celery, medium-sliced
4 carrots, medium-sliced
1 bunch green onions (both green
   and white parts), chopped

1 (10 ounce) can Ro-Tel tomatoes
10 corn tortillas
10 ounces sharp Cheddar cheese,
   grated

In a 4 quart pan, place 2 quarts of water. Bring to simmer. Add chicken stock base, coriander, celery, carrots, onions and Ro-Tel that has been puréed in a blender for 5 seconds. Tear or cut tortillas into 2 inch squares. Add to soup. Simmer for 2 hours. Serve with grated cheese on top of each bowl.

Morin Scott, Jr.
Houston, Texas

If a soup or sauce is too salty, add slices of raw potato and cook 5 to 10 minutes. Remove potato slices that have absorbed the excess salt.

VEGETABLE SOUP

Yield: 10 to 12 servings

3 pounds stew meat
1 soup bone
3 (13½ ounce) cans tomato juice
4 (13½ ounce) cans water
1 onion, chopped
½ green pepper, chopped
6 cloves garlic, minced
1 Tablespoon salt
1 teaspoon pepper
⅛ teaspoon cayenne pepper

1 Tablespoon chili powder
1 teaspoon garlic powder
1 teaspoon onion powder
2 Tablespoons Worcestershire
  sauce
1 teaspoon sugar
3 bay leaves
4 cups stewed tomatoes, chopped
4 (10 ounce) packages frozen mixed
  vegetables

Combine all ingredients except stewed tomatoes and frozen mixed vegetables. Bring to a boil, cover tightly, and simmer for 2 to 3 hours or until meat is tender. Return to a rolling boil, add tomatoes and frozen vegetables, and boil 5 minutes, uncovered. Cover, lower heat, and simmer until ready to serve. Better the second day.

Jo Ann Drew (Mrs. Tommy, Jr.)

VICHYSSOISE

Yield: 8 to 10 servings

3 cups peeled and sliced
  potatoes
3 cups sliced white portion of leeks,
  or 2½ cups chopped yellow
  onions
1½ quarts chicken stock or broth

2½ to 3 cups whipping cream
  (perhaps more)
Salt to taste
White pepper to taste
Minced chives or chopped fresh
  basil

Simmer the potatoes and leeks (or onions) in the broth approximately 45 minutes or until tender. Purée the mixture in the blender or food processor. Strain through a fine sieve. Stir in the cream. Season to taste with salt and pepper. Chill. If the soup is too thick after chilling, add cream to desired consistency. Also, check salt after chilling. Serve in chilled cups topped with sprinkling of chives or fresh basil.

Ben Hussman (Mrs. Walter, Jr.)

ALMOND, BACON AND CHEDDAR SANDWICH

Yield: 3 cups filling

½ cup finely chopped toasted almonds, unblanched
12 strips crisp bacon
2 cups grated Cheddar cheese (pack in measuring cup)

2 Tablespoons chopped green onions or chives
1 cup mayonnaise
½ teaspoon salt
Wheat bread

Finely chop almonds, crumble bacon, and add rest of ingredients and blend. Spread generously on wheat bread.

Ann Evans (Mrs. Thomas)

GARDEN SANDWICHES

Yield: 2 cups filling

1 (8 ounce) package cream cheese, softened
¼ teaspoon salt
2 Tablespoons lemon juice
1½ Tablespoons mayonnaise
⅔ cup grated carrots

¼ cup minced green pepper
¼ cup minced onion
¼ cup chopped cucumber
¼ cup chopped celery
Bread

Combine cream cheese, salt, lemon juice and mayonnaise. Beat until fluffy. Fold vegetables into cheese mixture and chill for several hours or overnight. Spread on bread.

Peg Smith (Mrs. George Rose)

CRAB BAKE SANDWICH

Yield: 4 to 6 servings

1 pound fresh lump white crabmeat
1 hard-boiled egg, grated
3 ribs celery, chopped
18 to 20 green stuffed olives, chopped
Juice of 1 lemon
¼ cup mayonnaise

⅛ teaspoon cayenne pepper
Salt to taste
Pepper to taste
English muffins
Avocado and/or tomato slices
Monterey Jack cheese

Rinse crabmeat several times, carefully checking for bone or fin that has been left in the meat. Drain and squeeze out excess liquid. Stir together the crabmeat, grated egg, celery, green olives, lemon juice, mayonnaise, cayenne, salt and black pepper. Chill. Spread muffin halves with butter. Toast. Place avocado and/or tomato slices on muffin halves. Cover with a mound of crabmeat mixture and top with sliced or grated Monterey Jack cheese. Place under broiler until cheese has melted and begins to brown. Serve 2 muffin halves per person.

Ben Hussman (Mrs. Walter, Jr.)

CRAB SOUFFLÉ SANDWICHES

Oven: 325°
Yield: 8 servings

16 slices bread, trimmed and
    buttered
2 (6½ ounce) cans crabmeat,
    drained, or 1⅓ pounds fresh
    crabmeat
4 Tablespoons chopped onion
⅔ cup mayonnaise
4 Tablespoons prepared mustard
½ teaspoon salt
Dash of pepper

Dash of paprika
Dash of celery salt
Dash of garlic (Optional)
8 slices American or pimiento
    cheese
4 eggs
2 cups milk
½ teaspoon salt
½ teaspoon dry mustard

Place 8 slices of bread, buttered side up, in a buttered 2 quart casserole dish. Combine crabmeat, onion, mayonnaise, mustard, salt, pepper, paprika, celery salt and garlic. Spread crabmeat mixture over bread in casserole. Top each piece of bread with a slice of cheese. Add other 8 slices of bread. Over the sandwiches, pour mixture of eggs, milk, salt and mustard. Bake at 325⁰ for 45 to 50 minutes.

Helen Anderson (Mrs. Bruce R.)

Cooked, cubed chicken may be substituted for the crabmeat.

"ET CETERA" SANDWICH

Yield: 8 sandwiches

4 large chicken breasts, boiled,
    boned and diced
Mayonnaise for spreading
    consistency
2 Tablespoons Durkees dressing
Salt to taste
24 slices thin white bread, toasted
    on one side only
1 bunch watercress, stems removed

1 (8 ounce) package cream cheese
3 ounces Bleu cheese
1 teaspoon onion salt
½ teaspoon garlic salt
½ teaspoon black pepper
1½ Tablespoons Worcestershire
    sauce
Large avocado, thinly sliced
16 slices bacon, crumbled

Combine chicken meat, mayonnaise, Durkees and salt. Spread chicken filling on untoasted side of 8 slices of bread. Cover with watercress. Combine cream cheese, Bleu cheese, onion salt, garlic salt, black pepper and Worcestershire sauce. Spread cheese filling on 8 slices of bread. Cover with avocado. Sprinkle with bacon. Place on top of first slices. Cover with remaining slices of bread, toasted side up. Cut into quarters.

Nancy Couch (Mrs. James)

JANE'S HOT HAM SANDWICHES

Oven: 325°
Yield: 12 servings

1 (8 ounce) container soft
   margarine
2 Tablespoons Reese's Bavarian
   wine mustard
1 Tablespoon prepared mustard

½ (2 ounce) box poppy seeds
   (Optional)
1 dozen onion buns
24 slices Swiss cheese
1½ pounds pre-cooked shaved ham

Combine margarine, mustards and poppy seeds. Split buns and generously spread mixture on both sides of buns. Place a slice of cheese on each bun half (2 slices per sandwich). Add a generous amount of shaved ham. Wrap each sandwich in heavy duty foil. Bake for 20 to 30 minutes at 325°. May be frozen before baking.

Jane Faust (Mrs. Norman R.)

HAYDON LAKE SPECIAL

Yield: 1 sandwich

1 slice bread, toasted
Mayonnaise

Red onion, thinly sliced and broken
   apart
Sharp Cheddar cheese, grated

On a slice of toasted bread, spread a generous portion of mayonnaise, then cover with a layer of onion and top with a generous amount of grated cheese. Place in a cold oven, turn on broiler and cook until cheese bubbles and browns slightly on top. Eat with a knife and fork.

Mrs. John E. Hawkins
Carmel, California

PENNSYLVANIA DUTCH SANDWICH

Yield: 6 sandwiches

4 slices boiled ham
4 slices Swiss cheese
½ teaspoon caraway seeds
¼ cup mayonnaise

½ cup sauerkraut, well drained
12 slices rye bread
3 Tablespoons soft butter or
   margarine

Cut ham and cheese into julienne strips. Blend caraway seeds and mayonnaise. Add ham and cheese. Stir to coat all pieces. Add sauerkraut. Spread bread with butter or margarine. Spread half of bread slices with ham-cheese mixture. Top with remaining bread slices. Wrap each sandwich with plastic wrap or foil and refrigerate.

Ceile Faulkner (Mrs. Jim)

LUNCHEON STUFFED ROLLS

Oven: 400°
Yield: 12 servings

1 pound lean pork sausage
2 Tablespoons margarine
1 clove garlic, crushed
½ cup chopped onion
12 Brown 'n Serve French Rolls
½ teaspoon salt
1 egg, slightly beaten

⅓ cup water
2 Tablespoons Grey Poupon Dijon
  mustard
Dash of pepper
Dash of oregano
2 teaspoons chopped parsley
Garlic butter

Cook sausage, margarine, garlic and onion in a large pan until brown. Cut a little slice off end of French Rolls and scoop out insides. Chop inside bread into crumbs and add to meat mixture. Add all other ingredients except garlic butter. Stir until mixed well. Stuff French Roll shells with mixture. Replace end slice and secure with a toothpick. Brush tops with garlic butter. Bake on cookie sheet at 400° for 15 to 20 minutes.

Jean Dixon
Blytheville, Arkansas

MEXICAN BURGER

Yield: 8 servings

¼ cup taco sauce
3 Tablespoons dried minced onion
2 cloves garlic, minced
2 teaspoons oregano leaves
2 teaspoons chili powder
1 teaspoon ground cumin
1½ teaspoons salt
2½ pounds lean ground beef
2 ripe avocados
3 Tablespoons lemon juice

Garlic salt to taste
Tabasco to taste
½ cup butter
1 Tablespoon chili powder
2 (4 ounce) cans whole green
  chilies, drained, split and
  flattened
2 tomatoes, sliced
Black olives, sliced

Mix first 8 ingredients and shape into patties. Grill. For topping, mash avocados and add lemon juice, garlic salt and Tabasco. Mix butter and chili powder. Brush on rolls to warm them. Place burger on warm roll, add avocado topping, chilies, tomato and black olives.

Fletcher Lord, Jr.

SPECIAL PIMIENTO CHEESE SANDWICH

Yield: 6 sandwiches

1 (8 ounce) package cream cheese
¼ cup grated onion

1 (3 ounce) jar chopped pimiento, drained
Raisin bread

Soften cream cheese. Add onion and pimiento. Spread on raisin bread.

Ann Wait (Mrs. Frank E., Jr.)

QUEEN'S ROYAL SANDWICH

Oven: 400°
Yield: 4 sandwiches

1 cup apple slices
2 teaspoons margarine
4 slices raisin bread or wheat bread

¼ cup strawberry preserves
½ pound turkey slices
4 cheese slices

Sauté apples in margarine. Spread each slice of bread with preserves. Cover with turkey, apples and cheese. Bake at 400° for 6 to 8 minutes.

Kathy Moore

QUESADILLA SUPREME

Yield: 4 servings

1 pound ground beef and/or 1 can refried beans with peppers
1 package taco seasoning mix
4 (12 inch) flour tortillas
10 ounces Cheddar cheese, grated
10 ounces Monterey Jack cheese, grated

2 cups prepared guacamole or 2 avocados, mashed
1 (2¼ ounce) jar sliced black olives, drained
2 tomatoes, chopped
1 bunch green onions, chopped
1 (8 ounce) carton sour cream

Brown beef and season according to taco seasoning directions. Butter 1 side of tortilla and place on a cookie sheet, buttered side down. Cover with the following layers: refried beans, taco seasoned beef, and two kinds of cheeses that have been mixed together. Cover with another flour tortilla that has been buttered on the top side. Bake 5 to 6 minutes at 500°. Broil for 2 to 3 minutes or until slightly brown and cheese has melted. Remove from oven and top with guacamole, black olives, tomatoes, green onions and a spoonful of sour cream. Cut into 4 wedges to serve.

Boopie Procter McInnis (Mrs. George)
Minden, Louisiana

SPINACH SANDWICHES

Yield: 10 large or
20 tea sandwiches

1 (10 ounce) package frozen
    chopped spinach
½ (8 ounce) can water chestnuts,
    chopped and drained
2 Tablespoons mayonnaise
2 Tablespoons sour cream
3 scallions or green onions and
    tops, chopped

½ teaspoon salt
Pepper to taste
Garlic powder to taste
Worcestershire sauce to taste
Mayonnaise
20 slices of bread

Thaw frozen spinach and squeeze all liquid out. Mix all other ingredients with spinach. Remove crust from bread. Spread 1 slice of bread with mayonnaise, then spread with spinach mixture. Cut in fourths, diagonally, to make tea sandwiches.

Mrs. J. Paul Faulkner
Jackson, Mississippi

SWISS TUNA GRILL

Yield: 4 sandwiches

1 (6½ to 7 ounce) can tuna, drained
½ cup (2 ounces) shredded Swiss
    cheese
½ cup chopped celery
2 Tablespoons finely chopped onion

¼ cup mayonnaise
¼ cup sour cream
Dash of pepper
Rye bread
Soft butter or margarine

Combine tuna, cheese, celery, onion, mayonnaise, sour cream and pepper to make the filling. Prepare sandwiches, spread outside of sandwiches with butter and cook on a hot griddle until toasted and filling is heated.

Diane Lord (Mrs. E. Fletcher, Jr.)

"That open sandwiches are not food,
And that love is not hate,
That is what at this time I know
About open sandwiches and love."
JOHAN HERMAN WESSEL
1742-1785

BREADS

Let them fill up on good bread and butter if they don't like salmon mousse.

CHEESE BREAD

Oven: 375°
Yield: 2 large loaves or
3 medium loaves

2 cups milk
⅓ stick margarine
⅛ cup white Karo syrup
1 Tablespoon brown sugar
5 to 6 cups flour
1 package yeast

1 teaspoon salt
1 to 2 teaspoons herbs (thyme, dill,
    oregano, sage, or a mixture)
1 (10 ounce) package extra sharp
    Cheddar cheese, grated

Bring milk, margarine, Karo syrup and sugar to boiling point. Cool to luke warm. Put 2 cups flour, yeast, salt and herbs in a large bowl. Add milk mixture, then grated cheese. Mix well and add more flour until the dough is dry enough to knead. Put on a flat surface and knead until very smooth, 8 to 10 minutes. Place in a greased bowl, cover, and let rise until double in bulk, 1½ to 2 hours. Punch down and let rest for 10 minutes. Shape into loaves (do not knead) and let double in bulk. Bake at 375° for 45 minutes for large loaves and 30 minutes for medium loaves. Remove from pan at once.

Mary Worthen (Mrs. Booker)

FRENCH BREAD

Oven: 400°
Yield: 2 loaves

1 package dry yeast
1 Tablespoon sugar
½ cup warm water (115°)
4 cups unsifted flour
1½ teaspoons salt

1 Tablespoon soft margarine
1 cup ice water
2 Tablespoons corn meal
Shortening
2 Tablespoons butter, melted

Combine yeast, sugar, and water. Set aside to proof for 5 to 10 minutes. Insert dough blade into food processor bowl. Add all of flour, salt and margarine. Process until well mixed. Add yeast mixture and process to mix. With machine running, slowly add ice water (it takes about 30 seconds). When all has been added and dough forms a ball, let machine run for 60 seconds to knead. Place in a greased bowl, cover, and let rise 1½ to 2 hours. Punch down and shape into 2 small loaves. Place on greased baking sheet which has been sprinkled with meal. Slash diagonally 3 to 4 times. Let rise. Bake at 400° for 25 to 35 minutes. Butter tops while hot.

Kathy Wilkins (Mrs. James H., Jr.)

CREAM CHEESE BRAIDS

(Must be prepared 1 day in advance)

Oven: 375°
Yield: 4 braids

1 cup sour cream
½ cup sugar
1 teaspoon salt
½ cup butter, melted

2 packages dry yeast
½ cup warm water
2 eggs, beaten
4 cups flour

Cream Cheese Filling
2 (8 ounce) packages cream cheese
¾ cup sugar

1 egg
⅛ teaspoon salt
2 teaspoons vanilla

Glaze
2 cups powdered sugar
4 Tablespoons milk

2 teaspoons vanilla

Heat sour cream over low heat. Stir in sugar, salt and butter. Cool to lukewarm. Sprinkle yeast over warm water in a large mixing bowl, stirring until it dissolves. Add sour cream mixture, eggs and flour. Mix well. Cover tightly and refrigerate overnight. The next day, divide the dough into 4 equal parts. Roll out each part on a well floured board into an 8 x 12 rectangle. Combine cream cheese and sugar in a small mixing bowl. Add egg, salt and vanilla and mix well. Spread ¼ of cream cheese filling on each rectangle and roll up like a jellyroll, beginning on a long side. Pinch edges together and fold ends under slightly. Place rolls, seam side down, on a greased baking sheet. Slit each roll at 2 inch intervals about ⅔ the way through dough to resemble a braid. Cover and let rise until double, about 1 hour. Bake at 375⁰ for 12 to 15 minutes. Combine powdered sugar, milk and vanilla for a glaze and spread over braids while warm.

Kay Anderson
Debra H. Browning, M.D.

CHEESE MUFFINS

Oven: 325°
Yield: 18 muffins

3¾ cups buttermilk biscuit mix
1¼ cups shredded Cheddar cheese
1 egg, beaten

1¼ cups milk
½ teaspoon HOT, prepared mustard
Generous dash of chili powder

Preheat oven to 325⁰. In a large bowl mix all of the ingredients to blend. Beat vigorously for 1 minute. Pour into well-greased muffin tins (do not use paper liners). Bake for 30 to 35 minutes.

Robyn Dickey

LA PETITE TEA ROOM LUSCIOUS LOAF

Oven: 350°
Yield: 2 loaves

1 package dry yeast
¼ cup warm water
1 cup hot scalded milk
½ cup butter
½ cup sugar

2 eggs, lightly beaten
2 teaspoons vanilla
1 teaspoon salt
4 to 4½ cups sifted flour
3 Tablespoons sesame seeds

Dissolve the yeast in the warm water. Combine the milk, butter and sugar in a large mixing bowl and cool to lukewarm. Stir in the 2 eggs (less 2 Tablespoons reserved for egg wash), vanilla, salt and yeast. Gradually add the flour to form a stiff batter, beating well after each addition. Cover and let rise in a warm place until light and doubled in bulk, about 1 hour. Beat down and let rise again until light and doubled in size, about ¾ hour. Turn into 2 (9x5) well-greased loaf pans. Let rise in a warm place until light, abut ¾ hour. Brush with reserved egg wash and sprinkle with sesame seeds. Bake at 350⁰ for 25 to 30 minutes or until golden brown. To store, wrap in aluminum foil and place in refrigerator. After 1 night's storage, this bread makes excellent sandwich bread.

Dora C. File
La Petite Tea Room

FAVORITE MONKEY BREAD

Oven: 375°
Yield: 1 loaf

1 package dry yeast
¼ cup warm water
1 cup milk
1 cup butter (DO NOT USE
    MARGARINE)

½ cup sugar
½ teaspoon salt
2 eggs
3 cups flour

Dissolve yeast in warm water. Scald milk. Add ½ cup of butter and cool. Add yeast, sugar, salt, eggs and half of flour. Beat well with mixer. Add rest of flour and beat until it is mixed in. Cover with a damp towel and refrigerate overnight. Remove from refrigerator 2 hours and 40 minutes before serving. Melt ½ cup butter in a regular-sized loaf pan. Drop batter in by spoonfuls and let rise for 2 hours. Bake at 375⁰ for 40 minutes. Turn out of the loaf pan and slice. Do not freeze. May be made ahead and reheated while still in pan.

Susan Brainard (Mrs. Jay)

WHOLE WHEAT BREAD

Oven: 350°
Yield: 2 (9x5) loaves

3 packages dry yeast
1 cup warm water
¾ cup milk
¾ cup water
1 Tablespoon sea salt (may
   substitute regular salt)

½ cup raw honey (may substitute
   regular honey)
3 eggs, beaten
½ cup unrefined oil (may substitute
   Mazola corn oil)
7 cups whole wheat flour

Dissolve the yeast in warm water. Stir in milk, water, salt and honey. Add eggs, oil, and ½ of the flour. Mix well, then add remaining flour by working in with hands. Turn the dough onto a floured board and allow it to rest for 10 minutes. Knead for 5 minutes. Place in an oiled bowl and cover with a damp cloth. Allow to rise until doubled. Punch down and let rise again for 30 minutes more. Divide the dough in half and shape into 2 loaves. Place in oiled loaf pans or shape into round loaves and place on oiled baking sheets. Cover the loaves with a damp cloth and let rise until doubled. Bake at 350° for 30 to 40 minutes. Cool on a rack.

Alice Lynn Overbey (Mrs. Thomas L.)

Wonderful texture. Delicious as buttered toast or sliced thin for sandwiches.

RED APPLE INN ROLLS

Oven: 425°
Yield: 60 small rolls

1 cup boiling water
1 cup butter
⅔ cup sugar
2 teaspoons salt
2½ packages dry yeast

1 cup warm water
2 eggs
6 cups flour
½ cup butter, melted

Pour the boiling water over the butter, sugar and salt. Let cool. Dissolve the yeast in the warm water and beat in the eggs. Add to the cooled butter mixture. Add the flour and mix well. Cover tightly and let dough sit overnight in the refrigerator. About 2 hours before baking, roll out on a floured board to ½ inch thick. Cut with a 2 inch biscuit cutter and fold in half to make pocketbook rolls. Place in a greased pan and let rise for 2 hours. Brush with melted butter. Bake in a 425° preheated oven for 12 minutes.

Ann Willis (Mrs. Ed)
Mrs. Don Harrison
Morrilton, Arkansas

Make cloverleaf rolls by placing 3 small balls of dough in greased muffin tins. Let rise for 2 hours and bake. You may also sprinkle with sesame or poppy seeds.

MARY'S HOMEMADE ROLLS

Oven: 375°
Yield: 3 dozen rolls

1 package dry yeast
1¼ cup lukewarm water
½ cup sugar
1 Tablespoon salt

1 egg
½ cup soft shortening
3 to 4 cups sifted flour
½ cup butter, melted

Warm a large bowl with warm water. Dissolve the yeast in the lukewarm water in this bowl. Add the sugar, salt, egg and shortening and stir. Slowly add the flour, stirring after each addition to fully incorporate the flour. Add the flour until the dough forms a ball. Cover the bowl with a damp cloth and let the dough rise in a warm, draft free place until it doubles in volume, or about 2 hours. Punch the dough down with your fist and turn it out onto a lightly floured board. The dough will be light and sticky. Knead the dough and add an extra cup of flour as needed. Knead until blisters form on the dough. Roll out or pat to ¼ to ½ inch thickness. Cut with a biscuit cutter. Fold with a piece of butter inserted in the fold. Place rolls in a well-buttered pan approximately 2 hours before baking and let rise. Bake in a preheated 375⁰ oven. When the rolls are just firm on top, brush with melted butter and continue baking until brown. Total cooking time should be about 15 minutes.

Mrs. Fred Kendrick
Water Valley, Mississippi

Important variation: After kneading the dough, you may return dough to a well-greased or buttered bowl, cover tightly with plastic wrap, and keep in the refrigerator until ready to be made out into rolls. If you do this, you will probably have to lightly knead the dough again when you turn it out of the bowl. Use a light touch when rolling out.

SIDNEY NISBET'S BUTTERY ROLLS

Oven: 425°
Yield: 1 dozen

2 cups Bisquick
1 cup sour cream

½ cup margarine, melted

Preheat oven to 425⁰. Combine all of the ingredients in a bowl and mix well. Spoon into greased muffin tins and fill half full. Bake for 12 to 14 minutes or until golden.

Elenia Keyes (Mrs. Cloud)
Rosie Ratley (Mrs. Richard H.)

May be made ahead of time and reheated.

REFRIGERATOR ROLLS

Oven: 425°
Yield: 2 to 3 dozen rolls

2 cups milk
½ cup butter
½ cup sugar
2 cups flour
1 package dry yeast

½ Tablespoon salt
½ teaspoon baking soda
1 teaspoon baking powder
2 cups flour

Heat the milk, butter and sugar to 125°. Add 2 cups of flour and dry yeast. Beat 2 minutes on medium speed of electric mixer. Cover with a damp cloth and let rise for 2 hours in a warm place. Punch down the dough and add the salt, soda and baking powder. Add 2 more cups of flour, mixing well. Place dough on floured board and knead, using additional flour as is necessary, until dough ceases to be sticky. Place in an air-tight, buttered container, buttering exposed surfaces, and refrigerate until needed. About 2 hours before serving, make the rolls, cover, and let rise. Bake in a 425° preheated oven until browned, about 12 to 20 minutes.

Linda Burrow VanHook (Mrs. Fred F.)

The dough will keep for 5 days in the refrigerator.

APPLESAUCE MUFFINS

Oven: 375°
Yield: 3 dozen muffins

1 cup butter or margarine
2 cups sugar
2 eggs
2 cups unsweetened applesauce
3 teaspoons ground cinnamon
2 teaspoons ground allspice

1 teaspoon ground cloves
1 teaspoon salt
2 teaspoons baking soda
4 cups flour
1 cup chopped nuts (Optional)
Powdered sugar (Optional)

Preheat oven to 375°. Cream butter and sugar. Add eggs, 1 at a time. Mix in applesauce and spices. Sift salt, soda and flour together and add to applesauce mixture. Mix well. Stir in nuts. Pour into greased muffin tins and bake for approximately 15 minutes for large muffins and 8 to 10 minutes for smaller muffins. Sprinkle tops with powdered sugar while still warm.

Carole Lynn Sherman (Mrs. William F.)

BLUEBERRY MUFFINS

Oven: 375°

Yield: 1 dozen large muffins

1 cup sugar
¼ cup margarine
1 cup milk
1 egg
¼ teaspoon salt
½ teaspoon vanilla

1½ cups flour
2 teaspoons baking powder
¾ teaspoon cinnamon
½ teaspoon nutmeg
1 cup fresh blueberries, or frozen
    dry-pack blueberries

Preheat oven to 375°. Cream sugar and margarine on low speed of mixer until smooth. Add milk, egg, salt and vanilla. Mix well. Sift flour, baking powder and spices and add half of mixture to creamed ingredients. Blend with mixer. Add the rest of flour mixture and gently mix by hand, just until moistened. Carefully fold in blueberries. Line muffin tins with paper liners and fill ¾ full. Bake 20 to 30 minutes until lightly browned.

Kathy Wilkins (Mrs. James H., Jr.)

CARROT MUFFINS

Oven: 350°

Yield: 1 dozen large muffins

¼ cup orange liqueur
¼ cup raisins
¼ cup chopped pecans
1 cup grated carrots
1 cup sugar
⅝ cup oil
2 eggs

1½ cups flour
1 teaspoon baking powder
½ teaspoon baking soda
¼ teaspoon salt
½ teaspoon cinnamon
½ teaspoon nutmeg

Preheat oven to 350°. Prepare muffin tins with paper liners. Heat orange liqueur just to boiling. Add raisins and remove from heat. Set aside to soak. Insert steel knife into food processor bowl and chop nuts with "on-offs". Remove and set aside. Cut carrots into chunks and use steel knife to coarsely chop. Add sugar, oil and eggs. Process until well blended, 5 to 10 seconds. Sift dry ingredients together. Add to processor bowl with chopped nuts. Process with "on-offs" just until ingredients are moist. Drain raisins and fold in by hand. Fill tins ⅔ full and bake for 35 to 40 minutes.

Kathy Wilkins (Mrs. James H., Jr.)

ICE BOX GINGER MUFFINS

Oven: 400°
Yield: 7 dozen
large muffins

1½ cups butter or margarine
1 cup sugar
½ cup dark corn syrup
½ cup sorghum molasses
4 large eggs
2 teaspoons baking soda
1 cup buttermilk

4 cups flour
Pinch of salt
2 teaspoons ginger
¼ teaspoon cinnamon
¼ teaspoon allspice
½ cup chopped raisins (Optional)
¾ cup chopped pecans

Cream butter and sugar well and then mix in syrup and molasses. Add eggs, 1 at a time. Stir soda into buttermilk and add to above while it foams. Sift other dry ingredients and add a little at a time to creamed mixture, which may look a little curdled. Add raisins and nuts. Store the mix in a covered jar in the refrigerator until ready to use. Bake in greased muffin tins at 400⁰ for 12 to 18 minutes, or 20 minutes according to the size of muffins.

Anabeth Ritter
Columbus, Indiana

May be kept 5 or 6 weeks in refrigerator. These are delicious with a luncheon. May be baked in small tins. They make a good dessert baked in large tins and served with sauce or whipped topping.

VERY SPECIAL LEMON MUFFINS

Oven: 375°
Yield: 5 dozen miniature muffins

1 cup butter
1 cup sugar
4 egg yolks, well beaten
½ cup lemon juice
2 cups flour

2 teaspoons baking powder
1 teaspoon salt
4 egg whites, stiffly beaten
2 teaspoons grated lemon peel

Preheat oven to 375⁰. Combine sugar and butter and cream until smooth. Add egg yolks and beat well. Sift dry ingredients together. Add alternately to creamed mixture with lemon juice, mixing well after each addition. DO NOT OVERMIX. Fold in the egg whites and lemon peel. Fill greased miniature muffin tins ¾ full and bake about 18 to 20 minutes.

A Very Special Tearoom

ORANGE MUFFINS

Oven: 400°
Yield: 2 dozen medium muffins

1 cup butter
1 cup sugar
2 eggs
1 teaspoon baking soda
1 cup buttermilk

2 cups sifted flour
Juice of 2 oranges and rind, finely
   grated
½ cup golden raisins
1 cup brown sugar, packed

Preheat oven to 400⁰. Cream butter and sugar, add eggs and beat. Dissolve soda in butter-milk and add this alternately with the flour to creamed mixture. (Do not overstir or beat as the mixture should look like rough corn pudding texture when finished, not like cake batter.) Add orange rind and raisins. Fill well-buttered muffin tins ⅔ full and bake in preheated oven for 20 to 25 minutes. In the meantime, mix orange juice with brown sugar and let stand while muffins are baking. Remove muffin pans from oven and while very hot, pour orange juice mixture down arund edges of each muffin so it goes in the cavity and coats the muffin sides. Remove from pans immediately.

Marilyn Hussman Augur (Mrs. James)
Dallas, Texas

RAISIN MUFFINS

Oven: 350°
Yield: approximately 2 dozen

1½ cups raisins
1½ cups water
1 cup sugar
½ cup butter
1 rounded teaspoon baking soda
2 Tablespoons hot water

1 egg
2 cups flour
½ teaspoon salt
2½ teaspoons cinnamon
2 teaspoons nutmeg
1 cup chopped pecans

Preheat oven to 350⁰. Simmer raisins in water for 20 minutes. Cream sugar and butter. Add ½ cup of the water in which the raisins were cooked, mixing well, and then add soda which has been dissolved in the hot water. Beat in the egg. The dry ingredients should be added and mixed until smooth. Stir in the raisins and pecans. Pour into greased muffin tins and bake for 20 minutes or until done.

Linda Burrow VanHook (Mrs. Fred F.)

PINEAPPLE APRICOT MUFFINS

Oven: 350°
Yield: 3 dozen miniature muffins

½ cup margarine
⅔ cup brown sugar
1 egg
⅔ cup crushed pineapple with juice
⅓ cup (3 ounces) dried apricots

1 cup flour
½ teaspoon baking soda
½ teaspoon salt
1 cup quick rolled oats

Preheat oven to 350°. Using a food processor, fit steel knife in bowl and cream margarine, brown sugar and egg until fluffy. Add crushed pineapple and dried apricots. Chop and combine with "on-offs" until apricots are finely chopped. Combine dry ingredients and mix well. Add to processor bowl and process with quick "on-offs" just until all is moist. Spoon into well-greased miniature muffin tins and bake for 20 minutes. Standard mixing procedure can be used if apricots are finely chopped or snipped.

Kathy Wilkins (Mrs. James H., Jr.)

APPLE SPICE BREAD

Oven: 325°
Yield: 2 (5 cup) pans or
3 small pans

2⅔ cups flour
1½ teaspoons baking soda
1 teaspoon salt
2 teaspoons cinnamon
1 teaspoon ground cloves
2 cups sugar
1 cup oil
4 eggs, beaten

2 teaspoons vanilla
4 cups coarsely chopped apples (1
  cup chopped apricots may be
  substituted for 1 cup apples)
1 cup raisins
1 cup chopped pecans
1 teaspoon sugar
Pecan halves

Preheat oven to 325°. Mix first 5 ingredients together. Mix sugar and oil in a large bowl. Add eggs and vanilla, then stir in apples, raisins and pecans. Add flour mixture and mix well. Grease pans and line bottom with waxed paper. Pour batter into pan and smooth top. Bake for 50 to 60 minutes. After 20 minutes, pull out rack and sprinkle tops with 1 teaspoon sugar and press in nut halves. Return and finish baking. Cool 10 minutes before turning out on rack. Freezes well.

Judy Burrow (Mrs. Larry)

APRICOT BREAD

Oven: 325°
Yield: 2 loaves

1 pound dried apricots, chopped
2 cups sugar
2 cups apricot nectar
1 teaspoon salt
¾ cup shortening

2 eggs, beaten
2 teaspoons baking soda
4 cups flour
½ cup chopped pecans

Preheat oven to 325°. In a large saucepan combine apricots, sugar, nectar, salt and shortening. Bring to a boil. Boil 5 minutes, remove apricots, and set aside. Cool liquid and add eggs, soda, flour and pecans, mixing well. Add reserved apricots. Place in 2 greased and floured 9x5 loaf pans and bake at 325° for 1 hour.

Ellon Cockrill (Mrs. Rogers)

This bread is delicious toasted.

BANANA APRICOT BREAD

Oven: 350°
Yield: 1 loaf

2 cups sifted all-purpose flour
1 cup sugar
1 teaspoon baking powder
½ teaspoon baking soda
½ teaspoon salt
1 cup chopped dried apricots

¾ cup mashed ripe bananas
½ cup milk
1 large egg
¼ cup butter, melted
Powdered sugar

Preheat oven to 350°. Sift dry ingredients together. Add apricots. Combine remaining ingredients and add to dry ingredients, stirring just until well blended. Turn into a 9x5 glass loaf pan that has been greased and lined with wax paper. Bake at 350° for 1 hour or until done. Cool in pan for 10 minutes, then turn out on wire rack. Sprinkle with powdered sugar.

Nancy Droege

" 'A loaf of bread,' the Walrus said,
'Is what we chiefly need.' "
LEWIS CARROLL
Through the Looking Glass
1832-1898

BANANA NUT BREAD

Oven: 350°
Yield: 1 loaf

1 cup sugar
1 (8 ounce) package cream cheese, softened
3 ripe bananas, mashed

2 eggs
2 cups Bisquick
½ cup chopped pecans

Preheat oven to 350⁰. In a bowl cream together the sugar and cream cheese until light and fluffy. Beat in mashed bananas and eggs. Add Bisquick and pecans. Pour into a greased 9x5 loaf pan. Bake for 1 hour or until done (may be done after 50 to 55 minutes). Note: Cover with foil the last 20 minutes of cooking time if the bread browns too quickly. Cool thoroughly before slicing.

Marilyn Fincher (Mrs. Edward)

This is wonderful sliced, spread with butter, and heated.

ZUCCHINI BREAD WITH PINEAPPLE AND NUTS

Oven: 350°
Yield: 2 (9x5) loaves

3 eggs, beaten
1 cup oil
2 cups sugar
2 teaspoons vanilla
2 cups zucchini, unpeeled and grated
1 cup crushed pineapple, drained
3 cups flour

2 teaspoons baking soda
1 teaspoon salt
1½ teaspoons baking powder
1½ teaspoons cinnamon
¾ teaspoon nutmeg
1 cup chopped pecans
1 cup raisins

Preheat oven to 350⁰. Mix eggs, oil, sugar and vanilla together. Add the zucchini and pineapple. Combine the dry ingredients and add to the zucchini mixture, mixing well. Add nuts and raisins and blend. Pour into 2 (9x5) greased and floured loaf pans. Bake for 1 hour. Cool 10 minutes in the pans and then turn on wire racks. Also may be cooked in small foil loaf pans and given as gifts. If so, reduce cooking time to 35 to 40 minutes.

Cherry Singleton Laughlin (Mrs. R.B., Jr.)
Aurora, Colorado

Very moist. Will last 2 weeks in the refrigerator. Freezes well.

POPPY SEED BREAD

Oven: 350°
Yield: 2 loaves

4 eggs
2 cups sugar
1½ cups salad oil
3 cups flour
½ teaspoon salt

1½ teaspoon baking soda
1 (13 ounce) can evaporated milk
1 Tablespoon vanilla
2 ounces poppy seed

Preheat oven to 350⁰. In a mixer, beat eggs with sugar until light and fluffy. Gradually add salad oil. Sift flour, salt, and soda. Add alternately with milk. Add vanilla and poppy seeds. Pour into 2 greased and floured 9x5 loaf pans. Bake for 1 hour. This bread has a sweet flavor.

Mrs. Michael O. Parker

EASY PATTY SHELLS FOR VEGETABLES, MEATS AND SEAFOODS

Oven: 300°
Yield: 6 shells

6 pieces of white bread

½ cup butter, softened

Preheat oven to 300⁰. Remove crust from bread and roll flat with a rolling pin. Butter both sides of bread. Stuff and pat into a custard cup or a muffin tin. Make sure the bread conforms to the tin. Bake until bread is brown and crisp.

Eva Riley (Mrs. Cooper)

TOASTED HERB BREAD

Oven: 325°
Yield: 4 to 8 servings

1 loaf thinly sliced bread
1 cup butter, softened
4 Tablespoons chopped chives

1 teaspoon basil
1 teaspoon savory

Preheat oven to 325⁰. Remove crust from the bread. Combine softened butter with the herbs and mix well. Spread herbed butter on both sides of slices of bread and cut in half. Place on a cookie sheet and bake for 45 minutes to 1 hour.

Georgea McKinley Greaves (Mrs. Thomas G.)
Greenville, South Carolina

Herb bread may be prepared and frozen in a tin. Reheat before serving. Leftover bread is delicious crumbled and sprinkled on top of casseroles.

JEANNE'S CORN BREAD

Oven: 475°
Yield: 4 servings

1 cup corn meal
1 heaping Tablespoon flour
½ teaspoon baking soda
1 teaspoon baking powder
½ teaspoon salt

1 pinch of sugar
1 cup buttermilk
1 egg
1 Tablespoon melted bacon grease
   or shortening

Preheat oven to 475⁰. Grease an iron skillet and put it in the oven to get very hot. Sift dry ingredients together in a bowl. Stir in the buttermilk and egg and beat until the batter is smooth. Add the grease and blend in well. Pour the batter into the very hot, greased skillet and bake for about 15 minutes or until browned.

MEXICAN CORN BREAD

Oven: 350°
Yield: 10 to 12 servings

1 (8 ounce) carton sour cream
1 (8½ ounce) can cream style corn
⅔ cup salad oil
2 eggs, lightly beaten
3 jalapeno peppers, chopped
2 Tablespoons chopped bell pepper

1½ cups yellow corn meal
1 teaspoon salt
3 tablespoons baking powder
8 ounces sharp Cheddar cheese,
   grated

Preheat oven to 350⁰. Combine sour cream, corn, oil, eggs and peppers. Add dry ingredients and mix well. Pour half of the mixture into a hot, greased skillet (for baking). Cover with half of the grated cheese and add remainder of the batter. Sprinkle with the rest of the cheese. Bake, uncovered, for about 40 minutes.

Nancy Mitcham (Mrs. Robert)

Great with chili and a green salad.

"With the bread eaten up, up breaks the company."
MIGUEL DE CERVANTES
1547-1616

SKIPPER'S HUSH PUPPIES

Yield: 6 servings

1 cup white corn meal	2 eggs, beaten
4 teaspoons baking powder	Buttermilk
1 cup all-purpose flour	2 large onions, chopped
2 teaspoons salt	1 (12 ounce) can beer

Mix dry ingredients in a large bowl. Mix beaten eggs with ¼ cup of the buttermilk and blend into the dry ingredients, adding more buttermilk to barely moisten the mixture. Add the beer to make a thick, soupy, pancake-like batter. (Skipper says it will take less than a can. The cook drinks the leftover to avoid waste.) Stir in the chopped onions. Drop the hush puppies from a Tablespoon into fat heated to about 370°. The batter should sink, then slowly rise and turn over. Fry until golden brown all over.

Julie Allen (Mrs. Wally)

Great with fried fish and lighter than ordinary hush puppies. If using self-rising flour, eliminate the baking powder and salt.

MOTHER'S SPOON BREAD

Oven: 350°
Yield: 6 to 8 servings

1 cup corn meal	1 teaspoon baking powder
1½ teaspoons salt	2 Tablespoons butter, melted
1 cup cold milk	3 egg yolks, beaten
2 cups hot milk	3 egg whites, stiffly beaten

Preheat oven to 350°. Combine corn meal, salt and cold milk and stir until smooth. Add this to hot milk and cook in a saucepan over medium heat for about 5 minutes or until thickened, stirring constantly. Add baking powder and butter. Place beaten egg yolks in a large bowl and slowly add corn meal mixture, stirring well. Gently fold in egg whites to mixture. Pour into a greased 2 quart casserole and bake for 1 hour or until firm. Serve immediately with lots of butter.

Robyn Dickey

"And the best bread was of my mother's making — the best in all the land!"
SIR HENRY JAMES
Old Memories
1843-1916

IRISH SODA BREAD

Oven: 350°
Yield: 1 large loaf

3¼ cups flour
¼ cup sugar
1 teaspoon baking soda
1 teaspoon baking powder
¾ teaspoon salt

½ cup margarine
1⅓ cups buttermilk
½ cup currants or raisins (Optional
    for breakfast bread)

Preheat oven to 350°. Combine dry ingredients in a large bowl. Cut in margarine until mixture resembles coarse crumbs. Add buttermilk, mixing just long enough to moisten. Shape dough into a ball and knead on floured surface 10 times. Place on a greased baking sheet. Shape into a round loaf 2½ inches thick and cut a ½ inch deep cross on top. Bake at 350° for 1 hour and serve warm. (May also be shaped into small 3 x 5 loaves and baked 20 to 25 minutes.)

Alice Lynn Overbey (Mrs. Thomas L.)

Makes good breakfast toast!

VEGETABLE BREAD

Oven: 350°
Yield: 8 to 10 servings

3 (10 ounce) cans biscuits
1 cup butter
¾ cup chopped onion
¾ cup chopped green or red bell
    pepper

¾ cup chopped celery
¾ cup grated Cheddar cheese or
    fresh Parmesan cheese
½ pound bacon, fried and
    crumbled

Preheat oven to 350°. Cut biscuits into quarters and place in a large bowl. Sauté the onions, bell pepper and celery in the butter for 5 to 10 minutes. Do not drain. Mix the grated cheese, bacon, and sautéed vegetables into the quartered biscuits. Spoon into a bundt cake pan. Bake for 30 to 35 minutes or until biscuits brown. Invert onto a plate. Watch for dripping butter.

Peggy Willbanks Jordan (Mrs. Don)

Wonderful for brunch or to serve with light soup and salad.

BARBARA FIREY'S CHEESE BREAD

Oven: 400°
Yield: 8 servings

1 loaf French bread
½ cup butter or margarine,
　softened
½ pound sharp Cheddar cheese,
　grated

5 Tablespoons mayonnaise
1 Tablespoon Miracle Whip
1 heaping Tablespoon finely
　chopped green onion tops

Preheat oven to 400°. Split the loaf of bread lengthwise and spread with the softened butter. Combine cheese, mayonnaise, Miracle Whip and onions. Spread on the buttered bread. Place on a cookie sheet and bake for 15 to 20 minutes until the cheese begins to bubble. Do not let it brown! Slice each half into 8 pieces.

Jane Miller (Mrs. G.R.)

This bread may be frozen but should be thawed before cooking.

"TOOTIE" BREAD

Oven: 400°
Yield: 6 to 8 servings

1 loaf French bread
1 (8 ounce) package Swiss cheese
　slices
½ cup margarine, softened
¼ cup finely chopped onion

1 Tablespoon prepared mustard
1 Tablespoon poppy seeds
4 slices uncooked bacon, cut into
　small pieces

Preheat oven to 400°. Partially slice the bread into 16 pieces. Cut each slice of cheese diagonally and place one triangle of cheese in between each piece of bread. Place the bread on a foil covered cookie sheet. Combine margarine, onion, mustard and poppy seeds and mix well. "Ice" the bread on top and sides. Place small pieces of bacon on top. Bake for 20 minutes and serve hot.

Ann Leek (Mrs. Stephen A.)

"We have a difficult time saying 'no' to third and fourth servings!"

"I must here observe that this double baked bread was originally the real biscuit prepared to keep at sea; for the word biscuit, in French, signifies twice baked."

BENJAMIN FRANKLIN
1706-1790

MONTEREY JACK BREAD

Oven: 400°
Yield: 8 to 10 servings

1 loaf French bread, cut in half
   lengthwise
½ cup butter
Garlic salt to taste
1 (3 ounce) can chopped green
   chilies, drained

¼ pound Monterey Jack cheese,
   grated
½ cup mayonnaise

Preheat oven to 400°. Melt butter in a saucepan and add garlic salt and green chilies. Mix the cheese and mayonnaise together. Spread the butter mixture on the 2 lengths of bread, then spread with the cheese and mayonnaise mixture. Place on a cookie sheet and bake, uncovered, for 20 minutes. Slice into serving pieces.

Mary Jane Robinson (Mrs. Robert L.)

POPOVERS

Oven: 450°
Yield: 12 large popovers

2 cups flour
1¼ teaspoons salt
6 eggs

2 cups milk
Butter

Preheat oven to 450°. Sift flour and salt together. Beat eggs lightly, add milk, and mix. Add dry ingredients and incorporate thoroughly. The batter should be like heavy cream. Heat popover pans in oven until hot. Butter generously. Fill each cup approximately half full. Bake for 20 minutes. Reduce heat to 375° and bake 20 to 30 minutes more. Serve immediately.

These are wonderful with any meal. Traditional servings are with butter and jam, or with roast beef.

"The destiny of nations depends on the manner in which they are fed."
BRILLAT-SAVARIN
1755-1826

CROUTONS

Oven: 275°
Yield: 6 cups croutons

½ cup butter
¼ cup finely chopped parsley
¼ cup grated Parmesan cheese

1 clove garlic, minced
12 slices white bread, cut into small cubes

Preheat oven to 275°. Melt the butter in a skillet and add the herbs and cheese. Remove the skillet from the heat and add the bread cubes. Toss the cubes in the butter until well coated. Place on a cookie sheet and bake for 30 minutes or until browned. Store in a covered container until ready to use.

Beverly Moore (Mrs. Richard N., Jr.)

BLUEBERRY BRUNCH CAKE

Oven: 350°
Yield: 1 (9 inch) square pan

¾ cup sugar
¼ cup shortening
1 egg
2 cups flour
1½ teaspoons baking powder
1 teaspoon salt
½ cup milk

2 cups blueberries (If frozen, do not thaw)
½ cup sugar
⅓ cup flour
1 teaspoon cinnamon
¼ cup cold butter

Preheat oven to 350°. Mix sugar and shortening thoroughly. Add egg and mix well. Sift together flour, baking powder and salt. Add flour mixture alternately with milk to creamed mixture. Fold in blueberries and pour into a buttered 9 x 9 pan. Blend together sugar, flour and cinnamon for topping. Cut in butter until crumbly and sprinkle over batter. Bake 45 minutes.

Judy Burrow (Mrs. Larry)

Flour and sugar mixture may be prepared ahead, then quickly put together with other ingredients for a great hot bread for breakfast.

"An hour in the morning is worth two in the evening."
NINETEENTH CENTURY PROVERB

CINNAMON NUT RING

Oven: 350°
Yield: 1 cake

½ to ¾ cup butter
6 to 8 Tablespoons brown sugar
1½ cups sifted powdered sugar,
   divided

2 teaspoons ground cinnamon
3 (9½ ounce) cans refrigerator
   biscuits
1 cup finely chopped pecans

Preheat oven to 350⁰. Melt butter in a small skillet over a low heat. Combine brown sugar, 1 cup powdered sugar and cinnamon in a small mixing bowl. Dip each biscuit in butter and then coat with sugar mixture. Place in a greased 10 inch tube pan or bundt pan, overlapping edges of biscuits. Sprinkle pecans over top and bake for 40 to 45 minutes. Remove from pan. Optional: Mix ½ cup powdered sugar with 3 Tablespoons water and drizzle over the coffee cake for a glaze.

Melinda Morse

Impressive and very easy.

NIGHT BEFORE COFFEE CAKE
(Must be prepared 1 day in advance)

Oven: 350°
Yield: 1 large coffee cake

⅔ cup butter, softened
1 cup sugar
½ cup brown sugar, packed
2 eggs
2 cups unsifted flour
1 teaspoon baking powder

1 teaspoon baking soda
1 teaspoon cinnamon
½ teaspoon salt
1 cup buttermilk
½ cup raisins, nuts or dates (all 3
   can be used)

Topping
½ cup brown sugar

1 teaspoon cinnamon

In a large bowl, cream butter and sugars. Add eggs, 1 at a time, beating well after each addition. Sift dry ingredients together. Alternately add flour and buttermilk to creamed mixture. Add raisins, nuts or dates. Pour batter into a greased 9 x 13 pan. Put topping on cake and cover tightly with foil. Refrigerate overnight. Remove cover in the morning and bake in a 350⁰ preheated oven for 35 to 40 minutes.

Mrs. C. Wallace Anderson
Vienna, West Virginia

CHEESE BLINTZES

Oven: 350°
Yield: Approximately 44 blintzes

2 loaves Pepperidge Farm very thin
  white bread
1 pound cream cheese
2 egg yolks

½ cup sugar
¾ cup butter, melted
6 Tablespoons brown sugar
1½ teaspoons cinnamon

Preheat oven to 350⁰. Cut the crusts off the pieces of bread and roll out very thin. Cream together the cream cheese, egg yolks and ½ cup sugar. Spread a layer of filling on each piece of bread and roll up like a jellyroll. Combine melted butter, brown sugar and cinnamon and mix well. Dip each roll-up into this mixture and line in a baking dish. Bake for 20 minutes or until golden brown.

Sharon Meehan
Garland, Texas

These are good warm or at room temperature. Can easily be reheated.

COTTAGE CHEESE PANCAKES

Yield: 12 pancakes

1 cup cottage cheese
3 eggs
⅓ cup flour
¼ teaspoon salt

2 Tablespoons sugar
2 Tablespoons butter, melted
1 teaspoon baking powder

Place all ingredients in a bowl and mix ONLY until combined. Cook on a lightly greased griddle, turning only once. Serve warm with melted butter and maple syrup or with sour cream and strawberries.

Aline Mobley (Mrs. Freeman)
Batesville, Arkansas

"Life, within doors, has few pleasanter prospects than a neatly arranged and well-provisioned breakfast-table."

NATHANIEL HAWTHORNE
The House of the Seven Gables
1804-1864

FRENCH TOAST

Oven: 400°
Yield: 6 servings

Cooking oil
4 eggs
1 cup whipping cream
¼ teaspoon salt

2 large thick slices bread, cut into 6
   triangles
Powdered sugar

Heat ½ inch cooking oil to 325⁰. Preheat oven to 400⁰. Beat eggs, cream and salt. Dip bread into batter. Allow batter to soak in. Fry bread until brown. Turn and fry until brown. Transfer to baking sheet. Bake 3 to 5 minutes until puffed. Drain. Sprinkle with powdered sugar. Serve hot.

Sissy Clinton (Mrs. David)

GINGERBREAD WAFFLES

Yield: 4 large waffles

2 cups sifted cake flour
1½ teaspoons baking soda
1½ teaspoons ginger
½ teaspoon cinnamon
½ teaspoon salt

1 egg, well beaten
1 cup molasses
½ cup buttermilk
⅓ cup butter, melted
Whipped cream

Sift dry ingredients together. Beat egg until light. Add molasses and buttermilk and blend well. Make a hole in dry ingredients. Add egg mixture and melted butter. Mix just to moisten all. Bake in well-greased waffle iron. Serve with whipped cream.

Sandy Ledbetter (Mrs. Joel Y., Jr.)

A great "snowy day" brunch idea.

VELVET WAFFLES

Yield: 6 waffles

2 cups flour
1 teaspoon salt
4 teaspoons baking powder

3 eggs, separated
1¾ cups milk
½ cup Wesson oil

Sift dry ingredients together. Beat egg yolks until light, stir milk into egg yolks, then add oil. Gradually stir this mixture into the dry ingredients and beat until smooth. Beat egg whites until stiff, but not dry, and fold them into flour mixture. Bake on a hot waffle iron.

Carol Vick Gross (Mrs. Ronald)

SALADS · DRESSINGS

Why honor more Balboa, who stumbled
upon the Pacific Ocean, than the unknown
hero who first bravely nibbled at a lettuce and
found it harmless?

CRISPY SALAD BOWLS

Vegetable oil   **Egg roll skins or corn tortillas**

Pour oil into deep fat fryer to a depth of 4 inches. Heat oil to 375º. Lay egg roll or tortilla on surface of oil and press down with soup ladle until completely covered. Fry until brown, about 1 to 2 minutes. Invert on paper towels and let cool. Fill egg rolls with salad or tortillas with guacamole.

Helen Sloan (Mrs. John C.)

They have a million uses. Just use your imagination.

BRIDGE DAY SALAD

Yield: 8 servings

1 head iceberg lettuce
1 head Boston lettuce
1 bunch spinach leaves, washed
1 (16 ounce) can pitted ripe olives,
    drained and sliced
2 avocados, diced
¾ cup alfalfa sprouts

1 cup broken walnut halves
2 cups cooked chicken breasts,
    diced
¾ cup grated Monterey Jack cheese
Italian seasonings or Fines Herbes
    (Optional)

Spicy Oil and Vinegar Dressing
½ cup vinegar
2 teaspoons salt
1 teaspoon sugar
½ teaspoon pepper
1 teaspoon paprika
1 teaspoon dry mustard
2 teaspoons prepared mustard

1½ cups Mazola oil
1 teaspoon Worcestershire sauce
1 teaspoon soy sauce
3 drops Tabasco
Dash of garlic salt
¼ onion

Prepare salad greens. Mix them in the bottom of a large salad bowl. Pile the following ingredients on top of the lettuce: sliced ripe olives, avocados, alfalfa sprouts, walnut pieces and chicken. Top with grated cheese. You may add your favorite salad seasonings (Italian seasonings or Fines Herbes). Serve with Spicy Oil and Vinegar Dressing. To make dressing, combine first 6 ingredients and shake well. Add remainder of ingredients, except onion, and shake well. Cut ¼ onion and place in jar and add the dressing. DO NOT pour onion on salad. Keep in refrigerator.

Susan K. Schallhorn (Mrs. Tom)

CAESAR SALAD

Yield: 8 servings

1 clove garlic, minced
⅓ cup salad oil or olive oil
½ teaspoon salt
1 scant teaspoon pepper
1 Tablespoon Worcestershire sauce
¼ cup lemon juice

½ teaspoon dry mustard
1 (2 ounce) can anchovies, drained
2 coddled eggs
½ cup Parmesan cheese
2 heads lettuce (Romaine or leaf)

Place all ingredients except eggs, cheese and anchovies in blender. Just before serving, add anchovies to blender mixture. Coddle eggs (place in boiling water for 1½ minutes). Add eggs to blender. Buzz at low speed about 30 seconds. Toss with greens and cheese, and serve. MUST BE SERVED IMMEDIATELY.

Mrs. Jack Meriwether

Rub bowl with a garlic pod for extra flavor.

COBB SALAD

Yield: 4 servings

1 head Romaine lettuce, chopped
5 slices bacon, cooked and
   crumbled
3 Tablespoons crumbled Bleu
   cheese

1 tomato, finely chopped
1 avocado, finely chopped
2 hard-boiled eggs, finely chopped

Dressing
¼ cup cider vinegar
½ cup salad oil
1 teaspoon lemon juice

¼ teaspoon garlic powder
1 teaspoon salt
½ teaspoon pepper

Combine all salad ingredients. If making ahead, add avocado and bacon at the last minute. Toss with dressing.

Julie Allen (Mrs. Wally)

Recipe can easily be doubled. Men love it.

When making a salad dressing, mix the seasonings with the vinegar before adding the oil. The oil will coat the herbs and not produce the fullest flavor.

FAR EASTERN SALAD

Yield: 8 servings

1 (5 ounce) can crisp Chinese noodles
3 Tablespoons butter, melted
1 teaspoon garlic salt
1 teaspoon curry powder

2 teaspoons Worcestershire sauce
Dash of liquid pepper seasoning
2 quarts salad greens
2 Tablespoons sliced ripe olives
French Dressing

French Dressing
½ teaspoon salt
¼ teaspoon paprika
½ teaspoon dry mustard
¼ teaspoon white pepper

1 Tablespoon fresh lemon juice
⅓ cup cider vinegar
1 small clove garlic, crushed
1 cup salad oil

Heat noodles with butter and seasonings in a slow oven, 200°, for 15 minutes. Toss hot noodles with greens, olives and French Dressing. For dressing, combine all ingredients except oil. Mix well, then add oil. Shake before use.

Mary Ann Wright
Naperville, Illinois

For salad greens use at least 3 to 4 different kinds of greens with very little head lettuce.

GREEK SALAD

Yield: 4 to 6 servings

1 clove garlic, split
Salt
1 head Boston lettuce
3 endives, shredded
3 celery hearts, diced
6 radishes, thinly sliced
1 bunch scallions or green onions, thinly sliced
1 cucumber, thinly sliced

1 green pepper, cut into rings
10 Greek olives
½ pound Feta cheese, diced
½ cup olive oil
Juice of 2 lemons
½ teaspoon oregano
½ teaspoon minced parsley
8 anchovies
3 tomatoes, cut in wedges

Rub a large salad bowl with garlic clove and salt. Discard garlic. In a large bowl, combine lettuce and endives, celery hearts, radishes, scallions, cucumber, green pepper rings, olives and Feta cheese. In a small bowl, beat oil with lemon juice and pour over salad. Toss. Sprinkle salad with oregano and parsley. Arrange anchovy filets in center and garnish with tomato wedges.

Judy Burrow (Mrs. Larry)

EGYPTIAN SALAD

Yield: 4 to 6 servings

1 large cucumber
Salt
8 to 12 ounces Feta cheese
½ cup finely chopped onion
¼ cup lemon juice

¼ cup olive oil
Pepper
½ cup sliced ripe olives
Lettuce
Mint leaves for garnish

Slice cucumber, sprinkle with salt, and let soak for 15 minutes. Drain and rinse. Crush cheese and mix with onion, lemon juice and oil. Season with pepper and add olive slices. Combine, serve over crisp greens, and sprinkle mint leaves over the top. Feta is salty, so watch salt added.

Judy Burrow (Mrs. Larry)

LAYERED SALAD

(Must be prepared 1 day in advance)

Yield: 10 servings

1 head iceberg lettuce
1 bunch red leaf lettuce OR 1
    bunch spinach
4 hard-boiled eggs, grated
1 bunch green onions (tops
    included), chopped
1 pound bacon, crisply fried and
    crumbled
1 (10 ounce) package frozen tiny
    peas, thawed

1 cup sliced fresh mushrooms
½ cup sliced almonds, toasted
1 cup grated cheese (Swiss or
    Cheddar)
2 teaspoons sugar
Salt to taste
Pepper to taste
Avocado slices
Optional ingredients: bell pepper,
    celery, tomato wedges, water
    chestnuts

Dressing

1½ cups mayonnaise

1½ cups sour cream

Wash, drain and tear lettuce into pieces. In a large bowl, layer ½ of the lettuce, eggs, onion, bacon, peas, mushrooms, almonds and cheese. Sprinkle with 1 teaspoon sugar, and salt and pepper. Frost with half the dressing. Repeat layers using the remaining half of the ingredients. Frost the top with the rest of the dressing. Cover with plastic wrap and refrigerate overnight. Before serving, garnish with avocado slices.

Janie Turner Lowe (Mrs. Chester, Jr.)

Salad may either be tossed before serving or served as is. This stays fresh for several days because the dressing seals the lettuce mixture.

CRUNCHY GUACAMOLE SALAD

Yield: 8 servings

1 head lettuce
2 tomatoes, chopped
½ cup chopped black olives

¼ cup chopped onion
½ cup shredded Cheddar cheese
1 cup small size corn chips

Dressing
1 ripe avocado, mashed
1 Tablespoon lemon juice
½ cup sour cream
⅓ cup salad oil

½ teaspoon chili powder
¼ teaspoon salt
¼ teaspoon Tabasco

Mix all salad ingredients except corn chips together. For dressing, beat all ingredients with mixer. Pour over salad which has been prepared. Chill. Add corn chips. Toss again and serve.   *Ginny Heiple (Mrs. Tim)*

MMM'S SALAD AND DRESSING

Yield: 6 servings

1 head Romaine lettuce
1 bunch spinach
1 (14 ounce) can hearts of palm,
   drained and chopped
8 slices bacon, cooked and
   crumbled
½ cup red onion OR 4 green
   onions, chopped (Optional)

½ cup Parmesan cheese or Romano
   cheese, or combination of both
Sesame buds or sticks, crumbled, or
   croutons
½ (8 ounce) can water chestnuts,
   chopped (Optional)

Dressing
½ to ¾ cup salad oil
1 egg
1 Tablespoon oregano, thyme or
   Italian seasoning herbs
1 Tablespoon lemon pepper
1 teaspoon Spike (found at Health
   Food stores)

2 teaspoons lemon dill seasoning
   (Optional)
1 to 2 teaspoons garlic salt
Juice of 1 to 2 fresh lemons

Mix all salad ingredients together and serve with salad dressing. To make dressing, beat egg and oil together. Add seasonings. Just before serving, add lemon juice and beat well. (Lemons will cook eggs and turn dressing white.) Pour over salad.

Melinda Morse

Try adding 1 to 2 teaspoons of Worcestershire sauce instead of herbs in the salad dressing for a Caesar Salad variation.

SPINACH SALAD WITH DRESSING

Yield: 6 servings

Dressing

1 hard-boiled egg yolk
1 small clove garlic
¼ cup red wine vinegar
¾ cup salad oil

1 teaspoon salt
1 teaspoon sugar
Freshly ground pepper to taste

Salad

1 pound fresh spinach, washed
½ pound mushrooms, sliced
6 slices bacon, crisply cooked and
    crumbled

2 hard-boiled eggs, sliced
1 medium purple onion, sliced

For dressing, combine egg yolk, garlic, vinegar, oil, salt, sugar and pepper in electric blender. Cover and blend well. For salad, combine spinach, mushrooms, bacon, eggs and onion in a large bowl. Add dressing and toss gently.

Sheila Wilson (Mrs. Philip)

Very easy. You may also use this dressing with a regular lettuce salad.

ARTICHOKE-RICE RING MOLD

Yield: 12 to 14 servings

2 (6 ounce) packages chicken
    flavored vermicelli rice mix
2 (14 ounce) cans artichoke hearts,
    drained and quartered
1 cup Italian salad dressing

½ cup sliced green olives
1 green pepper, sliced
4 green onions, sliced
⅔ cup mayonnaise
½ teaspoon curry powder

Cook rice mix following directions on the package, omitting the butter. Cool. Marinate artichokes in the Italian dressing for at least 2 hours. Spoon artichokes from the dressing and mix with rice, olives, green pepper and onions. Combine the Italian dressing in which the artichokes were marinated with the mayonnaise and curry powder. Then combine all the ingredients. Rub inside of an 11 inch ring mold with mayonnaise and spoon mixture into ring mold. Chill until firm. Loosen around side of mold with a knife and turn onto a round platter. Center of mold may be garnished with parsley or cherry tomatoes.

Jeanne Hamilton (Mrs. James K.)

RICE SALAD a la CHARCUTERIES de PARIS
(Must be prepared 1 day in advance)

Yield: 10 servings

Vinaigrette

4 Tablespoons good wine vinegar
¼ teaspoon salt
½ teaspoon dry mustard

¾ cup olive oil
½ teaspoon freshly ground pepper
½ teaspoon dry tarragon

2 cups uncooked long grain white rice
Chicken broth (Optional)
4 green onions, including green parts, chopped
1 (4 ounce) can black olives, drained and chopped or sliced
1 (4 ounce) jar green olives, drained and sliced
½ cup grated carrot

1 (10 ounce) package frozen green peas, cooked and drained
3 ribs celery, diced
¼ cup chopped parsley
2 (6 ounce) jars marinated artichoke hearts, drained (Optional)
2 Tablespoons capers
2 cups mayonnaise
Salt to taste
Pepper to taste

Make vinaigrette 1 hour ahead. Place all ingredients in a jar and shake for 1 minute until all is mixed well, or put in blender for 15 seconds. Add tarragon. Let spices be absorbed for about 1 hour. Taste for seasoning. Cook rice according to instructions on box. You may substitute part of the water with chicken broth. While rice is warm, toss in a large bowl with the vinaigrette and onions. Check the seasoning. Cover and refrigerate for 24 hours. Check seasonings again. Flavor should be perky. After 24 hours, add remaining ingredients and toss well. You may want to add more or less mayonnaise. Salt and pepper to taste. Chill until time to serve.

Debby Bransford Coates (Mrs. Wayne)

ZUCCHINI AND HEARTS OF PALM SALAD

Yield: 4 servings

2 (14 ounce) cans hearts of palm, drained
3 small zucchini
Small head bibb lettuce

Oil and vinegar dressing or French vinaigrette
Pimiento slices (Optional)

Split hearts of palm lengthwise. Slice zucchini into thin, lengthwise slices. Place lettuce leaf on salad plate. Alternate slices of hearts of palm with zucchini. Garnish with pimiento (Optional). Serve with favorite dressing.

Eden Ferguson Baber (Mrs. Tyler)

SPINACH, ARTICHOKE AND HEARTS OF PALM SALAD

Yield: 14 servings

1 pound fresh spinach, washed and
   torn into bite-sized pieces
1 (14 ounce) can hearts of palm,
   thinly sliced
1 (14 ounce) can artichoke hearts,
   drained and diced

6 slices bacon, cooked and
   crumbled
4 green onions, chopped
2 to 3 tomatoes, cut into wedges or
   cherry tomatoes, halved
2 hard-boiled eggs, chopped
Slivered almonds (Optional)

Dressing
1 small onion, minced
¾ cup sugar
½ cup vinegar
⅓ cup ketchup

¼ cup salad oil
2 Tablespoons Worcestershire
   sauce

Combine all salad ingredients in a large salad bowl. Toss. Chill, covered, until serving time. Serve with the following dressing. Combine all dressing ingredients in electric blender. Blend well. Chill before serving. Makes 2 cups of dressing.

Pam McKelvey

GARDEN SALAD

Yield: 12 small molds
or 1 large mold

2 (6 ounce) packages lemon jello
3 cups boiling water
3 Tablespoons vinegar
½ teaspoon salt
⅛ teaspoon pepper
1 cup mayonnaise

2 Tablespoons grated onion
¼ cup chopped green pepper
¾ cup chopped cauliflower
¾ cup shredded carrots
¾ cup diced celery
¾ cup chopped fresh tomatoes

Combine jello and boiling water. Add vinegar, salt and pepper. Cool. Add mayonnaise. Chill until slightly thick. Add grated onion and chopped vegetables. Pour into individual molds or a large round mold. Chill until set.

Mrs. J. G. Jackson
Fordyce, Arkansas

MOLDED GAZPACHO SALAD

Yield: 8 servings

2 envelopes unflavored gelatin
1 pint plus 2 ounces tomato juice
⅓ cup red wine vinegar
1 teaspoon salt
Few drops of Tabasco
2 small tomatoes, peeled and diced

½ medium green pepper, diced
1 medium cucumber, pared and
   diced
½ cup diced celery
¼ cup finely chopped red onion
1 Tablespoon chopped chives

In a medium saucepan, sprinkle gelatin over ¼ cup tomato juice to soften. Place over low heat, stirring constantly until gelatin dissolves. Stir in remaining tomato juice, vinegar, salt and Tabasco. Place in a bowl of ice, stirring occasionally until consistency of unbeaten egg whites, about 15 minutes. Fold in vegetables. Stir. Pour into a 1½ quart mold. Refrigerate until firm, at least 6 hours.

Marcia Johnston (Mrs. Richard S.)

SHRIMP ORIENTAL SALAD

Oven: 250°
Yield: 8 servings

1 (3 ounce) can Chinese noodles
3 Tablespoons butter, melted
2 teaspoons Worcestershire sauce
2 to 3 heads bibb lettuce
1 (8 ounce) can water chestnuts,
   drained and sliced

1 bunch green onions, white parts
   only, chopped
4 ribs celery, thinly sliced
1 (6 ounce) package frozen small
   precooked shrimp, thawed

Dressing
⅔ cup olive oil
⅓ cup red wine vinegar
2 teaspoons sugar
1 garlic clove, crushed
1 teaspoon dry mustard

1 teaspoon salt
½ teaspoon freshly ground pepper
1 Tablespoon lemon juice
3 to 4 mint leaves

Toss noodles in butter and Worcestershire sauce on a cookie sheet or large baking pan. Bake at 250⁰ for 30 minutes, stirring frequently. Cool. Wash and tear lettuce. Place in a large salad bowl. Add water chestnuts, onions, celery and shrimp. Just before serving, toss with Chinese noodles and dressing. For dressing, mix together all ingredients.

Carole Meyer (Mrs. Charles, III)

SHRIMP TOMATO ASPIC
(MISS MARGARET COUVILLON)

Yield: 12 servings

¾ cup cold water
4 envelopes Knox gelatin
4½ cups tomato juice, heated
3 Tablespoons lemon juice
1½ teaspoons salt
9 to 10 drops Tabasco
3 Tablespoons horseradish
½ cup diced green onions

1½ cups chopped celery
2 cups diced shrimp, or 2 (4½ ounce) cans small shrimp
1 (2 ounce) jar stuffed green olives, drained and sliced
1 (14 ounce) can artichoke hearts, drained and quartered

Pour cold water in a large mixing bowl. Sprinkle gelatin on top. Add heated tomato juice and stir until thoroughly dissolved. Add seasonings and put aside to cool in refrigerator. When mixture begins to congeal, add remaining ingredients. Pour into large decorative mold or individual molds that have been sprayed with Pam. Chill until set. Serve with homemade mayonnaise.

Jim Wilson

CRAB AND WILD RICE SALAD

Yield: 6 to 8 servings

½ (4 to 6 ounce) package wild rice
2 (6 ounce) packages frozen crabmeat, thawed, drained and flaked
1 (6 ounce) package cooked and peeled shrimp, thawed
½ cup cooked and drained English peas

½ cup chopped onion
2 Tablespoons chopped pimiento
½ cup mayonnaise
1 Tablespoon lemon juice
1 teaspoon curry powder
Lettuce
Cherry tomatoes or tomato wedges

Cook rice according to directions. Combine rice, crabmeat, shrimp, peas, onions and pimiento. Stir lightly. Combine mayonnaise, lemon juice and curry powder. Stir into crab mixture. Cover and chill. Serve on lettuce leaves. Garnish with tomatoes.

Ann R. Lewis (Mrs. Gene, Jr.)

Expensive but well worth the cost. White rice may be used instead of wild rice.

HEARTS OF PALM WITH SALMON

Yield: 8 servings

1 (14 ounce) can hearts of palm,
  drained
4 slices smoked salmon

1 head leaf lettuce
1 recipe vinaigrette with capers

Cut hearts of palm in half, horizontally. Cut salmon into 1½ inch wide strips. Wrap salmon around pieces of hearts of palm, with palm showing at both ends. Place 2 pieces of hearts of palm wrapped with salmon on each salad plate previously covered with leaf lettuce. Pour vinaigrette with capers over salad.

Anne Hickman (Mrs. Robert C.)

BASIL SHRIMP

Yield: 4 servings

1 pound shrimp
1 to 1½ cups olive oil
3 Tablespoons lemon juice
2 Tablespoons Pernod liqueur

⅓ cup fresh basil
Salt
Freshly ground white pepper

Shell, devein and butterfly shrimp. Heat olive oil in a large skillet. Mix basil, Pernod, lemon juice and then add to shrimp. Fry shrimp approximately 2 minutes or until just pink. Remove to a large bowl. Pour oil and herbs from skillet over shrimp. Chill. Serve at room temperature on a bed of lettuce with a wedge of lemon and a sprig of fresh basil.

Ben Hussman (Mrs. Walter, Jr.)

If fresh basil is not available, use dried basil in a smaller quantity.

PASTA-ARTICHOKE SHRIMP SALAD

Yield: 8 to 10 servings

2 cups tripolini or small sea shell
  macaroni
⅓ cup chopped green onions
½ cup chopped celery
1 (8 ounce) can artichoke hearts,
  quartered and drained

1 (4½ ounce) can shrimp, drained
  and rinsed
⅓ to ½ teaspoon curry powder
¾ cup Hellmann's mayonnaise
½ cup sour cream
Capers for garnish

Cook noodles as directed. Refresh and rinse immediately in cold water. Chill. Add remaining ingredients and mix. Adjust seasoning. Chill at least 4 hours. Serve on a bed of lettuce and garnish with capers.

Jane McGehee (Mrs. Frank E.)

CURRIED SHRIMP AND RICE SALAD
(Must be prepared 1 day in advance)

Yield: 6 servings

2 cups cooked tiny shrimp
2 cups cooked white rice
½ cup white raisins
½ cup slivered almonds
2 Tablespoons candied ginger,
   finely chopped

¼ cup sour cream
¼ cup mayonnaise
2 teaspoons curry powder
1 (8 ounce) can mandarin orange
   slices, drained (may use more if
   desired)

Mix all ingredients together except the orange slices. Let stand overnight in the refrigerator. Serve on a bed of chilled lettuce. Garnish with orange slices.

Judy Kane

Serve with hot rolls, pickled peaches and white wine. Easy luncheon dish.

SCALLOP AND SHRIMP PASTA SALAD

Yield: 6 servings

1 pound medium-sized raw shrimp,
   shelled and deveined
1 pound bay scallops, rinsed
½ pound shell shape pasta
1 cup frozen peas, rinsed and
   patted dry (DO NOT COOK)
½ cup diced sweet red pepper (if
   not available, use pimiento)
½ cup minced purple onion

¼ to ½ cup olive oil (best quality)
3 to 4 Tablespoons fresh lemon
   juice
⅛ to ¼ cup Basil Purée (see below)
Salt to taste
Freshly ground black pepper to
   taste
½ cup pitted and sliced ripe olives

Bring a large pot of salted water to boil, drop in shrimp (before shelling and deveining) and scallops. Cook 1 minute, then drain immediately. Bring a second pot of salted water to a boil. Drop in the pasta and cook until tender. Drain. Toss pasta and seafood, that has been shelled and deveined, in large bowl. Add the peas, red pepper and onion. In a small bowl, whisk the olive oil, lemon juice and basil purée. Season with salt and pepper. Pour over the salad and toss well. Mound the salad on a serving platter over lettuce leaves and scatter the olives over it. Serve immediately, or cover and refrigerate. Allow the salad to return to room temperature before serving.

Nancy Eakin Dickins (Mrs. Robert D., Jr.)

Basil Purée: Process or blend 7 cups of washed and dried fresh basil leaves with 3 to 4 Tablespoons olive oil. Cover and refrigerate, or freeze.

TUNA WITH WATER CHESTNUTS

Yield: 4 to 6 servings

1 (10 ounce) can tuna in spring
 water, drained
1 cup chopped celery
1 (8 ounce) can water chestnuts,
 drained and sliced
1 (6 ounce) can pitted black olives,
 drained and sliced

1 green onion, chopped
1 cup mayonnaise
Squeeze of lemon
Dash of salt
Dash of garlic salt
1 (3 ounce) can Chinese noodles

Mix all ingredients except Chinese noodles. Just before serving, sprinkle with noodles or serve over noodles.

Robyn Dickey

SCALLOP AND ORANGE SALAD

Yield: 4 servings

1 navel orange
1⅓ cups orange juice

1 pound bay or sea scallops

Dressing
¼ cup dry sherry or white wine
 vinegar
½ cup olive oil
½ teaspoon salt
Pepper to taste
1 Tablespoon minced coriander
 leaves or parsley

⅓ cup thinly sliced green onions
1 medium-sized red bell pepper, cut
 into ⅛ inch julienne strips
2 Tablespoons thinly slivered ginger
1 clove garlic, minced
1 Tablespoon honey

Prepare the orange. Use a swivel bladed peeler and remove peel in long strips. Cut into very thin strips. Cover with cold water and set aside. Working over a large bowl, section the orange, removing as much of the membrane as possible. Reserve the orange sections, measure the juice, and add more as needed to measure 1⅓ cups. Poach the scallops and cut scallops into wedge shaped sections. Rinse and pat dry. Place in a saucepan, add orange juice, cover, and bring to boil over moderate heat for 30 to 60 seconds. Do not overcook. Remove with slotted spoon. Set aside. Prepare the dressing. In a medium-sized bowl, whisk together vinegar, oil, salt, pepper and coriander. Chop ½ the orange peels, ½ the green onions and all the red pepper. Return to orange mixture. Add to the orange mixture that scallops were poached in, the ginger, garlic and honey. Bring to a boil over high heat, lower heat and cook until mixture is reduced to 1 cup. Let cool. Add scallops to dressing mixture and marinate 1 hour. To assemble salad, mound the scallop mixture in the center of a chilled plate. Dip orange sections into orange mixture and use these to garnish the salad mixture. Across the top add more orange peel strips and other half of sliced green onions.

Sheffield Landers Owings (Mrs. William Adolph)

SALAD NIÇOISE

Yield: 4 servings

1 (6 ounce) can tuna fish, drained
6 to 8 ounces French green beans, cooked (or peas, snow peas, etc.)
1 large cucumber, peeled and chopped
1 pound tomatoes, peeled and chopped

1 large cucumber, thinly sliced
10 to 15 cherry tomatoes, halved
10 anchovy filets
Black olives for garnish
1 cup vinegar and oil dressing

Put tuna fish on the bottom of a clear shallow dish. Add a layer of green beans, followed by layers of chopped cucumber and chopped tomatoes. Carefully place sliced cucumber in an overlapping pattern on top. Make sure the cucumbers cover the top of the salad. Make a lattice of anchovy filets on this and place the black olives between. Place the cherry tomatoes around the edge of salad and spoon over a well-seasoned vinegar and oil dressing.

Helen Sloan (Mrs. John C.)

This is a beautiful luncheon dish. Layers of sliced artichoke hearts, avocados or other vegetables may be added or substituted.

BEEF SALAD

(Must be prepared 1 day in advance)

Yield: 8 to 10 servings

2 pounds round steak, ¾ to 1 inch thick
1 cup salad oil (part olive oil if desired)
⅓ cup red wine vinegar
½ Tablespoon tarragon leaves
1 teaspoon salt
¾ teaspoon sugar
½ teaspoon dry mustard

½ teaspoon ground pepper
¼ teaspoon garlic powder
2 red onions, diced
½ pound fresh mushrooms, sliced
2 Tablespoons capers (Optional)
2 teaspoons freeze dried pink peppercorns (Optional)
Fresh parsley

Broil steak for 3 to 4 minutes on each side, cooking just to rare. Cool slightly. Using a very sharp knife, slice into thin strips 2 to 3 inches long. Combine dressing ingredients. Add beef strips, onions and mushrooms. Cover and refrigerate overnight. To serve, arrange lettuce on a large platter or on individual plates. Drain steak mixture and add capers and peppercorns. Place on leaves. Sprinkle lightly with parsley.

Sheila Foster Anthony (Mrs. Beryl, Jr.)
Washington, D.C.

MEXICAN TACO SALAD

Yield: 6 servings

1½ cups chopped onions
1 cup chopped green pepper
3 cloves garlic, chopped
3 Tablespoons butter or margarine
1½ pounds ground beef
1 Tablespoon cumin

1 Tablespoon chili powder
1 pound Velveeta cheese
1 (10 ounce) can Ro-Tel
1 head iceberg lettuce
2 tomatoes
1 (12 ounce) bag Fritos

Sauté onion, green pepper and garlic in butter until soft. Add ground beef and brown. Drain meat mixture and return to skillet. Toss meat with cumin and chili powder. Melt 1 pound Velveeta with can of Ro-Tel. BEFORE SERVING, shred lettuce into large bowl and cut up 2 tomatoes. Crush Fritos into bowl. Add beef mixture. Pour cheese over all and fold together. SERVE IMMEDIATELY.

Debby Bransford Coates (Mrs. Wayne)

A real crowd pleaser. Eat all, because it is *no good left over!*

CURRIED CHICKEN SALAD

Yield: 16 servings

½ cup uncooked rice
1 cup uncooked cauliflower,
    separated into flowerets
1 (8 ounce) bottle creamy French
    dressing
1 cup Hellmann's mayonnaise
1 Tablespoon curry powder

1 Tablespoon salt
1½ teaspoons pepper
½ cup milk
7 to 8 cups cooked chicken
½ cup thin strips green pepper
1 cup chopped celery
1 cup thinly sliced purple onion

Cook rice until tender and chill. Toss with cauliflower and French dressing. Refrigerate for 2 hours. In another bowl, combine mayonnaise, curry powder, salt and pepper. Slowly stir in milk. Add diced chicken and toss. Refrigerate 2 hours. When ready to serve, combine both mixtures. Add green pepper, celery and onion. May be served with condiments such as flaked coconut, slivered almonds, pineapple cubes, currant jelly, chutney, bacon or chopped hard-cooked eggs.

Diane Brownlee (Mrs. S. Porter, III)

May be made a day ahead.

CHICKEN SALAD

Yield: 8 to 10 servings

8 cups cooked chicken
8 Tablespoons sliced green olives
8 Tablespoons sliced ripe olives
8 Tablespoons India Relish
2 cups chopped celery
Slivered almonds, lightly toasted
1 (4 ounce) jar cocktail onions, drained

1 (8 ounce) can sliced water chestnuts, drained
Salt to taste
Pepper to taste
Dill weed to taste
Chives to taste
Hellmann's mayonnaise

Cut chicken in large chunks after removing the skin. Mix all other ingredients, adding mayonnaise slowly until moist. Best if refrigerated overnight. More mayonnaise may be needed before serving.

Jamie Sue Williams
Arkadelphia, Arkansas

Men love this.

CHILLED DUCK SALAD

Yield: 6 servings

3 cups cold roast duck, cut in chunks
3 green onions, chopped
½ green pepper, chopped

½ pound fresh mushrooms, sliced
¼ cup sliced stuffed green olives
1 (14 ounce) can artichoke hearts, drained and chopped

Dressing
4 Tablespoons red wine vinegar
7 Tablespoons olive oil
1 clove garlic, mashed
½ teaspoon dry mustard

Salt to taste
Pepper to taste
Pimiento strips for garnish

Combine first 6 ingredients in a large bowl. For dressing, combine all ingredients in a bowl and whisk until slightly thickened. Pour dressing over salad mixture and toss to coat lightly. Mound salad on individual lettuce lined plates and garnish with crossed pimiento strips.

Susan Gregory (Mrs. H. Watt)

Great for ladies luncheon.

CHINESE CHICKEN SALAD

Yield: 4 servings

2 Tablespoons sugar
1 teaspoon salt
1 teaspoon Accent
½ teaspoon cracked pepper
¼ cup salad oil
1 teaspoon sesame oil
3 Tablespoons vinegar

½ pound cooked chicken
2 ounces chow mein noodles
1 small head lettuce, shredded
3 green onions, chopped
2 Tablespoons chopped almonds, toasted
1 Tablespoon sesame seeds, toasted

Mix first 7 ingredients and chill. Boil chicken in small amount salted water, then shred. Toss together with other ingredients. May want to add chow mein noodles last before serving.

Mrs. Joseph Buchman

COLD CURRIED CHICKEN

Yield: 8 servings

½ cup mayonnaise
½ cup sour cream
⅓ cup milk
2 Tablespoons lemon juice
2 Tablespoons Dijon mustard
1 Tablespoon curry powder
½ teaspoon garlic salt

3 cups cooked chicken, cubed
1 cup diagonally sliced celery
½ cup sliced green onions
½ cup thinly sliced dried apricots
Crisp lettuce leaves
Toasted almonds for garnish

In bowl, combine mayonnaise, sour cream and milk. Blend in lemon juice, mustard, curry powder and garlic salt. Add chicken, celery, green onions and apricots. Chill for several hours. Serve on crisp lettuce leaves and garnish with slivered almonds if desired.

Arden Limerick Boyce (Mrs. Charles)
Russellville, Arkansas

"It's no wonder we have a tradition of eating well; nature has been good to us in Arkansas."

MRS. GEORGE ROSE SMITH
Little Rock Cooks

MARINATED ARTICHOKE SALAD
(Must be prepared 1 day in advance)

Yield: 8 servings

2 cups round ⅛ inch carrot slices
1 (14 ounce) can artichoke hearts,
   drained and quartered
½ cup finely sliced green onions

½ cup finely sliced celery
2 cups thinly sliced cauliflower
½ cup bottled Italian Dressing
Lettuce

Dressing
⅔ cup mayonnaise
2 Tablespoons chili sauce
1 Tablespoon lemon juice

⅛ to ¼ teaspoon dill weed
½ teaspoon salt

Combine all vegetables and marinate overnight in Italian Dressing. About 2 hours before serving, drain and toss with mayonnaise dressing. Chill until serving time. Serve on salad plate lined with lettuce and garnish with carrot curls.

Kathy Wilkins (Mrs. James H., Jr.)

Excellent for a buffet as well as a seated dinner.

ASPARAGUS AND NEW POTATO SALAD
(Must be prepared 1 day in advance)

Yield: 6 servings

1 cup vegetable oil
¼ to ½ cup wine vinegar
½ cup minced red onion
1 Tablespoon dry dill weed
1 Tablespoon Dijon mustard
Salt to taste
Pepper to taste
2 pounds small red potatoes,
   unpeeled, cooked until just
   tender, cooled and sliced

2 pounds fresh or 3 (8 ounce) boxes
   asparagus spears, cooked crisp
   tender
Hard-boiled eggs, quartered
   (Optional)
Fresh dill for garnish (Optional)

Combine oil, vinegar, onion, dill, mustard, salt and pepper in bowl or jar and mix well. Toss gently with potatoes in a large bowl. Cover and refrigerate overnight. To serve, arrange asparagus on a large platter in spoke pattern. Remove potatoes from dressing with a slotted spoon and mound in center of asparagus. Pour remaining dressing over asparagus and serve with quartered eggs and a garnish of fresh dill, if desired.

Helen Sloan (Mrs. John C.)

FRESH ASPARAGUS VINAIGRETTE A LA CRÈME

Yield: 8 servings

40 to 48 asparagus spears
2 Tablespoons minced shallots
2 Tablespoons Dijon mustard
1 Tablespoon crème fraîche (See Index)

1 Tablespoon red wine vinegar
Salt to taste
Pepper to taste
½ cup peanut oil
Lettuce

Cook asparagus until barely crisp tender. Drain well and set aside to cool. Combine next 4 ingredients with salt and pepper in small bowl and blend with whisk or mixer. Slowly add oil, drop by drop, beating constantly until thoroughly mixed and thickened. Line plates with lettuce and divide asparagus evenly. Drizzle with vinaigrette.

Mrs. Robert M. Eubanks, Jr.

CREAMY BROCCOLI AND CAULIFLOWER SALAD

Yield: 12 servings

1 cup mayonnaise
1 (8 ounce) carton sour cream
½ teaspoon dried parsley flakes
½ teaspoon dried dill weed
½ teaspoon onion salt
½ teaspoon Beau Monde seasoning
1 bunch fresh broccoli

1 head cauliflower
2 hard-boiled eggs, coarsley chopped
10 ripe olives, sliced
1 small onion, chopped
1 (2 ounce) jar pimiento, drained

Combine first 6 ingredients. Mix well and set aside. Trim off large leaves of broccoli. Remove tough ends of lower stalks, and wash broccoli. Remove flowerets and cut stems into 1 inch pieces. Remove outer leaves of cauliflower, break into flowerets, and wash. Combine broccoli (flowerets and stem pieces), cauliflower, eggs, olives, onions and pimiento in large bowl. Spoon dressing mixture over top and toss gently to coat. Refrigerate 8 to 10 hours or overnight.

Billie Jeanne Scroggin (Mrs. John H.)
Morrilton, Arkansas

"Cauliflower is nothing but cabbage with a college education."
MARK TWAIN
1835-1910

FRESH BROCCOLI SALAD

Yield: 4 to 6 servings

1 head fresh broccoli
1 ripe avocado, chopped
¼ to ½ pound fresh mushrooms,
   sliced
¼ purple onion, finely chopped
1 cup Hellmann's mayonnaise

1 teaspoon lemon juice
3 teaspoons Worcestershire sauce
Salt to taste
Coarsely ground pepper to taste
⅓ package Ranch dressing
   (Buttermilk style)

Peel broccoli and trim stems. Slice thinly at angle until all is sliced, including flowerets. Add avocado, mushrooms and onion. Toss with mayonnaise, lemon juice, Worcestershire, salt, pepper and sprinkle with Ranch dressing. Refrigerate several hours before serving. Garnish with an additional sprinkle of coarsely ground pepper.

Margaret Ann Cole, (Mrs. George R., Jr.)
Fayetteville, Arkansas

A dash of Cavender's Seasoning is also good - BUT JUST A DASH.

CARROT AND CAPER SALAD VINAIGRETTE

Yield: 4 to 6 servings

1½ pounds small baby carrots,
   fresh or frozen (may be cut in
   half)
4 scallions, chopped

½ cup sliced black olives
2 Tablespoons capers
2 Tablespoons chopped parsley
2 Tablespoons grated lemon rind

Dressing
½ cup olive oil
3 Tablespoons lemon juice
¼ teaspoon Dijon mustard

Salt to taste
Pepper to taste

Cook carrots for 5 minutes in boiling water. Drain and refresh under cold water. Drain and put in dish with the rest of the ingredients. Shake dressing and pour over mixture. Chill and serve.

Martha Grubbs

"According to the Spanish proverb, four persons are wanted to make a good salad: a spendthrift for oil, a miser for vinegar, a counsellor for salt, and a madman to stir all up."

ABRAHAM HAYWARD

FRESH CAULIFLOWER SALAD

Yield: 6 to 8 servings

1 medium head cauliflower, sliced
2 ribs celery, chopped
1 medium green pepper, chopped
¾ cup sliced stuffed olives
½ pound Cheddar cheese, cubed

1 (8 ounce) bottle Caesar salad
  dressing
1 cup sour cream
Dash of Worcestershire sauce
Salt to taste
Pepper to taste

Optional Dressing
In place of Caesar dressing mix:
1 cup Hellmann's mayonnaise

¼ cup Garlic French dressing with
  ½ cup sour cream

Combine all ingredients, mixing well. Refrigerate several hours or overnight.

Margaret Ann Cole (Mrs. George R., Jr.)
Fayetteville, Arkansas

CAULIFLOWER SALAD

Yield: 6 to 8 servings

1 cup mayonnaise
3 ounces (¾ cup) Parmesan cheese
¼ cup sugar
1 small head lettuce

1 medium red onion, chopped
1 head cauliflower, chopped
Crumbled bacon or Bacos

Mix mayonnaise, Parmesan cheese and sugar. Let stand before putting on salad. Tear lettuce and add onion and cauliflower. Add dressing just before serving. Add bacon. Toss.

Carol Ann Matthews
Knoxville, Tennessee

This salad has a sweet taste. Different.

CAULIFLOWER SLAW

Yield: 8 to 10 servings

1 head cauliflower, thinly sliced
½ purple onion, thinly sliced
½ cup chopped celery
½ cup chopped carrots
1 (14 ounce) can artichoke hearts,
  drained and chopped

1 (16 ounce) bottle Wishbone Italian
  Dressing
2 Tablespoons chili sauce
1 Tablespoon lemon juice
1 teaspoon dill weed
1 cup mayonnaise

Marinate vegetables in Italian Dressing for 2 hours. Drain. Mix the chili sauce, lemon juice, dill weed and mayonnaise. Toss with the vegetables. Chill for 2 hours.

LEMON SLAW

Yield: 10 to 12 servings

6 cups finely shredded cabbage
2 medium carrots, finely shredded
1 small onion, finely chopped
1 small green pepper, finely
   chopped
¾ cup oil
⅓ cup vinegar

⅓ cup water
1 cup sugar
¼ teaspoon mustard seed
1 teaspoon salt
1 teaspoon celery seed
1 (3 ounce) package lemon gelatin

Combine all vegetables and toss with oil. Set aside. Combine remaining ingredients except gelatin. Bring to a boil. Remove from heat. Add lemon gelatin. Stir to dissolve. Cool to lukewarm. Pour over slaw and toss well. Cover and chill overnight or at least 6 hours. This will keep 2 to 3 weeks in refrigerator.

Kathy Wilkins (Mrs. James H., Jr.)

Nice for picnics and safer than mayonnaise. Wonderful with chicken, barbecue or fried catfish. This is a *sweet* slaw.

FRESH MUSHROOM SALAD

Yield: 6 to 8 servings

Garden Dressing
½ cup salad oil
¼ cup vinegar
¼ cup sliced green onions
1 teaspoon salt
¼ cup snipped parsley

1 head Romaine lettuce, washed
   and chilled
1 head iceberg lettuce, washed and
   chilled

1 Tablespoon finely chopped green
   pepper (Optional)
1 teaspoon sugar
1 teaspoon dry mustard
⅛ teaspoon red pepper

½ pound fresh mushrooms,
   trimmed and sliced
Garden Dressing

Shake all ingredients for dressing in a tightly covered jar and refrigerate until well chilled. Shake again before using. About 30 minutes before serving, add mushrooms to dressing. Line large salad bowl with Romaine leaves. Tear remaining Romaine and iceberg lettuce into bite-sized pieces. Pour dressing with mushrooms over greens and toss.

Lynn Monk (Mrs. James W.)

MUSHROOM SALAD
"SIENISABALLI" (Finnish)

Yield· 6 servings

2 cups water
2 Tablespoons lemon juice
1 pound fresh mushrooms, cut in ⅛
   inch slices
½ cup whipping cream

2 Tablespoons grated onion
Pinch of sugar
1 teaspoon salt
¼ teaspoon white pepper
Lettuce leaves

In a 2 quart saucepan (not aluminum), boil water and lemon juice. Add mushrooms. Cover pan, reduce heat, and simmer for 2 to 3 minutes. Remove and drain. Pat dry with paper towels. Combine cream, onion, sugar, salt and pepper. May fix early in the day and refrigerate. Before serving, combine dressing and mushrooms. Toss lightly until well coated. Serve on crisp, dry lettuce.

Lynn Coates (Mrs. David B.)

PASTA SALAD

Yield: 6 servings

2 cups snow peas
1 (12 ounce) package egg noodles or
   noodles of your choice
1½ cups halved cherry tomatoes
1 Tablespoon dried basil OR 3
   Tablespoons fresh chopped basil

½ cup grated Parmesan cheese
Salt to taste
Freshly ground pepper to taste
Garlic salt to taste

French Dressing
⅓ cup fresh lemon juice
1 teaspoon salt

½ teaspoon freshly ground pepper
1 cup vegetable oil

Wash, trim and string snow peas. Blanch peas for 1½ minutes in salted water. Drain. Run cold water over peas until cooled. Pat dry in paper towels and chill. Cook pasta according to directions until just done. DO NOT OVERCOOK. Drain. Do not wash. Place in a bowl, add vegetables and enough dressing to coat well. Toss. Add basil, cheese, salt, pepper and garlic salt to taste. Chill. Remove from refrigerator, let come to room temperature, toss, adjust seasonings and more French Dressing if needed. To make dressing, combine lemon juice, salt and pepper in a container with a top. Swirl until salt dissolves. Add oil. Shake.

Ben Hussman (Mrs. Walter, Jr.)

Vegetables of your choice may be substituted (julienned zucchini, broccoli flowerets, fresh asparagus).

ONION LOVER'S SALAD

Yield: 6 to 8 servings

6 medium onions, finely sliced
¾ cup sliced stuffed olives
¾ teaspoon oregano
¾ teaspoon salt

3 Tablespoons vinegar or lemon
  juice
Olive oil, enough to cover
Shredded lettuce

Separate onions into rings. Add olives, oregano, salt, vinegar or lemon juice, and enough olive oil to lightly cover. Mix well. Serve on shredded lettuce. May be made a day ahead.

Mrs. John M. Bransford

Serve with fish, steak or Italian foods.

ENGLISH PEA - BACON SALAD

Yield: 12 servings

2 (10 ounce) packages frozen green
  peas, thawed
1 cup sour cream
2 green onions, chopped
6 slices bacon, crisply cooked and
  crumbled

1 (8 ounce) can water chestnuts,
  drained
Salt to taste
Pepper to taste

Combine peas, sour cream, onions, bacon and water chestnuts. Season to taste.

Virginia Downie

May be made ahead of time.

BLEU CHEESE AND BACON POTATO SALAD

(Must be prepared 1 day in advance)

Yield: 8 servings

3 pounds new potatoes, peeled
⅓ cup dry white wine
⅓ cup chicken broth
⅓ cup minced parsley
⅓ cup sliced scallions
8 ounces Bleu cheese

¾ cup vinaigrette dressing
¼ pound bacon, fried and
  crumbled
Salt to taste
Pepper to taste

Steam new potatoes, let them cool slightly, and quarter them. In a large bowl, combine warm potatoes with wine, chicken broth, parsley and scallions, tossing mixture gently. Let cool. Then crumble Bleu cheese, add vinaigrette dressing and toss mixture gently. Chill overnight. Transfer salad to a salad bowl. Sprinkle with crumbled bacon and serve at room temperature.

Kim Eubanks (Mrs. Robert, III)

HOT PARMESAN POTATO SALAD

Yield: 6 servings

**8 slices bacon, cooked and
  crumbled**
4 cups sliced cooked potatoes

½ cup sliced green onions
⅓ cup Italian Dressing
½ cup Parmesan cheese

Combine bacon, potatoes, onions and dressing in a medium saucepan. Cook over low heat until thoroughly heated, stirring occasionally. Remove from heat and stir in cheese. Variation: Cook and slice potatoes and put in a casserole. Pour sauce over and heat in oven.

Linda Buzbee (Mrs. Dick)

TOMATO AND SQUASH SALAD

Yield: 6 servings

**4 yellow crookneck squash, 4 to 5
  inches long**
Boiling water
1 teaspoon salt

6 firm ripe tomatoes, chilled
Salad greens
Parmesan cheese

Marinade
1 clove garlic, crushed
1 teaspoon salt
2 teaspoons sugar
½ teaspoon dry mustard
2 Tablespoons water

¼ teaspoon Tabasco
⅓ cup cider or tarragon vinegar
¾ cup salad oil
4 to 6 green onions, sliced

Place whole squash in a saucepan and cover with boiling water. Add salt. Cover and boil for 8 to 10 minutes until tender, but firm. Drain and cool. Slice in ¼ inch slices. Combine marinade ingredients and pour over slices. Let stand in refrigerator 6 hours or overnight. Cut tomatoes into thick slices and place in rings on crisp greens. Spoon squash on top of each serving. Drizzle a little marinade over all. Sprinkle with Parmesan cheese.

Burke J. Coleman (Mrs. Randy)

Squash part may be made and held for several days. This is a very pretty, colorful salad and tastes best when fresh tomatoes are available.

*"I feel a recipe is only a theme, which an intelligent cook can play each time
with a variation."*

MADAME BENOIT

TOMATO BEAN SALAD
(Must be prepared 1 day in advance)

Yield: 8 servings

2 (16 ounce) cans French cut green
  beans, drained
2 small tomatoes, chopped
1 small purple onion, chopped
⅔ cup sugar

¼ cup salad oil
½ cup cider vinegar
Salt to taste
Pepper to taste

Combine all ingredients. Blend well. Chill overnight.

Sandy Ledbetter (Mrs. Joel Y., Jr.)

A very attractive dish and easy to make. Men enjoy this.

VEGETABLE SALAD PLATTER

Yield: 10 to 12 servings

6 red potatoes
2 cups chicken broth
1 (10 ounce) package frozen green
  beans or 1 (16 ounce) can whole
  green beans, drained
1 (10 ounce) package frozen green
  peas or 1 (16 ounce) can green
  peas, drained
½ green pepper, chopped
6 radishes, sliced
3 ribs celery, sliced

8 large mushrooms, sliced
1 (8 ounce) can water chestnuts,
  drained and sliced
1 (14 ounce) can artichoke bottoms,
  drained and sliced
1 can Belgium (small) carrots,
  drained
1 (8 ounce) can pitted black olives,
  drained
1 bunch green onions, chopped
Cherry tomatoes or tomato wedges

Dressing
1 (10 ounce) jar Durkees Dressing
1 pint sour cream
5 Tablespoons mayonnaise

1 Tablespoon lemon juice
1 teaspoon dill weed

Peel and dice potatoes. Boil in broth until barely done. Drain potatoes, but save broth. If using frozen beans and peas, cook in broth according to package directions. Drain and cool. On a large platter, place vegetables in layers starting with potatoes, carrots and celery. Then add peas, beans, mushrooms, radishes, green peppers, water chestnuts, artichoke bottoms and green onions. Garnish with olives and tomatoes. Blend together all ingredients for dressing. Dressing can be poured over all, then sprinkle with dill, or serve dressing on the side.

Julie Truemper (Mrs. John J., Jr.)

Place 4 to 5 cups of cooked and sliced chicken breasts or crabmeat on top of the vegetables and cover with dressing and dill for a different flare. Dressing is also good on sandwiches.

MARINATED VEGETABLE SALAD

Yield: 6 to 8 servings

1½ cups thinly sliced mushrooms
1½ cups halved cherry tomatoes
1½ cups thinly sliced zucchini
1½ cups thinly sliced carrots
1½ cups thinly sliced scallions
1½ cups thinly sliced green pepper
 rings
1½ cups broccoli flowerets
1½ cups cauliflower flowerets

1 clove garlic, split
1½ teaspoons salt
½ teaspoon freshly ground pepper
½ teaspoon dry mustard
2 teaspoons chopped fresh chives
2 Tablespoons red wine vinegar
1 Tablespoon lemon juice
2 Tablespoons olive oil
Lettuce or spinach leaves

Prepare vegetables and set aside. Rub large salad bowl with garlic. Combine remaining ingredients and whisk or shake. Place vegetables in salad bowl and pour dressing over them. Cover bowl and marinate vegetables for at least 2 hours. May be served on lettuce or spinach leaves.

Helen Harrison (Mrs. Fred H.)

Keeps well in refrigerator.

VEGETABLE SALAD

(Must be prepared 1 day in advance)

Yield 10 to 12 servings

1 (20 ounce) package frozen
 chopped broccoli
1 (20 ounce) package frozen French
 style green beans
1 (15 ounce) can cut asparagus
 spears, drained

1 (14 ounce) can artichoke hearts,
 drained and halved
1 green pepper, chopped
1 cucumber, pared and thinly sliced

Dressing
¾ cup Half and Half
2 Tablespoons lemon juice
2 Tablespoons vinegar
1½ cups mayonnaise

¾ cup chopped fresh parsley
½ cup finely chopped onion
3 Tablespoons anchovy paste

Cook frozen vegetables half as long as directed on package. Drain and cut in bite-sized pieces. Add canned vegetables, green pepper and cucumber. Chill. Mix dressing ingredients and toss together with chilled vegetables in large salad bowl. Refrigerate. Make at least 1 day ahead.

Janie Turner Lowe (Mrs. Chester, Jr.)

CRANBERRY OR RASPBERRY FROZEN SALAD

Yield: 10 to 12 servings

2 (3 ounce) packages cream cheese
2 Tablespoons mayonnaise
2 Tablespoons sugar
2 (10 ounce) boxes frozen raspberries or 1 (16 ounce) can whole cranberry sauce

1 (9 ounce) can crushed pineapple, drained
½ cup chopped nuts
⅓ (10 ounce) package miniature marshmallows
1 cup whipped cream or 1 cup Cool Whip

Cream cheese, mayonnaise and sugar. Add fruit, nuts and marshmallows. Fold in Cool Whip or whipping cream. Freeze in a 9 x 13 shallow pan or pour into styrofoam cups and freeze.

Lynn Benham (Mrs. Paul B., III)

FROZEN PEACH SALAD

Yield: 10 servings

1 (3 ounce) package cream cheese, softened
2 Tablespoons mayonnaise
¼ teaspoon salt
½ pint whipping cream, whipped
1⅔ cups miniature marshmallows

1 (16 ounce) can cling peach slices, drained
1 (15 ounce) can pineapple chunks, drained
½ cup sliced maraschino cherries
½ cup chopped pecans

Cream cheese and mayonnaise until smooth. Add salt and mix well. Fold in whipped cream and add marshmallows. Lightly fold fruits and nuts into creamed mixture. Turn into 2 regular ice cube trays, freezing until firm. Cut into squares. Serve on crisp greens.

Mrs. Vernon Miles
Newport, Arkansas

JANET'S STRAWBERRY SALAD

Yield: 24 small servings

2 (8 ounce) packages cream cheese
2 Tablespoons mayonnaise
2 Tablespoons sugar
2 (10 ounce) packages frozen strawberries, partially thawed
⅓ (10 ounce) package small marshmallows

1 (12 ounce) can crushed pineapple, drained
¾ (12 ounce) carton Cool Whip
½ cup chopped pecans

Mix all the ingredients. Pour into a mold or dish and return to freezer. Take out about 15 minutes before serving so it can be cut into squares or sliced.

Mandy Dillard (Mrs. William, II)

APRICOT NECTAR SALAD

Yield: 12 servings

1 (6 ounce) package orange jello
1½ cups boiling water
1 (46 ounce) can apricot nectar
1½ cups miniature marshmallows
½ cup sugar
¼ teaspoon salt

2 Tablespoons flour
1 egg
1 (12 ounce) carton Cool Whip or 2
   cups whipped cream
½ cup chopped pecans or walnuts

Dissolve gelatin in water. Stir in 2½ cups apricot nectar. Sprinkle 1½ cups miniature marshmallows over top of gelatin mixture in a 9 x 13 pan or dish. Chill for 2 hours or until set. For topping, combine sugar, salt, flour and egg in a medium saucepan. Add 1 cup apricot nectar. Cook over medium heat to thicken, stirring constantly. Cool 20 minutes. Add Cool Whip or whipped cream. Spread over gelatin mixture and sprinkle with nuts.

Jan Gattis (Mrs. James D.)

This could also be used for a summer dessert. It's light and refreshing.

MOLDED CRANBERRY AND ORANGE SALAD

Yield: 8 servings

1⅓ Tablespoons gelatin (equals 2
   envelopes of Knox gelatin)
¼ cup cold water
1¼ cups orange juice
4 Tablespoons sugar
½ teaspoon salt
¼ cup lemon juice

1 teaspoon grated orange rind
1 cup raw cranberries, chopped, or
   whole berry cranberry sauce,
   drained
½ cup chopped orange sections
⅓ cup chopped walnuts

Dressing
½ to ¾ cup mayonnaise
½ cup unsweetened pineapple juice

1 teaspoon sugar

Soften gelatin in cold water. Stir in a double boiler over boiling water until dissolved. Add orange juice, sugar and salt. Stir until sugar is dissolved. Add lemon juice and grated orange rind. Chill until partially set. Fold in cranberries, oranges and nuts. Put in mold or pan. Chill until firm. Serve topped with additional chopped walnuts and pineapple/mayonnaise dressing. To make dressing, add enough unsweetened pineapple juice to make the mayonnaise of salad dressing consistency. Add sugar. Beat until well blended.

Kem Embrey Aburrow (Mrs. Harry J.)

This is good for Thanksgiving and Christmas.

FRUIT SALAD WITH NUTS

Yield: 4 to 6 servings

1 small honeydew melon
2 oranges
3 kiwi

1 cup purple or blue grapes
12 walnut halves
Lettuce leaves

Scoop out melon with melon baller. Remove peel and white membrane from oranges and slice crosswise. Peel kiwi and slice crosswise. Cut grapes in half and remove seeds. Arrange the fruit on the lettuce leaves, then top with walnut halves.

Daryl Newcomb

Drizzle favorite fruit dressing over the top of each fruit salad. This is a wonderful combination of different fruits.

BLENDER MAYONNAISE

Yield: 1¼ cups

1 whole egg
2 Tablespoons lemon juice, strained
¼ teaspoon dry mustard
¼ teaspoon paprika

Dash of cayenne pepper
½ teaspoon salt
1 cup salad oil plus 1 teaspoon olive oil

In blender, put egg, lemon juice, mustard, paprika, cayenne pepper, salt and ¼ of the salad oil. Turn on blend. Pour the remaining ¾ cup of oil in a steady stream into blender while mixing. Refrigerate.

Kenan Keyes (Mrs. Griff)

For Basil Mayonnaise add ¼ cup fresh basil, 1 teaspoon lemon juice to 1 cup mayonnaise and blend. This is excellent served with fresh sliced tomatoes, grilled fish or on turkey sandwiches.

SALAD DRESSING LA RAT

Yield: 2 cups

2 ounces tarragon vinegar
4 cloves garlic, peeled
1 Tablespoon peppercorns
¼ lemon, peeled and seeded

8 ounces Mazola salad oil
1 Tablespoon sugar
½ Tablespoon salt
3 ounces Bleu cheese

Place first 4 ingredients in blender and blend on high until peppercorns are pulverized. Add balance of ingredients and blend for 1 minute. Will keep in sealed jar for 1 week. Do not refrigerate. Best served over plain head of lettuce, broken and separated.

L. A. Ratley

RANCH STYLE DRESSING MIX

Yield: ½ cup mix

2 teaspoons salt
2 teaspoons dried minced garlic
8 teaspoons instant minced onion
2 teaspoons black pepper

2 teaspoons sugar
2 teaspoons paprika
2 teaspoons parsley flakes

Combine spices. Store tightly covered.

Uses: Sprinkle directly on salads to season,

Or: Add 1 Tablespoon mix to 1 cup mayonnaise and 1 cup buttermilk. Mix with spoon. Refrigerate.

Or: Add 1 Tablespoon mix to 8 ounces of plain yogurt and use as dip with fresh vegetables.

Or: Combine 2 Tablespoons water with ¼ cup vinegar. Stir in 2 teaspoons mix, then ⅔ cup salad oil. Shake well.

Kenan Keyes (Mrs. Griff)

BLEU CHEESE DRESSING

Yield: 2 cups

4 ounces Bleu cheese, crumbled
1 (16 ounce) jar Hellmann's
    mayonnaise
¼ cup water
¼ teaspoon garlic powder

1½ Tablespoons monosodium
    glutamate
Coarsely ground pepper to taste
2 Tablespoons salad oil

In a bowl, mix Bleu cheese and mayonnaise. Add water, garlic powder, MSG, pepper and oil. Mix well. Chill before serving. A small amount of water can be added if dressing is too thick.

Cindy Miller (Mrs. Patrick)

For a creamy Bleu cheese dressing, mix all ingredients together in a blender until smooth. Keeps well in refrigerator.

MOTHER'S FRENCH DRESSING

Yield: 1½ cups

½ cup sugar
1 teaspoon salt
1 teaspoon dry mustard
½ cup vinegar

1 cup tomato soup
1 cup oil
1 clove garlic
½ onion

Beat first 6 ingredients together. Add garlic clove and ½ onion on a toothpick to season.
Nancy Eakin Dickins (Mrs. Robert D., Jr.)

DUTCH "SWEET-SOUR" SALAD DRESSING

Yield: 1 pint

2 Tablespoons flour
1 cup sugar
2 eggs
1 teaspoon salt

3 teaspoons French mustard
¾ cup cider vinegar
¼ cup water
1 Tablespoon butter

Sieve flour. Blend flour and sugar together. Add eggs, 1 at a time, and blend well. Add salt and mustard. Blend well. Add vinegar and water. Cook over moderate heat, stirring constantly until mixture thickens and starts to boil. Remove from heat and add butter. If too thick, correct by adding cream.

Tony Franke (Mrs. William)

This dressing is good for Apple Salad or Potato Salad.

ITALIAN DRESSING

(Must be prepared 1 day in advance)

Yield: 1 quart

1 (10¾ ounce) can tomato soup
½ cup cider vinegar
1 cup oil
1 Tablespoon Worcestershire sauce
1 to 2 cloves garlic
1 Tablespoon grated onion
1 cup chopped sweet pickles

1 cup chopped olives, green and/or
   ripe
1 teaspoon dry mustard
2 Tablespoons sugar
Salt to taste
Hot sauce (Optional)

Shake all ingredients together in a jar and refrigerate overnight. Remove garlic before serving on green salad. Shake before using.

Almeda W. Elliott (Mrs. Frank)

This was an original recipe by my mother, Elizabeth M. White

MUSTARD VINAIGRETTE

Yield: 1½ cups

1 cup salad oil
⅓ cup wine vinegar
4 Tablespoons Dijon mustard
2 Tablespoons Worcestershire
   sauce

1 teaspoon sugar
1 to 2 cloves garlic
Salt to taste
Pepper to taste

Combine all ingredients, mixing well with a wire whisk.

Lynda H. Hannal

CREAMY SPINACH SALAD DRESSING
(Must be prepared 1 day in advance)

Yield: 1 pint

1 cup Wesson oil
5 Tablespoons wine vinegar
4 Tablespoons sour cream
1½ teaspoons salt

½ teaspoon dry mustard
2 Tablespoons sugar
2 Tablespoons chopped parsley
2 garlic cloves, minced

Mix ingredients in a jar and shake well. Best when served with spinach and crumbled bacon.

Cindy Feltus (Mrs. Greg)

Dressing needs to be made a day in advance. It will keep for several days in refrigerator.

BEST OIL AND VINEGAR DRESSING

Yield: 1½ pints

1 teaspoon Colman's dry mustard
1 teaspoon salt
2 teaspoons sugar
¼ teaspoon white pepper

¼ teaspoon paprika
½ cup cider vinegar
1 cup salad oil (Mazola or Wesson)
1 large clove garlic, split

Mix first 6 ingredients in bottle. Shake well. Add the oil and garlic. Cover. Keeps well in refrigerator. Take out and let come to nearly room temperature before using.

Carrie Dickinson (Mrs. Tyndall)

One recipe will cover a large party salad. This is good to keep on hand.

SAUCE VINAIGRETTE FOR ASPARAGUS

Yield: 2 quarts

3 cups olive oil
1 cup white vinegar
1 cup tarragon vinegar
2 medium Kosher dill pickles
2 medium onions
1 hard-boiled egg
2 Tablespoons chopped parsley

3 Tablespoons capers
4 cloves garlic
1 Tablespoon Dijon mustard
2 Tablespoons salt
10 good grinds fresh black pepper
Juice of ½ lemon
Juice of ½ lime

Place all ingredients in blender and blend. Refrigerate.

Paul Bash
Restaurant Jacques and Suzanne

This recipe can be easily cut in half.

VINAIGRETTE DRESSING

Yield: 1 cup

¼ cup wine vinegar
2 Tablespoons lemon juice
Scant ⅓ cup olive oil
Scant ⅓ cup cooking oil
½ teaspoon dry mustard

½ teaspoon salt
½ teaspoon pepper
¼ teaspoon paprika
Dash of red pepper
1 clove garlic, crushed

Combine all ingredients and mix thoroughly. (Note: Liquid ingredients are in the same proportions as the "Good Seasons" bottles, substituting lemon juice for water and olive oil for ½ of the oil.)

Ted Glusman

VINAIGRETTE DRESSING

Yield: 3 bottles

3 teaspoons salt
2 teaspoons ground black pepper
1 teaspoon dry mustard
1 teaspoon Dijon mustard
1 Tablespoon lemon juice
⅓ cup tarragon vinegar
¼ cup olive oil

1¾ cups vegetable oil
1 garlic clove, bruised
1 hard-boiled egg, separately rub
    white and yellow through sieve
    (Optional)
Capers (Optional)

In a bowl, mix salt, pepper, dry and Dijon mustards, lemon juice, vinegar and stir well. Slowly add oils and beat until creamy consistency. Add garlic. After tossing salad, dust with eggs. You may add capers to dressing.

Judy Burrow (Mrs. Larry)

This dressing may be mixed in food processor very successfully.

TARRAGON DRESSING FOR FRESH SPINACH SALAD

Yield: 1⅛ cups

1 cup salad oil
4 Tablespoons wine vinegar
2 teaspoons sugar
1 teaspoon salt

½ teaspoon pepper
2 Tablespoons fresh or dried
    tarragon

Combine all ingredients in a small jar. Shake well, then refrigerate for several hours. Dressing will keep in refrigerator for months.

Betty Kate Carney

CELERY SEED DRESSING

Yield: 4 cups

1¼ cups sugar
2 teaspoons dry mustard
2 teaspoons salt

1 Tablespoon onion juice
⅔ cup vinegar
2 cups salad oil
1 Tablespoon celery seed

Combine sugar, mustard, salt, onion juice and ½ teaspoon vinegar. Beat well with rotary beater. Add oil gradually, alternating with remaining vinegar. Add 1 Tablespoon celery seed.

Helen Sloan (Mrs. John C.)

Great for fruit salads. You may also substitute poppy seeds for celery seeds.

SAUCE FOR FRUIT SALAD

Yield: 1½ cups

1 (3 ounce) package cream cheese,
   softened
2 Tablespoons mayonnaise
5 ounces pineapple, apricot or
   peach preserves

1 Tablespoon fresh lemon juice
1 Tablespoon sherry
¼ teaspoon curry powder
½ cup whipping cream, whipped
Fresh fruit

Blend cream cheese and mayonnaise until smooth by mixing with a spoon. Stir in preserves, lemon juice, sherry and curry. Chill until just before serving. (Up to 1 hour before serving can add whipping cream.) Stir in whipped cream and keep refrigerated until served. Serve with fresh fruit salad.

Robyn Dickey

For a lighter sauce, add more whipped cream.

FRENCH DRESSING FOR FRUIT

Yield: 1½ cups

⅓ cup sugar
1 teaspoon celery seed
1 teaspoon salt
1 teaspoon dry mustard

1 teaspoon paprika
1 teaspoon grated onion
4 Tablespoons cider vinegar
1 cup salad oil

Put all ingredients except oil in blender. Blend for 30 seconds, add oil and blend for 30 to 45 seconds.

Mrs. Bill Meriwether

Great on fruit. EASY. Keeps for weeks.

HONEY DRESSING FOR FRESH FRUIT

Yield: 1¼ cups

⅔ cup sugar
1 teaspoon dry mustard
1 teaspoon paprika
1 teaspoon celery seed
¼ teaspoon salt

⅓ cup strained honey
5 Tablespoons vinegar
1 Tablespoon lemon juice
1 teaspoon grated onion
1 cup salad oil

Mix dry ingredients. Add honey, vinegar, lemon juice and onion. Pour oil in mixture very slowly, beating constantly. Mix with electric mixer or blender at low speed. Keeps in refrigerator indefinitely.

Mrs. John Darwin
Cookeville, Tennessee

PECAN SALAD DRESSING

Yield: 1½ cups

⅓ cup mayonnaise
⅓ cup chopped pecans
¼ cup light corn syrup

¼ teaspoon salt
1 (6 or 8 ounce) carton plain yogurt

Stir together mayonnaise, pecans, syrup and salt. Fold in yogurt. Chill. Serve over fruit.
Nancy Couch Lee (Mrs. James M., Jr.)

STRAWBERRY DRESSING

Yield: 3 cups

2 Tablespoons powdered sugar
2 Tablespoons lemon juice
1 cup freshly crushed strawberries

1 cup sour cream
1 cup mayonnaise

Combine first 3 ingredients. Then add sour cream and mayonnaise. Chill. Serve over fully ripened fruit.

Mrs. Morin M. Scott
Austin, Texas

"There is no love sincerer than the love of food."
GEORGE BERNARD SHAW
1856-1950

VEGETABLES

Vegetables in their profusion, beauty and delectability compare as the music of Mozart to the Bach of robust meats.

ARTICHOKES WITH FLAIR

Oven: 350°
Yield: 4 to 6 servings

1 (8½ ounce) can artichoke hearts,
   drained
2 (10 ounce) packages frozen
   chopped spinach, cooked and
   drained

1 (8 ounce) package cream cheese
1 stick butter
½ pound bacon, cooked and
   crumbled
Parmesan cheese

Quarter drained artichoke hearts and spread over bottom of an 8 x 8 casserole. Spoon spinach over artichokes. Melt butter and cream cheese in a small saucepan. (Cream cheese will be lumpy.) Pour and spread over spinach. Sprinkle crumbled bacon over cream cheese mixture. Sprinkle well with Parmesan cheese. Bake at 350⁰ for 30 minutes or until bubbly.

Robyn Dickey

An easy and elegant side dish with beef.

ARTICHOKE CASSEROLE

Oven: 350°
Yield: 6 to 8 servings

1 (14 ounce) can artichoke hearts,
   drained and quartered

1 pound Longhorn or rat cheese,
   grated
6 eggs, beaten

Place artichokes on the bottom of a greased 8 x 8 pan. Top with cheese. Pour beaten eggs over cheese. Bake at 350⁰ for 45 minutes.

Marilyn Loyd
Lake Village, Arkansas

Good for brunch or supper.

EASY COMPANY ASPARAGUS

Oven: 350°
Yield: 4 servings

¼ cup margarine
¼ cup sauterne wine
1 (15 ounce) can asparagus spears,
   drained

Parmesan cheese
Salt to taste
Pepper to taste

Melt margarine and mix with wine. Pour over drained asparagus. Sprinkle heavily with Parmesan cheese. Salt and pepper to taste. Bake until heated through.

Nancy Couch (Mrs. James)

ASPARAGUS CASSEROLE

Oven: 350°
Yield: 4 servings

Cream Sauce
¼ cup margarine
2 Tablespoons flour
1 cup milk
Juice of canned asparagus

1 cup grated sharp Cheddar cheese
Salt to taste
Pepper to taste

1 (12 ounce) can asparagus
2 hard-boiled eggs, thinly sliced

1 cup crushed Ritz crackers

To make cream sauce, melt margarine and add flour. Mix well. Add milk and juice of asparagus. Cook in a saucepan, stirring constantly, until thick. Add Cheddar cheese, salt and pepper. In a casserole layer ½ can asparagus, 1 egg, ½ cream sauce. Repeat. Top with Ritz cracker crumbs and heat at 350⁰ for 20 to 30 minutes.

Cindy Wage (Mrs. Olin)

SALLY'S TWO BEANS AND A POD

(Must be prepared 1 day in advance)

Oven: 350°
Yield: 16 servings

2 (10 ounce) packages frozen cut
    green beans
2 (10 ounce) packages frozen baby
    lima beans
2 (10 ounce) packages frozen
    English peas
1½ cups mayonnaise
3 hard-boiled eggs, finely chopped
1 medium onion, finely chopped

1 teaspoon prepared mustard
1 teaspoon Worcestershire sauce
4 Tablespoons vegetable oil
Dash of Tabasco
2 (8½ ounce) cans water chestnuts,
    drained and sliced
2 (4 ounce) cans sliced mushrooms,
    drained
Buttered bread crumbs

Cook the green beans, lima beans and peas according to package directions, being careful not to overcook. Make a sauce mixing mayonnaise, eggs, onion, mustard, Worcestershire sauce, oil and Tabasco. Combine cooked vegetables, water chestnuts, mushrooms and sauce. Let stand overnight in refrigerator. Top casserole with buttered bread crumbs. Bake in a 9 x 13 pyrex dish at 350⁰ for 30 minutes. The casserole should just come to a bubbling stage.

Cotsy Chenault (Mrs. Harry)

Great for pot luck supper.

BEEFY BAKED BEANS
(Must be prepared 1 day in advance)

Oven: 300°
Yield: 10 to 12 servings

1½ pounds ground chuck
2 medium onions, chopped
½ stick margarine
2 (20¾ ounce) cans pork and beans
3 (15 ounce) cans Ranch Style
  Beans

¼ cup prepared mustard
½ cup brown sugar
¼ cup syrup (maple preferred)
1 cup ketchup

Brown beef and onions in margarine. Add beans. Mix remaining ingredients and add to meat and beans. Place it all in a casserole or beanpot and refrigerate overnight. Bake at 300⁰ for 1½ hours.

Julie Truemper (Mrs. John J., Jr.)

CALICO BEANS

Oven: 350°
Yield: 8 servings

½ pound bacon, cut up
½ pound ground beef
½ cup chopped onion
1 (16 ounce) can pork and beans
1 (16 ounce) can kidney beans
1 (16 ounce) can butter beans

½ cup ketchup
¾ cup brown sugar
1 teaspoon salt
1 teaspoon mustard
1 teaspoon vinegar

Brown and drain bacon, ground beef and onions. Mix with remaining ingredients and place in a 3 quart casserole. Bake at 350⁰ for 1½ hours.

Patti Turner Lueck (Mrs. Daniel)
Northfield, Minnesota

A delicious substitute for baked beans. For a meatier dish, add 1 pound of ground beef.

"If pale beans bubble for you in a red earthenware pot, you can often decline the dinners of sumptuous hosts."

MARTIAL
A.D. 40-102

GREEN BEANS WITH EGG SAUCE
(Must be prepared 1 day in advance)

Yield: 6 servings

2 pounds fresh green beans or
   2 (16 ounce) cans French style
   green beans
1 onion, sliced

6 Tablespoons Wesson oil
3 Tablespoons vinegar
½ teaspoon salt
½ teaspoon pepper

Egg Sauce
6 Tablespoons mayonnaise
2 teaspoons prepared mustard
4 teaspoons vinegar

Salt
3 hard-boiled eggs, chopped

Steam fresh beans until tender or cook canned beans for 10 minutes with no seasonings. Drain. Layer green beans and sliced onion and marinate overnight in oil and vinegar, salt and pepper. Drain EXTRA WELL before serving. Serve with egg sauce

Nancy Lichty (Mrs. Larry)

FRENCH QUARTER GREEN BEANS

Oven: 375°
Yield: 8 servings

3 (9 ounce) packages frozen French
   style green beans
3 Tablespoons butter or margarine
1 (10¾ ounce) can cream of
   mushroom soup
1 (3 ounce) package cream cheese,
   softened
1 teaspoon dried onion flakes
1 (8 ounce) can sliced water
   chestnuts, drained

¼ teaspoon garlic salt
½ teaspoon salt
¼ teaspoon pepper
1½ cups grated Cheddar cheese
1 (2½ ounce) package slivered
   almonds
Paprika

Cook beans according to package directions. Drain. Melt butter in a saucepan and add soup and cream cheese. Cook over low heat, stirring constantly, until cream cheese is melted and mixture is smooth. Remove from heat and stir in green beans, onion flakes, water chestnuts, garlic salt, salt, pepper and Cheddar cheese. Spoon mixture into a lightly greased 2 quart casserole dish. Top with almonds and sprinkle with paprika. Bake, uncovered, at 375° for 45 minutes or until bubbling around edges.

Martha Laurens Taylor

PLANTATION GREEN BEANS

Oven: 400°
Yield: 8 servings

80 fresh long pole or green beans
8 slices bacon, partially cooked

8 toothpicks

Sauce
4 Tablespoons bacon grease
3 Tablespoons cider vinegar
2 Tablespoons tarragon vinegar
1 teaspoon salt

½ teaspoon paprika
1 Tablespoon chopped parsely
1 Tablespoon grated onion

Partially cook beans in salted water until tender. Drain. Secure 10 beans in a bundle wrapped with bacon and secured with a toothpick. Place on foil covered cookie sheet and bake at 400° until bacon is done on all sides (10 to 15 minutes). Pour sauce over beans and serve hot. To make sauce, boil ingredients over medium heat for 5 minutes. Pour 1 to 1½ Tablespoons over each bundle.

Rosie Ratley (Mrs. Richard)

Looks pretty for buffet.

SWISS GREEN BEANS

Oven: 350°
Yield: 6 servings

4 Tablespoons butter
2 Tablespoons flour
1 teaspoon salt
½ teaspoon pepper
1 teaspoon minced, dried onion
1 Tablespoon sugar

1 cup sour cream
2 (10 ounce) packages frozen
  French cut green beans, cooked
  and drained
1½ cups grated Swiss cheese
¼ cup crushed Ritz crackers

Over low heat melt 2 Tablespoons of butter. Add flour, salt, pepper, onion and sugar. Stir in sour cream and green beans. Put in a 2 quart greased casserole. Cover with cheese. Melt remaining butter and mix with crackers. Spread over cheese. Bake at 350° for 30 minutes.

Anne Arnold (Mrs. Scott A., III)
Tunica, Mississippi

SALLY'S RED BEANS AND RICE

Yield: 6 to 8 servings

1 pound red or kidney beans
1 quart water
1 ham bone with ham
1 large onion, chopped
2 garlic cloves, crushed
¼ cup chopped celery

½ teaspoon Tabasco
1 teaspoon salt
¼ teaspoon thyme
1 bay leaf
1 pound package hot sausage links

Soak beans. Pour into a large, heavy pan. Add remaining ingredients except sausage and simmer 3 hours until beans are tender. Add water when necessary during cooking. Remove ham bone, cut off meat and add to beans. Liquid should barely cover beans at end of cooking time. Cut sausages into ½ inch slices and add to beans. Let simmer. Serve beans and meat over rice.

Carol Lord (Mrs. Robert C.)

EASY BEETS

Yield: 4 servings

2 Tablespoons butter
¼ cup sugar
½ cup vinegar
3 Tablespoons cornstarch

½ cup beet liquid
1 (16 ounce) can sliced or whole beets

Combine all ingredients in a saucepan. Add beets. Simmer for 10 minutes.

Margaret Windsor Clark (Mrs. William)

Thin orange slices may be added during simmering for a change of taste.

BROCCOLI WITH PINE NUTS

Yield: 6 servings

1 bunch fresh broccoli
½ cup butter or margarine
½ cup golden raisins

½ cup (2¾ ounce jar) pine nuts
2 Tablespoons lemon juice

Steam broccoli until tender but crisp. Melt butter. Stir in raisins and pine nuts. Sauté gently until pine nuts are golden, about 3 minutes. Stir in lemon juice and pour over broccoli. If made ahead and kept warm, do not add lemon juice until ready to serve.

Irene Vratsinas (Mrs. Gus)

Slivered almonds may be substituted for the pine nuts.

STIR-FRIED BROCCOLI

Yield: 8 servings

3 Tablespoons salad oil
2 bunches broccoli, cut into small
   pieces
¼ to ½ cup chopped green onions

¼ cup water
1 Tablespoon lemon pepper
2 dashes soy sauce (Optional)
1 hard-boiled egg, minced

Heat oil in a large skillet over high heat. Cook broccoli, stirring quickly until well-coated with oil. Add green onions, water, lemon pepper and soy sauce. Turn heat to medium high, cover and cook 2 minutes. Uncover and stir-fry about 5 minutes or until tender but crisp. Sprinkle hard-boiled egg on top of vegetables.

Melinda Morse

BROCCOLI CASSEROLE

Oven: 350°
Yield: 6 to 8 servings

4 (10 ounce) packages frozen
   broccoli spears, cooked and
   drained
6 hard-boiled eggs, finely chopped
3 Tablespoons butter or margarine
½ medium onion, chopped
6 Tablespoons flour

2 cups milk
10 to 12 ounces sharp cheese,
   grated (reserve ¼ cup)
1 teaspoon salt
6 slices bacon, cooked and
   crumbled

Layer broccoli and eggs in a buttered 2 quart casserole. Melt butter over medium heat and sauté onions until clear. Stir in flour. Add milk slowly while stirring. Cook until it begins to thicken. Reduce heat. Add cheese (reserving ¼ cup) and salt. Cook until cheese is completely melted. Pour sauce over broccoli and eggs. Top with ¼ cup grated cheese and bacon. Bake at 350° for 30 minutes.

Nancy Bishop (Mrs. William E.)

May be made ahead and refrigerated.

"...Only I stick to asparagus, which still seems to inspire gentle thoughts."
CHARLES LAMB
1775-1834

BROCCOLI-RICE QUICHE

Oven: 375°
Yield: 10 to 12 servings

3 cups cooked rice
1½ cups grated sharp Cheddar
  cheese
6 eggs
1 teaspoon salt
½ cup chopped onion

2 (10 ounce) packages frozen
  chopped broccoli
½ cup milk
¼ teaspoon pepper
1 (4 ounce) can sliced mushrooms,
  drained

Combine rice, ¾ cup cheese, 2 slightly-beaten eggs and ½ teaspoon salt. Press mixture firmly and evenly over bottom and sides of a greased 12 inch pizza pan or 2 (9 inch) pie pans. Set aside. Add onions to broccoli and cook according to package directions. Drain well. Beat remaining eggs slightly and stir in milk, pepper, mushrooms, and remaining ½ teaspoon salt. Add to broccoli and mix well. Pour into rice crust. Bake at 375° for 20 minutes. Sprinkle cheese on top and bake 10 more minutes. Cool some before cutting.

Ann R. Lewis (Mrs. Gene, Jr.)

BROCCOLI SOUFFLÉ

Oven: 325°
Yield: 6 servings

1 (10 ounce) package frozen
  chopped broccoli
3 Tablespoons butter
3 Tablespoons flour
1 teaspoon salt

1 cup milk
2 teaspoons lemon juice
4 egg yolks
4 egg whites

Sauce
½ cup sour cream

½ cup mayonnaise

Cook broccoli, drain well and finely chop. Melt butter, add flour, salt and milk to make white sauce. Cook until thick. Add lemon juice and broccoli. Place all ingredients in blender and purée. Cool slightly and add beaten egg yolks. Beat egg whites until stiff and fold into broccoli mixture. Pour all into a buttered 1½ quart casserole. Place in pan of 1 inch hot water. Bake at 325° for 1 hour or until firm. Serve immediately with mixture of sour cream and mayonnaise.

Grace McCaskill (Mrs. Austin)

This soufflé can be mixed ahead of time except for adding the egg whites.

BRUSSELS SPROUTS AND ARTICHOKES

Oven: 425°
Yield: 6 servings

1 (10 ounce) package frozen
   Brussels sprouts
1 (14 ounce) can artichoke hearts,
   drained
⅔ cup mayonnaise

½ teaspoon celery salt
¼ cup grated Parmesan cheese
¼ cup margarine, melted
2 teaspoons lemon juice
¼ cup sliced almonds

Cook Brussels sprouts according to package directions. Drain. Arrange Brussels sprouts
and artichokes in a greased 1 quart casserole. Combine remaining ingredients and spoon
over vegetables. Bake, uncovered, at 425° for 8 to 10 minutes.

Mrs. Jack L. Graham

DUCK HUNTERS' CABBAGE

Oven: 350°
Yield: 8 servings

1 large head cabbage
½ cup butter or margarine,
   softened
Cavender's Greek Seasoning

Lemon pepper
Worcestershire sauce
Wine vinegar

Wash and core cabbage. Place cabbage on heavy-duty aluminum foil. Line cavity of cabbage with butter and fill with Worcestershire sauce. Season to taste with Cavender's
and lemon pepper. Seal tightly and place on cookie sheet. Bake at 350° for 2½ to 3 hours.
Remove foil and place in a large bowl. Cut into bite-sized pieces and toss with wine vinegar
to taste (approximately ½ cup). Serve immediately.

Rogers Cockrill
J. D. Simpson, III

There is no cabbage odor to perfume your home!

SCALLOPED CABBAGE

Oven: 350°
Yield: 4 servings

4 cups shredded cabbage
1 cup canned or fresh tomatoes,
   diced
1 cup grated sharp cheese

1 cup bread crumbs
½ teaspoon salt
Pepper to taste
1 Tablespoon butter or margarine

Cook cabbage in a small amount of boiling, salted water until tender but slightly crisp,
about 5 minutes. Drain. Layer half of cabbage, tomatoes, cheese and bread crumbs. Drizzle
with butter. Repeat. Cover and bake at 350° for 30 minutes.

Ann Willis (Mrs. Ed)

CREOLE CABBAGE

Yield: 6 servings

1 large head cabbage, cut into chunks
1 large onion, chopped
1 bell pepper, chopped
2½ cups canned tomatoes
1 meaty ham hock
6 whole allspice

3 bay leaves
1 teaspoon chili powder
1 teaspoon salt
½ teaspoon pepper
Potatoes, peeled and quartered
  (Optional)

Combine all ingredients in a Dutch oven or heavy saucepan and cook, covered, until cabbage is tender (about 1½ hours). Peeled and quartered potatoes may be added for the last 20 minutes of cooking time. When cabbage is done, remove the ham from the bone, cut into bite-sized pieces and serve with the cabbage. Remove allspice and bay leaves before serving. May be served in soup plates or bowls.

Mrs. E. D. Polk

CARROTS CHABLIS

Yield: 8 to 10 servings

2 pounds carrots
2 Tablespoons butter
¾ cup chablis wine
⅛ teaspoon sugar

Salt to taste
Pepper to taste
1 cup red grapes, cut in half and
  seeded

Cut carrots into thick, diagonal slices or into julienne strips. Sauté carrots in butter. Add wine and cook, covered, until tender. Add seasonings and grapes. Continue cooking for 5 minutes.

Eva Rand (Mrs. Benjamin A.)

CHINESE CARROTS AND MUSHROOMS

Yield: 4 to 6 servings

3 Tablespoons butter
12 carrots, sliced paper thin
2 onions, thinly sliced
1½ cups fresh mushrooms, thinly sliced
½ cup water
Juice of ½ lemon
¾ teaspoon salt

¼ teaspoon savory
¼ teaspoon ginger
⅛ teaspoon mace
⅛ teaspoon nutmeg
⅛ teaspoon thyme
⅛ teaspoon pepper
2 Tablespoons chopped parsley

Melt butter in a large skillet. Add carrots, onion and mushrooms and sauté until onion is tender. Add water and remaining ingredients and simmer until tender, about 25 minutes.

Mary Ann Wright
Naperville, Illinois

CARROT SOUFFLÉ

Oven: 350°
Yield: 6 to 8 servings

2 cups cooked and mashed carrots
1 cup milk
1 stick butter
¼ cup grated onion
1 teaspoon salt
¼ teaspoon pepper

⅛ teaspoon cayenne pepper
1 cup cracker crumbs
¾ cup grated sharp Cheddar
    cheese
3 eggs, lightly beaten

Peel and cook carrots until tender. Mash carrots and combine with milk, butter, onion and seasonings. Add cracker crumbs and cheese. Fold eggs into carrot mixture and place in a 1½ quart casserole. Bake, uncovered, at 350⁰ for 40 to 45 minutes.

Cynthia Weber (Mrs. James R.)

For a special touch, cook soufflé in a 1½ quart well-greased ring mold. When unmolded on platter fill the center with green peas.

CELERY CASSEROLE

Oven: 350°
Yield: 8 servings

3 cups celery, sliced diagonally in
    ½ inch pieces
¼ cup slivered almonds
½ cup sliced water chestnuts
1 (4 ounce) can sliced mushrooms,
    drained
¼ cup plus 1 Tablespoon butter or
    margarine

3 Tablespoons flour
1 cup chicken broth
¾ cup Half and Half
½ cup grated Parmesan cheese
½ cup soft bread crumbs
3 Tablespoons butter, melted
Parsley sprigs

Cook celery in small amount of boiling water until just tender (about 5 minutes). Drain. Combine celery, almonds, water chestnuts and mushrooms. Mix well. Pour into a greased 9 x 13 baking dish. Melt ¼ cup plus 1 Tablespoon butter in a saucepan over low heat. Blend in flour. Cook 1 minute, stirring constantly. Gradually add chicken broth and Half and Half. Cook over medium heat, stirring constantly until thickened. Pour sauce over celery mixture. Combine cheese and bread crumbs. Sprinkle over casserole. Drizzle melted butter over top. Bake at 350⁰ for 25 minutes. Garnish with parsley.

Sunny Hawk (Mrs. Boyce)

CELERY SAUTÉ

Yield: 4 to 6 servings

1 bunch celery
1 (8 ounce) can water chestnuts,
   drained and chopped

1 (2 ounce) package almonds,
   toasted
¼ cup margarine, melted

Chop celery diagonally and boil in salted water until just tender and still crisp. Drain well. Toss water chestnuts in margarine. Add toasted almonds and water chestnuts to drained celery. Toss lightly. Serve hot.

Katherine Rather (Mrs. Gordon)

COLACHE

Yield: 8 servings

¼ cup bacon fat or other
   shortening
2 yellow crookneck squash, thinly
   sliced
2 zucchini, thinly sliced
1 medium onion, finely chopped
1 red bell pepper, seeded and
   chopped
1 green bell pepper, seeded and
   chopped

1 (4 ounce) can chopped green
   chilies, drained (Optional)
1 clove garlic, minced
3 ears corn
1 large tomato, peeled and diced
1 cup green beans, cut in ½ inch
   slices
½ cup water
1 teaspoon salt
Freshly ground pepper to taste

Melt bacon fat in a heavy pan and add squash, onion, peppers, chilies and garlic. Cook, stirring for about 5 minutes. Cut kernels from corn cobs and add corn, tomato, beans, water and salt to mixture. Cover and simmer until the vegetables are tender. Correct seasonings and add freshly ground pepper.

Mary Ann Wright
Naperville, Illinois

SOUTHERN-STYLE CREAMED CORN

Yield: 6 servings

6 ears fresh corn
¼ cup butter or margarine
¼ cup water
1 teaspoon sugar

1 Tablespoon flour
½ teaspoon salt
½ teaspoon coarsely ground pepper
¾ cup milk

Cut corn from cobs. Scrape cobs with a sharp knife to remove milk. Melt butter in a skillet, stir in corn and corn milk, water and sugar. Cook corn until done. Stir in flour, salt and pepper. Gradually add milk, stirring constantly. Cook a few minutes longer. Do not boil.

Diane Lord (Mrs. E. Fletcher, Jr.)

FRESH CORN AND BACON CASSEROLE

Oven: 350°
Yield: 6 servings

6 slices bacon
6 ears fresh corn
½ cup chopped green pepper
½ cup chopped onion

1 teaspoon salt
⅛ teaspoon pepper
2 fresh tomatoes, peeled and sliced

In a large skillet, cook bacon until crisp. Remove from skillet, drain on paper towels and crumble. Remove all but 2 Tablespoons bacon fat from skillet. Cut corn from cobs. Add corn, green pepper and onion to bacon fat. Cook over high heat for 5 minutes. Add crumbled bacon, salt and pepper. In a 2 quart casserole, alternate layers of the corn mixture and tomato slices. Bake, uncovered, at 350° for 30 to 40 minutes, until corn is tender.

Karen Valentine Sanders (Mrs. Brant)
Birmingham, Alabama

HOT CORN

Oven: 350°
Yield: 6 servings

1 stick butter or margarine
1 (8 ounce) package Philadelphia
  cream cheese
2 (12 ounce) cans shoe peg white
  corn, drained

1 (4 ounce) can chopped green
  chilies, drained
Salt to taste
Pepper to taste
1 or 2 jalapeño peppers, finely
  chopped (Optional)

Melt butter or margarine in a small saucepan over low heat. Add cream cheese and stir until melted. Remove from heat. Combine cheese mixture with remaining ingredients in a 2 quart baking dish. Add jalapeño peppers, if desired, for an extra spicy taste. Bake, uncovered, for 35 minutes at 350°.

Jane Johnson

CORN AND SOUR CREAM WITH BACON

Yield: 6 to 8 servings

½ pound bacon
2 Tablespoons bacon drippings or butter
2 Tablespoons minced onion
2 Tablespoons flour
1 teaspoon salt

Pepper to taste
1 cup sour cream
2 (12 ounce) cans whole kernel
  corn, well drained
1 teaspoon chopped parsley

Brown bacon until crisp. Reserve 2 Tablespoons drippings. Drain and crumble bacon. Cook onion in drippings until soft. Blend in flour, salt and pepper. Add sour cream very slowly. Stir constantly to keep smooth. Heat to boiling. Add corn and heat. Just before serving, add half the crumbled bacon. Place in serving dish and sprinkle remaining bacon on top. Garnish with parsley.

Marcia Johnston (Mrs. Richard S.)

EGGPLANT PIE

Oven: 375°
Yield: 2 pies

4 to 6 medium eggplant
Salt
Olive oil
4 to 6 medium onions, sliced
4 to 6 medium tomatoes, sliced
Freshly ground black pepper
1 to 2 cups freshly grated Parmesan
   cheese

1 to 2 cups freshly grated Gruyère
   cheese
3 cups cream
Butter
2 (9 inch) pie crusts

Peel eggplant, cut in thin slices, sprinkle with salt and let stand at room temperature in a bowl for 2 hours. Drain and wipe eggplant. Fry lightly in olive oil until soft and golden. Drain on paper towels. Sauté the onions. In pie crusts layer the eggplant, pepper, cheeses, cream and dots of butter. Repeat the layers with the onions and then the tomatoes. Bake at 375° for 45 to 60 minutes.

Joe Brogdon

Wonderful as a main dish. Serve with salad.

SCALLOPED EGGPLANT CASSEROLE

Oven: 350°
Yield: 10 to 12 servings

3 medium eggplant, peeled and
   sliced
½ cup butter
½ onion, grated
Salt to taste

Pepper to taste
3 eggs
1 cup milk
1 cup cracker crumbs
1 cup grated Cheddar cheese

Cook eggplant in boiling salted water until soft. Drain and mash. Add butter, onion, salt and pepper, stirring well. Beat the eggs and add milk. Add mixture to the eggplant. Add cracker crumbs and ½ cup grated cheese. Bake in a 2½ quart casserole at 350° for 45 minutes or until firm in the middle. During last few minutes sprinkle remaining ½ cup cheese on top and allow to bubble.

Mrs. Richard Allin, Sr.
Helena, Arkansas

EGGPLANT PARMIGIANA

Oven: 350°
Yield: 6 servings

1 Tablespoon olive oil
2 Tablespoons vegetable oil
2 cloves garlic, minced
2 cups Total cereal, crushed (or use bread crumbs)
1 Tablespoon parsley
¼ teaspoon oregano

1 teaspoon salt
½ teaspoon pepper
½ cup Parmesan cheese
1 pound Mozzarella cheese, sliced
1 large eggplant or 2 small eggplant
1 egg, beaten

Sauce
1 Tablespoon olive oil
2 Tablespoons vegetable oil
2 onions, chopped
2 cloves garlic, minced
2 Tablespoons parsley

¼ teaspoon oregano
¼ teaspoon salt
⅛ teaspoon pepper
4 (8 ounce) cans tomato sauce

Heat oil in skillet until smoking. Remove from heat and add garlic. Add cereal and seasonings. Pour into bowl and add Parmesan cheese. Slice eggplant lengthwise. Dip each piece into beaten egg, then cereal mixture. Heat 2 Tablespoons oil in wok or skillet. Cook eggplant less than 30 seconds on each side. Drain. To make sauce, heat oils and sauté onion and garlic until soft. Add spices and tomato sauce. Simmer 30 minutes. To assemble, layer eggplant, Mozzarella cheese, Parmesan cheese and sauce. Repeat. Sprinkle top with Parmesan cheese and bake at 350° for 30 minutes or until cheeses are melted.

Anne Arnold (Mrs. Scott A., III)
Tunica, Mississippi

MUSHROOMS AU GRATIN

Oven: 425°
Yield: 4 servings

1 pound fresh mushrooms, sliced
2 Tablespoons butter
⅓ cup sour cream
1 egg yolk

Salt to taste
Pepper to taste
¼ cup finely chopped parsley
¼ cup grated Swiss cheese

Sauté mushrooms in butter until light brown. Simmer 2 minutes. Blend sour cream, egg yolk, salt and pepper until smooth. Add to mushrooms. Heat, stirring constantly, until blended. Pour into a shallow baking dish and sprinkle with parsley and cheese. Bake 10 minutes at 425° until cheese is melted.

Sissy Clinton (Mrs. David)

Can be made ahead and cooked just before serving.

ONION-MUSHROOM-BACON PIE

Oven: 350°
Yield: 6 to 8 servings

1 pound mushrooms, sliced
6 slices bacon, diced
½ medium onion, sliced
2 garlic cloves, minced
2 Tablespoons chopped parsley
3 Tablespoons olive oil

4 eggs, beaten
1 cup Parmesan cheese
½ teaspoon salt
¼ teaspoon pepper
1 (9 inch) pie shell, unbaked

Sauté mushrooms, bacon, onion, garlic and parsley in olive oil until tender. Drain well and cool. Combine eggs, cheese and seasonings. Stir into onion-bacon mixture. Pour into pie shell and bake for 30 minutes at 350⁰.

Cindy Miller (Mrs. Patrick)

Add a green salad and you have lunch.

MUSHROOMS IN PASTRY

Yield: 10 servings

10 frozen patty shells
2 Tablespoons butter
1 pound fresh mushrooms, sliced
1½ cups sour cream

¾ cup grated Parmesan cheese
3 Tablespoons dry sherry
Dash of garlic powder
Fresh parsley

Bake patty shells according to package directions. Melt butter in a large skillet. Add mushrooms and sauté. Drain. Stir in sour cream, cheese, sherry and garlic powder and cook over low heat until thoroughly heated. Spoon into patty shells. Garnish with parsley. Serve immediately.

Alice Gazette (Mrs. Gary)

CREOLE OKRA

Yield: 6 to 8 servings

3 cups sliced okra
½ cup chopped onion
½ cup chopped green pepper
¼ cup butter or margarine

3 cups chopped tomatoes
4 teaspoons sugar
1¼ teaspoon salt
½ teaspoon pepper

Sauté okra, onion and green pepper in butter for 5 minutes, stirring constantly. Add remaining ingredients and cook over low heat for 10 to 15 minutes, stirring occasionally.

Diane Lord (Mrs. E. Fletcher, Jr.)

BEST CHEESE GRITS

Oven: 350°
Yield: 8 servings

1 cup grits
4 cups water
1 teaspoon salt
¼ pound butter or margarine
1 (6 ounce) roll Kraft garlic cheese

3 eggs
½ cup milk
1 cup sour cream
1 cup crushed and buttered
  cornflakes (Optional)

Cook grits in 4 cups water and 1 teaspoon salt as directed on package. Cool 15 minutes. Melt butter or margarine and ¾ roll of cheese together and add to grits. Beat eggs and milk. Add sour cream. Add mixture slowly to grits. Pour into a greased 2 quart casserole. Top with remaining cheese that has been grated or cut into small pieces and cornflakes. Bake for 45 minutes at 350⁰.

Janet Hurley (Mrs. Harry)
Kirkwood, Missouri

BAKED CURRIED ONIONS

Oven: 350°
Yield: 6 servings

1 pound onions, sliced
1 cup water
3 Tablespoons butter
2 Tablespoons flour
¼ teaspoon cayenne pepper
¼ teaspoon curry powder

¼ teaspoon paprika
2 bouillon cubes
1 cup milk
3 ounces sharp cheese, grated
4 to 6 slices bread, cut in triangles
  and toasted

Place onions in a saucepan with water. Cover and simmer for 10 minutes. In a double boiler, melt the butter and stir in the flour and seasonings. Add bouillon cubes and stir in milk gradually. Add cheese, saving a few Tablespoons to spread on top. Stir constantly until mixture is very thick. Place toast in a buttered 2 quart casserole dish and cover with drained onions. Pour sauce over them and sprinkle with cheese. Bake at 350⁰ for 20 to 30 minutes.

Margaret Windsor Clark (Mrs. William)

Delightful, different and excellent with game.

"This is every cook's opinion,
No savory dish without an onion,
But lest your kissing should be spoil'd
Your onions must be thoroughly boiled..."
JONATHAN SWIFT
1667-1745

ONIONS ALMONDINE

Oven: 350°
Yield: 6 to 8 servings

½ cup butter
½ cup blanched, slivered almonds
1 Tablespoon dark brown sugar
2 cloves garlic, pressed
½ teaspoon salt

¼ teaspoon pepper
¼ cup dry white wine or sherry
4 dozen small white onions, fresh or
    canned

Melt butter. Stir in almonds and brown sugar. Add pressed garlic, seasonings and wine. Add onions and stir until well coated. Cover and bake at 350° for 1 hour, stirring or shaking pan occasionally to coat onions.

Nancy Mitcham (Mrs. Robert)

Great with the Thanksgiving turkey!

SPICY BLACK-EYED PEAS

Yield: 8 servings

½ pound bacon
2 cups chopped onion
2 cups chopped green pepper
2 cups chopped celery
3 tomatoes, peeled, seeded and
    chopped

3 (15 ounce) cans black-eyed peas
1 (10 ounce) can Ro-Tel tomatoes
Salt to taste
Pepper to taste
White vinegar to taste (Optional)

Cook bacon until it has rendered the fat. Transfer bacon to a 6 to 8 quart soup pot. Sauté the onion, green pepper and celery in the bacon fat. Pour peas into the soup pot. Add the sautéed vegetables, chopped tomatoes, Ro-Tel tomatoes, salt and pepper. Cook over medium to medium low heat for 30 minutes. Correct seasonings. Serve hot.

Katie Tufts (Mrs. Mitchell)
Dallas, Texas

Great served in mugs as a soup on a cold day.

"Peas
I eat my peas with honey,
I've done it all my life,
It makes the peas taste funny,
But it keeps them on the knife."
ANONYMOUS

PEAS AND ARTICHOKE HEARTS SAUTÉ

Yield: 4 to 6 servings

2 Tablespoons olive oil
2 cloves garlic, minced
1 Tablespoon chopped parsley
¼ teaspoon fennel seed
Salt to taste

Pepper to taste
1 (14 ounce) can artichoke hearts,
  drained and quartered
1 (16 ounce) can green peas,
  drained

Sauté garlic in olive oil until softened. Add parsley, fennel seed, salt and pepper. Add artichoke hearts and sauté for 5 minutes. Add peas and simmer until heated through and flavors have blended.

Julie Truemper (Mrs. John J., Jr.)

SNOW PEAS ORIENTAL

Yield: 4 servings

1 chicken bouillon cube
¼ cup boiling water
1 teaspoon cornstarch
1 teaspoon cold water
1 Tablespoon salad oil
1 teaspoon soy sauce
1 garlic clove, minced

1 (6 ounce) package frozen snow
  peas, thawed, or 1 cup fresh
  snow peas
1 (8½ ounce) can bamboo shoots,
  drained
1 (8½ ounce) can water chestnuts,
  drained and sliced
1 (4 ounce) can sliced mushrooms,
  drained (Optional)

Dissolve bouillon cube in boiling water, then set aside. Combine cornstarch in cold water and set aside. Heat oil and soy sauce over low heat in a large skillet or wok and add garlic. Sauté until brown. Add snow peas, bamboo shoots, water chestnuts and mushrooms and stir-fry for 1 minute over high heat. Add chicken bouillon and cornstarch mixtures and stir until thickened, about 1 minute.

POTATOES AU GRATIN

Oven: 350°
Yield: 8 servings

½ pound Velveeta cheese
1 pint Half and Half
1 (4½ ounce) package shredded
  Cheddar cheese

1 stick butter or margarine
1 (2 pound) package frozen hash
  brown potatoes

Melt first 4 ingredients in a saucepan. Place frozen hash browns in a 9 x 13 dish. Pour cheese mixture over potatoes and bake, uncovered, for 1 hour at 350⁰.

Rita Massey (Mrs. Don)

POTATO CASSEROLE

Oven: 325°
Yield: 6 to 8 servings

6 potatoes, peeled, sliced and
   boiled
2 cups grated Cheddar cheese
¼ cup melted butter
⅓ cup chopped green onions

2 cups sour cream, at room
   temperature
1 teaspoon salt
¼ teaspoon pepper
2 Tablespoons butter

While potatoes are still quite warm, mix lightly with cheese and melted butter. Mix onions and sour cream together and add to potatoes. Add salt and pepper. Place mixture in a 9 x 13 pan and dot with butter. Bake at 325⁰ for about 20 minutes or until thoroughly heated.

Jo Ann Drew (Mrs. Tommy, Jr.)

SIMPLY ELEGANT POTATOES

Yield: 4 servings

8 to 10 new potatoes
1 stick butter or margarine
½ cup chopped parsley

Salt to taste
Pepper to taste

Slice unpeeled potatoes ¼ inch thick. Steam for 10 minutes or until tender. Melt butter and add parsley, salt and pepper. Place potatoes in a shallow dish, pour butter mixture over, and serve immediately.

Ellen Golden (Mrs. Lex)

CREAMY NEW POTATOES

Yield: 16 servings

4 pounds new potatoes, unpeeled
   and quartered
4 medium onions, sliced
3 cloves garlic, crushed
½ pound butter
¾ cup sour cream
4 ounces cream cheese, softened

1 to 1½ ounces finely crumbled
   Bleu cheese
1 Tablespoon Cavender's Greek
   Seasoning
1 teaspoon pepper
2 teaspoons dillweed
Salt to taste

Cook potatoes, onions and garlic in boiling water until potatoes are tender. Drain thoroughly. Add rest of the ingredients and beat until creamy.

Becky McKinney (Mrs. Richard H., Jr.)

GOLDEN SWEET POTATOES

Oven: 350°
Yield: 6 to 8 servings

2 eggs
1 cup sugar
1½ sticks (¾ cup) margarine
½ cup milk
1 teaspoon vanilla

3 cups cooked sweet potatoes,
   mashed
1 cup brown sugar
⅓ cup flour
¼ stick margarine
½ cup chopped nuts

Beat eggs, sugar and margarine. Add milk and vanilla. Add mixture to mashed sweet potatoes and place in a greased 2 quart baking dish. Mix brown sugar, flour and margarine together making fine crumbs. Place on top of sweet potatoes, then cover with chopped nuts. Bake for 45 minutes at 350⁰.

Anne Rucker
Mrs. Max A. Mitcham
Smackover, Arkansas

SWEET POTATO PINEAPPLE CASSEROLE

Oven: 375°
Yield: 6 to 8 servings

2 (10 ounce) cans sweet potatoes,
   drained
1 (8¼ ounce) can crushed
   pineapple, drained

⅛ teaspoon nutmeg or cinnamon
½ teaspoon salt
2 Tablespoons brown sugar
¼ cup butter or margarine, melted

Topping
½ cup butter or margarine, melted
⅓ cup brown sugar, firmly packed

2 cups cornflakes

Mash potatoes in a large bowl until smooth. Add pineapple, nutmeg or cinnamon, salt, brown sugar and butter. Mix well with a fork. Spread evenly into a shallow dish. To make topping, mix brown sugar with melted butter. Add cornflakes and stir until cereal is well coated. Sprinkle evenly over potato mixture. Bake at 375⁰ until topping is brown and crisp.

Deborah Beard (Mrs. Michael)

"Next to eating good dinners, a healthy man with a benevolent turn of mind must like, I think, to read about them."
WILLIAM M. THACKERAY
1811-1863

ROAST POTATOES

Oven: 425°
Yield: 4 servings

12 even-sized potatoes
Oil for frying
Salt

Peel potatoes and boil for about 7 to 10 minutes. Drain. With a fork scratch each potato to roughen the surface. Have a roasting pan ready with about ½ inch of smoking hot oil, put in the potatoes, and turn to baste at once. Roast in a 425° oven for about 30 minutes or until golden brown and crisp. Drain and salt lightly before serving.

Helen Sloan (Mrs. John C.)

FRIED RICE

Yield: 6 to 8 servings

3 Tablespoons oil
½ cup chopped green onions
1 cup diced celery
1 cup sliced mushrooms

3 cups cooked rice
2 Tablespoons soy sauce
1 egg, slightly beaten
½ pound crisp bacon, crumbled

In a large skillet, heat oil. Add onions and celery. Cook until tender. Add mushrooms, rice and soy sauce. Cook for 10 minutes on low heat, stirring occasionally. Stir in beaten egg and cook only until egg is done. Add bacon and mix well. Extra soy sauce may be served with rice.

Martha H. Carle (Mrs. Kenneth)
Stuttgart, Arkansas

RICE PILAF

Oven: 350°
Yield: 6 to 8 servings

1½ cups uncooked rice
1 stick butter
2 (13 ounce) cans chicken broth
Salt to taste

Pepper to taste
½ cup blanched almonds
1 (4 ounce) can mushrooms, drained
½ cup chopped onion

Sauté rice in melted butter until light brown. Pour into 9 x 11 baking dish. Add chicken broth. Add any or all of the last 3 ingredients. Bake at 350° for about 45 minutes.

Marcia Johnston (Mrs. Richard S.)

GREEN RICE

Oven: 350°
Yield: 12 servings

1 cup uncooked rice
¾ stick butter
½ large bell pepper, chopped
1 onion, chopped
2 celery rib tops, chopped
1 (10¾ ounce) can cream of
   mushroom soup

½ teaspoon basil
½ teaspoon marjoram
½ teaspoon curry
Salt to taste
Pepper to taste
1 cup grated mild Cheddar cheese
1 cup grated sharp Cheddar cheese

Cook rice in 3 cups of water until tender. Sauté bell pepper, onion and celery in butter. Dilute mushroom soup with ¾ can water, and heat to a boil. Add sautéed pepper, onion and celery. Add basil, marjoram, curry, salt and pepper. Mix with rice and transfer to a buttered baking dish. Top with the mixed cheeses and bake at 350° for 20 minutes or until hot.

Cindy Wage (Mrs. Olin)

RICE SUPREME

Oven: 375°
Yield: 8 servings

1 stick butter or margarine
1 large onion, chopped
1 cup diced celery
½ cup chopped bell pepper
½ cup sliced green onion tops
¼ cup chopped pimientos
¼ cup chopped parsley, fresh or
   dried
2 cups cooked rice

1 (10¾ ounce) can cream of
   chicken or cream of mushroom
   soup
Dash of garlic powder
Salt to taste
Pepper to taste
6 thick slices Velveeta cheese
½ cup buttered bread crumbs

In skillet, melt butter or margarine and sauté onion, celery, bell pepper and green onion tops over medium heat. When vegetables are tender, add pimientos, parsley, rice, soup and seasonings. Cook 5 minutes longer. Put mixture into a 2 quart casserole dish and top with cheese slices and bread crumbs. Place in a 375° oven for approximately 10 minutes, making sure cheese is melted.

Cindy Miller (Mrs. Patrick)

May be prepared ahead of time and refrigerated.

EASY RAISIN RICE

Oven: 350°
Yield: 6 servings

¼ cup butter
¼ cup chopped green onions,
　including tops
1 (10½ ounce) can chicken broth
1 soup can water

1 cup uncooked long grain
　converted rice
1 cup golden raisins
¼ cup finely chopped parsley
½ cup shelled sunflower seeds

Sauté onions in butter until clear. Put in a 2 quart baking dish with all other ingredients except sunflower seeds. Stir and cover. Bake at 350° until liquid is absorbed, approximately 45 minutes. Mix in sunflower seeds and serve.

Catherine B. Morse (Mrs. Tuck)

May be made ahead and reheated in microwave, adding sunflower seeds after microwaving.

WILD RICE WITH SNOW PEAS

Yield: 6 servings

1 cup wild rice
2 scallions
1 Tablespoon margarine
1 teaspoon salt
2 cups or more chicken broth
1 (6 ounce) package frozen snow
　peas, thawed and drained

1 (3 ounce) can sliced mushrooms,
　drained
1 (4 ounce) can water chestnuts,
　drained and sliced
2 Tablespoons vegetable oil
½ teaspoon salt
¼ teaspoon freshly ground pepper

Wash rice, changing the water several times. Cut the green scallion stems diagonally into 2 inch lengths. Finely chop the white part of the scallions. Melt margarine in a large saucepan. Add white scallion pieces and sauté. Add rice, 1 teaspoon salt and 2 cups chicken broth. Bring to a boil, stir and reduce heat. Cover and cook over low heat until rice is tender and the liquid is absorbed, about 35 minutes. If necessary, add more broth as rice cooks. Heat oil in a skillet. Add scallion stems, peas, mushrooms and water chestnuts, and sauté lightly. Mix vegetables together with the rice. Add salt and pepper. Keep warm in low oven.

Irene Vratsinas (Mrs. Gus)

You may substitute ½ cup white rice and ½ cup wild rice for the 1 cup of wild rice. If using packaged wild rice, omit the herb seasonings.

WILD RICE WITH SAUSAGE

Oven: 350°
Yield: 6 servings

1 pound hot or mild sausage
1 onion, chopped
1 pound fresh mushrooms, chopped
1 (6 ounce) box long grain and wild
   rice

⅓ cup whipping cream
1⅓ cups chicken broth
⅓ cup chopped almonds, toasted

Preheat oven to 350⁰. Brown sausage and sauté mushrooms and onion in fat. Drain fat. Cook rice according to directions for 20 minutes. Mix cream and chicken broth. Combine all ingredients except almonds. Put into a 2½ quart casserole and bake for 25 minutes. Top with almonds and bake 5 more minutes.

Robyn Dickey

SPINACH AND MUSHROOM ROLL

Oven: 350°
Yield: 8 servings

3 (10 ounce) packages frozen
   chopped spinach
¼ cup bread crumbs
2 teaspoons salt
1 teaspoon pepper
¼ teaspoon nutmeg
6 Tablespoons melted butter or
   margarine

4 eggs
⅛ teaspoon cream of tartar
4 Tablespoons Parmesan cheese
1½ pounds mushrooms, sliced
¼ cup butter or margarine
1½ Tablespoons flour
1½ cups Hollandaise sauce (See
   Index)

Thaw spinach and squeeze out all excess moisture. Butter a jellyroll pan (10 x 15) and line with waxed paper. Spread bread crumbs over waxed paper. Add to uncooked spinach 1 teaspoon salt, ¼ teaspoon pepper, nutmeg and melted butter. Separate eggs. Beat yolks into spinach 1 at a time. Beat whites with cream of tartar to foamy stage. Fold into spinach. Spoon spinach into jellyroll pan. Sprinkle with Parmesan cheese. Bake at 350⁰ until center is barely firm (about 15 minutes). While baking spinach, sauté mushrooms in ¼ cup butter. Add flour and remaining salt and pepper. After spinach is baked, place a sheet of buttered waxed paper, buttered side down, on spinach. Invert on cookie sheet. Remove bottom paper, spread mushroom mixture and roll up jellyroll fashion. Serve immediately or wrap in foil and reheat when ready to serve. Pour Hollandaise sauce over roll or serve on the side.

Courtney Jackson (Mrs. J. Presley)

BAKED CREAMED SPINACH

Oven: 350°
Yield: 12 to 15 servings

¼ cup butter or margarine
¾ cup chopped onion
¼ cup flour
Salt to taste
⅛ teaspoon pepper
2 cups milk

3 eggs
Tabasco
4 (10 ounce) packages frozen
    chopped spinach, thawed and
    drained

In a saucepan over medium heat, cook onion in butter until tender (about 5 minutes). Stir in flour, salt and pepper until blended. Gradually stir in milk. Cook, stirring constantly, until sauce is thickened. In a small bowl, beat egg slightly with fork. Add Tabasco to taste. Slowly pour egg mixture into cream sauce, stirring rapidly to prevent lumping. Cook, stirring constantly, until mixture is thickened. Do not boil. Add spinach. Stir until blended. Pour mixture into a 9 x 13 pan. Bake at 350⁰ for 40 minutes or until firm in the center. Cut into servings.

Cynthia Weber (Mrs. James R.)

BROILED SPINACH

Yield: 6 servings

2 (10 ounce) packages frozen
    chopped spinach
2 teaspoons butter or margarine,
    melted
1 teaspoon salt
⅛ teaspoon pepper

½ teaspoon nutmeg
2 Tablespoons butter or margarine,
    melted
¾ cup canned mushrooms, stems
    and pieces
2 ounces Cheddar cheese

Topping

¾ cup sour cream
2 Tablespoons prepared
    horseradish

2 teaspoons Dijon mustard
½ teaspoon salt
Paprika

Add frozen spinach to butter in skillet. Cover and cook until spinach is defrosted. Stir seasonings into spinach. Sauté mushrooms in butter. Add cheese and cook until melted. Combine with spinach. Pour into a shallow 2 quart buttered casserole. Combine topping ingredients (except paprika) and spread over hot spinach. Sprinkle with paprika. Broil 2 inches from heat until browned.

Ginna Simpson (Mrs. James D., III)

GREEK SPINACH CASSEROLE

Oven: 350°
Yield: 12 to 14 servings

7 eggs
7 Tablespoons flour
1 pound Feta cheese
2 pounds cottage cheese
12 ounces sharp Cheddar cheese, grated

3 (10 ounce) packages frozen chopped spinach, drained
¼ pound butter, melted
1 large onion, chopped
1½ teaspoons oregano

Mix eggs and flour. Rinse Feta cheese to remove salty brine, and crumble into egg mixture. Add all other ingredients. Pour into a buttered 9 x 13 casserole. Bake at 350° for 1 hour.

Dianne Tucker (Mrs. Robert W.)

Freezes well.

SPINACH SOUFFLÉ

Oven: 325°
Yield: 8 to 10 servings

4 Tablespoons butter, melted
2 Tablespoons all-purpose flour
2 cups milk
1 teaspoon salt
½ teaspoon pepper

8 eggs, separated
2 (10 ounce) packages frozen chopped spinach, cooked and pressed dry
¼ cup Parmesan cheese

Melt butter in a saucepan. Add flour and combine well. Gradually add milk, stirring until sauce thickens. Add salt and pepper. Beat egg yolks. To yolks add about a cup of hot white sauce. Then add spinach and cheese. Stir well. Beat egg whites until stiff. Fold into spinach mixture. Pour into individual greased baking dishes and bake at 325° for 30 minutes or until firm.

Mary Wilson Allison (Mrs. John)

Two individual dishes may be cooked in the microwave on medium high for 4 to 5 minutes.

"It is computed that eleven thousand persons have at several times suffered death, rather than submit to break their eggs at the smaller end."
JONATHAN SWIFT
1667-1745

SQUASH CASSEROLE

Oven: 375°
Yield: 6 to 8 servings

2½ to 3½ pounds yellow squash, sliced
1 medium onion, chopped
1 teaspoon salt
1½ Tablespoons sugar
½ pound Cheddar cheese, grated
4 Tablespoons butter or margarine

3 Tablespoons flour
¼ teaspoon pepper
Beau Monde seasoning or Accent to taste
2 eggs, beaten
1 cup milk
Buttered bread crumbs

Boil squash and onion until tender in a covered pan containing 1 inch water, salt and sugar. Drain well and mash. Combine with remaining ingredients, except bread crumbs. Place in a buttered casserole and top with bread crumbs. Bake at 375⁰ for 25 minutes or until edges are puffy and brown.

Nancy Jennings (Mrs. Boo)

This is best when made ahead and refrigerated a few hours or overnight until baking time.

MY FAVORITE SQUASH CASSEROLE

Oven: 350°
Yield: 6 to 8 servings

2 pounds (6 cups) yellow summer squash, sliced
¼ cup chopped onion
1 (10¾ ounce) can cream of chicken soup

1 cup sour cream
1 cup shredded carrots
1 (8 ounce) package herb seasoned stuffing mix
½ cup margarine, melted

In a saucepan cook squash and onion in boiling salted water for 5 minutes. Drain. Combine soup and sour cream. Stir in shredded carrots. Fold in drained squash. Combine stuffing mix and margarine. Spread half of stuffing mixture in the bottom of a 7 x 12 baking dish. Spoon vegetable mix on top. Sprinkle remaining stuffing over vegetables. Bake at 350⁰ for 25 to 30 minutes.

Sunny Hawk (Mrs. Boyce)

"Life is like an onion; you peel it off one layer at a time, and sometimes you weep."

CARL SANDBURG
1878-1967

SKILLET SQUASH

Yield: 6 servings

¼ cup margarine
4 cups sliced yellow squash
1 onion, sliced or chopped
1 teaspoon salt
Dash of pepper

1 (16 ounce) can tomatoes, drained,
　or 2 tomatoes, peeled and sliced
½ cup grated cheese (American or
　Cheddar)

Melt margarine in large skillet. Add squash, onion, salt and pepper. Cook, covered, for 10 to 15 minutes. Add tomatoes after 5 minutes. Remove lid and allow most of the moisture to cook out. Turn squash often to prevent sticking. Sprinkle with cheese and remove quickly to serving bowl. Cheese will melt as squash is served.

Nancy Hamilton (Mrs. Barry S.)

TOMATOES WITH ARTICHOKE

Oven: 400°
Yield: 8 servings

4 large, firm tomatoes
1 (14 ounce) can artichoke hearts,
　drained and chopped
1 stick butter
¼ teaspoon thyme
1 garlic clove, crushed

1 bay leaf
2 teaspoons lemon juice
1 teaspoon salt
½ teaspoon pepper
Parmesan cheese
1 cup vermouth

Wash and dry tomatoes. Cut out stems and cut tomatoes in half. Scoop out pulp and reserve. Salt and pepper tomato shells and place a thin slice of butter in each. Arrange in a buttered casserole. In a skillet melt 4 Tablespoons of butter and add chopped artichoke hearts, tomato pulp, thyme, garlic and bay leaf. Sauté 10 minutes over medium heat. Add lemon juice, salt and pepper. Remove bay leaf. Place about 2 Tablespoons of artichoke mix in each tomato. Top generously with Parmesan cheese. Pour vermouth in bottom of pan and bake at 400° for 25 minutes. Arrange on a serving platter and top each with a little of the pan liquid.

Dianne Tucker (Mrs. Robert W.)

Butter is at the right temperature for sautéing when the foam from heating subsides.

BASIL CHERRY TOMATOES

Yield: 10 servings

3 pints cherry tomatoes
3 Tablespoons butter

1 Tablespoon dried basil or 3
Tablespoons fresh basil

Rinse, stem and pat dry tomatoes. In a large skillet melt the butter over medium heat. Add the basil. Cook, stirring, for 2 minutes. Add tomatoes and cook, tossing them, for 5 minutes or until heated through. Serve immediately. Be careful not to overcook as tomatoes will become mushy.

Ben Hussman (Mrs. Walter, Jr.)

BROCCOLI STUFFED TOMATOES

Oven: 400°
Yield: 4 servings

4 medium tomatoes
1 (10 ounce) package frozen
   chopped broccoli

1 (6 ounce) roll garlic cheese
Salt to taste
Pepper to taste

Cut tops off tomatoes and scoop out the pulp being careful not to pierce skin. Cook broccoli according to package directions and drain. Combine cooked broccoli, cheese, salt and pepper in food processor and process to a smooth, not runny, consistency. Stuff tomatoes with broccoli mixture. Bake at 400° for 10 minutes.

Jo Ann Drew (Mrs. Tommy, Jr.)

Especially pretty served at Christmas time.

BROILED TOMATOES WITH DILL SAUCE

Yield: 6 servings

3 large, firm tomatoes
Butter or margarine
½ cup sour cream
¼ cup mayonnaise

2 Tablespoons chopped onion
¼ teaspoon dill
¼ teaspoon salt
Pepper to taste

Cut tomatoes in half and core. Dot tomato halves with butter and broil 3 inches from heat for 5 minutes. Make sauce with remaining ingredients and spoon on tomato halves. Sauce may be served at room temperature or heated.

Susan Freeling Carr (Mrs. Phil)
Washington, D.C.

TOMATOES ROCKEFELLER

Oven: 350°
Yield: 12 servings

12 thick slices tomato
2 (10 ounce) packages frozen
   chopped spinach
1 cup soft bread crumbs
1 cup seasoned bread crumbs
1 to 1½ cups finely chopped green
   onions

6 eggs, slightly beaten
¾ cup melted butter or margarine
½ cup grated Parmesan cheese
½ teaspoon minced garlic
1 teaspoon salt
1 teaspoon thyme
Hot sauce to taste

Arrange tomato slices in a lightly greased 9 x 13 baking dish. Set aside. Cook spinach according to package directions, drain well, and squeeze to remove excess water. Add remaining ingredients, stirring well. Mound mixture on tomato slices. Bake at 350⁰ for about 15 minutes.

Sheila Wilson (Mrs. Philip)

STUFFED ZUCCHINI

Oven: 350°
Yield: 4 to 6 servings

½ cup long grain brown rice
1 egg, beaten
1¼ cups water
½ cup sliced tart apple
½ cup pine nuts
½ cup fresh chopped spinach
   leaves

½ medium onion, chopped
½ teaspoon herb salt
¼ teaspoon minced fresh garlic
4 to 6 zucchini, about 6 inches long
2 teaspoons sea salt or coarse salt
2 medium tomatoes, peeled and
   thinly sliced

Preheat oven to 350⁰. Combine rice and half the egg in a heavy ovenproof 1 quart saucepan and stir over medium heat until grains are dry and separate. Add water, apples, nuts, spinach, onion, herb salt, garlic and bring to a boil. Cover and bake until rice is tender and all liquid is absorbed, about 30 minutes. Adjust seasoning. Meanwhile, halve zucchini lengthwise. Scoop out seeds using top of small spoon. Transfer zucchini halves to large saucepan and barely cover with water. Add salt to pan. Place over low to medium heat and bring to a boil. Drain immediately. Pat dry with paper towels. Reduce oven temperature to 275⁰. Arrange zucchini in shallow baking dish and fill with rice mixture. Arrange tomato slices over top of each filled zucchini. Bake until heated through (about 5 minutes).

Rosie Ratley (Mrs. Richard H.)

DEEP FRIED ZUCCHINI

Yield: 8 servings

10 large zucchini
2 eggs
3 cups milk
4 cups bread crumbs
½ teaspoon salt

Black pepper
½ teaspoon paprika
1 Tablespoon chopped parsley
Flour
Grated Parmesan cheese

Cut ends off zucchini and cut lengthwise into ½ inch spears. Soak in enough cold water to cover for 15 minutes. Mix together eggs and milk. Mix bread crumbs, salt, pepper, paprika and parsley. Dredge zucchini in flour, then dip into egg and milk mixture. Roll in bread crumbs to coat evenly. Chill at least 30 minutes. Heat oil to 375° and drop zucchini into hot oil. Do not overcrowd. Cook until golden brown, about 3 to 5 minutes. Drain on paper towels and sprinkle generously with Parmesan cheese.

Betty Biggadike Scroggin (Mrs. Carroll)
Palos Verdes, California

ZUCCHINI-PEPPER PIE

Oven: 350°
Yield: 6 to 8 servings

1 (9 inch) pie shell
3 medium zucchini (1 pound), thinly
   sliced
2 green onions with tops, thinly
   sliced
1 large clove garlic, minced, or ¼
   teaspoon garlic powder
2 Tablespoons oil
1 medium tomato, peeled and
   chopped

1 medium bell pepper, chopped
¾ teaspoon salt
½ teaspoon basil
¼ teaspoon pepper
3 eggs
½ cup whipping cream
¼ cup grated Parmesan cheese

Prick bottom of pie shell and bake at 450° for 5 to 8 minutes or until lightly browned. Cool. Saute zucchini, onions and garlic in oil about 5 minutes, stirring occasionally. Stir in tomato, bell pepper, salt, basil and pepper. Cook over low heat, stirring occasionally, until vegetables are tender and liquid has evaporated (about 15 minutes). Spread vegetables evenly in pie shell. Beat eggs and cream until well mixed. Pour over vegetables. Sprinkle with Parmesan cheese. Bake at 350° for 30 minutes.

Mrs. R. B. Oliver
Stuttgart, Arkansas

EGGS·CHEESE·PASTA

A man who lost his goatskin filled with milk, found it only to discover cheese. Bless him, the chicken, and the glutton who gave the world pasta.

SAUSAGE AND EGG CASSEROLE

Oven: 350°
Yield: 8 to 10 servings

6 slices buttered bread
1 pound hot ground sausage
6 eggs
1 pint (2 cups) Half and Half
1 teaspoon salt
Pepper to taste

Dash of Worcestershire sauce
1 teaspoon dry mustard
1 pound sharp Cheddar cheese, grated
Paprika

Remove crust from bread. Lightly toast buttered bread. Cube toast. Butter the bottom of a 9 x 13 pyrex baking dish. Brown sausage and crumble and drain. Spread sausage over bread cubes. In a large bowl, lightly beat eggs and Half and Half with a fork. To this add salt, pepper, Worcestershire sauce and dry mustard. Pour over sausage and bread. Top with cheese. Sprinkle top with paprika. Bake at 350° for 35 to 45 minutes or until brown.

Margaret Ann Cole (Mrs. George R., Jr.)
Fayetteville, Arkansas

May be made ahead and frozen. Thaw before baking.

DUTCH BABY

Oven: 450°
Yield: 4 servings

4 Tablespoons butter, melted
3 eggs
½ teaspoon salt
½ cup sifted flour
½ cup milk

Juice of ½ lemon
2 Tablespoons butter, melted
Powdered sugar
½ cup almonds, toasted (Optional)

Preheat oven to 450°. Paint the sides and bottom of a cold 8 inch iron skillet with the melted butter. Place skillet in refrigerator. Beat eggs in bowl with mixer on medium speed. Gradually add flour and salt. Add milk and blend thoroughly. Pour the batter into the cold, buttered skillet and bake in the preheated oven until it forms a brown crust, approximately 20 minutes. Mix the lemon juice with the remaining 2 Tablespoons of melted butter. Pour over the cooked batter and sprinkle with powdered sugar and toasted almonds, if desired.

Claudia Hammans Stallings (Mrs. Walt)

This is a cross between an omelet and a soufflé. It puffs during baking and falls when served. Great with coffee and crisp bacon.

MIGAS

Yield: 12 servings

4 Tablespoons butter
3 large bell peppers, chopped
3 large onions, chopped
3 large tomatoes, chopped
2 garlic cloves, minced
1 pound bulk pork sausage,
    crumbled, fried and drained

12 eggs
½ cup milk
1½ cups grated Cheddar cheese
½ to 1 teaspoon cumin
Salt to taste
Pepper to taste

Sauté vegetables and garlic in butter. Cook until most of liquid has been reduced. Remove half of vegetable mixture from skillet and reserve to pass as a sauce. Beat eggs, milk, cheese, cumin, salt and pepper together. Add egg mixture and cooked sausage to skillet and scramble until eggs are cooked to taste. Serve immediately and pass vegetable sauce to top the eggs.

Helen Harper (Mrs. Tom)
Fort Smith, Arkansas

SPICY EGG CASSEROLE
(Must be prepared 1 day in advance)

Oven: 350°
Yield: 8 servings

6 eggs
½ cup flour
1 teaspoon baking powder
1 cup milk
1 (3 ounce) package cream cheese
1 (8 ounce) carton small curd
    cottage cheese
10 ounces Monterey Jack cheese,
    grated
6 ounces mild Cheddar cheese,
    grated

1 pound Jimmy Dean sausage,
    cooked, crumbled and drained
⅛ teaspoon salt
1 bunch green onions, chopped
2 (6 ounce) cans sliced mushrooms,
    drained
6 Tablespoons butter
Paprika

In a large bowl, beat eggs well with a wire whisk. Add flour, baking powder and milk. Cut cream cheese into small cubes. Add cream cheese and cottage cheese to egg mixture. Add the grated Monterey Jack and Cheddar cheeses, along with the cooked sausage, salt, chopped green onions and mushrooms. Butter a 9 x 13 casserole and pour mixture into dish, dot with butter and top with a sprinkling of paprika. Cover and refrigerate overnight. Next day, bring to room temperature and bake at 350° for 45 minutes.

Marilyn Porter (Mrs. Rob)

STEEPLECHASE BRUNCH
(Must be prepared 1 day in advance)

Oven: 350°
Yield: 8 to 10 servings

12 slices white bread
2 to 3 Tablespoons butter, softened
½ cup butter
½ pound fresh mushrooms, sliced
2 cups thinly sliced yellow onions
Salt to taste
Pepper to taste
1½ pounds mild sausage
¾ pound Cheddar cheese, grated

5 eggs
2⅓ cups milk
1 Tablespoon Dijon mustard
1 teaspoon dry mustard
1 teaspoon ground nutmeg
1 teaspoon salt
⅛ teaspoon pepper
2 Tablespoons finely minced
  parsley

Remove crust from bread. Butter one side of bread with softened butter and set aside. Melt ½ cup butter. Add mushrooms and onions and sauté over medium heat for 5 to 8 minutes or until tender. Season with salt and pepper. Drain and set aside. Cook the sausage, drain, and break into bite-sized pieces. In a buttered 7 x 11 shallow pan, layer half the bread with the buttered side down, mushrooms and onions, sausage, then cheese. Repeat. In a bowl mix the eggs, milk, Dijon mustard, dry mustard, nutmeg, 1 teaspoon salt and ⅛ teaspoon pepper. Pour over sausage and cheese. Cover and refrigerate overnight. Remove from refrigerator 1 hour before baking. Sprinkle parsley over the top. Bake, uncovered, in a preheated 350° oven for 1 hour.

Kem Embrey Aburrow (Mrs. Harry J.)

WESTERN EGG CASSEROLE

Oven: 350°
Yield: 8 servings

3 (4 ounce) cans green chilies,
  drained and chopped
1½ pounds Monterey Jack cheese,
  grated

2 teaspoons seasoned salt
1 teaspoon pepper
12 eggs, lightly beaten
¾ cup evaporated milk

Butter and flour a 9 x 13 pyrex dish. Sprinkle half of the green chilies on the bottom of the dish. Spread half of the cheese over the chilies. Sprinkle with 1 teaspoon seasoned salt. Repeat these layers of chilies, cheese and seasoned salt. Beat pepper, eggs and milk together. Pour over cheese mixture. Bake at 350° for 35 minutes. Cool slightly. Cut into squares to serve.

Morin M. Scott, Jr.
Houston, Texas

DADDY'S EGGS

Oven: 450°
Yield: 4 servings

4 ramekins or individual casseroles
8 link sausages
8 eggs
½ cup butter
8 Tablespoons Half and Half (or
   milk)

Chives, chopped
2 cups grated Cheddar cheese
Salt
Pepper
Tabasco
Paprika

Preheat oven to 450°. Cook link sausages and set aside. Coddle eggs by placing in a pan of cold water and bringing to a boil. Remove from heat. Place 1 Tablespoon of butter and 2 Tablespoons of Half and Half (or milk) in each casserole. Place in oven just long enough to melt the butter. Take out of oven and place 2 link sausages in each casserole on the sides of the dish, break 2 eggs in the center of each casserole, and sprinkle with salt, pepper, Tabasco and chives. Cover with cheese. Sprinkle with paprika. Place in hot oven. Watch carefully. Cook only until set, about 5 minutes. Serve immediately.

James M. Coates, Jr.
Birmingham, Michigan

EGG BRUNCH

Oven: 275°
Yield: 12 servings

Sauce
4 slices bacon, diced
½ pound chipped beef, shredded
½ cup butter
1 (8 ounce) can sliced mushrooms,
   drained

½ cup flour
Pepper to taste
1 quart (4 cups) milk

Eggs
16 eggs
¼ teaspoon salt

1 cup evaporated milk
½ cup butter, melted

Sauté bacon. Remove pan from heat and drain grease. Add chipped beef, butter and mushrooms to pan with bacon. Sprinkle flour and pepper over mixture. Gradually stir in milk. Cook until sauce is thickened and smooth. Stir constantly. Set aside. Combine eggs with salt and milk. Scramble in butter in a large skillet. In a 9 x 13 casserole dish, alternate layers of ½ eggs, ½ sauce, ½ eggs, ½ sauce. Cover with foil or casserole lid and bake at 275° for 1 hour.

Elaine Schuppe
Memphis, Tennessee

This dish, if prepared 1 day ahead, must be brought to room temperature before baking.

BACON AND SOUR CREAM OMELET

Yield: 2 servings

2 eggs
1 Tablespoon water
4 or 5 strips bacon

3 scallions, chopped
⅓ cup sour cream
1 Tablespoon butter

Using a fork, beat the eggs and water until barely mixed. Fry bacon until crisp. Drain, reserving the grease. Crumble the bacon into the sour cream. Sauté the scallions in a bit of bacon grease and stir into sour cream mixture. Melt butter in an omelet pan. Pour in egg mixture. When omelet is set, spoon sour cream mixture along the center and fold omelet out onto a warm plate.

Cathy Mallard

MORNING AFTER THE NIGHT BEFORE OMELET

Oven: 350°
Yield: 5 to 6 servings

1 Tablespoon butter
7 eggs
1 cup milk
1 cup grated Cheddar cheese
¼ cup chopped onion
1 cup chopped mushrooms

1 cup chopped ham (may substitute
   with radishes, bacon buds,
   chopped chicken, steak, etc.)
Salt to taste
Pepper to taste

Preheat oven to 350°. Butter a 3 inch deep, approximately 10 inch square, baking dish. Beat eggs and stir in milk, cheese, onions, mushrooms, ham, salt and pepper. Pour into baking dish. Place in oven and bake 20 minutes. Check for doneness by inserting a knife in the middle of the omelet. If juice comes out, then cook longer until the omelet is fluffy.

Jack M. East

MISS MARY WILLARD'S CHEESE PUDDING

Oven: 350°
Yield: 4 to 6 servings

2 eggs, well beaten
¼ cup milk
18 soda crackers, finely rolled

½ pound Cheddar cheese, grated
¼ teaspoon salt
1½ cups milk

Combine eggs, crackers, and ¼ cup milk. Let stand a few minutes. Add cheese, salt and 1½ cups milk. Stir. Butter a 1 quart casserole. Pour mixture into casserole. Bake at 350° for 50 minutes.

Carol Vick Gross (Mrs. Ronald)

BEVERLY'S QUICHE

Oven: 425° and 325°
Yield: 8 servings

1 (9⅝ inch) pastry shell
1 pound hot ground sausage
1 (4 ounce) can chopped
   mushrooms, drained
1 Tablespoon butter
½ cup chopped onion
¼ cup chopped bell pepper
1 teaspoon minced fresh parsley

½ teaspoon dried basil
Dash of garlic powder
½ cup mayonnaise
½ cup milk
2 eggs
1 Tablespoon cornstarch
1½ cups grated Cheddar cheese

Bake pastry shell at 425° for 10 minutes. Cook sausage until done in a skillet. Drain well. Melt 1 Tablespoon butter in a skillet and sauté onions and bell pepper. In a large bowl, stir cooked sausage, mushrooms, onions and bell peppers, parsley, basil and garlic powder. In a separate bowl blend mayonnaise, milk, eggs and cornstarch until smooth. Stir sausage mixture, egg mixture and cheese together. Pour into baked pastry shell. Bake at 325° for 50 minutes.

Rosie Ratley (Mrs. Richard H.)

VEGETABLE QUICHE

Oven: 425° and 350°
Yield: 6 servings

1 (9 inch) pie shell
1 pound fresh spinach, cooked and
   well drained
½ cup chopped green onions
1 garlic clove, minced
2 Tablespoons butter
1½ cups (6 ounces) shredded Swiss
   cheese

3 eggs, lightly beaten
¾ cup milk
1 teaspoon salt
1 teaspoon fresh chopped basil, or
   ⅓ teaspoon dried basil
2 tomatoes, sliced

Press water out of spinach. Finely chop. Sauté green onions and garlic in butter until golden. Add spinach, cook over medium heat, stirring constantly, until excess moisture evaporates. Combine spinach mixture, cheese, eggs, milk and spices in a large bowl. Mix well. Turn into the pie shell. Place sliced tomatoes around edges. Bake at 425° for 25 to 35 minutes, then reduce heat to 350° for an additional 20 minutes.

Susan Terry Borné (Mrs. Robin)

SPINACH QUICHE

Oven: 350°
Yield: 4 servings

1 (9 inch) pie pastry
1 (10 ounce) package frozen
　chopped spinach
1 (8 ounce) package Swiss cheese
　slices

2 Tablespoons all-purpose flour
3 eggs, beaten
1 cup whipping cream
½ teaspoon salt
Pepper to taste

If you are using a frozen pie shell, let it thaw 20 minutes. Cook spinach and drain well. Do not overcook the spinach. Cut cheese into ½ inch strips. Toss cheese with the flour and set aside. Combine eggs, whipping cream, salt and pepper, beating well. Add spinach and cheese. Pour mixture into the pastry shell. Bake at 350° for 1 hour. Can be made ahead and reheated.

Lisa Foster (Mrs. Vincent, Jr.)

MY VERY BEST QUICHE

Oven: 450° and 325°
Yield: 6 servings

1 Tablespoon butter
1 (9 inch) pie shell, unbaked
6 slices bacon
½ small onion, diced
5 eggs, beaten
½ (5⅓ ounce) can Pet evaporated
　milk
2 cups grated Swiss cheese
1 (4½ ounce) can sliced mushrooms,
　drained

1 Tablespoon flour
¼ teaspoon salt
Pepper to taste
¼ teaspoon marjoram
¼ teaspoon dried basil
⅛ teaspoon ground cumin
¼ cup grated Parmesan cheese
2 Tablespoons butter, melted and
　browned over a low flame

Preheat oven to 450°. Butter pie shell with 1 Tablespoon butter. Fry bacon and drain on paper towel. Sauté onion in bacon grease. Drain. Beat eggs, add milk and Swiss cheese. Mix well. Break bacon into pieces. Add bacon, mushrooms and onions to egg mixture. Sift dry ingredients together and add to egg mixture. Combine well. Pour mixture into unbaked pie shell. Bake for 10 minutes. Cover loosely with foil, reduce heat to 325°, and bake 25 minutes longer. Drizzle browned butter over top and sprinkle with Parmesan cheese. (Can cool and freeze at this point.) Bake 10 minutes more or until knife comes out clean. Cut and serve.

Alice Lynn Overbey (Mrs. Thomas L.)

Frozen quiche should be thawed at room temperature and reheated, uncovered, at 350°.

ITALIAN QUICHE

Oven: 375°
Yield: 6 servings

1 (9 inch) pie shell
½ cup diced pepperoni
1 cup shredded Swiss cheese
1 cup shredded Mozzarella cheese
1 (4⅛ ounce) can sliced ripe olives, drained
½ bell pepper, chopped

1 cup chopped mushrooms
3 small green onions, chopped
3 eggs, well beaten
1 cup Half and Half
¼ teaspoon salt
½ teaspoon oregano

Mix pepperoni, cheeses, olives, bell pepper, mushrooms and onions and arrange evenly in the pie shell. Mix eggs, Half and Half, salt and oregano and pour evenly over cheese mixture. Place pie on a cookie sheet for easy handling and place in a 375⁰ oven. Bake approximately 30 to 40 minutes until light brown and a toothpick comes out clean. Cool 10 minutes before serving.

Sally Ferguson

CHEESE AND ONION PIE

Oven: 350°
Yield: 6 to 8 servings

4 Tablespoons butter
2 large white onions, chopped
10 ounces Swiss cheese, grated
2 Tablespoons flour
1 (10 inch) pastry shell

2 large tomatoes, cut into wedges
2 extra-large eggs
¾ cup Half and Half
1 teaspoon basil

Melt butter in a skillet. Add chopped onions and saute until golden and sweet (about 30 minutes). Toss the grated cheese with the flour. Spread half of the cheese over the bottom of the pastry shell. Spread the onions over the cheese. Arrange tomato wedges in a ring around the outside edge of the pastry shell. Sprinkle remaining cheese over top. Beat the eggs with the basil and the Half and Half. Pour over the pie. Bake at 350⁰ for 35 to 40 minutes. Let the pie rest a few minutes before serving.

A Very Special Tea Room

"Cheese—milk's leap toward immortality."
CLIFTON FADIMAN

SPINACH FRITTATA

Oven: Broil
Yield: 6 servings

½ **pound fresh spinach, trimmed or**
  1 (10 ounce) package frozen
  chopped spinach
3 **Tablespoons butter**
½ **pound fresh mushrooms, sliced**
1 **small onion, finely diced**

8 **eggs**
½ **teaspoon salt**
1⅓ **teaspoon pepper**
1½ **cups grated fresh Parmesan**
  cheese

Cook spinach. Drain and squeeze out excess liquid. In a large ovenproof skillet, sauté the mushrooms and onions. Beat eggs, salt and pepper. Stir spinach into eggs. Mix well and pour over mushrooms and onions in skillet. Cook over medium heat until eggs are set. Sprinkle with Parmesan cheese. Place in oven on broil and broil until cheese melts and top is lightly brown. Cut into wedges to serve.

Betty Ann Bullard (Mrs. Allen)

EASY CHEESE SOUFFLÉ

Oven: 350°
Yield: 6 to 8 servings

6 **eggs, separated**
4 **Tablespoons butter**
6 **Tablespoons flour**

1 **cup whipping cream**
1½ **cups shredded Cheddar cheese**
1 **teaspoon salt**

Butter a 2 quart soufflé dish. Also, butter the inside of a piece of foil that is folded to 3 layers of thickness and long enough to fit around your soufflé dish. Wrap around the dish and secure with string or tape. Beat egg yolks and set aside. Melt butter in a saucepan over low heat and slowly add flour, stirring constantly with a wire whisk. Add cream gradually and cook, stirring constantly, until thickened. Add cheese, beaten egg yolks and salt. Cook over low heat until cheese is well incorporated. Be sure mixture is smooth. Cool 45 minutes to 1 hour. Beat egg whites to stiff peaks. Fold into cheese sauce. Pour into prepared soufflé dish. Bake at 350⁰ for about 30 minutes. Remove collar and serve at once.

Georgia McKinley Greaves (Mrs. Thomas G.)
Greenville, South Carolina

"Soufflé is more important than you think. If men ate soufflé before meetings, life could be much different."

JACQUES BAEYENS

VEGETABLE AND HAM SOUFFLÉ

Oven: 375°
Yield: 6 servings

3 Tablespoons butter
1¼ cups chopped ham
2 Tablespoons minced green onions
4 eggs, separated
½ cup plus 1 Tablespoon sour cream
¼ cup flour
6 Tablespoons grated Gruyère cheese
6 Tablespoons freshly grated Parmesan cheese

1 teaspoon salt
¼ teaspoon white pepper
⅛ teaspoon freshly grated nutmeg
Pinch of salt
2¼ cups broccoli flowerets, cooked and drained
1 cup English peas, cooked and drained
2 Tablespoons butter

Butter the inside of a 2 quart soufflé or casserole and set aside. Melt 3 Tablespoons butter. Add ham and green onions. Sauté 5 minutes and set aside to cool. In a bowl, beat the egg yolks, add sour cream, flour, 2 Tablespoons of both cheeses, 1 teaspoon salt, white pepper and nutmeg. Stir to incorporate ingredients.** In another bowl, beat the egg whites with pinch of salt until they hold stiff peaks. Fold ⅓ of the egg whites into the egg and cheese mixture. Now fold this mixture back into remaining egg whites. Be sure the whites are well incorporated. Spread half of the egg mixture in the bottom of the soufflé dish. Top with broccoli. Add peas to the ham mixture. Spread half of the peas and ham over the broccoli. Sprinkle with 2 Tablespoons each of Gruyère and Parmesan cheese. Add remaining half of egg mixture. Spread with remaining ham and pea mixture. Top with 2 Tablespoons each of Gruyère and Parmesan cheese. Dot with butter. Bake at 375⁰ for 35 to 40 minutes or until it is puffed and golden brown.

**Can be prepared ahead to this point. Cover all ingredients with plastic wrap, and finish just before baking. Also, cauliflower can be substituted for broccoli. Corn is also good added to the ham and pea mixture.

FUSILLI CON POMODORI AND MOZZARELLA

Yield: 8 servings

6 to 8 ripe tomatoes, peeled and chopped
½ pound Mozzarella cheese, coarsely grated
¼ cup chopped fresh basil, or 1 Tablespoon dried basil

5 Tablespoons olive oil
2 garlic cloves, minced
1 Tablespoon chopped fresh parsley
Salt to taste
Freshly ground pepper to taste
16 ounces pasta

In a large bowl, combine all ingredients except the pasta. Let stand at room temperature 1 hour. Cook pasta al dente. Drain. Toss pasta with tomato mixture until cheese has melted. Serve immediately.

Ann Montedonico
Memphis, Tennessee

FRESH PASTA
(Use Food Processor)

Yield: 4 to 6 servings

3 cups flour
3 eggs
3 Tablespoons vegetable oil

1 teaspoon salt
6 Tablespoons water

Put flour in food processor bowl and add eggs. Blend for a few seconds. Scrape sides of work bowl and blend a few more seconds. Add vegetable oil and salt. Blend into flour mixture. While processor is running, add water in a slow stream. When dough forms a ball, it is ready. If a ball does not form, add 1 Tablespoon of water at a time until it does form a ball. (Do not let the dough get too gummy. If this does happen, take the dough out of the processor and knead in a little more flour.) When the dough forms a ball, take it out of the processor and knead a few minutes in flour, form into a ball, cover with a bowl and let rest at least 20 minutes. Cut small fistfulls of dough off, pound out with your fist, and run through the pasta machine.

Becky McKinney (Mrs. Richard H., Jr.)

PESTO SAUCE

Yield: 3½ to 4 cups

3 packed cups fresh basil leaves
⅓ cup pine nuts (Optional)
2 to 4 garlic cloves, sliced

1½ cups fresh grated Parmesan
 cheese
1 to 1½ cups olive oil

Place basil in food processor or blender. (Blender method - partially chop leaves before putting in blender jar.) Add pine nuts, garlic and cheese. Blend until ingredients form a thick paste. You may need to scrape down the sides of the container during this process. Next, add the olive oil slowly through the feeding tube or cover hole in the blender Add oil only until it forms a thick sauce. Add to your favorite pasta and toss. A good measure is 3 Tablespoons per serving of pasta. To store, pour into jars and pour a thin coating of olive oil over top of sauce. Put tops on jars and place in refrigerator or freezer. This sauce will keep indefinitely in refrigerator or freezer as long as there is a seal of olive oil on top of the sauce.

Ben Hussman (Mrs. Walter, Jr.)

Try using this sauce in twice-baked potatoes, spread on tomato halves and broil, or add to a pasta salad or soup for flavor. Be creative!

"After a good dinner, one can forgive anybody, even one's own relations."
OSCAR WILDE
1856-1900

ARTICHOKE OR TOMATO PASTA

Yield: 4 servings

8 ounces tomato, artichoke or
    spinach fettuccini, or any pasta
    of your choice
½ cup cooking oil
6 Tablespoons butter
¼ cup olive oil
Salt to taste
Pepper to taste (freshly ground is
    best)

1 pint Half and Half
½ pound Prosciutto, cut into thin
    strips
2 large zucchini, coarsely grated
1 cup finely grated Parmesan
    cheese or 1 cup of any other
    cheese, finely grated

In a large pot, boil the pasta in 3 quarts of water. Add ½ cup cooking oil to keep pasta from sticking together. When soft to the bite (about 8 minutes), drain. In a large saucepan, melt the butter, add olive oil, salt and pepper. Add the Half and Half, meat and squash. Cook about 3 minutes, stirring constantly. Toss the hot pasta with the sauce and cheese.

Catherine Hipp
New York, New York

Other meats good in this are pastrami, chipped beef or ham, always cut in thin strips. Shrimp is also good.

FETTUCCINI ALFREDO

Yield: 6 to 8 servings

2 packages spinach pasta
2 ounces olive oil
3 ounces butter
4 garlic cloves, chopped and soaked
    in a little olive oil
1 pint whipping cream
4 egg yolks
8 ounces chicken stock

4 ounces grated Parmesan cheese
Salt
Pepper
Lemon juice
Worcestershire sauce
4 ounces ham, diced (Optional)
4 ounces mushrooms, sliced and
    sautéed in butter (Optional)

Cook noodles in 8 quarts boiling water with salt and oil. Slightly undercook pasta, drain and rinse with cold water. Melt butter in a large skillet. Add chopped garlic and noodles. Toss until hot. Mix cream with egg yolks and add to pasta. Toss. Bring almost to a boil and immediately reduce heat. Correct consistency of sauce with chicken stock. Add Parmesan cheese. Season with salt, pepper, lemon juice and Worcestershire sauce. If you are adding ham and/or mushrooms, do so now. Toss and serve immediately.

Lisa Foster (Mrs. Vincent, Jr.)

FETTUCCINI WITH MUSHROOMS AND ZUCCHINI

Yield: 6 servings

Sauce

¼ cup butter
½ pound fresh mushrooms, sliced
1¼ pounds zucchini, julienned

1 cup whipping cream
½ cup butter

5 quarts water
1 pound fettuccini
1 Tablespoon olive oil

2 Tablespoons salt
¾ cup grated Parmesan cheese
½ cup minced parsley

Sauté mushrooms over moderate heat for 2 minutes. Add zucchini, cream and ½ cup butter. Bring to a boil, reduce heat, and simmer for 3 minutes. Meanwhile, add 2 Tablespoons salt and 1 Tablespoon olive oil to 5 quarts water. Bring water to a boil, add fettuccini and boil for 7 minutes. Drain fettuccini, add to ingredients in skillet. Add Parmesan cheese and parsley. Toss. May be served with more cheese.

Arden Limerick Boyce (Mrs. Charles)
Russellville, Arkansas

GNOCCHI WITH MUSHROOMS AND ARTICHOKES

Yield: 6 servings

4 Tablespoons olive oil
1 garlic clove, chopped
1½ pounds mushrooms, sliced
Freshly ground black pepper
Salt to taste
2 teaspoons chopped fresh parsley

1 (14 ounce) can artichoke hearts, drained
1 package gnocchi or any other short noodle
1½ to 2 cups freshly grated Parmesan cheese

In a large skillet, sauté mushrooms and garlic in olive oil for 15 minutes. Add salt, pepper, parsley and artichokes. Cook 5 minutes longer to heat artichokes. Cook gnocchi in salted water. Drain but DO NOT RINSE. Pour gnocchi onto a heated platter, pour mushrooms and artichokes over gnocchi and sprinkle liberally with Parmesan cheese.

Ann Montedonico
Memphis, Tennessee

"No man is lonely while eating spaghetti—it requires so much attention."
CHRISTOPHER MORLEY
1890-1957

LINGUINI WITH WHITE CLAM SAUCE

Yield: 4 to 6 servings

½ cup olive oil
½ cup butter
10 garlic cloves, minced
2 Tablespoons snipped parsley
½ teaspoon dried oregano or to taste

1½ teaspoons salt
4 (7 ounce) cans minced or chopped
  clams, drain and reserve liquid
8 to 12 ounces linguini

Heat butter and olive oil in a medium skillet. Sauté garlic in oil and butter until golden. Add liquid from clams, parsley, salt and oregano to garlic. Simmer, uncovered, for 10 minutes. Meanwhile, cook linguini by package directions. Drain. Add clams to garlic mixture and simmer 2 minutes. Place hot linguini on a heated platter. Pour sauce over and serve immediately.

Colin Reeves (Mrs. R. Scott, III)

SPINACH LASAGNE

Oven: 350°
Yield: 8 to 10 servings

1 pound ground chuck
½ pound sweet Italian sausage (if
  not available, increase to 2
  pounds of ground chuck)
2 large onions, chopped
1 garlic clove, minced
1 (2 pound 3 ounce) can tomatoes,
  undrained
1 (6 ounce) can tomato paste
3 teaspoons salt
¼ teaspoon pepper

2 teaspoons Italian herbs
1 Tablespoon sugar
½ package lasagne noodles
2 eggs
2 (10 ounce) packages frozen
  chopped spinach, thawed and
  well drained
1 (16 ounce) carton small curd
  cottage cheese
1 cup Parmesan cheese
2 (6 ounce) packages Mozzarella
  cheese

Brown beef and sausage in a large Dutch oven, remove with a slotted spoon and reserve meats. Pour off all but 3 Tablespoons of fat. Sauté onions and garlic in fat until tender. Return meat to pan, add tomatoes, tomato paste, 2 teaspoons salt, pepper, Italian herbs and sugar. Bring to a simmer and simmer over low heat for 30 minutes. Stir frequently to pervent sticking. While the sauce is cooking, boil the noodles according to the package directions. Drain and place in a large bowl of ice water to prevent sticking together. Beat eggs in a large bowl. Add spinach, cottage cheese and remaining 1 teaspoon salt. To assemble, drain noodles, place on towel and pat dry with paper towels. Prepare the inside of 1 large lasagne pan or 2 (2 quart) casseroles, with butter or olive oil. Place 1 layer of noodles on bottom of pan. Next, add a layer of the spinach mixture, then meat sauce and next Parmesan cheese, then Mozzarella cheese. Repeat layers until all ingredients have been used. Make top layer Mozarrella cheese. Bake at 350° for 30 minutes.

Sandy Ledbetter (Mrs Joel Y., Jr.)

MAMA DONIMO'S LASAGNE

Oven: 375°
Yield: 10 servings

Tomato Sauce

3 Tablespoons olive oil
½ pound ground beef
½ pound ground sausage
1 medium onion, chopped
2 garlic cloves, minced

3 Tablespoons minced fresh parsley
1 (6 ounce) can tomato paste
1 (28 ounce) can tomatoes, roughly
   chopped with the juice

1 pound lasagne noodles
3 Tablespoons olive oil

8 quarts water

Bechamel Sauce

3 Tablespoons butter
3 Tablespoons flour
2¼ to 2½ cups milk

Salt
Pepper

1 pound Mozzarella cheese, sliced

2 cups Parmesan cheese, grated

In a large saucepan heat the olive oil. Add meats and all remaining sauce ingredients and brown, crumbling the meats with a fork. Combine well. Cover and simmer 45 minutes. Stir occasionally. While the sauce is simmering, cook the lasagne noodles in salted water and olive oil for 12 to 15 minutes. Stir to prevent sticking. Drain, rinse and lay side by side on paper towels to drain.

Make the Bechamel sauce as follows: Melt the butter in a medium-sized saucepan over low heat. Gradually stir in the flour. Slowly add the milk, stirring. Season with salt and pepper. Cook over a low flame, stirring constantly, until sauce begins to thicken. This should be a fairly thin sauce. (It's purpose is to keep the noodles moist.) To assemble: Butter a lasagne pan or a 3 quart casserole and layer as follows: a thin layer of tomato sauce, lasagne noodles, a thin coating of Bechamel sauce, a layer each of Parmesan and Mozzarella cheese. Keep repeating layers until all ingredients have been used, ending with cheeses on top. Bake in preheated oven for 20 minutes or until a light, golden crust forms on top. Let cool slightly before serving.

Ann Montedonico
Memphis, Tennessee

May be made a day ahead or frozen.

"He who flatters the cook never goes hungry."
OLD PROVERB

MANICOTTI CREPES

Oven: 350°
Yield: 20 to 25 crepes

Tomato sauce

2 (28 ounce) cans Italian plum
   tomatoes, undrained
¼ cup olive oil
2 large onions, diced
2 garlic cloves, minced
1 (6 ounce) can tomato paste

1 Tablespoon sugar
¼ cup minced fresh parsley
1½ teaspoons dried oregano
1 teaspoon dried basil
½ teaspoon marjoram

Crepes

8 eggs
2 cups milk
2 cups water
4 cups flour

1 teaspoon salt
¼ cup butter, melted
¼ cup oil

Filling

2 (10 ounce) packages frozen
   chopped spinach
2 Tablespoons olive oil
2 garlic cloves, minced
2 onions, chopped
2 pounds ground lean pork
2 pounds ground veal
4 cups Ricotta cheese

6 eggs, beaten
1 cup chopped fresh parsley
½ teaspoon nutmeg
1 cup freshly grated Parmesan
   cheese
Salt to taste
Pepper to taste
3 cups grated Monterey Jack cheese

Purée small batches of undrained tomatoes in blender or food processor. Heat olive oil in a large pot and sauté onions and garlic. Add tomatoes, tomato paste, sugar and herbs. Cover and simmer 1 hour. Uncover and simmer 1½ hours longer. Stir occasionally.

To make crepes, beat eggs, then add milk and water. Mix well. Beat in flour, salt, butter and oil until smooth. Cover batter and allow to rest in refrigerator 1 to 2 hours. Remove batter from refrigerator and check for lumps. If there are any, strain through a sieve to remove lumps. Cook crepes in a well-seasoned 5 to 7 inch crepe pan. As each crepe is done, place it on a tea towel to cool. Stack crepes between pieces of waxed paper to keep or freeze. (If freezing, stack between waxed paper and wrap stacks in plastic wrap, then foil to seal crepes. Be sure to freeze any extra crepes.)

To make filling, cook spinach, drain and squeeze. In a very large, deep skillet or a large pot, mix together all filling ingredients except Monterey Jack cheese. Sauté until the pork and veal are well browned. Spoon off any excess fat that may rise to the top. Check seasonings and correct.

To assemble crepes: Preheat oven to 350°. Butter 2 (9 x 13) dishes. Place 2 to 3 Tablespoons filling on outer edge of crepes. Roll crepes and place in buttered dishes, seam side down. Divide the tomato sauce between the 2 dishes, pouring over the rolled crepes. Sprinkle each dish with 1½ cups Monterey Jack cheese. Bake at 350° for 25 minutes.

Boopie Porter McInnis (Mrs. George)
Minden, Louisiana

Takes time, but is well worth the effort! Freezes well.

MOCK RAVIOLI

Oven: 350°
Yield: 6 to 8 servings

Sauce

1 medium onion, chopped
1 garlic clove, pressed
1¼ cups plus 1 Tablespoon olive oil
1½ pounds ground round
2 (14 ounce) jars prepared spaghetti sauce (Ragu, etc.)
¾ cup beef broth

½ teaspoon dried basil
½ teaspoon dried thyme
¼ pound mushrooms, sliced and sautéed in 3 Tablespoons butter or 1 (2¼ ounce) can sliced mushrooms, drained

Filling

2 (10 ounce) packages frozen chopped spinach
½ cup bread crumbs
½ cup finely chopped parsley
1 cup grated fresh Parmesan cheese

1 teaspoon sage
4 eggs, well beaten
Dash of nutmeg

½ pound bow pasta, cooked and drained (use lasagne noodles if you cannot find bow pasta)

Sauté onion and garlic in olive oil. Add meat, brown and drain. Add spaghetti sauce, broth, basil, thyme and mushrooms. Simmer, covered, for 1 hour. Stir occasionally. Cook spinach and drain. Mix spinach, bread crumbs, parsley, ½ cup of Parmesan cheese, sage, eggs, and a dash of nutmeg. Combine to form a thick paste. Cook and drain the pasta.

To assemble: Grease a 3 quart casserole. Layer in casserole dish as follows: sauce, pasta, filling. Repeat. Finish the top with a layer of pasta, then sauce. Sprinkle with remaining ½ cup Parmesan cheese. Cook at 350°, covered, for 45 minutes.

Mary Ellen Pugno
Upper Montclair, New Jersey

INSIDE OUT RAVIOLI

Oven: 350°
Yield: 8 to 10 servings

1 (10 ounce) package large
   macaroni shells

Sauce

1 Tablespoon olive oil
1 pound ground beef
½ onion, chopped
1 garlic clove, minced
1 (15½ ounce) jar Ragu sauce with
   mushrooms

1 (10 ounce) package frozen
   chopped spinach
2 cups shredded Cheddar cheese

1 (8 ounce) can tomato sauce
1 (6 ounce) can tomato paste
Salt to taste
Pepper to taste

½ cup bread crumbs
2 eggs, beaten
¼ cup olive oil

Cook noodle shells and drain. In 1 Tablespoon olive oil, brown meat, onions and garlic. Drain excess fat. Cook spinach and reserve juice. Add enough water to spinach juice to make 1 cup. Add juice to meat mixture. Add Ragu sauce, tomato sauce, tomato paste, salt and pepper to meat mixture. Stir and cook 10 minutes. In a separate bowl, combine spinach, cooked shells, bread crumbs, 1 cup cheese, eggs, and olive oil. Butter a 9 x 13 casserole. Spread spinach mixture in the casserole and top with meat mixture. Top with ¾ to 1 cup cheese. Bake at 350⁰ for 30 minutes. Let stand 10 minutes before serving.

Kathy Palazzi (Mrs. Robert)

Can be made ahead and frozen.

PASTA WITH GORGONZOLA SAUCE

Yield: 8 servings

3 to 4 Tablespoons butter
5 ounces Gorgonzola cheese
½ cup Half and Half
Salt to taste

1 (10 ounce) package your favorite
   pasta
⅓ cup whipping cream
¼ cup Parmesan cheese

In an enamel saucepan, melt the butter over low heat, add the Gorgonzola cheese, Half and Half, and salt. Mash the Gorgonzola with a wooden spoon and stir to mix over a low flame. Cook about 1 minute until sauce becomes thick and creamy. In the meantime, cook the pasta according to the package directions and drain. Just before fettuccini is done, stir the whipping cream into the cheese sauce over a low flame. Place the pasta on a warm platter and pour sauce over. Toss until coated. Add Parmesan cheese and toss to mix well. Serve immediately with more Parmesan cheese on the side.

Ben Hussman (Mrs. Walter, Jr.)

PASTA WITH SCALLOPS, MUSHROOMS AND CREAM SAUCE

Yield: 6 servings

6 Tablespoons butter
1 garlic clove, whole
1 pound fresh mushrooms, washed
   and sliced
2 pounds scallops, cleaned
1 box twist (curled) pasta

1½ cups whipping cream
¾ cup grated Parmesan cheese
Salt to taste
Pepper to taste
¼ cup chopped parsley

In a large skillet, melt the butter over medium heat with the garlic clove. Add the cleaned and sliced mushrooms. Sauté in the butter until they appear done. Remove the whole garlic clove and add the cleaned scallops. Stir the mixture to avoid scalding the scallops. Cook about 6 minutes. In a large pan, boil the pasta according to the directions on the box. When tender, drain and return to the cooking pot. Add the cream and cheese. Toss well. Pour the scallops, mushrooms and liquid in the skillet over the pasta. Toss. Correct seasoning with salt and pepper. Serve topped with parsley.

Mark Robertson

SAUSAGE RIGATONI

Oven: 350°
Yield: 6 to 8 servings

2 cups rigatoni noodles, uncooked
1 pound ground sausage, mild or
   hot
Basil to taste
Oregano to taste
Garlic powder to taste
Salt

Pepper
4 cups tomato sauce
½ cup sour cream
½ pound Mozzarella cheese, sliced
½ pound Provolone cheese, sliced
½ to 1 cup Parmesan cheese

Boil noodles in salted water until tender. Drain. Sauté sausage until brown. Drain. Butter a 2 quart casserole and assemble as follows: rigatoni, ½ of tomato sauce, 1 layer of Provolone cheese, sour cream, meat, sprinkle seasonings over meat, Mozzarella cheese, and remaining tomato sauce. Top with Parmesan cheese. Bake at 350° for 30 minutes. May also substitute ground beef for sausage.

Joy McGinnis (Mrs. Tom)
Johnson City, Tennessee

Easy and delicious. A real hit! May be made ahead and frozen.

PASTA PRIMAVERA

Yield: 4 to 6 servings

⅓ cup unsalted butter
1 medium white onion, finely
    minced
1 garlic clove, finely minced
1 carrot, halved lengthwise and
    sliced thinly on diagonal
1 pound thin asparagus, trimmed
    and cut on the diagonal
5 ounces broccoli flowerets
1 medium zucchini, sliced ¼ inch thick
½ pound mushrooms, stems
    removed and thinly sliced

½ cup chicken broth
1 cup whipping cream
4 Tablespoons fresh chopped basil
    (or 1⅓ Tablespoons dried basil)
1 cup lightly cooked green peas
⅔ cup chopped ham
5 green onions, chopped
Salt to taste
Freshly ground pepper to taste
1 pound fettuccini
Parmesan cheese

In a large skillet, melt butter over medium high heat and sauté onion and garlic until tender (approximately 2 minutes). Add carrots, asparagus and broccoli flowerets. Stir fry for 1½ to 2 minutes. Add zucchini and mushrooms and stir-fry for 1 to 2 more minutes. Increase heat to high, add stock, cream and 3 Tablespoons fresh basil. Allow to boil (watch carefully so it does not boil over) until sauce is slightly reduced, or about 3 minutes. Add peas, ham and green onion and cook 1 more minute. Season with salt and freshly ground black pepper. In the meantime, cook the pasta al dente and drain. Do not rinse. On a warm platter, toss the pasta with the vegetable/ham sauce and Parmesan cheese. Garnish with remaining fresh basil and more cheese.

Kay Kennedy (Mrs. Frazier)
Libby Strawn (Mrs. Jim)

SHRIMP AND FETA CHEESE SAUCE WITH PASTA

Yield: 6 servings

1½ pounds medium shrimp, cooked,
    shelled and deveined
1¼ pounds Feta cheese, rinsed,
    patted dry and crumbled
4 to 6 whole green onions, chopped
2 Tablespoons fresh minced
    oregano (2¼ teaspoons dried
    oregano)

4 to 5 tomatoes, peeled, cored,
    seeded and chopped
10 to 12 pitted black olives, sliced
    or chopped
Salt to taste (be careful as Feta
    cheese is salty)
Freshly ground pepper to taste
10 ounce package pasta

In a large bowl, combine the shrimp, cheese, onions, oregano, tomatoes, olives and salt and pepper. Let stand at room temperature for at least 1 hour. Cook pasta until just done. Drain but do not rinse. Add pasta to the shrimp mixture in the bowl and toss. Serve immediately.

Ben Hussman (Mrs. Walter, Jr.)

FISH · SHELLFISH

As an antidote to a natural caution concerning fish and shellfish, always serve them with your most assured manner, as if you were a famed seafood restaurateur.

BAKED CATFISH PARMESAN

Oven: 375°
Yield: 6 servings

6 skinned catfish filets
1 cup dry bread crumbs (plain, whole wheat or Italian)
¾ cup grated Parmesan cheese
¼ cup chopped parsley
1 teaspoon paprika
½ teaspoon oregano

¼ teaspoon basil
2 teaspoons salt
½ teaspoon pepper
⅓ cup butter or margarine, melted
Lemon wedges
Parsley

Clean, wash and pat fish dry. Combine bread crumbs, Parmesan cheese, parsley, paprika, oregano, basil, salt and pepper. Dip catfish in melted butter and roll in crumb mixture. Arrange fish in a well greased 9 x 13 baking dish. Bake at 375° for about 30 minutes or until fish flakes easily when tested with a fork. Garnish with lemon wedges and parsley.

Mrs. Edwin Patterson
Minta Speights (Mrs. Burton)

The best way to cook fish without making a mess in your kitchen.

BAKED FRESH FISH

Oven: 375°
Yield: 4 servings

Cooking oil
1 pound fish filets
Crazy Jane salt

Black pepper, freshly ground
Dill weed, crushed
Butter

Sauce
3 Tablespoons butter or margarine
1 teaspoon tarragon

2 teaspoons capers with juice
2 Tablespoons lemon juice

Spray or brush cookie sheet with cooking oil. Place filets on greased surface and sprinkle with salt, pepper, dill weed and dots of butter. Bake at 375° for 6 to 8 minutes. Turn and bake another 6 to 8 minutes or until fish is flaky. To make sauce melt the butter, tarragon, capers and lemon juice together. Serve sauce over warm fish.

Jackie Kelley (Mrs. G. Larry)

CEVICHE
(Must be prepared 1 day in advance)

Yield: 4 to 6 servings

1 pound firm, fleshed white fish
  filets (such as lake bass, red
  snapper or sea bass), cut into ½
  inch pieces
1 cup fresh lime juice
Salt to taste
¼ cup olive oil
½ garlic clove, minced

1 small onion, chopped
1 small green pepper, chopped
¾ teaspoon salt
¼ teaspoon pepper
Lettuce leaves
Chopped tomatoes
Sliced avocados

In a ceramic or glass bowl, combine the fish with the lime juice and salt to taste. Chill the mixture overnight. Be sure fish is covered by lime juice as this cooks the fish. Next day, combine oil, garlic, onions, pepper, salt and black pepper in a small bowl and mix well. Drain fish well. Return to dish. Pour oil mixture over fish and toss gently. Let stand 30 minutes. Arrange lettuce leaves in chilled dishes and top with fish. Garnish with chopped tomatoes and avocado slices. Serves 4 to 6 as a first course. If used for an appetizer, arrange in dish and serve cocktail sauce (omit tomatoes and avocado).

Dr. Albert Johnson

Along with fish try adding ½ pound sea scallops.

MUSTARD FISH

Yield: 14 to 16 servings

5 pounds fish filets (preferably bass
  or crappie)
2½ cups flour
1 (24 ounce) jar prepared mustard

1 ounce (½ bottle) Tabasco
1 (5 ounce) jar horseradish
½ to 1 cup water (Optional)

Mix all ingredients together except water in a large bowl. Coat each fish filet with the mustard batter. If batter is too thick and will not coat filets well, add water to thin batter. Deep fry fish in a heavy pan or Dutch oven in very hot grease. Do not be scared to add the large amount of Tabasco and horseradish because the hot flavor will cook out while the fish are being fried.

Mike Miller

Variation: after coating your fish with the mustard batter, roll in equal amounts of yellow corn meal and cajun seasoning. This gives a spicier flavor.

CHEESE SALMON CASSEROLE WITH CELERY SAUCE

Oven: 350°
Yield: 6 to 8 servings

1 (16 ounce) can salmon, drained
1 egg, beaten
½ cup cream
3 Tablespoons butter, melted
1 Tablespoon lemon juice

⅛ teaspoon pepper
1¼ cups grated Cheddar cheese
1 cup bread crumbs
2 Tablespoons margarine

Celery Sauce
4 Tablespoons butter
4 Tablespoons flour
1 teaspoon salt
¼ teaspoon pepper

2 cups milk
1 cup chopped celery, cooked until
   crisp tender

Combine first 7 ingredients. Mix thoroughly. Put into a greased 1 quart casserole. Top with buttered bread crumbs. Bake at 350⁰ for 40 minutes. Serve hot or cold with celery sauce. Make sauce by melting butter over low heat. Add flour, salt and pepper. Stir until well blended. Gradually stir in milk. Cook, stirring constantly until thick and smooth. Add celery.

Mescal Johnston

A good family dish.

SALMON CROQUETTES

Yield: 4 servings

1 (1 pound) can salmon, drained
½ teaspoon salt
Dash of cayenne pepper
1 Tablespoon chopped parsley
¼ cup cracker crumbs

½ teaspoon grated onion
1 egg, beaten
1 cup bread crumbs
1 egg, beaten

Finely mince fish. Add salt, pepper, parsley, cracker crumbs, onion and egg. Mix well. Roll in cones. Dip these into beaten egg, roll in bread crumbs. Drop into deep hot fat and fry until light brown. Drain on paper towels. Serve immediately with your favorite tartar sauce.

Helen Sloan (Mrs. John C.)

SALMON WITH DILLED CREAMED PEA SAUCE

Oven: Microwave
Yield: 6 servings

1 (16 ounce) can salmon, drained
  and flaked
2 eggs, beaten
½ cup Italian bread crumbs

2 Tablespoons milk
½ teaspoon grated lemon peel
½ cup chopped green onions
½ teaspoon salt

Sauce
1 (10 ounce) package frozen peas,
  cooked
1 Tablespoon margarine
1 Tablespoon flour

½ teaspoon salt
Dash of pepper
⅔ cup milk
¼ teaspoon dill

Mix all ingredients (except sauce ingredients). Press into 6 (6 ounce) custard cups or muffin cups. Arrange in a circle in microwave. Cook on high for 3 minutes. Rearrange cups. Microwave until set, 2 to 3 minutes. To make sauce, microwave margarine in a 2 cup container until melted. Blend in flour, salt, pepper and dill. Stir in milk. Microwave for 1 minute. Stir in peas. Cook until mixture boils and thickens.

Martha H. Carle (Mrs. Kenneth)
Stuttgart, Arkansas

A good family dish.

RED SNAPPER MAXIMS

Yield: 4 servings

1 pound fresh mushrooms
Butter
1 pound lump crabmeat
Cooking oil
4 red snapper, red fish or sea trout
  filets cleaned of bones and skin

Flour
2 eggs, beaten with small amount of
  milk
2 Tablespoons chopped parsley
Lemon wedges

Slice mushrooms and sauté in a small amount of butter. After mushrooms start to turn brown add crabmeat and set aside. Heat 1 inch of oil to 350⁰ in a large iron skillet. Put filets in flour, then egg, then flour and place in skillet. Cook fish until golden brown, turn and cook the same on other side. Reheat mushroom/crabmeat mixture and add one large spoonful to each filet. Brown butter in pan and add chopped parsley and pour over each filet. Serve with lemon wedges.

Morin Scott, Jr.
Houston, Texas

SNAPPER BÉARNAISE

Oven: 450°
Yield: 4 to 6 servings

2 pounds of snapper filets
Worcestershire sauce
Lemon Juice
Salt
White pepper
Flour
1 egg, beaten with small amount of
   milk

Clarified butter
4 slices tomato per serving
½ small avocado per serving in ¼
   inch slices
Béarnaise sauce (See Index)
Butter, melted
Lemon juice
Fresh parsley, chopped

Season the filets with Worcestershire sauce, lemon juice, salt and white pepper to taste. Dip filets in flour, then in egg. In a skillet, sauté the filets in butter on one side only; then place them cooked side up in a baking pan single layer. Top each filet with a layer of tomato slices and then a layer of avocado slices. Bake the fish in a preheated 450⁰ oven for 8 to 10 minutes. Make Béarnaise sauce. When the filets are done, remove them to an ovenproof serving platter. Pour Béarnaise sauce over the fish. Place under preheated broiler just until brown. Heat butter, lemon juice and parsley. Pour over fish to serve.

Robert M. Eubanks III

SOUFFLÉED SOLE

Oven: 350°
Yield: 4 servings

8 small sole filets
Lemon juice
Salt
Pepper
¾ cup butter, softened
¼ cup minced parsley

1 Tablespoon minced fresh dill
1½ teaspoons minced fresh
   tarragon
1 cup mayonnaise
¼ cup chopped chives
1 egg white, stiffly beaten

Preheat oven to 350⁰. Rinse filets in salt water. Pat dry with paper towels. Sprinkle with lemon juice, salt and pepper. Blend butter with parsley, dill and tarragon using electric mixer. Spread butter on skinned side of filets. Roll lengthwise and place seam side down in a buttered casserole. Bake for 20 minutes. Combine mayonnaise and chives. Fold ½ egg white into mixture. Carefully place rolled filets in individual ovenproof serving dishes. Cover each with mayonnaise mixture. Broil until golden, 2 to 3 minutes.

Richard N. Moore, Jr.

FILETS OF SOLE WALEWSKA

Oven: 350°
Yield: 6 servings

2 rock lobster tails	**1 stick butter**
¼ cup dry sherry	**4 Tablespoons cognac**
¾ cup dry white wine	**1 Tablespoon chopped parsley**
½ cup water	**2 shallots, chopped**
½ pound fresh mushrooms	**1 teaspoon tomato paste**
Salt	**4 Tablespoons flour**
Pepper	**⅔ cup Half and Half**
6 large filets of sole	**2 egg yolks**
Lemon juice	**1 Tablespoon brandy**

Remove the meat from the lobster tails. Put the shells in a pot with sherry, wine, water, 1 sliced mushroom. salt and pepper. Bring mixture to a boil. Simmer for 20 minutes, strain and reserve liquid. Wash sole in water to which approximately 1 Tablespoon of lemon juice has been added. Pat fish dry. For stuffing, quarter remaining mushrooms and sauté in ½ stick butter. Sprinkle with lemon juice, salt and pepper. Turn off heat. Chop lobster meat and add to pan. Flame the mixture with warm cognac. Add chopped parsley. Place the sole filets with dark sides up, spread with stuffing, and roll up. Place in a buttered baking dish. Pour the reserved stock over the stuffed sole and poach for 15 minutes in a preheated 350⁰ oven. Remove, carefully strain stock, and reserve. Keep filets warm. Melt ½ stick butter in a heavy saucepan. Add chopped shallots and sauté briefly. Remove from heat and stir in tomato paste, flour, and 1 cup reserved stock. Return to low heat and stir until sauce thickens. Do not let it boil. Add Half and Half. In a separate bowl, mix the egg yolks with 1 Tablespoon brandy. Enrich the sauce by gradually adding the hot sauce to the egg mixture. When warm, add the egg mixture back into the sauce. On a warm platter, arrange the sole and spoon sauce over them. Sprinkle with any reserved stuffing. Watercress makes a nice additional garnish.

Eden Ferguson Baber (Mrs. Tyler)

"He ordered himself a dozen oysters; but, suddenly remembering that the month contained no 'r', changed them to a fried sole."
JOHN GALSWORTHY
1867-1933

CHARCOAL GRILLED TROUT

Yield: 4 servings

**Fish grill brushed or sprayed with
  cooking oil**
4 (10 ounce) trout
½ cup mayonnaise

1 large tomato, sliced
4 lemons, sliced
2 onions, sliced

Light grill and let coals burn down. Clean trout and leave heads on. Spread mayonnaise on inside of trout. Put sliced tomatoes inside trout. Open fish grill and put half sliced onions and lemons, trout and remainder of onions and lemons. Close fish grill. Either put on a rotisserie for 15 minutes or cook for 6 to 7 minutes on one side and turn for 5 to 6 minutes. Serve with dill sauce or other favorite sauce.

Dan Robinson

In the absence of a fish grill, the lemons and onions may be placed directly on the charcoal grill.

RAINBOW TROUT IN MUSTARD DILL SAUCE

Yield: 6 servings

2 to 3 cups dry white wine
6 rainbow trout
¼ cup Dijon mustard
¼ cup prepared mustard
1 Tablespoon sugar
2 Tablespoons chopped fresh dill

¼ teaspoon salt
⅛ teaspoon white pepper
3 Tablespoons olive oil
2 Tablespoons lime juice
1 Tablespoon white wine vinegar

Heat wine in a large skillet. Lower heat and add fish. Cover and simmer (3 minutes for filets or 5 minutes for whole fish), turning once if fish is whole. Lift out of wine. Try not to break fish. Drain on paper towels. Take skin off fish. Combine mustards, sugar, dill, salt, pepper, oil, lime juice and vinegar in bowl. Whisk until creamy. Place fish in a glass dish 1 layer deep. Pour on mustard sauce and cover with plastic wrap. Refrigerate overnight or at least 8 hours. Serve cold on a platter lined with lettuce.

Diane Lord (Mrs. E. Fletcher, Jr.)

"To a Baked Fish
Preserve a respectful demeanor
When you are brought into the room;
Don't stare at the guests while they're eating
No matter how much they consume."
CAROLYN WELLS

LOBSTER MUSHROOM COQUILLES

Oven: 350°
Yield: 12 to 14 servings

½ pound mushrooms, minced
3 Tablespoons butter
¼ cup minced shallots
3 Tablespoons flour
1½ cups Half and Half
½ teaspoon salt
½ teaspoon dry mustard
½ teaspoon paprika
¼ teaspoon garlic powder

¼ teaspoon white pepper
2 egg yolks
¼ cup sherry
2 teaspoons lemon juice
½ teaspoon curry powder
2½ cups cooked lobster meat
3 Tablespoons minced parsley
Buttered bread crumbs
Grated Parmesan cheese

Sauté mushrooms in butter until slightly browned. Add shallots and cook 2 minutes. Sprinkle in flour, stir and cook 3 minutes. Slowly add Half and Half, stir and cook until thickened. Add seasonings. Beat yolks and sherry. Whisk yolk mixture into 1 cup hot mushroom sauce. Beat yolk and mushroom sauce into remaining sauce and add lemon juice and curry powder. Cook and stir without boiling for 5 minutes. Adjust seasonings and add lobster and parsley. Divide lobster between buttered scallop or oyster shells. Sprinkle with crumbs and cheese. Bake at 350° for 15 minutes until bubbly and browned. Garnish with parsley and lemon curls.

Marcie Scriber (Mrs. Ladd)
Jonesboro, Arkansas

MARYLAND CRABCAKES

Yield: 4 servings

1 pound fresh crabmeat
½ cup cracker crumbs
2 Tablespoons mayonnaise
1 Tablespoon prepared mustard
1 egg, beaten

1 teaspoon minced parsley
1 teaspoon Lea & Perrins
4 Tablespoons butter
Lemon wedges

Gently mix crab with cracker crumbs. In another bowl, combine mayonnaise, mustard, egg, parsley and Lea & Perrins. Blend this mixture with meat. Make patties about 3 inches across. Sauté in butter for about 3 to 5 minutes on each side.

Victoria Hall (Mrs. A. David)

Great with slaw!

CRAB-SPINACH SOUFFLÉ

Oven: 350°
Yield: 10 to 12 servings

1 (12 ounce) package Stouffer's
   Spinach Soufflé, thawed
2 pounds small curd cottage cheese
6 Tablespoons flour
6 eggs, beaten

1 stick butter or margarine, melted
½ pound sharp Cheddar cheese,
   grated or cut in small pieces
1 (6 ounce) can crabmeat

Mix all ingredients together. Bake in a 9 x 13 baking dish for 1 hour at 350⁰.

Nancy Couch (Mrs. James)

GOURMET OYSTER LOAF

Oven: 300°
Yield: 1 loaf

1 long loaf sourdough French bread
Butter

1 teaspoon garlic powder
2 dozen oysters, fried

Sauce
½ stick butter
3 Tablespoons flour
1 cup milk
½ teaspoon salt
¼ teaspoon pepper
1 Tablespoon Worcestershire sauce
½ teaspoon paprika

¼ teaspoon thyme
¼ teaspoon mace
Dash of hot sauce
Dash of cayenne
⅓ cup sauterne wine
½ cup chopped ripe olives

Cut a lengthwise slice from top of bread. Scoop out inside, leaving shell. Mix ¼ cup butter with garlic powder and spread inside of shell and lid. Place fried oysters in shell. Make sauce by melting butter, then blend in flour. Add milk gradually, stirring constantly until thick. Stir in seasonings. Add sauterne. Pour over oysters. Add olives. Place lid on shell. Wrap in damp cloth and place on a baking sheet. Bake at 300⁰ for 20 to 30 minutes. Cut into 2 to 3 inch slices. Can be garnished with parsley.

"Mme. Denis will eat your oysters tomorrow; I might eat some too provided they were roasted; I feel there is something barbarous in eating a pretty little animal raw."

VOLTAIRE
1694-1778

BATTER FRIED OYSTERS

Yield: 4 servings

2½ dozen medium-sized oysters,
    freshly shucked
Vegetable oil for deep frying
2 eggs
2 Tablespoons water
Horseradish sauce to taste

1½ cups flour
1½ teaspoons salt
½ teaspoon freshly ground black
    pepper
⅛ teaspoon cayenne

Drain oysters. Preheat oil in deep fryer to 375⁰. Combine eggs, water and horseradish sauce. Combine flour, salt, pepper and cayenne in a bowl and mix thoroughly. Dip oysters in egg mixture, then in seasoned flour to coat. Place side by side but not touching on a platter and allow to dry for a few minutes. When ready to fry the oysters, dip again in seasoned flour. Fry in batches of 6 to 8 until golden brown (about 3 minutes). Drain oysters by placing on a platter lined with paper towels. Can be set in a 200⁰ oven until ready to serve.

Try serving in an oyster loaf, or with brown sauce.

HELENA, ARKANSAS OYSTER LOAF

Yield: 3 to 5 servings
per loaf

1 loaf of white bread, unsliced and
    staled 1 day if possible
Melted butter
1 to 2 pints fresh oysters, drained
Corn meal
Salt
Pepper

¼ to ½ cup Crosse and Blackwell
    mustard pickle (Optional)
½ cup ketchup
Green olives, preferably with pits
1 lemon, thinly sliced
¼ cup bite-sized pieces of celery

Slice top from bread loaf. Remove as much of the crumb as possible to leave an empty crust. Brush melted butter generously inside the empty loaf and on the top. Toast crust and top in oven. Roll oysters in meal, salt and pepper, and fry until crisp and golden. Place a layer of oysters on bottom of loaf followed by small amounts of mustard pickle and ketchup. Press the garnish of olives and lemon slices amongst the oysters. Add more oysters and repeat the process until the loaf is filled. Replace top, reheat briefly in oven, and serve by slicing loaf into several pieces.

Richard Allin

OYSTERS MOSCA

Oven: 375°
Yield: 4 servings

2 dozen raw oysters, shucked
½ stick butter
4 shallots, chopped
1 teaspoon lemon juice
6 to 8 unseasoned artichoke hearts,
   mashed

Salt
Pepper
½ cup Italian bread crumbs
Parmesan cheese

Place oysters, single layer, in a 9 x 9 dish or larger depending upon the size of the oysters. Sauté shallots in butter. Add lemon juice, salt and pepper to taste, if desired. Pour over oysters. Top each oyster with some mashed artichoke. Top with bread crumbs. Sprinkle Parmesan cheese over all. Bake at 375⁰ for 15 to 20 minutes

Steve Canone
New Orleans, Louisiana

COQUILLES SAINT-JACQUES

Oven: 450°
Yield: 8 servings

1 pound scallops
1½ cups water
¾ cup dry white wine
2 sprigs fresh parsley
1 bay leaf
½ pound mushrooms, chopped
1 cup finely chopped onion
2 Tablespoons sherry

1 teaspoon lemon juice
6 Tablespoons butter
3 Tablespoons flour
2 egg yolks
4 Tablespoons whipping cream
1¼ teaspoons salt
¼ teaspoon white pepper
½ cup bread crumbs

Combine scallops, water, wine, parsley and bay leaf in saucepan. Bring to a boil and cook over low heat for 5 minutes. Drain scallops, reserving liquid. In a saucepan, combine mushrooms, onion, sherry, lemon juice and 2 Tablespoons butter. Bring to a boil, cover and cook over low heat for 10 minutes. Strain and reserve liquid. Dice scallops and mix with mushroom/onion mixture. Set aside. Melt 3 Tablespoons butter in saucepan. Blend in flour. Add reserved liquids, stirring constantly to boiling point. Cook over low heat 3 minutes. Beat egg yolks and whipping cream in bowl. Add a little hot liquid, stirring. Then pour egg yolk and cream mixture into saucepan with liquids and cook until thickened (do not boil). Season with salt and pepper. Add scallops/onion/mushrooms. Mix well and spoon into 8 ramekins. Dot with butter and bread crumbs. Bake in 450⁰ oven for 10 minutes.

Kenneth E. Carle
Stuttgart, Arkansas

SCALLOPS IN MUSHROOM TOMATO SAUCE

Yield: 8 servings

3 pounds bay scallops
Flour
Salt to taste
Pepper to taste
½ cup olive oil
1 stick unsalted butter
1 small onion, chopped
½ pound mushrooms, sliced
1 teaspoon dried thyme

1 teaspoon dried basil
1 cup dry white wine
4 large tomatoes, peeled, seeded
  and chopped
1 to 2 garlic cloves, minced
1 bunch fresh minced parsley
  leaves (approximately 1 cup)
Fresh lemon juice to taste

Dust scallops with flour and salt and pepper. Sauté scallops in 6 Tablespoons of the olive oil and 2 Tablespoons of the butter for 3 to 4 minutes. Transfer to a bowl. Add remaining oil and butter and cook onion for 1 minute. Add mushrooms, thyme, basil and cook 2 or 3 minutes. Add wine and reduce by half. Add tomatoes and juice from scallops and cook until mixture is thick. Stir in scallops and garlic and heat thoroughly. Add parsley, lemon juice and salt and pepper to taste.

Ellen Golden (Mrs. Lex)

SHRIMP ÉTOUFÉE

Yield: 6 servings

½ stick butter
2 Tablespoons flour
1 cup chopped onion
½ cup chopped celery
⅓ cup chopped bell pepper
1 large clove garlic, mashed
1 Tablespoon Worcestershire sauce

1 Tablespoon minced parsley
1 teaspoon salt
⅛ teaspoon cayenne pepper
1 cup water
1½ pounds shrimp, peeled and
  deveined

In a heavy 2 quart saucepan, melt butter. Add flour and cook over low heat, stirring constantly to make a light brown roux. Add onion, celery, bell pepper and garlic. Cook until vegetables are soft. Add remaining ingredients except for shrimp. Simmer for 15 minutes, stirring occasionally. Add shrimp and cook until done, 3 to 5 minutes. Turn off and let cool. Flavor is enhanced if refrigerated overnight and reheated. Serve over hot rice.

Mrs. Vincent Foster
Hope, Arkansas

SHRIMP ST. TROPEZ

Yield: 4 servings

4 ounces butter
½ large onion, finely chopped
24 large shrimp, peeled
2 ounces Pernod liqueur
1 pint whipping cream
1 Tablespoon dill
2 Tablespoons butter, room
   temperature

2 Tablespoons flour (mix with
   butter)
Salt
Pepper
Lemon juice
Worcestershire sauce
Cooked rice

Melt butter in a large skillet. Add onion and cook quickly. Add shrimp and cook over high heat until shrimp are half-cooked. Add Pernod and flambé. Add whipping cream and reduce by one-third. Add dill and small bits of butter/flour mixture until sauce is the consistency desired. Season to taste with salt, pepper, lemon juice and Worcestershire sauce. Serve over rice.

Vincent W. Foster, Jr.

GINGER SHRIMP WITH PEA PODS

Yield: 4 servings

2 Tablespoons oil
¾ pound shrimp, shelled
1 garlic clove, crushed
1½ cups snow peas
1 (8 ounce) can sliced water
   chestnuts, drained
½ cup chicken broth

2 Tablespoons soy sauce
1 Tablespoon cornstarch
1 Tablespoon cold water
1 Tablespoon grated fresh ginger
Chow mein noodles or freshly
   cooked rice

Heat oil in a heavy skillet or wok until hot but not smoking. Add shrimp and sauté 2 minutes. Take shrimp out. Add garlic to skillet and stir for 15 seconds. Add snow peas, water chestnuts, broth and soy sauce. Stir for 2 minutes. Combine cornstarch and water, blending until smooth. Add to skillet. Return shrimp to skillet with ginger and stir until sauce thickens and is heated through. Serve immediately over chow mein noodles or rice.

Martha H. Carle (Mrs. Kenneth)
Stuttgart, Arkansas

"Fish dinners will make a man spring like a flea."
THOMAS JORDAN
1612-1685

THE JUDGE'S BROILED SHRIMP

Oven: 300°
Yield: 4 to 6 servings

2 pounds medium or large shrimp
   with shells
Garlic salt

5 Tablespoons lemon juice
1 stick butter, melted
½ to ⅓ cup olive oil

Place shrimp in a large pan with sides about 1 inch high. Sprinkle with garlic salt, lemon juice, butter and olive oil. Marinate in refrigerator at least 1 hour. Bake at 300º until pink, 8 to 10 minutes. Then, broil until oil and butter bubbles, about 4 minutes. Serve with French bread which is delicious dipped in the sauce.

Judge William Culpepper
Alexandria, Louisiana

KIWI FRUIT AND SHRIMP SAUTÉ

Yield: 4 servings

3 kiwi fruits
2 to 3 Tablespoons olive oil
1 pound shrimp, peeled
3 Tablespoons flour

¾ cup Prosciutto or thinly sliced
   sandwich ham, cut into thin strips
3 shallots, finely chopped
¼ to ⅓ teaspoon chili powder
¾ cup dry white wine

Peel kiwi. Reserve 4 slices for garnish and chop remaining fruit. In a heavy skillet or wok, heat oil. Toss shrimp in flour and sauté 30 seconds. Add Prosciutto, shallots and chili powder. Sauté another 30 seconds. Add the chopped kiwi and sauté 30 seconds. Add wine and reduce by half. Serve immediately.

Julie Allen (Mrs. Wally)

SHRIMP AND VEGETABLES, ORIENTAL STYLE

Yield: 6 servings

3 Tablespoons butter
1 cup sliced fresh green beans
   (frozen may be used)
1½ cups sliced celery
1½ cups sliced fresh mushrooms
1 cup thinly sliced onions

2 cups shredded lettuce
1 pound shrimp, cooked
¼ cup soy sauce
1 teaspoon cornstarch
¼ teaspoon ground ginger
⅛ teaspoon pepper

Melt butter. Add green beans and cook, covered, for 5 minutes. Add next 3 ingredients and cook slowly for 8 to 10 minutes. Add lettuce and shrimp and heat for 2 minutes. Blend soy sauce with remaining ingredients and add to heated mixture. Cook until sauce has thickened, usually less than 1 minute.

Carol H. Rasco (Mrs. Terry)

GAME

Game must be given your most affectionate
attention if you are to convince your guests you
didn't shoot it yourself.

TARRAGON DOVE

Oven: 450°
Yield: 10 to 12 servings

15 to 20 dove breasts
Lemon pepper
Dried tarragon
Sage
1 cup chicken broth or stock
⅓ (12 ounce) can frozen orange
juice concentrate

2 apples, quartered
2 onions, quartered
1 cup white wine
3 Tablespoons butter
3 Tablespoons flour

Place dove breasts in a 9 x 13 roasting pan, breasts up. Sprinkle liberally with lemon pepper and lightly with tarragon and sage. Roast at 450° for 10 minutes. Remove from oven and turn breasts down. Add chicken stock to pan and spoon the orange juice over the dove breasts. Add apples and onions. Seal with foil. Bake at 325° for 30 minutes. Add wine, bake, resealed, for another 30 minutes or until tender. Remove dove to platter briefly and strain liquid into heavy saucepan. Return dove to pan and reseal to keep warm (this can be done ahead). Reduce liquid over medium high heat to about 1½ cups. With back of spoon, mix butter and flour and drop little balls of this into reduced liquid, stirring constantly until sauce thickens to your liking. Spoon over breasts placed on platter or serving plates. Cooking time for dove will naturally depend on the age and size of the birds. They should be tender but short of falling off the bone.

Sheila Foster Anthony (Mrs. Beryl, Jr.)
Washington, D.C.

A Beaujolais wine is nice with this.

J.J.'S SMOTHERED DOVE

Yield: 4 servings

½ stick butter
¼ cup minced onion
½ cup flour
20 dove breasts

½ cup sherry
1 (4 ounce) can mushrooms, drained
Bacon slices
1 cup chicken bouillon

Melt butter in a large skillet. Sauté onion until clear. Shake dove breasts in a bag of flour. Brown doves in butter. Be sure to brown all sides. Add sherry, cover and cook slowly, about 45 minutes. Add mushrooms and place bacon slices over top. Cook another 45 minutes very slowly. Serve over wild rice. (Water or chicken bouillon should be added as the doves are cooking to prevent their drying out.)

Jean Ann Kidd (Mrs. Judson)

DUCK À L'AMATA

Oven: 350°
Yield: 4 to 6 servings

2 wild ducks (average 2 pounds each)
½ to 1 cup water
½ cup vinegar
4 Tablespoons curry powder

3 teaspoons garlic powder
2 teaspoons tumeric
1½ teaspoons Tabasco
1 apple

Basting sauce
1 cup honey
½ cup orange juice

½ cup lemon juice
3 Tablespoons curry powder

Soak ducks in cold water with ½ cup vinegar for 2 or 3 hours. Remove and pat dry with a towel. Rub the ducks inside and out with the next 4 ingredients. Slice apple in small pieces and place in cavity of ducks. Place in roasting pan with approximately ½ to 1 cup water and cover with foil. Bake at 350° until tender (about 1 to 1½ hours). To make basting sauce, combine honey, orange juice, lemon juice and curry powder. Remove foil, carve ducks and cover with basting sauce. Return to oven and bake, uncovered, until glaze thickens (about 1 hour). Serve on a bed of white rice and garnish with chutney.

Amata Smith (Mrs. C. Aubrey)

BARBECUED DUCK

Yield: 6 servings

3 ducks, well washed
Salt to taste
Pepper to taste
1 (14 ounce) bottle ketchup
2 Tablespoons Worcestershire sauce
1 Tablespoon vinegar
¼ teaspoon cayenne pepper

1 stick butter
1½ cups hot water
2 garlic cloves
1 small onion, chopped
1 (4 ounce) can mushrooms, chopped and drained, or fresh mushrooms, chopped

Place ducks breast down in an electric skillet. Mix remaining ingredients, pour over ducks, cook on very low heat, covered, for 4 hours or until meat is very tender. Add water if needed. The last hour of cooking add chopped onion and mushrooms. This makes a good gravy.

Kathy Cobb (Mrs. Thomas)

This is so easy and delicious. Any leftovers may be put with spaghetti for duck spaghetti!

FRIED DUCK STRIPS
(Must be prepared 1 day in advance)

Deep Fry
Yield: 6 to 8 servings

Breasts of 4 ducks, skinned and
boon
3 cups Bulgarian buttermilk
2 large eggs (or 3 smaller)
3 large cloves garlic, minced

2 teaspoons salt
1 large onion, quartered and then
sliced
½ teaspoon pepper
2 cups flour

Slice duck breasts across the width in about 1 inch wide strips. Set aside. Combine remaining ingredients EXCEPT flour. Pour marinade over duck strips and stir to coat each piece. Marinate at least overnight or longer. It is best to let the mixture come to room temperature, then drain and coat with flour. Let set at least 30 to 45 minutes. Then deep fry quickly for 2 to 3 minutes. Serve immediately.   *Becky Powell Jacobs*
Wynne, Arkansas

This may be frozen in the marinade. Especially good as an appetizer or delicious as a main course served with DeWitt Duck Gravy (See Index).

GRANDMOTHER'S CASSEROLED DUCK
(Must be prepared 1 day in advance)

Oven: 300°
Yield: 6 servings

3 wild ducks or 1 (6 pound)
domestic duck
1 pint red wine
2 large onions, sliced
2 bay leaves
Olive oil or vegetable oil
2 Tablespoons minced parsley
1 Tablespoon thyme

1 clove garlic, minced
Salt
Pepper
½ pound mushrooms, quartered
Butter
1 Tablespoon flour
Water

Cut duck up as for frying. Place pieces in a china dish, cover with wine, sliced onions and bay leaves. Marinate overnight. Drain, reserving liquid and the onions. Brown each piece of the duck in olive oil, just enough to cover the bottom of the skillet. When each piece is well browned, transfer to a casserole. Brown the onion slices in the remaining oil. Pour the wine marinade into the skillet and heat. Ladle the contents of the skillet over the duck. Add parsley, thyme, garlic, salt and freshly ground pepper. Cover and bake in 300° oven for 2 to 2½ hours for wild duck, (1 hour for domestic duck) until tender. About 5 minutes before the dish is ready to serve, sauté mushrooms in butter. Spoon off any excess liquid in the casserole and add the mushrooms to the liquid. Thicken with the flour which has been mixed with a little water to form a creamy consistency. Serve with wild rice.   *Helen Sloan (Mrs. John C.)*

GRILLED DUCKS ORIENTAL
(Must be prepared 1 day in advance)

Yield: 4 servings

2 ducks
¾ cup sherry
2 Tablespoons soy sauce

1 teaspoon dry mustard
¾ teaspoon powdered ginger
¼ cup apricot jam

Cut ducks into halves. Combine all remaining ingredients to make a smooth mixture. Pour over the ducks and refrigerate, covered, overnight. Grill ducks, covered, over hot coals, setting high enough above the coals so that ducks will COOK SLOWLY for about 1 hour. Baste with remaining marinade. Ducks should be moist and tender with a crunchy skin. Variation: Cook ducks in a 325° oven, covered, for 2½ to 3 hours or until tender. Remove cover during last 30 mintues.

Robyn Dickey

It is important to cook the ducks slowly when prepared on the grill.

MOIST TENDER DUCK

Crockpot
Yield: 4 servings

2 wild ducks
1 apple
1 potato
Salt to taste
Pepper to taste

4 ribs celery or 4 carrots
1 (10¾ ounce) can beef consommé
  plus 6 ounces water or 2 cups
  beef bouillon

To prepare ducks for baking in crockpot, wash ducks and pat dry. Quarter apple and potato. Stuff each duck with apple and potato. Sprinkle ducks with salt and pepper. Place celery or carrots in bottom of crockpot. Lay ducks on top. Pour bouillon over ducks and cover. Cook ducks on high heat for 4 to 4½ hours. Test breasts for doneness. Remove ducks and cover with your favorite sauce.

Susan K. Schallhorn (Mrs. Tom)

This is especially good with Raspberry Sauce (See Index).

"Then all of us prepare to rise
And hold our bibs before our eyes,
And be prepared for some surprise
When father carves the duck."
ERNEST VINCENT WRIGHT
1872-1939

GLAZED DUCK

Oven: 325°
Yield: 1½ cups glaze
1 duck per person

Duck

1 cup Burgundy wine

Glaze
½ cup granulated sugar
⅓ cup brown sugar
1 Tablespoon cornstarch

1 cup orange juice
1 Tablespoon grated orange rind
¼ teaspoon salt

Brown duck in Dutch oven. Add wine and bake, covered, at 325⁰ until tender, basting and turning often (about 2½ to 3 hours). Combine sugars and cornstarch in a heavy saucepan. Add juice, rind and salt. Simmer and stir until thick. Serve over duck.

Julie Allen (Mrs. Wally)

WILD DUCK AND RICE CASSEROLE

Oven: 350°
Yield: 4 servings

2 ducks
2 apples, quartered
2 onions, quartered
1 onion, chopped
1 bell pepper, chopped
¾ cup chopped celery
1 stick butter or margarine
1 cup Uncle Ben's converted rice

1 (10½ ounce) can beef consommé
1 (10½ ounce) can water
1 (8 ounce) can mushrooms, drained
1 (6 ounce) can water chestnuts, drained
Salt to taste
Pepper to taste

Place ducks, apples and onions into a large pan. Cover with water, sprinkle with salt and pepper, and boil for 3 hours. Ducks should be tender. Sauté chopped onions, bell pepper and celery in butter. Mix all other ingredients in a 1½ quart casserole. Add sautéed mixture. Debone ducks and cut into bite-sized chunks and add to mixture. Check for seasoning. Add salt and pepper to taste. Cover casserole and cook for 1 hour at 350⁰.

Nancy Boyd (Mrs. Mike S.)
Carolyn Boshears (Mrs. Gaylon)

May be reheated and served later.

To help remove the game taste from wild duck, soak in salted water in the refrigerator overnight.

PIN OAK TEAL

Oven: 500°
Yield: 2 teal per serving

**2 teal killed at Pin Oak (or at least
  in Arkansas)**
Pepper

**Sauerkraut (fresh bulk style in jar
  or plastic bag)**

Sprinkle teal (inside and out) with pepper. Stuff cavity with sauerkraut and then wrap bird in aluminum foil and cook for 10 minutes at 500⁰. Turn oven to 300⁰ and cook for 2½ hours. Make sure teal is wrapped properly so juice does not leak out. After cooking, turn over so juice goes throughout the bird. Meat should fall off the bone and the kraut is great.

Charles B. Whiteside, III

If you use canned sauerkraut, you might as well stuff a coot!!

ROAST DUCK

Oven: 325°
Yield: 1 duck per person

2 ducks or more
Garlic powder
Salt
Pepper
1 cup chopped celery
1 large onion, chopped
2 garlic cloves

2 cups Kraft Hot Barbecue Sauce
1 Tablespoon Worcestershire sauce
1 Tablespoon dry mustard
1 Tablespoon lemon juice
1 cup water
Paprika

Rub ducks with garlic powder, salt and pepper. Put breast down in a large roaster. Combine other ingredients (except paprika) and pour over ducks. Bake, covered, for 3 hours at 325⁰. When ducks are tender, turn ducks breast side up and sprinkle with paprika. Bake, uncovered, until golden brown. Serve gravy over ducks. (If thicker gravy is desired, add small amount of flour and cook until thickened.)

Patrick D. Miller

Good way to serve duck without the "wild" flavor.

"Cookery has become an art, a noble science; cooks are gentlemen."
ROBERT BURTON
1577-1640

RED CURRANT DUCK

Oven: 325°
Yield: 8 to 10 servings

6 apple wedges
6 onion wedges
6 ducks

1 (10 ounce) jar red currant jelly
⅓ cup Worcestershire sauce
½ cup butter

Put a piece of apple and piece of onion in each duck cavity. Place ducks into a baking pan at least 2 inches deep. Add about ½ inch of water to pans. Cover and bake, at 325° for 3 hours. Prepare sauce by simmering jelly, Worcestershire sauce and butter in a double boiler for 15 minutes. Skin and debone breasts. Place breasts in a pan and cover with sauce. Place in refrigerator overnight. Bring to room temperature and heat at 325° until hot. Serve warm with sauce accompanying it. (Refrigerating overnight may be omitted.)

Winifred Smith Watkins (Mrs. Larry)

JACK'S STEAMED DUCK WITH ALMONDS AND ORANGES

Oven: 275°
Yield: 6 servings

3 wild ducks
Salt
Pepper
1 large onion, chopped
1 bunch celery, chopped
1½ cups dry sherry (more may be used if needed)

1 (4 ounce) can sliced mushrooms with liquid
1 (4.5 ounce) package slivered almonds (or more if desired)
3 oranges, peeled (reserve larger pieces of peeling)

Preheat oven to 275°. Wash ducks thoroughly and rub well with salt and pepper (inside breast cavity also). Stuff a generous handful each of chopped onions and celery into each breast cavity. Line a large 9 x 13 baking dish with enough aluminum foil to pull over tops of ducks and make a steam tent (or use a covered roasting pan). Make a bed of remaining onions and celery in pan and place ducks, breasts down, in it. Pour sherry, mushrooms with liquid, and almonds over ducks. Take 2 of the peeled oranges and squeeze juice liberally over ducks. Place some larger orange peelings over the duck bodies (like aprons). Seal foil tent tightly and place in the oven at 275° for about 4 hours. After the first 2 hours, baste ducks and add more sherry if needed. Squeeze third orange over ducks, reseal and continue baking until tender (approximately 2 hours). Discard cooked orange peels before serving. Arrange cooked ducks on serving platter over a bed of wild rice. Spoon remaining pan juices over ducks. Wild rice may also be served on the side, if preferred.

Debby Cross (Mrs. Junius, Jr.)

This recipe has always produced tender, juicy meat without any gamey taste.

ROASTED WILD DUCK IN FOIL

Oven: 425°
Yield: 2 to 3 servings

1 medium to large duck
Salt
1 apple, quartered and cored
1 Tablespoon butter
¼ cup honey

¼ cup orange juice
1 teaspoon orange peel
¼ teaspoon ginger
¼ teaspoon basil leaves

Preheat oven to 425°. Wash duck well and dry with paper towel. Salt body cavity and outside of duck and stuff cavity with pieces of apple. In a saucepan, heat the next 6 ingredients until the butter melts. Place duck on a piece of heavy duty foil, large enough to cover when folded. Pour ½ of the liquid mixture into duck cavity and the rest over duck and seal edges with a double fold. Place in a shallow pan and roast in 425° oven for 1 hour and 45 minutes. Open foil and roast for 10 to 15 minutes more until brown. Remove and discard apple.

Mrs. Brooks Norfleet

Very easy and truly delicious.

BILL'S SMOKED DUCK

Yield: 1 breast per person

Duck breasts, skinned
Soy sauce
Bacon drippings

Celery salt
Black pepper
Cayenne pepper

Wash breasts thoroughly and drain on paper towels. Rub each breast with soy sauce and bacon drippings, coating thoroughly. Sprinkle each breast with celery salt, black pepper, and cayenne pepper (easy on cayenne). Build a low charcoal fire (a little charcoal and lot's of hickory). Do not use a smoker. Place ducks at opposite end (NOT DIRECTLY OVER FIRE) with vent open over ducks and under fire. Close lid and smoke 30 minutes. Baste with bacon drippings. Turn and baste again. Smoke 4 to 6 hours, turning every hour or so but no need to baste again. Serve immediately or freeze for another day. When frozen, thaw in slow oven or microwave, slice and serve.

William B. Sigler

This is a wonderful appetizer. To serve, slice breast in VERY thin slices, serve with crackers if you want, but this is so good, you don't need them! The key to this is to smoke VERY SLOWLY with ducks at opposite end of a low fire.

DEWITT DUCK GRAVY

Yield: Gravy for 4 duck breasts

½ cup duck drippings
2 Tablespoons flour, rounded
1 cup Half and Half
1 (4 ounce) can sliced mushrooms
    and juice

Garlic salt
Worcestershire sauce
2 Tablespoons creme sherry

In a medium-sized saucepan, make a roux with ½ cup duck drippings and 2 Tablespoons flour, stirring until flour is absorbed. Pour in 1 cup of Half and Half, 1 can of sliced mushrooms, a dash of garlic salt, 2 dashes of Worcestershire sauce and 2 Tablespoons of creme sherry. Stir until thickened. Pour gravy over duck breasts and serve.

Tom Schallhorn

RASPBERRY SAUCE FOR BAKED DUCKS

Yield: 4 servings

¼ cup butter
¼ cup flour
1 cup chicken bouillon or consommé
3 shallots, chopped

¼ cup sherry
1 (10 ounce) package quick thaw
    raspberries and juice

Melt butter in skillet. Add flour and stir until dissolved. Add chicken bouillon, chopped shallots and ¼ cup sherry. Cook over medium heat until thickened. Add raspberries and juice. Cook for a few minutes more until raspberries are warm. Pour sauce over duck breasts. This sauce should be the consistency of a medium white sauce. Remove baked duck breasts from duck. Place on bed of rice and cover with raspberry sauce.

Susan K. Schallhorn (Mrs. Tom)

Use your favorite baked duck recipe or try this with Moist Tender Duck for the crockpot (See Index).

"In England there are sixty different religions, and only one sauce."
MARQUIS DOMENICO CARACCIOLO
1715-1789

FRIED FROG LEGS

Frog legs
Milk
Eggs
Flour seasoned with salt and
  pepper

Premium saltine cracker crumbs
Crisco

Rinse thawed frog legs lightly with cold water and place them in a bowl. Cover with milk and refrigerate for 8 to 24 hours. Take them directly from the milk and shake in a bag with flour, salt and pepper. Then, dip the frog legs in an egg batter and roll them in cracker crumbs. Fry in plenty of hot grease for 3 to 4 minutes on each side. Do not overcook or STEAM.

Debbie Morgan (Mrs. Biff)

May use the same procedure for bass filets. Good with tartar sauce and hush puppies.

WILD GOOSE ORANGE

Oven: 375 degrees
Yield: 4 to 6

1 (14 x 20) oven bag
1 (¾ ounce) package brown gravy
  mix
¼ cup flour
1½ teaspoons salt
2 Tablespoons sugar

1 cup hot water
2 Tablespoons orange marmalade
1 (6 ounce) can frozen orange juice,
  thawed
1 (4 to 5 pound) dressed wild goose

Preheat oven to 375°. Place oven bag in a 2 inch deep roasting pan. Combine all ingredients except goose and pour into the oven bag. Add the goose to the bag, turning well to moisten all sides. Tie the bag and make 6 (½ inch) slits in the top of the bag. Cook for 2 to 2½ hours or until tender. Pour sauce into a bowl and skim off excess fat. Serve sauce with goose.

Mrs. Brooks Norfleet

The above sauce may be used as a marinade for other wild game.

"What is sauce for the goose may be sauce for the gander but is not necessarily sauce for the chicken, the duck, the turkey or the guinea hen."
ALICE B. TOKLAS

BAKED PHEASANT

Oven: 350°

1 (10¾ ounce) can cream of
   chicken soup
½ cup apple cider
1 Tablespoon plus 1 teaspoon
   Worcestershire sauce
¾ teaspoon salt

⅓ cup chopped onion
1 small clove garlic, minced
1 (4 ounce) can sliced mushrooms,
   drained
Pheasants
Paprika

Blend all ingredients except pheasants and paprika. Pour over pheasants and sprinkle with paprika. Bake, covered, for 1½ to 2 hours. Remove cover the last 30 minutes of cooking. After 1 hour, sprinkle again with paprika.

Carol Lord (Mrs. Robert C.)

STEAMED PHEASANT OR CHUKKAR

Oven: 150°
Yield: 1 to 2 birds
per serving
(depending on size)

Game birds
Salt
Pepper
¼ onion, sliced (per bird)

1 small garlic clove (per bird)
Orange peel (per bird)
1 Tablespoon white wine (per bird)
Butter or margarine

Place each bird on a sheet of heavy foil large enough to wrap and seal. Salt and pepper each and place onion, garlic and orange peel inside. Rub butter on breast, add 1 Tablespoon wine. Wrap and seal tightly. Place birds in a large roaster or iron pot and fill with water to cover. Add orange peel, a few slices of onion, butter, salt, pepper and wine to the water. Bring water to a boil, cover with lid and place in oven for 3 hours at 150⁰. Remove birds and, in a small skillet, make enough roux for gravy. Use remaining liquid in cooking pot with roux to make gravy. Season to taste.

Irene Davis (Mrs. George H.)

"Pheasant exceedeth all fowls in sweetness and wholesomeness, and is equal to capon in nourishment."

SIR THOMAS ELYOT

PHEASANT DIVINE

Oven: 300°
Yield: 4 servings

Breast and legs of 2 pheasant	2 cups milk
Flour	1 (10¾ ounce) can cream of
Salt	mushroom soup
Pepper	1 cup white wine
Shortening	1 heaping teaspoon curry powder

Flour, salt and pepper pheasant pieces. Brown in shortening. Mix milk, soup, wine and curry together. Place browned pheasant pieces in baking dish and cover with milk mixture. Bake, covered, for 3 hours at 300⁰. Baste 2 or 3 times. Add more milk if it cooks down too much.

Joyce Steele (Mrs. H. William)
Nashville, Tennessee

RED WINE QUAIL

Yield: 6 servings

6 quail	1 cup dry red wine
Brandy	1 rib celery, cut up
Flour	Salt to taste
6 Tablespoons butter	Pepper to taste
2 cups sliced, fresh mushrooms	Juice of 2 oranges
½ cup melted butter	Wild rice, cooked
1 cup consommé	

Clean quail and rub with brandy. Dust with flour. Melt 6 Tablespoons of butter in a heavy skillet and sauté quail for 10 minutes. Sauté mushrooms in ½ cup melted butter and pour over quail. Add consommé, wine, celery, salt and pepper. Cover and simmer for 25 to 30 minutes or until tender. Remove celery and stir in orange juice. Heat well. Serve over wild rice.

"An honest fellow enough, and one that loves quails."
WILLIAM SHAKESPEARE
Troilus and Cressida
1564-1616

SQUIRREL AND DUMPLINGS

Yield: 4 servings

2 squirrels
2 bay leaves
1 cup sliced onion
1 cup chopped celery

10 medium carrots, quartered
2 teaspoons salt
½ teaspoon pepper
1½ cups hot water

Dumplings
2 cups flour
½ teaspoon salt

4 teaspoons baking powder
¾ cup milk

Cut 2 squirrels into serving pieces. Place in a kettle and cover with 1 inch of water. Add 2 bay leaves and simmer for 1¼ hours, skimming as necessary. Add onions, celery and carrots. Season with salt and pepper. Add 1½ cups hot water and cook 15 minutes longer. Add dumplings. To make dumplings, mix dry ingredients and gradually add milk. Turn dough onto a floured board, roll to ½ inch thickness and cut in 3 inch squares. Place on top of ingredients in kettle, cover tightly, and cook 15 minutes.

Jane Gulley (Mrs. Thomas H.)

VENISON CHILI

Yield: 4 to 6 servings

2 medium onions, chopped
½ cup chicken broth (or ½ stick of butter if you don't mind the calories)
2 pounds ground venison hamburger
1 (28 ounce) can whole tomatoes, undrained

2 cloves garlic, minced
2 teaspoons salt
1 teaspoon pepper
3 Tablespoons chili powder
1 Tablespoon ground cumin
1 Tablespoon oregano

Simmer onions in broth or butter until clear. Brown venison until all the red is gone. Add tomatoes that have been cut up with scissors while still in can. Add rest of ingredients. Simmer at least 1 hour. Better if made a day ahead or at least several hours for flavors to blend.

Kenan Keyes (Mrs. Griff)

This freezes well and is great for chili dogs! Also great for a low-fat diet as venison is almost void of fat.

VENISON NORMAN

Yield: 6 servings

4 Tablespoons butter
2 pounds venison, cut in 1 inch
  cubes
1 medium onion, chopped
1 Tablespoon flour
1 (10¾ ounce) can consommé
1 cup warm water

1 teaspoon salt
¼ teaspoon pepper
1 clove garlic, crushed
1 teaspoon thyme
2 bay leaves
½ pound mushrooms, sliced
Peel of 1 lemon, grated

Melt butter in skillet. Cut venison into 1 inch cubes and brown slowly in butter. When nearly brown, add onion and brown. Add flour and stir. Add consommé and water. Blend well. Add salt, pepper, garlic, thyme and bay leaves. Cover and cook slowly for 1 hour. Add mushrooms and lemon peel. Let all cook for an additional hour. Serve over rice.

Linda Burrow VanHook (Mrs. Fred F.)

VENISON PARMESAN

Oven: 350°
Yield: 4 servings

1½ pounds venison steaks, thinly
   sliced
Italian bread crumbs
½ pound Mozzarella cheese, sliced
3 (4 ounce) cans tomato purée

Basil
Italian seasoning
Parmesan cheese
½ pound Mozzarella cheese, grated

Grease a 9 x 13 casserole. Preheat oven to 350⁰. Pound the venison steak to tenderize. Coat the steaks with Italian bread crumbs. Place a layer of the coated venison steaks in the bottom of the casserole. Next place layers of sliced Mozzarella cheese, tomato purée, ¼ teaspoon basil and ¼ teaspoon Italian seasoning. Sprinkle with Parmesan cheese. Repeat layers and then sprinkle with the grated Mozzarella cheese. Bake for 1 hour at 350⁰.

Nancy Tomosieski

May be made ahead. Freezes well.

"The discovery of a new dish does more for the happines of man than the discovery of a star."

BRILLAT-SAVARIN
1755-1826

POULTRY

When you are on the verge of calling the whole thing off, calm yourself with a poultry recipe.

CHICKEN WITH ARTICHOKE HEARTS AND MUSHROOMS

Oven: 375° to 400°
Yield: 4 to 6 servings

6 chicken breast halves, boned and
  skinned
Salt
Pepper
Paprika
1 stick butter

½ to 1 pound large fresh
  mushrooms
2 Tablespoons flour
1 (13½ ounce) can chicken broth
½ to 1 cup sherry
1 (14 ounce) can artichoke hearts,
  drained

Sprinkle chicken breasts with salt, pepper and paprika. Sauté in ½ stick butter. Put chicken aside. In same skillet (do not use iron skillet) add other half of butter and sauté mushrooms. Add 2 Tablespoons flour to the mushrooms, salt and pepper, chicken broth and sherry (to taste). Simmer for 5 to 10 minutes. Place chicken breasts in a 2 quart casserole dish, pour sauce over, cover and cook for 1 hour at 375° to 400°. After an hour, remove from oven and add artichoke hearts. Cover and cook an additional 30 minutes.

Teresa Osam (Mrs. Patrick N.)

CHICKEN AND ARTICHOKE DELIGHT

Oven: 350°
Yield: 8 servings

1 large chicken
1 cup butter
½ cup flour
3½ cups milk
1 teaspoon cayenne pepper
1 Tablespoon Accent
½ teaspoon garlic powder

¾ to 1 cup grated Cheddar cheese
3 ounces Gruyère cheese
2 (8 ounce) cans whole mushrooms,
  drained
2 (14 ounce) cans artichoke hearts,
  drained and cut into large pieces

Cook chicken in seasoned water. Skin, bone and cut into bite-sized pieces. Melt butter in a saucepan. Add flour, milk and seasonings. Add cheeses and cook until mixture thickens. Mix together chicken, mushrooms, artichokes and sauce in a 3 quart casserole. Cook for 30 minutes at 350° or until bubbly.

Cindy Miller (Mrs. Patrick)

CHICKEN CYNTHIA

Oven: 350°
Yield: 4 to 6 servings

1 (3 pound) chicken, cut up
3 Tablespoons oil
Lawry's seasoned salt
Pepper
Flour
1 (6 ounce) jar marinated artichoke
  hearts, drained
1 (6 ounce) jar marinated
  mushrooms, drained

2 cups tomatoes, fresh or canned,
  drained
2 cloves garlic, minced
½ teaspoon basil
½ teaspoon oregano
Cavender's Greek Seasoning to taste
½ cup sherry

Preheat oven to 350°. Heat oil in frying pan. Season chicken with salt and pepper and dredge in flour. Brown chicken in oil. Place in a 9 x 13 casserole. Add marinated artichokes and mushrooms. Mix together tomatoes, garlic, basil and oregano and pour over chicken. Sprinkle with Cavender's. Bake, uncovered, at 350° for 1½ hours or until tender. Add sherry during last 30 minutes.

Cynthia Weber (Mrs. James R.)

Great served with a Caesar salad and fettuccini plus a good dry white wine.

CHICKEN DELIGHT

Oven: 300°
Yield: 8 servings

8 chicken breasts, boned and
  skinned
8 slices boiled ham
8 slices bacon
1 (10¾ ounce) can cream of
  mushroom soup

1 (10¾ ounce) can cream of
  chicken soup
1 (4 ounce) can chopped
  mushrooms, drained
1 (8 ounce) can water chestnuts,
  sliced and drained
1 (8 ounce) carton French onion dip

Wrap chicken around rolled ham and bacon around chicken. Place in a 9 x 13 casserole dish. Mix last 5 ingredients and pour over chicken. Bake at 300° for 2½ hours or until tender. Serve with wild rice.

Norma C. Rauch

"And we meet, with champagne and a chicken, at last."
LADY MARY WORTLEY MONTAGU
The Lover
1689-1762

CHICKEN AND ASPARAGUS CASSEROLE

Oven: 350°
Yield: 12 servings

12 chicken breast halves
1 medium onion, chopped
1 stick butter
1 (8 ounce) can button mushrooms,
  drained
1 (10¾ ounce) can cream of
  chicken soup
1 (10¾ ounce) can cream of
  mushroom soup
1 (5⅓ ounce) can Pet milk

½ pound sharp Cheddar cheese,
  grated
Tabasco to taste
2 teaspoons soy sauce
1 teaspoon salt
1 teaspoon monosodium glutamate
1 (4 ounce) jar pimientos, drained
  and chopped
2 (10 ounce) packages frozen
  asparagus spears
½ cup slivered almonds

Cook chicken in seasoned water until done. Cut into bite-sized pieces and set aside. Sauté onion in butter until limp and add remaining ingredients except asparagus and almonds. Cook asparagus according to directions on package and drain well. When cheese has melted in the sauce, begin to layer ingredients in a 3 quart casserole: a layer of chicken, layer of asparagus and a layer of cheese sauce. Repeat layers. Top with almonds and bake at 350⁰ until bubbly.

A great company dish.

CHICKEN DIVAN

Oven: 350°
Yield: 6 to 8 servings

3 whole chicken breasts
2 (10 ounce) packages broccoli
  spears
2 (10¾ ounce) cans cream of
  mushroom soup
1 cup mayonnaise
1 (8 ounce) carton sour cream
1 cup grated sharp cheese

1 Tablespoon lemon juice
1 teaspoon curry
Salt to taste
Pepper to taste
Parmesan cheese
Paprika
Butter

Cook chicken breasts. Simmer in well-seasoned chicken stock. Cook broccoli according to directions on package. Drain well. Mix soup, sour cream, mayonnaise, grated cheese and seasonings. Arrange broccoli in the bottom of a flat, greased 3 quart casserole dish. Sprinkle generously with Parmesan cheese. Remove skin from chicken and take chicken from bone, pulling apart into pieces. Spread over broccoli. Sprinkle again with Parmesan cheese. Pour sauce over all. Sprinkle with Parmesan cheese and paprika. Dot with butter. Cook 30 to 40 minutes at 350⁰ or until bubbly and heated through.

Jann Scott (Mrs. Bob)

CHICKEN MORNAY

Oven: 325°
Yield: 6 to 8 servings

8 large fresh broccoli spears,
   cooked (or frozen broccoli
   spears)
8 large slices chicken breasts,
   cooked

3 cups Mornay Sauce
1 cup grated American cheese
¼ teaspoon paprika

Mornay Sauce
3 Tablespoons butter
3 Tablespoons flour
1 cup milk (or chicken stock)
⅛ teaspoon cayenne pepper

1 teaspoon salt
1 cup cubed sharp cheese
1 cup cream

Arrange broccoli in a 9 x 13 baking dish. Cover with chicken breasts. Top with grated cheese and pour mornay sauce over. Sprinkle with paprika. Brown slowly under broiler or bake for 30 minutes at 325⁰ until hot. To make sauce, melt butter slowly. Add flour, then milk, stirring constantly. Add cayenne, salt and cheese. When cheese is melted, slowly add cream.

Anne Turner Dawson (Mrs. Michael)
Denver, Colorado

A good luncheon dish. Serve with fruit or a green salad and hot bread.

CHICKEN WITH CUCUMBERS IN PAPRIKA SAUCE

Yield: 4 servings

2 cucumbers, peeled and cut into ¼
   inch slices
4 whole chicken breasts, boned and
   cut into strips
2 Tablespoons paprika, divided
2 ounces butter
2 ounces oil

1 small onion, finely diced
4 ounces white wine
1 pint whipping cream
Salt
Pepper
Lemon juice
Worcestershire sauce

Blanch cucumbers in 2 quarts of boiling, salted water. Remove and refresh cucumbers in cold water. Season chicken strips with salt and 1 teaspoon paprika. Melt butter in skillet. Add oil. Allow to start browning and add diced onion. Stir. Add chicken and brown on all sides. Remove chicken from skillet and keep warm. Add paprika and cook for 2 minutes over moderate heat. Add white wine and reduce by half. Add whipping cream and reduce until thick. Season with salt, pepper, lemon juice and Worcestershire sauce to taste. Add chicken and cucumbers. Serve immediately.

CHICKEN BREASTS FLORENTINE

Oven: 325°
Yield: 8 servings

8 chicken breast halves, boned and
    skinned
Flour
2 eggs, beaten
1 stick butter
Fresh chopped spinach, cooked, or
    1 (10 ounce) box frozen chopped
    spinach, cooked and drained

Parmesan cheese, freshly grated
8 slices Mozzarella cheese
¼ cup chicken broth
¼ cup white wine
¼ cup lemon juice

Dip breasts in flour and then in eggs. Sauté breasts in butter for 4 minutes on each side (should be lightly browned). Remove breasts to a large 3 quart flat casserole dish and top each with cooked spinach. Sprinkle each breast with Parmesan cheese and top with a slice of Mozzarella cheese. Add chicken broth to the same pan used to sauté breasts (to deglaze). Then, add the wine and lemon juice. Stir. Pour sauce over chicken. Bake at 325° for 25 to 30 minutes. Cheese should be melted and breasts heated thoroughly.

Julie Headstream Haught (Mrs. William D.)

May be assembled earlier in the day and then cooked in oven before serving. Especially good served with fettuccini.

CHICKEN CURRY

Yield: 4 to 6 servings

4 Tablespoons butter
1 (2½ pound) chicken fryer, cut in
    pieces
2 onions, thinly sliced
1 garlic clove, minced
1 to 2 Tablespoons curry powder
½ teaspoon ginger
1 teaspoon seasoned salt, or to taste

Lemon pepper to taste
½ teaspoon coriander
¼ to ½ teaspoon tumeric
1 tomato, chopped
¾ cup buttermilk
¼ cup slivered almonds
2 Tablespoons whipping cream

Melt 2 Tablespoons butter in a heavy skillet and brown chicken on both sides. Remove chicken. Melt remaining butter and sauté onions and garlic until limp. Return chicken to skillet and sprinkle with curry powder, ginger, salt, pepper, coriander and tumeric. Add tomato, buttermilk and almonds. Cover and cook for 1 hour or until chicken is tender. Stir frequently. Before serving, add cream and stir. Serve over rice.

Cynthia Weber (Mrs. James R.)

CRABMEAT STUFFED BREAST OF CHICKEN

Oven: 450°
Yield: 4 servings

1 Tablespoon butter
1 Tablespoon flour
½ cup cream
Salt
Pepper
1 cup crabmeat

1 cup chopped mushrooms
Bread crumbs
4 whole chicken breasts, boned and
    skinned
2 or 3 eggs, beaten
Oil

Sauce
2 Tablespoons butter
2 Tablespoons flour
1½ cups cream
Salt
Pepper

2 Tablespoons dill
1 cup sliced mushrooms
¼ cup white wine
Juice of 2 limes

Melt butter and add flour to make a roux. Slowly add cream to make a smooth sauce. Season with salt and pepper to taste. Add crabmeat, mushrooms and enough bread crumbs to bind the stuffing. Pound each breast thin and fill each with stuffing. Roll to enclose. Dip each breast first into the beaten eggs, then into bread crumbs. Sauté in oil until golden brown. Remove from pan and drain. Bake at 450° for 5 minutes to finish cooking. To make sauce, melt butter and add flour to make a roux. Slowly add cream. Add seasonings to taste, mushrooms, wine and lime juice. Heat. Serve over stuffed chicken breasts.

Robert M. Eubanks, III

CHICKEN REGAL PARMESAN

Oven: 350°
Yield: 6 to 8 servings

8 chicken breast halves, boned and
    skinned
1 cup sherry
1 cup seasoned or Italian bread
    crumbs
1 teaspoon salt

½ teaspoon pepper
1 cup Parmesan cheese
2 Tablespoons parsley
1 garlic clove, crushed
1 cup slivered almonds
1½ sticks butter, melted

Marinate chicken breasts in sherry for 3 hours. Pat dry with paper towel. Combine bread crumbs, salt, pepper, Parmesan cheese, parsley, garlic and ¾ cup almonds. Dip chicken in melted butter, then roll in bread crumb mixture. Arrange in a 9 x 13 baking dish and top with remaining almonds. Bake for 45 minutes to 1 hour at 350°.

Etta Smith (Mrs. Stephen G.)

CHICKEN WITH HAM AND CHEESE

Oven: 350°
Yield: 6 servings

6 chicken breast halves, skinned
   and boned
6 ounces Swiss cheese, sliced
6 thin slices of ham
¼ cup flour
⅓ cup butter
½ cup water

2 Tablespoons instant chicken
   bouillon
⅓ cup white wine
1 (3 ounce) can sliced mushrooms,
   drained
2 Tablespoons flour
½ cup water

Preheat oven to 350°. Place chicken breasts, boned side up, on a cutting board and pound chicken lightly with a mallet to make ¼ inch thick cutlets, working from the center out. Place a slice of cheese and ham on each piece of chicken. Tuck in sides, roll and fasten well with wooden toothpicks. Coat with ¼ cup flour. Heat butter in skillet and brown chicken in butter. Remove chicken and place in a 7 x 11 baking dish. Combine ½ cup water, bouillon, mushrooms and wine in the same skillet. Heat and stir to remove crusty bits from skillet. Remove toothpicks from chicken and pour sauce over chicken. Bake for 1 to 1¼ hours at 350° or until tender. Transfer chicken to warm serving platter. Blend 2 tablespoons flour with ½ cup water. Stir into drippings from pan. Cook on top of stove, stirring until thick. Pour over chicken and serve.

Daryl Newcomb

CHICKEN BREASTS WITH CURRY SAUCE

Oven: 350°
Yield: 4 servings

4 chicken breast halves
Salt
Butter pats
2 Tablespoons butter
3 Tablespoons flour
2 teaspoons curry powder
Freshly ground pepper to taste

Salt to taste
1½ cups Swanson's chicken broth
½ cup Half and Half
¼ cup Major Grey's Chutney,
   chopped
1 (3½ ounce) bag Success Rice
1 cup raisins

Lightly salt and butter each chicken breast and wrap in foil. Bake for 1½ hours at 350°. Cool chicken until it can be handled and carefully remove skin and bone. Make sauce by melting butter in a 2 quart saucepan. Add flour and seasonings using a wire whisk. Add broth, stirring constantly until smooth. Stir in Half and Half and chutney. Cook rice according to package directions and mix with raisins. Place chicken on rice and spoon sauce over all.

Nancy Sloan (Mrs. Neill)

Peanuts or chow mein noodles may be sprinkled on top for "crunch."

PICCATA CHICKEN

Yield: 4 to 6 servings

4 whole chicken breasts, skinned,
  boned and halved
½ cup flour
1 teaspoon salt
¼ teaspoon freshly ground pepper
Paprika
½ cup butter

1 Tablespoon olive oil
4 Tablespoons dry sherry or dry
  red wine
3 Tablespoons fresh lemon juice
1 lemon, sliced
3 Tablespoons capers
⅓ cup fresh minced parsley

Flatten chicken breasts until about ¼ inch thick. Combine flour, salt, pepper and paprika in a bag. Add breasts and shake well. Heat butter and olive oil in skillet until bubbly. Sauté chicken breasts a few at a time for 3 to 5 minutes on each side. Drain and keep warm. Drain off all but 2 Tablespoons oil. Stir in sherry or wine, scraping the bottom of the skillet to loosen any browned bits. Add lemon juice and slices and heat. Add capers and sprinkle with parsley. Pour sauce over the chicken breasts.

Mrs. Robert M. Eubanks, Jr.

BONED BREAST OF CHICKEN WITH GREEN PEPPERCORN SAUCE

Yield: 2 servings

3 Tablespoons butter, clarified and
  unsalted

1 or 2 whole chicken breasts,
  skinned, boned and split

Green Peppercorn Sauce
2 Tablespoons minced onion
¼ cup dry white wine
½ cup whipping cream
1 teaspoon green peppercorns,
  rinsed, drained and mashed
1 teaspoon whole green
  peppercorns, rinsed and drained

1 teaspoon fresh tarragon leaves or
  ¼ teaspoon dried tarragon,
  crumbled
Salt to taste
Freshly ground pepper to taste

Melt butter in a heavy skillet. Add chicken and sauté until golden brown on both sides, turning once. Transfer to heated platter and keep warm. DO NOT CLEAN SKILLET. Add onion to skillet and place over low heat. Sauté until limp. Blend in wine. Boil until wine is reduced by half, scraping up browned bits clinging to bottom of skillet. Stir in cream, mashed and whole peppercorns and tarragon. Continue boiling until sauce is syrupy. Remove from heat and add salt and pepper. Pour over chicken and serve immediately.

Libby Strawn (Mrs. Jim)

May easily be doubled or tripled. Delicious served with rice.

CHICKEN ROSEMARY

Yield: 8 servings

8 chicken breast halves, boned
1 (16 ounce) bottle Wishbone Italian
   Salad Dressing
½ cup dry vermouth or white wine
¼ cup soy sauce

¼ heaping cup brown sugar
2 teaspoons rosemary
1 teaspoon salt
1 teaspoon pepper

Place chicken breasts in a deep bowl. Mix remaining ingredients together, stirring well. Pour marinade over chicken, arranging chicken so that all pieces are covered. Cover bowl and refrigerate 8 hours or overnight. (If shallow dish has been used to marinate, turn chicken several times during 8 hours.) Cook chicken over charcoal fire. Brush with marinade during cooking. Cook until done.

Robyn Dickey

MANDARIN CHICKEN BREASTS

Yield: 6 servings

6 whole chicken breasts, boned
1½ cups hot cooked rice
1 Tablespoon butter
¼ teaspoon salt
1 Tablespoon chopped parsley
¼ teaspoon rosemary
¼ teaspoon basil
½ cup flour
1 teaspoon paprika
1 teaspoon salt
3 Tablespoons butter

2 teaspoons instant chicken broth
   crystals
1¾ cups water
1 Tablespoon minced dried onion
2 Tablespoons lemon juice
1 bay leaf
1 Tablespoon cornstarch
1 (11 ounce) can mandarin oranges,
   drained
1 cup seedless grapes

Sprinkle insides of chicken breasts with salt. Combine rice, 1 Tablespoon butter, ¼ teaspoon salt, parsley, rosemary and basil in bowl. Mix together. Spoon into middle of breasts. Fold edges and fasten with wooden toothpicks. Mix flour, paprika and ½ teaspoon salt and dip chicken breasts into mixture, coating well. Brown breasts in 3 Tablespoons butter in a large skillet. When brown, stir in chicken broth, 1¾ cups water, onion, lemon juice and bay leaf. Bring to a boil and cover. Simmer for 30 minutes. Remove bay leaf, then remove chicken (keep warm). Reheat liquid to boiling and smooth cornstarch to paste and add to liquid. Cook until sauce thickens. Stir in oranges and grapes. Reheat until bubbly. Spoon over chicken and serve.

Genny Doramus (Mrs. W. Michael)
Dallas, Texas

A colorful dish with a wonderful flavor.

CHICKEN IN ORANGE SAUCE

Yield: 4 servings

1 whole chicken, cut up
1 stick butter
¼ cup flour
2 Tablespoons brown sugar
1 teaspoon salt
½ teaspoon ground ginger

½ teaspoon pepper
1½ cups orange juice
½ cup water
2 oranges, peeled and sectioned, or
   1 (16 ounce) can mandarian
   oranges, drained

In large skillet, brown chicken in butter. Set aside. Blend flour, brown sugar, salt, ginger and pepper into drippings and cook, stirring frequently, just until it bubbles. Add orange juice and water slowly until sauce thickens. Boil 1 minute. Return chicken to skillet. About 45 minutes prior to serving, reheat chicken and sauce mixture just to boiling and simmer, covered, for 30 minutes. Lay orange sections around chicken and cook for 15 more minutes. Serve over rice.

Robin Coates
Dallas, Texas

RUTH AGAR'S CHICKEN DELLA ROBBIA

(Must be prepared 1 day in advance)

Yield: 6 to 8 servings

8 chicken breast halves
½ stick butter
2 medium onions, sliced
16 ounces fresh mushrooms
1 cup dark raisins, sliced
4 teaspoons salt
¼ cup lemon juice
2 teaspons monosodium glutamate
½ teaspoon ground cloves
½ teaspoon allspice
½ teaspoon ginger
¼ cup brown sugar

¼ cup walnut halves
4 teaspoons cornstarch
1¾ cups chicken broth
¼ cup brandy
3 Tablespoons Orange Curacao
2 cups seedless grapes
2 cups mandarin oranges, drained
6 green maraschino cherries, cut in
   half
6 red maraschino cherries, cut in
   half

Cook chicken in small amount of water until tender. Cut into large chunks. Sauté onions and mushrooms in butter. Add raisins, salt, lemon juice, monosodium glutamate, cloves, allspice, ginger, brown sugar and 1¼ cups chicken broth. Simmer for ½ hour. Add walnuts. Add cornstarch to ½ cup chicken broth; slowly add this to the sauce to thicken it. Add chicken. Stir well. Add brandy and Orange Cucacao. Cool and refrigerate overnight. When ready to serve, heat gently and transfer to a chafing dish. Decorate with fruit. Serve over wild rice.

Kristin Agar
Cynthia East (Mrs. Robert C.)

A colorful Christmas buffet dish.

CHICKEN BREASTS TARRAGON

Oven: 375°
Yield: 8 servings

1 stick butter
8 chicken breast halves
1 teaspoon salt
½ teaspoon tarragon

¼ teaspoon pepper
1 cup sour cream
¼ cup Parmesan cheese
2 cups fresh sliced mushrooms

Melt butter in a 9 x 13 pan. Dip chicken breasts in butter and put skin side up in pan. Sprinkle with salt, tarragon and pepper. Bake, covered, for 50 minutes at 375º. Combine sour cream and cheese. Blend sour cream and cheese mixture with drippings from chicken. Add mushrooms to chicken and pour sour cream and drippings mixture over chicken. Bake, uncovered, for 10 more minutes and serve.

Julie Fulgham (Mrs. Edward)

CHICKEN BREASTS SPECIAL

Oven: 350°
Yield: 8 servings

8 chicken breast halves, boned and
skinned
Salt
Freshly ground pepper
Paprika
½ stick butter
½ pound fresh mushrooms

½ stick butter
¼ cup sherry
1 (10¾ ounce) can cream of
mushroom soup
1 cup sour cream
1 (2.8 ounce) can Durkees onion
rings (Optional)

Place chicken breasts in a 9 x 13 baking dish. Sprinkle each piece of chicken with salt, pepper, and lots of paprika. Cut ½ stick of butter into pats and top chicken breasts. Bake, covered, for 1 hour at 350º. Wash mushrooms. Slice some in half, leave some whole. Sauté in butter and sherry over medium heat in a heavy skillet. When chicken is done, remove from baking dish. Add mushrooms (including juice), soup, and sour cream to drippings. Mix well. Return chicken to dish and partially cover with sauce mixture. Top with onion rings and bake, uncovered, for 10 to 15 more minutes. Serve with sauce spooned on top.

Elegant to be so easy.

"I want there to be no peasant in my kingdom so poor that he is unable to have a chicken in his pot every Sunday."

HENRY IV OF FRANCE
1553-1610

CHICKEN BREASTS SUPREME
(Must be prepared 1 day in advance)

Oven: 350°
Yield: 12 servings

6 whole chicken breasts, boned
2 cups sour cream
2 Tablespoons lemon juice
2 cloves garlic, finely chopped
2 teaspoons Worcestershire sauce
2 teaspoons celery salt

2 teaspoons paprika
2 teaspoons salt
Dash of pepper
1¾ cups bread crumbs or fine
  stuffing crumbs
½ cup butter or margarine, melted

Cut breasts in half. In large bowl combine sour cream, lemon juice, garlic and seasonings. Add chicken, coating each piece well. Cover bowl and let stay in refrigerator overnight. Next day roll chicken breasts (still coated with sour cream mixture) in bread crumbs. Arrange in a single layer in greased 9 x 13 baking dish. Drizzle melted butter over the chicken evenly. Save a little butter. Bake, uncovered, at 350⁰ for 45 minutes. Drizzle reserved butter over chicken. Serve as is, or with a mushroom sauce.

Becky Slater (Mrs. John)
Linda Shollmier (Mrs. Dudley)
Kathy Wilkins (Mrs. James H., Jr.)

DEE DEE'S CHICKEN ROMA

Oven: 400°
Yield: 4 servings

1 (2½ to 3 pound) chicken fryer,
  cut up
1 envelope Shake and Bake
  Seasoning for Chicken
½ teaspoon oregano
½ teaspoon basil
1 teaspoon McCormick's Italian
  Seasoning

¼ teaspoon rosemary
¼ pound sharp Cheddar cheese,
  grated
¼ cup mayonnaise
4 slices raw bacon, chopped
½ green pepper, chopped

Coat chicken pieces with Shake and Bake that is seasoned with oregano, basil, McCormick's Italian Seasoning and rosemary. Coat according to directions on envelope. Arrange chicken in a single layer in an ungreased shallow 9 x 13 baking pan. Bake at 400⁰ for 40 to 50 minutes or until tender. While chicken is cooking, combine cheese, mayonnaise, bacon and pepper, blending well. Spread over baked chicken and broil for 5 minutes.

Carol Lord (Mrs. Robert C.)

COUNTRY CAPTAIN

Oven: 325°
Yield: 8 to 10 servings

2 (3 pound) chickens
⅔ cup all-purpose flour
1 teaspoon salt
½ teaspoon black pepper
¼ teaspoon paprika
1 clove garlic, chopped
½ cup olive oil
1 cup finely chopped onion
1 bell pepper, sliced
4¾ cups canned tomatoes

2 teaspoons parsley, chopped
1 teaspoon curry powder
½ teaspoon powdered thyme
⅛ teaspoon cayenne pepper
½ cup water
1 cup seedless raisins
½ cup toasted almond slivers
2 cups hot cooked rice
Parsley

Cut chicken into frying-sized pieces. Flour chicken by shaking in a paper bag containing flour, salt, pepper and paprika. Make garlic oil by adding chopped garlic to olive oil and let stand until flavor is absorbed. Use ½ cup hot garlic oil to brown chicken. Remove chicken to 9 x 13 casserole and cover. Cook onion and bell pepper in oil until limp, stirring constantly. Add tomatoes, parsley, curry, thyme, cayenne pepper, and water. Cook slowly for 5 minutes. Pour over chicken. Cover and bake for 45 minutes at 325°. Add raisins the last 15 minutes. Arrange chicken in the center of a large, heated platter. Pour sauce over it and pile cooked rice around edges. Sprinkle toasted almonds on top and garnish with fresh parsley.

Mrs. Joseph Fearis Caldwell
Columbus, Georgia

"County Captain" was a favorite dish of President Franklin Roosevelt's when he visited Warm Springs, Georgia. This is the original recipe.

CHICKEN SUPREME

Yield: 4 servings

2 Tablespoons butter or margarine
4 chicken breast halves, boned and
   skinned
Pepper
¼ cup chicken bouillon

¼ cup white wine
½ pint whipping cream
2 Tablespoons cornstarch
½ cup water

Melt butter or margarine in a large Dutch oven. Add chicken and cook for 10 minutes over low heat. Sprinkle with pepper. Remove chicken and set aside. Add bouillon, wine and whipping cream. Stir well. Combine cornstarch and water. Add to liquid mixture, stirring constantly. Pour over chicken and serve with rice.

Harriet Harper Baker (Mrs. Brian)

DELICIOUS CHICKEN

Oven: 350°
Yield: 8 servings

½ cup butter
½ large onion, chopped
1 (10¾ ounce) can cream of
    mushroom soup
1 (8 ounce) carton sour cream
1 (4 ounce) can mushrooms, drained
¼ cup wine

¼ teaspoon salt
Ground pepper to taste
1 (3 pound) chicken, cooked and cut
    into bite-sized pieces
½ cup slivered almonds, or
    cashews

Sauté onion in butter until limp. Add cream of mushroom soup, sour cream, mushrooms, wine, salt and pepper. Simmer over low heat for 5 minutes. Combine sauce with chicken in a 3 quart casserole dish. Top with almonds or cashews and bake, uncovered, for 30 minutes at 350⁰, or until bubbly. Serve as is, or over rice. Especially good if served in patty shells.

Tish Nisbet (Mrs. Wyck)

A versatile dish that's good and easy - can be served so many different ways!

CHICKEN AND RICE AU VIN

Yield: 4 servings

4 chicken breast halves
Salt
Freshly ground pepper
2 Tablespoons butter
½ cup chopped onion
1 teaspoon chopped garlic
½ pound fresh mushrooms, sliced,
    or 1 (8 ounce) can mushrooms,
    sliced and drained

1 bay leaf
½ cup dry white wine
½ teaspoon dried thyme leaves
1 cup Uncle Ben's Converted Rice,
    uncooked
1 cup chicken broth

Season chicken with salt and pepper. Melt butter in a skillet and add chicken, flesh side down. Cook about 5 minutes and turn. Add onion, garlic, mushrooms and bay leaf. Cook 5 minutes more. Add remaining ingredients, being careful not to put rice on top of chicken. Cover and cook until liquid is absorbed and rice is tender, about 15 minutes.

Suzanne Hamilton (Mrs. Don F.)

For variety, substitute fresh or dried rosemary for the thyme, and dry red wine for the white.

CHICKEN BREASTS WITH MUSHROOM SAUCE

Oven: 350°
Yield: 8 servings

8 whole chicken breasts, skinned and boned
Sauterne wine
Margarine or butter
2 (10¾ ounce) cans cream of mushroom soup

¼ cup sherry
1 cup sour cream
½ teaspoon salt
⅛ teaspoon pepper
⅛ teaspoon garlic powder
10 large fresh mushrooms, sliced

Simmer chicken breasts in ½ inch of sauterne wine for 1 hour. Drain breasts and brown in margarine or butter. Mix mushroom soup, sherry, sour cream, salt, pepper and garlic powder for sauce. Heat. Put breasts in 9 x 13 pyrex dish and cover with sauce. Sauté sliced mushrooms in butter and place on top of breasts and sauce. Heat at 350° until bubbly.

Cindy Feltus (Mrs. Greg)

May be made a day ahead. Great served with wild rice.

CHICKEN TETRAZINNI

Oven: 350°
Yield: 12 to 16 servings

4 pounds of chicken
2 (13½ ounce) cans chicken broth
1 cup diced celery
Salt
Pepper
2 green peppers, diced
2 onions, diced
20 ounces vermicelli

20 ounces sharp Cheddar cheese, grated
2 (10¾ ounce) cans cream of mushroom soup
1 (2 ounce) can sliced mushrooms, drained
4 to 6 ounces pimientos, drained and chopped

Place chicken in a large pot and cover with 2 cans of chicken broth and water. Add 1 cup diced celery and salt and pepper. Cook. Skin, bone and cut into chunks. Bring chicken broth back to a boil with green peppers and onions. Cook vermicelli in broth. Drain but save 2 cups of the liquid to put back in a large bowl. Add vermicelli, celery, peppers, onions, grated cheese, mushroom soup and mushrooms to the 2 cups of broth. Stir until cheese is melted into the mixture. Add chicken chunks and pimiento. Bake at 350°, uncovered, for 30 to 45 minutes.

Jann Scott (Mrs. Bob)

CHICKEN-WILD RICE CASSEROLE

Oven: 350°
Yield: 8 to 10 servings

4 to 6 chicken breast halves
1 cup water
1 cup sherry
1½ teaspoons salt
Pepper to taste
½ teaspoon curry powder
1 medium onion, sliced
2 ribs celery, sliced
12 ounces fresh mushrooms, sliced

½ stick butter
1 (6 ounce) package Uncle Ben's
    long grain and wild rice with
    seasonings
1 cup sour cream
1 (10¾ ounce) can cream of
    chicken soup
½ cup slivered almonds

Boil chicken in water seasoned with sherry, salt, pepper, curry powder, onion and celery. Cover and bring to a boil. Reduce heat and simmer for at least 1 hour. Remove from heat and strain, reserving broth. Bone and skin the chicken breasts and cut meat into bite-sized pieces. Sauté mushrooms in butter. Cook rice according to the directions on the package, using the reserved broth as part of the liquid for cooking rice. Combine chicken, mushrooms and rice in a 3 quart casserole. Add sour cream and cream of chicken soup. Mix well. Top with slivered almonds. Bake, covered, for 1 hour at 350°. Uncover for the last 15 minutes of cooking.

Beth Jackson (Mrs. Douglas W.)

May be completely prepared and frozen ahead of time.

CHICKEN AND RICE DELUXE

Oven: 350°
Yield: 6 to 8 servings

2 Tablespoons butter
2 Tablespoons chopped green
    pepper
2 Tablespoons chopped onion
2 cups cooked chicken, cut into
    bite-sized pieces.
1 (6 ounce) package wild rice, or
    long grain and wild rice, cooked
½ cup mayonnaise

1 (16 ounce) can French style green
    beans, drained
1 (10¾ ounce) can cream of celery
    soup
½ cup sliced water chestnuts
¼ teaspoon salt
Pepper to taste
Juice of 1 lemon (Optional)
1 cup grated Cheddar cheese

Sauté green pepper and onion in 2 Tablespoons butter. Combine all ingredients and place in a greased 2 quart casserole dish. Bake at 350°, uncovered, for 25 to 30 minutes. Top with grated cheese and cook 5 more minutes or until cheese is melted.

Robin Lawrence (Mrs. Scott)

The wild rice gives this dish an unusual taste!

CHICKEN OLÉ
(Must be prepared 1 day in advance)

Oven: 400°
Yield: 8 servings

8 chicken breast halves, boned and skinned
1 (7 ounce) can diced green chilies, drained
¼ pound Monterey Jack cheese, cut into 8 strips
½ cup dry bread crumbs

¼ cup grated Parmesan cheese
1 Tablespoon chili powder
½ teaspoon salt
¼ teaspoon cumin
¼ teaspoon pepper
6 Tablespoons butter, melted

Tomato sauce
1 (15 ounce) can tomato sauce
½ teaspoon cumin
½ cup sliced green onions

Salt to taste
Pepper to taste
Pepper sauce to taste

Pound chicken to ¼ inch thickness. Place chilies and a strip of cheese in the center of each breast. Roll up and tuck ends under. Combine bread crumbs, Parmesan cheese, chili powder, salt, cumin and pepper. Dip each stuffed breast in 6 Tablespoons melted butter and roll in crumb mixture. Place seam side down in an oblong 7 x 11 baking dish. Drizzle with melted butter. Cover and refrigerate overnight. Bake, uncovered, at 400° until done (30 to 45 minutes). To make tomato sauce, combine all ingredients in a saucepan and heat thoroughly. Serve with chicken breasts.

Betty Biggadike Scroggin (Mrs. Carroll)
Palos Verdes, California

TAMALE PIE

Oven: 300°
Yield: 6 to 8 servings

1 dozen tamales, shucked
1 (3 pound) chicken, boiled, boned and shredded
1 onion, chopped
1 clove garlic, minced
½ green pepper, chopped
Olive oil or vegetable oil

1 (16 ounce) can tomato sauce
1 (4 ounce) can chopped ripe olives, drained
2 Tablespoons chili powder
1 (14 ounce) can cream style corn
½ pound Cheddar cheese, grated

Line a 9 x 13 casserole dish with tamales. Cover with a layer of chicken. Sauté onion, garlic and pepper in oil and add to combined tomato sauce, olives, corn and chili powder. Pour sauce over chicken and top with cheese. Bake at 300° for 1 hour or until cheese is bubbly.

Norma C. Rauch

ENTOMATADOS
(SOUR CREAM CHICKEN ENCHILADAS)

Oven: 350°
Yield: 8 servings

2 cups cooked, chopped chicken
1 large onion, chopped
4 cloves garlic, minced
2 teaspoons basil or oregano
1 (15 ounce) can tomato sauce or
   red enchilada sauce
½ cup chicken broth

Salt to taste
Pepper to taste
1 dozen corn tortillas
½ cup cooking oil
1 pound Monterey Jack cheese,
   grated
1 pint sour cream
1 avocado, sliced

Boil chicken and reserve broth. Chop chicken. Sauté onion, garlic and spices in scant amount of cooking oil. Heat tomato or enchilada sauce with ½ cup chicken broth. Add onion mixture. Add salt and pepper. Fry tortillas lightly in oil, just to soften. Roll chicken in tortillas. Cover with sauce, cheese, sour cream and avocado. Bake, covered, for 20 minutes at 350°. Tortillas and chicken can be layered in a 9 x 13 casserole dish and baked.

Edwynne M. Horner (Mrs. Lawson D.)
West Helena, Arkansas

CHICKEN RO-TEL

Oven: 300° to 350°
Yield: 16 to 20 servings

1 (5 pound) hen
2 large green peppers, chopped
2 large onions, chopped
1½ sticks margarine
1 (7 ounce) package vermicelli
1 (10 ounce) can Ro-Tel tomatoes

2 Tablespoons Worcestershire sauce
1 (17 ounce) can tiny English peas,
   drained
1 (8 ounce) can mushrooms, drained
2 pounds Velveeta cheese, cut up
Salt to taste
Pepper to taste

Season and bake hen in enough water so that you will have ½ to 1 quart broth in which to cook vermicelli. Cook hen according to size. Chop and sauté green pepper and onions in margarine. Cook vermicelli in chicken broth. When almost done, add Ro-Tel tomatoes (mashed) but only ½ the juice. Add Worcestershire sauce, sautéed onions and peppers. Cool together until it begins to thicken. Add peas, mushrooms and cheese. When cheese has melted, add chicken that has been cut to desired size. Season to taste with salt and pepper. Cook, uncovered, in 2 (2½ quart) casserole dishes at 300° to 350° until bubbly.

Miriam F. Hasson (Mrs. Leonard)

Freezes beautifully.

CHICKEN CHILI CASSEROLE

Oven: 350°
Yield: 12 servings

1 Tablespoon oil, preferably olive oil

1 (8 ounce) package small egg noodles

1 large onion, chopped

1 green pepper, chopped

3 Tablespoons butter or margarine

3 (10¾ ounce) cans cream of mushroom soup

1 (4 ounce) jar pimientos, chopped and drained

2 (4 ounce) cans green chilies, chopped and drained

1 jalapeño pepper, chopped

2 chicken fryers, cooked and cut into large, bite-sized pieces (5 to 6 cups)

Salt to taste

Pepper to taste

1½ pounds sharp Cheddar cheese, grated (4 to 5 cups)

Bring 3 quarts water to boil. Add oil and noodles. Return to boil. Cook, uncovered, for 2 minutes. Drain, rinse and set aside to cool. Sauté onions and green pepper in butter. Add soup, pimientos, green chilies and jalapeño pepper. In a buttered 4 quart casserole dish, layer half of the ingredients as follows: noodles, chicken, salt, pepper, soup mixture and cheese. Repeat. Bake for 45 minutes, uncovered, at 350º. Add grated cheese on top to serve.

Mrs. Morgan Jones
Abilene, Texas

BRUNSWICK STEW

Yield: 6 servings

1 (3 pound) chicken

3 cups water

1½ teaspoons salt

1 (16 ounce) can new potatoes, drained, or fresh new potatoes

1¾ cups canned lima beans, drained

1¾ cups tomato sauce

⅔ cup chopped onion

1¾ cups corn

1 teaspoon sugar

Salt to taste

⅛ teaspoon pepper

⅛ teaspoon oregano

⅛ teaspoon poultry seasoning

Simmer chicken in salted water until tender. Drain broth and set aside. Cut meat from bones. Skim fat from broth. Boil broth to concentrate it to about 2 cups. If using fresh new potatoes, add to broth and simmer for 10 minutes. Add lima beans, tomato sauce and onion. (Add canned new potatoes with other canned vegetables). Cook 20 minutes longer. Add chicken, corn and seasonings. Cook 15 to 20 minutes longer.

Beth Bridgforth (Mrs. John D.)
Forrest City, Arkansas

CHICKEN CHILI SPAGHETTI

Oven: 350°
Yield: 8 to 10 servings

1 (4 to 5 pound) hen, or 2 fryers
2 large onions, chopped
1 cup chopped celery
1 clove garlic, minced
2 (4 ounce) cans sliced mushrooms, drained
Margarine
2 (15 ounce) cans whole tomatoes

1 or 2 (15 ounce) bricks of chili
Ripe olives (Optional)
1 (2¼ ounce) package slivered almonds
1 (12 ounce) package vermicelli
Salt to taste
Pepper to taste
Cheddar cheese, grated

Cook chicken until tender. Reserve broth. Sauté onion, celery, garlic and mushrooms in margarine. Add tomatoes. Add chili bricks, olives and almonds. Heat broth and cook spaghetti in broth. Add remaining ingredients, chicken last. If too dry to mix, add more broth. Salt and pepper to taste. Place in a 3 quart casserole and top with grated cheese. Bake, uncovered, at 350⁰ or until bubbly.

Mrs. Jo Ann Sandlin
Fayetteville, Arkansas

EASY CHICKEN SPAGHETTI

Oven: 350°
Yield: 6 to 8 servings

1 (4 pound) hen (approximately 4 cups cubed chicken)
4 Tablespoons butter
½ cup chopped celery
½ green pepper, chopped
1 onion, chopped
1 (4 ounce) can mushrooms, sliced and drained

2 (10¾ ounce) cans cream of mushroom soup
1 cup milk
½ pound yellow cheese, grated
7 ounces vermicelli, cooked
Salt to taste
Pepper to taste
Tabasco to taste

Boil hen in seasoned water until done. Cut into bite-sized pieces. Sauté onion, celery and green pepper in butter. Mix soup with milk and add to sautéed ingredients. Add mushrooms. Add cheese and stir until melted. Add chicken, vermicelli, salt, pepper and Tabasco. Pour into a buttered 2 quart casserole and bake, uncovered, for 35 minutes at 350⁰.

Ann Cashion (Mrs. Ted)

Quick and easy. Perfect for the working woman who likes to entertain but doesn't have all day to spend in the kitchen. Freezes beautifully.

LAKE VILLAGE CHICKEN SPAGHETTI

Oven: 350°
Yield: 10 to 12 servings

1 hen
1 cup chopped green pepper
1 cup chopped celery
1 large onion, chopped
1 stick margarine
1 (16 ounce) can tomatoes
1 (10¾ ounce) can cream of
   mushroom soup
2½ Tablespoons lemon juice
2 Tablespoons Worcestershire
   sauce
2 teaspoons chili powder
1 bay leaf

1 teaspoon paprika
½ teaspoon garlic salt
1 teaspoon salt
½ teaspoon black pepper
1 (4 ounce) can mushrooms,
   undrained
1 pint chicken broth
¼ cup sliced black olives
¼ cup sliced pimiento
¼ cup sliced almonds
4 ounces spaghetti (or more if
   desired), cooked
Sharp Cheddar cheese, grated

Cook hen and reserve broth. Sauté green pepper, celery and onion in margarine. Add next 10 ingredients and stir. Add the juice from the can of mushrooms and 1 pint of chicken broth. (Add water if there is not enough broth.) Cook for 45 minutes. Add mushrooms, olives, pimientos, almonds and cut up chicken. Stir into cooked spaghetti and place in a 3 quart casserole. Cover with grated cheese. Bake, covered, at 350⁰ for 30 minutes or until bubbly.

Mrs. Gaither C. Johnston
Hot Springs, Arkansas

JULIE'S 15 MINUTE CHICKEN

Yield: 6 servings

2 chicken breasts, skinned, boned
   and cut into finger-sized pieces
   about 3 inches long
¼ cup flour
¼ cup butter
Salt to taste
Freshly cracked white pepper to
   taste

1 Tablespoon fresh rosemary,
   crushed or ¼ teaspoon dried
   rosemary
3 Tablespoons raspberry vinegar,
   lemon or orange juice, sherry, or
   red or white wine
1 Tablespoon finely chopped fresh
   parsley

Roll chicken pieces, a few at a time, in the flour. Pat off excess. In a large skillet, melt butter until it sizzles. Add chicken and toss or stir over high heat for 3 to 5 minutes or until chicken is no longer pink. Stir in salt, pepper and rosemary. Add vinegar or alternative ingredient to deglaze the pan. Sprinkle parsley on top.

Mrs. Fletcher Long, Jr.
Forrest City, Arkansas

CHICKEN SPECTACULAR

Oven: 350°
Yield: 12 to 14 servings

1 (5 ounce) package fine egg
  noodles
1 (10¾ ounce) can cream of
  chicken soup
1 (10¾ ounce) can cream of
  mushroom soup
1 (5⅓ ounce) can Pet milk
1 cup shredded cheese

3 cups cooked, diced chicken
  breasts
1 cup diced celery
¼ cup diced pimiento
½ cup diced green pepper
4 dashes Tabasco
1 teaspoon salt
Pepper to taste
1 cup sliced almonds

Cook noodles in chicken broth (from cooking chicken). Boil for 8 minutes. Drain. Combine all remaining ingredients except almonds. Salt and pepper to taste and place in a buttered 3 quart casserole dish. Top with almonds. Bake, uncovered, at 350⁰ for 45 minutes. Extra shredded cheese may be added to top.

Carrie Dickinson (Mrs. Tyndall)

Try adding either sherry or curry to make casserole even more interesting!

CASHEW CHICKEN

Yield: 4 to 6 servings

2 pounds boneless chicken breasts
Flour
4 eggs, beaten
1 cup milk

Salt to taste
Pepper to taste
Peanut oil

Sauce
4 cups water
8 chicken bouillon cubes
2 Tablespoons cornstarch
1 teaspoon sugar

2 teaspoons oyster flavor sauce, or
  to taste
1 (6 ounce) can cashew nuts
1 cup chopped green onions

Cut chicken in bite-sized pieces. Flour well. Let stand in flour for 15 minutes. Mix eggs, milk, salt and pepper. Remove chicken from flour and place in egg mixture for 10 minutes. Roll in flour and deep fry in oil (350⁰ to 400⁰). Chicken will cook in about 15 minutes. Chicken may be kept warm in a covered pan in a warm oven. For sauce, boil water and add bouillon cubes. When bouillon cubes are dissolved, remove ½ cup bouillon broth and mix with cornstarch until smooth. Pour back into broth and add remaining ingredients. Let thicken over low heat. Pour sauce over chicken and top with cashews and onions. Serve with rice and soy sauce.

Mary Powell

CHICKEN AND SPINACH LASAGNE

Oven: 350°
Yield: 10 to 12 servings

8 to 10 chicken breast halves
6 Tablespoons butter
8 Tablespoons flour
1½ cups buttermilk
1 cup milk (or Half and Half)
Salt to taste
Pepper to taste
3 (10 ounce) packages frozen
   chopped spinach, thawed and
   drained
4 to 5 ounces Ricotta cheese

6 ounces cream cheese, softened
8 ounces Jarlsberg cheese, grated
2½ cups dry white wine
Lemon pepper to taste
Dash or two cayenne pepper
Salt to taste
Pepper to taste
Nutmeg to taste
¾ package (16 ounce) lasagne
   noodles, uncooked
½ cup grated Parmesan cheese

Place chicken breast halves in a small stockpot with enough water to cover. Simmer and cook for 15 to 20 minutes. Make a Béchamel sauce by melting butter in saucepan. Stir in flour to form a stiff paste, then add buttermilk, milk, salt and pepper to taste. Stir until thick. Cook chicken and cut into small pieces. In a large bowl, combine chicken, spinach, cheeses and a small amount of wine to moisten. Season with lemon pepper, a dash or two of cayenne pepper, salt, pepper and nutmeg to taste. Pour a small amount of Bechamel sauce into a 9 x 13 baking dish or a lasagne dish. Add a layer of UNCOOKED lasagne noodles. Sprinkle liberally with white wine. Add layer of chicken mixture filling, then sauce, then noodles, wine, and top with more filling. End with sauce. Sprinkle with ½ cup Parmesan cheese. Bake, uncovered, at 350⁰ for 1 hour.

Melinda Morse

A delicious and unusual way to serve lasagne.

FRENCH ROAST CHICKEN

Oven: 400°

1 (3 to 4 pound) chicken
2 ounces butter
½ teaspoon tarragon

½ teaspoon rosemary
½ pint chicken broth

Preheat oven to 400⁰. Rub the chicken well with butter. Put 1 ounce of butter inside the chicken with the herbs and seasonings. Set in a roasting pan with half the chicken broth. Roast for 1 hour to 1 hour and 15 minutes. Baste and turn frequently. The chicken should be well browned on all sides. Add remaining chicken broth and reduce. Adjust seasonings and serve with chicken.

CHINESE VELVET CHICKEN

Yield: 8 servings

3 whole chicken breasts, boned
2 egg whites
2 Tablespoons cornstarch
1 teaspoon sugar
½ teaspoon salt
½ teaspoon Accent
¼ teaspoon pepper
2 Tablespoons sherry

Flour
½ cup oil
½ pound fresh mushrooms
¼ cup water
1 cup chicken broth
1 (6 ounce) package frozen snow
  peas
½ cup water chestnuts

Partially freeze chicken. Slice lengthwise (⅛ inch). Make batter by mixing egg whites, cornstarch, sugar, salt, Accent, pepper and sherry. Dredge chicken in flour. Shake off excess. Dip in batter. Heat oil. Place chicken in oil but do not let pieces touch. Sauté for 3 to 4 minutes, stirring constantly. Drain on paper towels. Pour off all but 3 Tablespoons oil. Add mushrooms. Sauté for 5 minutes. Remove and add ¼ cup water. Stir to loosen particles on bottom of skillet. Combine 1 Tablespoon cornstarch and chicken broth. Add to skillet and boil. Add snow peas, water chestnuts, chicken and mushrooms. Heat. Serve immediately.

Susan Owens (Mrs. Robert W.)

BARBECUED HERB CHICKEN

Yield: 6 servings

¼ pound margarine
1 Tablespoon minced parsley
¼ teaspoon tarragon
½ teaspoon marjoram
3 halved broiler chickens, or 6
  chicken breast halves

½ cup vegetable oil
1 cup dry white wine
¼ cup Chinese soy sauce
1 garlic clove, crushed
¼ teaspoon salt

Make a mixture of the margarine, parsley, tarragon and marjoram. Using a dull knife, lift the skin from the breast meat of the halved chickens and insert the blend of margarine and seasonings. Spread the blend under the skin as widely as possible, making sure the skin is not so detached it will come off when the chicken is turned on the grill. Make a marinade of the oil, wine, soy sauce, crushed garlic clove and salt. Let chicken stand in marinade overnight, or at least several hours. Turn chicken once during this period. Grill chicken halves over glowing coals on a greased rack. Turn halves occasionally while basting with marinade until golden brown, which should take about ½ hour.

Wanda C. Shaw

The longer the chicken marinates, the better. Also, try using chicken breast halves. It's just as good.

DADDY'S BARBECUED CHICKEN

Yield: 6 to 8 servings

Sauce

Juice of 6 lemons
6 teaspoons Worcestershire sauce
1 teaspoon Tabasco
1 teaspoon pepper
1 Tablespoon celery salt

1 Tablespoon salt
1 Tablespoon garlic salt
2 Tablespoons honey
½ pound butter (NOT margarine)

6 to 8 chicken halves, or 12 to 14
  chicken breasts

Mix all sauce ingredients together and simmer for 30 minutes. Place chicken on gas or charcoal grill and cook over low heat. Baste and turn chicken frequently until done.

Sandy Jones (Mrs. Eugene M.)

Different because the barbecue sauce has a non-tomato base. Unused sauce stores well in refrigerator.

OVEN BARBECUED CHICKEN

Oven: 350°
Yield: 4 to 6 servings

1 chicken fryer, cut up
Salt

Cracked pepper
Lawry's garlic salt

Sauce

2 Tablespoons butter
4 Tablespoons water
1 Tablespoon white vinegar
3 Tablespoons ketchup
3 Tablespoons light brown sugar

2 Tablespoons Worcestershire
  sauce
1 Tablespoon lemon juice, freshly
  squeezed
1 teaspoon chili powder
1 teaspoon prepared mustard

Preheat oven to 350°. Grease a 9 x 13 baking dish with butter. Wash and pat dry chicken. Place pieces in a greased dish, skin side down. Season with salt, cracked pepper and garlic salt. Turn chicken and repeat seasoning. Make sauce by melting butter over low heat in a medium-sized pan. Add remaining ingredients and stir over low heat until sauce comes to a boil. Pour sauce over chicken, making sure each piece is coated. Bake, uncovered, at 350° for 1 hour. Baste each piece every 15 minutes. For the second hour of baking, cover the pan with foil but do not seal.

Carol Hodges (Mrs. Thomas L.)

HOT CHICKEN SALAD

Oven: 450°
Yield: 8 servings

3 cups cooked, diced chicken
1½ cups diced celery
Salt to taste
Pepper to taste
2 Tablespoons finely diced onion
1 cup chopped almonds
1 cup Hellmann's mayonnaise
2 Tablespoons fresh lemon juice
1 Tablespoon grated lemon rind

1 (8 ounce) can water chestnuts,
    sliced and drained
1 (8 ounce) can black olives, diced
    and drained
1 cup whole white seedless grapes
½ cup capers (Optional)
1 cup grated Cheddar cheese
Potato chips, crushed (Optional)

Combine all ingredients except cheese in a 7 x 12 casserole dish. Sprinkle cheese on top with crushed potato chips, if desired. Bake at 450⁰, uncovered, for 15 minutes

Helen McLarty Peck (Mrs. George)

This is also good served as a cold chicken salad.

CHICKEN PIE

Oven: 350°
Yield: 6 to 8 servings

1 (11 ounce) package pie crust mix
2 cups cooked chicken, cut into
    bite-sized pieces
2 to 3 ribs celery, chopped
2 carrots, sliced
1 medium onion, chopped
1 teaspoon salt
Pepper to taste

1 (8½ ounce) can green peas,
    drained
1 (10¾ ounce) can cream of
    chicken soup
¾ cup chicken broth
1 (4 ounce) jar pimiento, drained
    and chopped

Mix pie crust according to package directions. Roll out half and cover the bottom of a 1½ or 2 quart casserole dish. Cook chicken with the celery, carrots, onions, salt and pepper. Drain. Add peas and place chicken and vegetables in the bottom of the casserole over crust. Mix broth and chicken soup with pimiento and pour over chicken and vegetables. Roll out remainder of crust and cover the top with dough. Pierce the dough to let out steam during cooking. Bake according to crust recipe directions. If you make your own crust, bake at 350⁰ until crust top is golden brown.

Allison Denman Holland

A super way to use leftover chicken or turkey and easy to prepare. Recipe can be frozen and the crust browned at a later date.

SWISS CHICKEN QUICHE

Oven: 425°
Yield: 6 to 8 servings

1 (9 inch) pastry shell, unbaked
1 cup shredded Swiss cheese
2 Tablespoons flour
1 Tablespoon Wyler's chicken
  bouillon
2 cups cooked, cubed chicken

1 cup milk
3 eggs, well-beaten
¼ cup chopped onion
2 Tablespoons chopped green
  pepper
2 Tablespoons chopped pimiento

Preheat oven to 425°. Bake pastry shell for 8 minutes. Remove from oven. Reduce oven to 350°. In a medium bowl, toss cheese with flour and bouillon. Add remaining ingredients. Mix well. Pour into prepared shell. Bake 40 to 45 minutes or until set. Let stand 10 minutes before serving.

Pam Skokos (Mrs. Ted)

A nice luncheon dish served with a tossed green salad.

SAVORY SOUR CREAM CORNISH HENS

Oven: 350°
Yield: 4 servings

2 (1½ pound) Cornish hens, split
  lengthwise by butcher
Garlic powder
Salt
Pepper
1 medium to small onion, chopped

8 ounces fresh mushrooms, sliced
1 stick butter or margarine, melted
½ cup dry white wine
½ to 1 teaspoon salt
½ cup sour cream
1 teaspoon dry basil

Generously sprinkle hens with garlic powder, salt and pepper. Place cut side down in a lightly greased 9 x 13 baking dish. Cover with foil and bake in a preheated 350° oven for 30 minutes. Remove foil and bake an additional 30 minutes. Sauté onions and sliced mushrooms in 1 stick butter over medium heat for 5 minutes. Stir in wine and ½ to 1 teaspoon salt, according to taste. Pour mixture over hens and bake an additional 30 minutes or until juices run clear. Place hens on a serving platter, reserving pan juices. Blend in sour cream with a wire whisk. Add basil. Pour over hens. Garnish with fresh parsley and whole fresh mushrooms.

Martha Laurens Taylor

BRANDY CORNISH HENS

Oven: 375°
Yield: 2 servings

2 Cornish hens	Pepper to taste
⅓ cup fresh parsley, finely chopped	½ cup butter
½ teaspoon salt	½ cup red currant jelly
	½ cup brandy

Rinse hens in cold water and pat dry. Combine parsley, salt, pepper and ¼ cup butter. Mix well. Stuff cavity of hens with parsley mixture and secure well. Place hens in a 9 x 9 pan breast side up. Rub hens with ¼ cup butter. Bake for 30 minutes at 375°. In a small saucepan, combine jelly and brandy. Cook over low heat until jelly melts. Pour over hens and cook an additional 30 minutes. Baste frequently.

Marian Goff (Mrs. Robert M.)

Recipe can easily be doubled or tripled. For a different flare, try using chicken breasts instead of hens.

CORNISH HENS WITH TOMATOES

Oven: 400°
Yield: 4 servings

2 Cornish hens	½ pound fresh mushrooms, sliced
¼ teaspoon salt	½ cup dry white wine
¼ teaspoon garlic salt	2 tomatoes, peeled, seeded and cubed
⅛ teaspoon pepper	⅓ cup sour cream
3 Tablespoons butter	1 Tablespoon flour
1 medium onion, chopped	

Cut the Cornish hens into halves, lengthwise. Sprinkle lightly with salt, garlic salt and pepper. Arrange in a 9 x 13 baking dish. Bake, uncovered, in a 400° oven for 35 minutes. Cover and bake 15 more minutes or until done. Melt butter in a frying pan. Add onion and mushrooms to the butter and cook for about 5 minutes. Remove vegetables from heat. Add wine and tomatoes. Pour this mixture over the cooked hens. Reduce oven temperature to 350° and continue cooking hens and vegetables, uncovered, for 15 more minutes. Remove from oven and place hens on a warm serving platter. Blend sour cream and flour until smooth. Stir into pan juices and vegetables. Cook this mixture on top of the stove until it boils and thickens. Serve sauce over the hens.

Gayle Leonard (Mrs. Donald)

SEASONED TURKEY

Oven: 325°

1 turkey (any size)
2 Tablespoons oil
2 Tablespoons salt
1 teaspoon pepper

1 teaspoon paprika
1 Tablespoon garlic powder
Water

Wash turkey and pat dry. Combine oil, salt, pepper, paprika and garlic powder. Make a paste by adding water to a spreading consistency. Spread over inside and outside of turkey. Place turkey on a rack in a shallow pan. Bake at 325⁰ for 20 minutes per pound.

Kem Embrey Aburrow (Mrs. Harry J.)

May easily be doubled if an extra large turkey is used.

BAKED TURKEY AND GIBLET GRAVY
(Must be prepared ahead)

Oven: 300° to 350°

1 turkey (hen or Tom)
Salt
Pepper

Pam
Cheesecloth, turkey size
½ pound melted butter

Giblet Gravy
1 cup flour
Turkey neck, liver and gizzard
Broth

Turkey drippings
Salt
Pepper

Thaw turkey in refrigerator for several days or in a large grocery sack for 24 hours. Remove liver, gizzard and neck from insides. Salt and pepper the bird, inside and out. Spray roasting pan with Pam and line the bottom with a large piece of heavy duty foil. Dip cheesecloth in melted butter and wrap around turkey to cover completely. Cook at 300⁰ to 350⁰ for approximately 25 minutes per pound. Baste turkey often with butter while cooking until it is gone, then baste with pan drippings. Turkey is done when leg moves easily.

To make gravy, put flour in pie pan. Heat oven to 350⁰. Brown flour, watching it carefully. Shake and stir the pan often. Cook flour. Wrap in waxed paper and store in a jar until ready to use. Boil turkey neck, liver and gizzard in water to cover for approximately 15 minutes. Save broth. In a food processor with plastic blade or in a bowl, put flour and enough turkey drippings to make a paste. Put into a skillet and add drippings and broth. Add chopped liver and gizzard if desired. Cook until thick and season with salt and pepper.

Debby Bransford Coates (Mrs. Wayne)

CORN BREAD TURKEY DRESSING

Oven: 350°
Yield: 10 to 12 servings

1 recipe your favorite corn bread (9 inch skillet)
1 pound chicken necks or wings
1 medium onion, quartered
2 ribs celery
Salt
Peppercorns
2 bunches green onions, chopped
2 cups chopped celery, leaves and all
4 Tablespoons butter
¼ teaspoon freshly ground black pepper
¼ teaspoon white pepper
¼ teaspoon cayenne pepper
½ teaspoon paprika
1 (8 ounce) bag Pepperidge Farm Herb Stuffing mix
3 eggs, lightly beaten
Dry parsley
Sage to taste
Thyme to taste
Basil to taste
Dry mustard to taste
Garlic salt to taste
Lemon juice to taste
Worcestershire sauce
Cavender's Greek Seasoning

Bake corn bread and cool. Cook necks or wings with onion, celery, salt and peppercorns in water to cover for 30 minutes. Strain and reserve broth. Sauté green onions and celery in butter until tender. Crumble corn bread into a large bowl. Add sautéed vegetables, peppers, paprika and bag of stuffing mix. Add enough broth to soften and mix well. Add 3 eggs and mix. All of the other various spices should be added to taste, but start with a dash of each. Mix all together well. Bake, uncovered, at 350° for 1 hour in a greased 9 x 13 casserole.

Debby Bransford Coates (Mrs. Wayne)

Add a jar of drained raw oysters just before baking for oyster dressing.

SMOKED TURKEY
(Must be prepared in advance)

1 (10 to 15 pound) turkey
Kosher salt
Coca-cola
White wine
Vinegar

Rub turkey generously with salt, inside and out. Put in a plastic bag. Secure and refrigerate for 5 days. Wash thoroughly inside and out to remove all the salt. Prepare smoker. Be sure and use damp hickory chips on fire. In drip pan put ½ water and ½ a mixture of equal parts of coca-cola, wine and vinegar. Put turkey on rack and baste with the mixture of equal parts of coke, wine and vinegar. Pour some of the mixture in the cavity of the turkey. Rebaste every 1 to 2 hours and check the fire. Cook for 8 to 12 hours.

Sharon Bale (Mrs. John H., Jr.)

MEATS

Many of the petty dissatisfactions which guests bring to the table often turn out to be only a craving for meat.

ELEGANT FILET MIGNON

Yield: 4 servings

4 thick filets mignon
2 Tablespoons butter
Salt to taste
Pepper to taste
½ cup Arrow coffee flavored
  brandy

1 large clove garlic, minced
½ pound fresh mushrooms, sliced
1 (6 ounce) jar Bearnaise sauce
1 Tablespoon lemon juice
1 Tablespoon finely minced parsley

In a large skillet, cook filets in butter 4 or 5 minutes per side over medium high heat. Sprinkle with salt and pepper. Pour ¼ cup brandy over the steaks. IGNITE CAREFULLY. When flame dies, remove steaks to heated serving platter. Add garlic and mushrooms to drippings in pan. Cook until softened. Stir in remaining ¼ cup brandy, Béarnaise sauce and lemon juice. Heat through but do not boil. Spoon sauce over steaks and garnish with parsley.

Lynn Monk (Mrs. James W.)

BEEF TENDERLOIN IN CREAM AND MUSHROOM SAUCE

Yield: 6 servings

⅔ pound fresh mushrooms, sliced
4 Tablespoons minced green onions
4 Tablespoons butter
½ teaspoon salt
⅛ teaspoon freshly ground pepper
2½ to 3 pounds tenderloin of beef,
  cut in ½ inch slices
4 Tablespoons butter
⅓ cup Madeira wine

¾ cup beef bouillon
1¼ cups whipping cream
2¼ teaspoons cornstarch
Salt
Pepper
2 Tablespoons butter
Parsley
Cooked rice or noodles

Sauté mushrooms and green onions in 4 Tablespoons butter for 5 minutes until lightly browned. Season with salt and pepper and set aside. Heat 4 Tablespoons butter in a large skillet until foamy. When foam begins to subside, sauté beef on both sides until brown and medium rare. Set beef aside and keep warm. Add wine and bouillon to pan and boil rapidly, scraping the pan and reducing juices to ⅓ cup. Combine cornstarch and cream. Whisk in the cream and cornstarch mixture and simmer briefly. Add mushrooms and simmer 1 minute longer. Add salt and pepper to taste. Add beef and any collected juices to cream sauce and baste beef with sauce. Cover and heat on very low heat for 3 to 4 minutes. Add 2 Tablespoons of butter, a little at a time, and blend well. Garnish with parsley and serve over rice or noodles.

IMPERIAL TENDERLOIN

Oven: 450°
Yield: 8 servings

1 tenderloin of beef
¼ cup olive oil
1 clove garlic
1 Tablespoon Worcestershire sauce
¼ pound Bleu cheese
¼ pound butter

1 pound mushroom caps
2 Tablespoons butter
1 teaspoon onion salt
½ teaspoon caraway seeds
Pepper to taste

Trim fat from tenderloin, brush with olive oil and roast at 450° for 30 minutes or until meat thermometer registers 140°. Meanwhile, mash garlic into Worcestershire sauce and combine with Bleu cheese and ¼ pound of butter. Spread over the top of the cooked tenderloin. Brown mushrooms in 2 Tablespoons of butter for 5 minutes. Toss with onion salt, caraway seeds and pepper. Serve immediately with tenderloin.

Deirdre Newcomb

MARINATED TENDERLOIN

(Must be prepared in advance)

Oven: 450°
Yield: 6 to 10 servings

2 carrots, sliced
2 onions, sliced
10 black peppercorns
1 whole clove
2 bay leaves
Fresh parsley
¼ teaspoon thyme
4 garlic buds

½ cup wine vinegar, red or white
2 Tablespoons oil
2 shallots, chopped
2 Tablespoons lemon juice
2 cups sherry
1 Tablespoon Worcestershire sauce
1 (3 to 5 pound) tenderloin of beef
Butter

Combine the first 14 ingredients. Marinate meat in refrigerator for 24 hours. Drain, dot with butter and roast at 450° for 30 to 45 minutes depending on degree of doneness desired.

Mandy Dillard (Mrs. William, II)

"For its merit, I will knight it and make it sir-loin!"
CHARLES II OF ENGLAND
on being told that a piece of beef which particularly pleased him was called the loin.
1630-1685

BEEF WELLINGTON

(Must be prepared day before or morning of serving)

Oven: 425°
Yield: 10 servings

**1 (5 pound) filet of beef, well
trimmed**

Forcemeat

¼ **cup chopped onion**
½ **cup chopped pecans**
¼ **cup butter**
¼ **pound fresh mushrooms,
chopped**
¼ **cup cognac**
½ **pound ground chuck**
½ **pound ground pork**
1 egg, lightly beaten

¼ **cup whipping cream**
¼ **cup chopped parsley**
1 teaspoon salt
¼ **teaspoon basil**
¼ **teaspoon thyme**
¼ **teaspoon rosemary**
⅛ **teaspoon allspice**
⅛ **teaspoon pepper**

Pastry

½ **pound butter**
⅔ **cup shortening, chilled**
4 cups sifted flour
1 teaspoon salt

10 Tablespoons cold water
2 Tablespoons flour
1 egg white, lightly beaten

Turn tail of beef under and tie with string to make even thickness for roasting. Roast at 425° for 40 minutes. Remove from oven, cool, wrap in foil and chill for 4 hours or overnight. Sauté onion and nuts in butter until onion is tender and nuts toasted. Stir in mushrooms and cognac. Cook over medium heat for 5 to 10 minutes. In a large bowl, combine the onion mixture with the remaining forcemeat ingredients. Mix well, let cool, cover and refrigerate. In a large bowl, cut the butter and shortening into the flour and salt until the mixture resembles small peas. Sprinkle cold water over all and work quickly into the flour mixture until it forms a ball. Sprinkle with flour. Pastry may be rolled out at this time or wrapped in waxed paper and refrigerated. Pastry must be removed from refrigerator 2 to 3 hours before rolling. On a generously floured board, roll pastry into a square approximately 18 inches by 18 inches. Trim uneven edges. Remove string from filet and lay along one edge of the pastry. Spread the forcemeat evenly over the filet. Lift pastry over all, overlapping it under the meat and sealing the edges. Cut designs from remaining pastry to decorate the Wellington. Brush entire pastry with egg white. Place on an ungreased baking sheet and bake at 425° for 40 minutes. Transfer carefully to serving platter and allow to set for 10 to 20 minutes before serving. This recipe may be halved.

Marti Thomas (Mrs. A. Henry)

Place the unbaked Wellington on a narrow, folded sheet of aluminum foil strong enough for lifting and with the ends extending for grasping. This prevents the pastry from breaking when transferring to the serving platter.

BEEF AND ASPARAGUS WITH OYSTER SAUCE

Yield: 4 servings

½ pound steak (flank or sirloin)
2 Tablespoons soy sauce
1 teaspoon peanut oil
1 teaspoon cornstarch
2 Tablespoons peanut oil
2 slices fresh ginger
2 cloves garlic

Fresh asparagus, washed, with
   tough parts removed, cut
   diagonally into 2 inch lengths
4 to 5 large, dried oriental
   mushrooms, reconstituted and
   cut into strips
3 green onions, sliced

Oyster Sauce
¼ cup bottled oyster sauce
¼ cup chicken broth

1 teaspoon sugar
1 Tablespoon cornstarch

Slice ½ pound steak across the grain into strips. Marinate for ½ hour in 2 Tablespoons soy sauce, 1 teaspoon peanut oil and 1 teaspoon cornstarch. In wok, heat 2 Tablespoons peanut oil. Add ginger and garlic. Sauté until brown. Remove and discard ginger and garlic. Stir-fry meat for about 2 minutes. Add asparagus, mushrooms and onions. Stir-fry until asparagus turns bright jade green. Stir sauce ingredients together until well blended. Pour over vegetable-meat mixture. Reduce heat. Cook 1 to 2 minutes until sauce is thickened.

Robert Henderson

ALMOND BEEF WITH BROCCOLI

Yield: 2 servings

⅓ pound beef sirloin, cut into thin
   strips
1 Tablespoon soy sauce
3 Tablespoons white wine
½ teaspoon cornstarch
½ teaspoon sugar
¼ teaspoon garlic powder

⅛ teaspoon ground ginger
¾ pound fresh broccoli, cut in 2
   inch lengths
Boiling water
4 Tablespoons vegetable oil
½ cup blanched almonds, toasted

Combine beef, soy sauce, wine, cornstarch, sugar, garlic powder and ginger. Marinate for ½ hour. Split each length of broccoli into 4 pieces. Drop into boiling water and boil for 2 minutes. Drain. Heat 2 Tablespoons of oil in wok or skillet, add broccoli and stir-fry for 2 minutes. Arrange broccoli in ring at edge of a serving plate. Add remaining 2 Tablespoons of oil to wok. Lift beef from marinade and stir-fry for 1 minute. Add marinade and cook, stirring until glazed. Pour into center of broccoli. Sprinkle almonds over all.

Gaye White (Mrs. Frank)

FIERY HUNAN BEEF

Yield: 4 servings

1 pound lean beef round, sliced into
    paper thin strips
¼ cup soy sauce
2 Tablespoons sherry
1 clove garlic, chopped
3 Tablespoons oil
1 bunch scallions, cut into 1 inch
    lengths

1 cup thinly sliced carrots
2 cups thinly sliced celery
1 (6 ounce) can button mushrooms,
    drained
1 teaspoon salt
¼ cup whole blanched almonds
½ teaspoon ground ginger
½ to 1 teaspoon hot pepper flakes

Combine beef, soy sauce, sherry and garlic and let stand at room temperature for 1 hour. Remove beef and reserve marinade. In a large skillet, heat oil until it sizzles. Add beef and stir-fry for 2 or 3 minutes or until browned. Add marinade and remaining ingredients and stir-fry over high heat for 4 to 5 minutes or until vegetables are tender but still crisp. Add pepper flakes a little at a time to taste.

Ellon Cockrill (Mrs. Rogers)

Serve with hot cooked rice and egg rolls.

PEPPER STEAK WITH TOMATOES

Yield: 6 servings

1 pound sirloin, cut in ¼ inch strips
2 Tablespoons shortening
¼ cup chopped onion
1 clove garlic, minced
1 teaspoon salt
1 teaspoon pepper
1 beef bouillon cube
1 cup hot water

1 (14 ounce) can tomatoes, drained
    and cut in bite-sized pieces
1 large green pepper, cut in strips
2 Tablespoons cornstarch
¼ cup cold water
2 Tablespoons soy sauce
Rice or noodles, cooked

Slowly brown meat in shortening. Add onion and garlic, then salt and pepper. Dissolve bouillon cube in hot water and add to meat. Cover and simmer for 25 minutes. Add tomatoes and green peppers and continue cooking for 10 minutes. Combine cornstarch, cold water and soy sauce. Add to meat mixture. Cook 5 minutes longer. Serve over rice or noodles.

Cindy Clifton

When slicing meat for a Chinese stir-fry recipe, slice while frozen.

STEAKABOBS
(Must be prepared in advance)

Oven: Broil
Yield: 4 to 6 servings

½ cup soy sauce
½ cup cooking oil
½ cup peach or pineapple juice
1 teaspoon ginger
⅛ teaspoon garlic powder

1½ pounds round steak, cut in ¼
   inch strips
Canned peach slices
Pineapple chunks
Cherries
Cooked rice

Combine soy sauce, oil, juice, ginger and garlic powder and pour over steak strips, coating both sides. Cover and refrigerate 4 hours or overnight. Thread steak strips on skewers, accordian style, with peaches, pineapple and cherries between strips. Brush with marinade and broil 3 to 4 inches from heat for 3 minutes. Turn, brush with marinade, and broil 3 or 4 minutes longer. Serve on a bed of rice.

Linda Deloney (Mrs. Phil)

STEAK AND MUSHROOM CARBONADE

Yield: 4 servings

3 strips bacon, cut in small pieces
1 pound sirloin, cut into 1½ inch by
   2 inch strips
½ pound fresh mushrooms, sliced
1 clove garlic, minced
¼ cup butter
3 Tablespoons flour
½ cup beer

1 cup beef consommé
½ teaspoon salt
¼ teaspoon thyme
1 Tablespoon minced parsley
1 bay leaf
1 (8 ounce) package wide noodles,
   cooked according to package
   directions and drained

In a large skillet sauté bacon until crisp, remove and set aside. Brown meat in bacon grease, remove and set aside. Sauté mushrooms and garlic, remove and set aside. In skillet, melt butter and add flour, stirring until mixed. Slowly add consommé and beer. Stir until thick. Add bacon, meat, mushrooms, garlic, salt, thyme, parsley and bay leaf. Cover and simmer for 1 hour, stirring occasionally. Add more beer if thinner sauce is desired. Serve over noodles.

GRILLED FLANK STEAK
(Must be prepared in advance)

Yield: 6 servings

1 (3 pound) flank steak
Lawry's seasoned salt
Lawry's seasoned pepper

Worcestershire sauce
Liquid Smoke

Generously sprinkle one side of the steak with seasoned salt, seasoned pepper and Worcestershire sauce. Sprinkle lightly with Liquid Smoke. Turn steak and repeat on the other side. Cover and marinate for at least 3 hours in refrigerator. Remove from refrigerator and leave at room temperature for 1 hour before cooking. Grill over charcoal for 7 to 8 minutes on each side. Turn steak 4 times during cooking. Slice on diagonal to serve.

William D. Haught

MARINATED FLANK STEAK
(Must be prepared in advance)

Yield: 6 servings

1½ cups vegetable oil
½ cup soy sauce
½ cup honey
¼ cup wine vinegar
1 medium onion, chopped

4 to 6 cloves garlic, minced
3 teaspoons ginger
3 pounds flank steak, trimmed of
   excess fat
1 pound fresh mushrooms, sliced

Up to 3 days before serving, combine first 7 ingredients in a large pan. Add steak and turn over to fully coat. Spoon marinade over the steak. Cover and refrigerate, turning steak several times each day. On the day of serving, remove steak from marinade. Grill over VERY HOT charcoals, cooking 5 minutes per side for medium rare. Baste the steak with marinade only when almost done. Locate the grain which runs the length of the steak. Holding a sharp knife at an angle almost horizontal to the cutting board, slice ¼ inch slices totally on the bias. Slice diagonally through to the bottom. With a basting tube remove the bottom portion of the marinade which has separated from the oil. Discard oil. Add mushrooms to marinade and heat until mushrooms are tender. Serve sauce with the steak.

Becky McKinney (Mrs. Richard H., Jr.)
Cathie Matthews (Mrs. Bill)

RUTH AGAR'S STANDING RIB ROAST

1 standing rib roast
Coarsely ground pepper
Seasoned salt

Crazy Jane's Mixed Up Salt
Meat thermometer

Coat roast GENEROUSLY with spices. Place in a roasting pan with meat thermometer in center. Cook over indirect fire on outside grill with grill lid down. Open to check internal temperature at 30 minute intervals until thermometer registers desired degree of doneness.

Kristin Agar
Cynthia East (Mrs. Robert C.)

POT ROAST DIJON
(Must be prepared in advance)

Yield: 8 to 10 servings

1 (4 pound) pot roast or rump roast
1 onion, thinly sliced
2 cloves garlic, chopped
2 teaspoons seasoning salt
¼ teaspoon pepper
⅓ cup olive oil

3 Tablespoons wine vinegar
2 Tablespoons vegetable oil
1 cup water
1 Tablespoon Dijon mustard, mixed
    with 1 cup water

In a large bowl, marinate meat in onion, garlic, salt, pepper, oil and vinegar. Marinate at least 2 hours, turning meat at least once. Drain and save marinade. In a Dutch oven, heat vegetable oil, add meat and brown on all sides. Add marinade and 1 cup of water, cover tightly and simmer for 3 or more hours until meat is tender. Add mustard to meat and cook until liquid is reduced and sauce is thickened somewhat. To serve, carve meat in thin slices and pour sauce over the slices.

BRISKET BARBECUE
(Must be prepared in advance)

Oven: 200° to 225°
Yield: 2 whole briskets

2 ounces Liquid Smoke
1 Tablespoon salt
2 Tablespoons chili powder
1 Tablespoon cayenne pepper
1 Tablespoon sugar

2 Tablespoons Lea & Perrins
2 or 3 Tablespoons A-1 sauce or
    Heinz 57 sauce
2 cups vinegar
2 whole briskets

Combine first 8 ingredients in a saucepan and bring to a boil. Remove from heat and let cool. When cool, pour over briskets and marinate overnight in refrigerator. Cover briskets and marinade with foil and cook for 10 to 12 hours in a 200⁰ to 225⁰ oven. Remove briskets from marinade and chill. When cold, slice and layer in baking dishes. Baste with your favorite barbecue sauce, cover and reheat before serving.

Cindy Wage (Mrs. Olin)

CARBONADA

Oven: 300°
Yield: 6 to 8 servings

1 Tablespoon Chefway oil
1 Tablespoon butter
2 Tablespoons minced onion
2½ to 3 pounds chuck roast, cubed
1 teaspoon minced garlic
½ cup dry vermouth
1 cup beef broth
1 teaspoon salt
¼ teaspoon pepper

6 medium carrots, sliced
1 Tablespoon canned chopped
  green chilies
3 medium yellow squash, cubed
1 (10 ounce) package frozen green
  beans, partially thawed
5 canned tomatoes
4 small frozen ears of corn
1 cup beef broth

In a 5 quart Dutch oven, heat oil and butter. Add onion and sauté. Add meat, browning on all sides, and garlic. Add vermouth, beef broth, salt and pepper. Bring to a boil over high heat. Cover, reduce heat and simmer for 20 minutes. Add carrots, cover and bake at 300⁰ for 30 minutes. Add remaining ingredients, cover and continue baking for 30 minutes longer, stirring once.

Ruby Hampton (Mrs. F. Barnes)
DeWitt, Arkansas

FRENCH BEEF STEW

Yield: 6 to 8 servings

3 slices bacon, cut into pieces
2 pounds beef stew meat
1 cup water
1 cup dry red wine
1 beef bouillon cube
2 garlic cloves, chopped
1 Tablespoon instant minced onion
2 teaspoons salt
¼ teaspoon thyme

1 strip orange peel
18 small white onions, fresh or
  canned
¾ pound small mushrooms
2 Tablespoons cornstarch
2 Tablespoons water
1 (10 ounce) package frozen peas
½ cup pitted ripe olives, drained

Fry bacon until crisp in a large Dutch oven over medium high heat. Push bacon bits to side of pan. Add stew meat and brown. Stir in water, wine, bouillon cube, garlic, onion, salt, thyme and orange peel. Reduce heat to low, cover and simmer for 1 hour or until meat is tender. In a covered saucepan over high heat, cook onions in 1 inch of boiling, salted water for 10 minutes. Add mushrooms and cook 5 minutes longer. Drain. If using canned onions, skip this step and cook mushrooms in a small amount of butter. In a small bowl, mix cornstarch and water and add to stew. Heat to boiling, stirring constantly, and continue cooking until thickened. Add onions, mushrooms, peas and olives. Cover and heat for 10 minutes.

Judy Burrow (Mrs. Larry)

OVEN BEEF STEW

Oven: 250°
Yield: 15 servings

2½ pounds beef stew meat
1 (28 ounce) can tomatoes,
   undrained
1 cup coarsely chopped celery
4 medium carrots, sliced
3 medium potatoes, cubed
3 medium onions, chopped
1 (10 ounce) package frozen peas or
   green beans

3 to 4 Tablespoons flour
2 to 3 beef bouillon cubes
1 Tablespoon salt
1 Tablespoon sugar
Pepper, freshly ground
⅛ teaspoon thyme
⅛ teaspoon rosemary
⅛ teaspoon marjoram
½ cup red wine

Combine all ingredients in a 5 quart casserole. Cover and cook at 250° for 5 hours. After 3½ hours of cooking, stir well, cover and continue cooking.

Mero McCreery (Mrs. David G.)

BEEF-BROCCOLI PIE

Oven: 350°
Yield: 6 servings

1 pound ground beef
¼ cup chopped onion
2 Tablespoons flour
¾ teaspoon salt
¼ teaspoon garlic salt
1¼ cups milk
1 (3 ounce) package cream cheese,
   softened
1 egg, well-beaten

1 (10 ounce) package frozen
   chopped broccoli, cooked
   according to package directions
   and drained
Pastry for double crust 9 inch pie
   (See Index)
4 to 6 ounces Monterey Jack
   cheese, sliced

Brown beef and onion in a 10 inch skillet. Drain off fat. Add flour, salt and garlic salt. Stir. Add milk and cream cheese. Cook and stir until smooth and bubbly. Add some of hot cream cheese mixture to beaten egg. Return mixture to skillet and cook and stir over medium heat until thickened (1 to 2 minutes). Stir in broccoli. Divide pastry into 2 balls. Roll 2 pie crusts on floured board and place bottom crust in a 9 inch pie pan. Spoon broccoli mixture into pie pan and top with slices of Monterey Jack cheese. Cover with the top pie crust and seal. Bake at 350° for 40 to 45 minutes. Let stand for 10 minutes before slicing.

Margaret Kelly Balch (Mrs. Fred, III)

ENCHILADAS

Oven: 350°
Yield: 12 enchiladas

1 pound ground beef
12 frozen tortillas
⅓ cup salad oil
1 (10 ounce) can enchilada sauce
¼ cup butter
¼ cup flour
½ teaspoon salt

¼ teaspoon paprika
2 cups milk
6 ounces sharp American cheese, grated
3 drops hot pepper sauce
4 tomatoes, peeled and diced
½ cup finely chopped onion

Brown ground beef. Fry tortillas in hot salad oil, one at a time, just to soften. Heat enchilada sauce and dip tortillas in sauce. Melt butter in a saucepan and blend with flour, salt and paprika. Add milk. Cook and stir until mixture thickens and bubbles. Blend in cheese and hot pepper sauce. Spoon 1 or 2 Tablespoons of cheese sauce on each tortilla. Sprinkle with browned ground beef, 2 Tablespoons tomato and 2 teaspoons onion. Roll up and place seam side down in a greased 9 x 13 baking dish. Combine remaining cheese sauce with enchilada sauce and pour over enchiladas. Bake at 350⁰ for 25 minutes.

Ashley Allen Ingalls (Mrs. George)

HOT SPAGHETTI SAUCE

Yield: 3 quarts

2 pounds hamburger meat
1 green pepper, chopped
5 ribs celery, chopped
1 medium onion, chopped
1 teaspoon celery salt
1 teaspoon oregano
1 teaspoon monosodium glutamate
1 teaspoon red pepper (Optional)
1 teaspoon onion salt

1 teaspoon garlic salt
1 teaspoon salt
1 teaspoon pepper
1 bay leaf
2 (16 ounce) cans stewed tomatoes
1 (10 ounce) can Ro-Tel tomatoes
1 (46 ounce) can V-8 juice
1 (6 ounce) can tomato paste

Brown hamburger meat in a 6 quart pan. Add green pepper, celery and onion, cooking about 5 minutes. Add rest of ingredients and simmer for 2 hours. Serve with spaghetti cooked according to package directions.

Phyllis McKuin (Mrs. Barry)
Morrilton, Arkansas

A wonderful and pleasingly different spaghetti sauce. It is hotter than most. Freezes well.

UNCLE JOE'S SPAGHETTI SAUCE

Yield: 4 to 6 servings

1 Tablespoon cooking oil
1 pound ground beef
¼ cup coarsely chopped green
   pepper
1 medium onion, coarsely chopped
4 garlic cloves, chopped
½ teaspoon oregano
½ teaspoon thyme
½ teaspoon basil
Salt to taste

Pepper to taste
1 (10 ounce) can beef bouillon
1 (12 ounce) can tomatoes
1 (6 ounce) can tomato paste
¼ pound or 4 inches hot Italian link
   sausage, sliced
½ cup mushrooms, chopped
1 generous splash sherry or cooking
   wine

In a deep 10 inch skillet or Dutch oven, heat oil and brown meat. Add green pepper, onion and garlic and cook, stirring until tender. Add all remaining ingredients. Reduce heat and cook slowly for 1 hour. Serve over spaghetti and top with Parmesan cheese.

Jess Askew

STUFFED MEXICAN MEAT LOAF

Oven: 375°
Yield: 8 servings

2 pounds ground chuck
⅓ cup chopped green pepper
⅓ cup finely chopped onion
1½ slices soft white bread, torn
   into crumbs
1 egg, slightly beaten
1 (8 ounce) can tomato sauce

½ cup plus 2 Tablespoons French's
   Taco Seasoning
½ cup sour cream
2 cups shredded Cheddar cheese
Cheddar cheese slices
Avocado slices
Cherry tomatoes

Mix first 7 ingredients together thoroughly. Place half the meat mixture in a 9 x 5 loaf pan. Mix the sour cream and shredded cheese together. Make a deep well the length of the loaf pan and place the cheese mixture in the middle. Cover with the remaining meat mixture and seal well. Bake at 375° for 1½ to 1¾ hours. During the last few minutes of baking time, place triangles of cheese on top of loaf and continue cooking until melted. Let meat loaf set for 8 to 10 minutes. Place on serving platter and garnish around the loaf with avocados and cherry tomatoes.

Ginny Shell (Mrs. Bob)

REUBEN CASSEROLE

Oven: 425°
Yield: 4 to 6 servings

1¾ cups sauerkraut, drained
½ pound corned beef, thinly sliced
2 cups shredded Swiss cheese
3 Tablespoons Thousand Island
    dressing

2 tomatoes, thinly sliced
2 Tablespoons butter
½ cup butter
1 cup Rye Krisp crackers, crumbled
¼ teaspoon caraway seeds

In a 2 quart casserole, spread sauerkraut evenly over the bottom. Top with corned beef and cheese. Spread dressing on top of cheese. Layer tomatoes and dot with 2 Tablespoons butter. Sauté Rye Krisp crumbs in ½ cup butter. Add caraway seeds. Spread over other layers and bake at 425⁰ for 30 minutes.

Patsy Frost (Mrs. H. G. "Jack")

VEAL SCALLOPS WITH AVOCADO

Yield: 4 servings

1 pound veal scallops
1 egg, beaten
2 Tablespoons flour
3 Tablespoons butter
1 Tablespoon oil
¼ cup vermouth
½ cup chicken broth

3 Tablespoons lemon juice
¾ teaspoon salt
½ teaspoon white pepper
¼ cup chopped parsley
1 large avocado

Soak scallops in egg for at least 1 hour, then coat evenly with flour. Melt butter and oil in skillet and sauté ½ the veal scallops at a time for about 3 minutes per side and remove to a warm plate. After browning all veal, return meat to the skillet. Add vermouth, stirring gently. Add the broth, 2 Tablespoons lemon juice, salt and pepper. Stir well until sauce is creamy. Cover and simmer 10 to 15 minutes. Add parsley during the last 5 minutes. While veal is cooking, peel and slice avocado and sprinkle with remaining lemon juice. Bake the slices at 300⁰ for 5 minutes. Place veal on serving platter, surround with avocado slices and pour on sauce. Serve at once.

Helen Harrison (Mrs. Fred H.)

"Show me another pleasure like dinner which comes every day and lasts an hour."

TALLYRAND
1754-1838

ÉMINCÉ DE VEAU A LA CRÈME

Yield: 4 servings

1⅓ pounds veal round steak, thinly
 sliced into small strips
Salt to taste
Pepper to taste
Flour
1 Tablespoon butter
1 Tablespoon oil
1 Tablespoon finely chopped
 shallots

4 ounces dry white wine
⅔ pound fresh mushrooms, sliced
10 ounces whipping cream
⅜ cup basic brown sauce (See
 Index for Marchand de Vin
 Sauce)
1 small clove garlic, finely minced
1 - 2 teaspoons lemon juice
2 Tablespoons chopped parsley

Season veal with salt and pepper. Sprinkle with flour and sauté quickly in hot butter-oil combination until very slightly colored. Remove from pan. Add shallots to pan and deglaze with the white wine. When wine reaches boiling, add mushrooms and cook for several minutes to reduce wine. Add whipping cream and brown sauce and continue reducing. Add garlic, lemon juice, parsley and veal to mushroom sauce. To serve, garnish with sprigs of parsley.

Restaurant Jacques and Suzanne

LES MIGNONS DE VEAU AU CITRON

Yield: 4 servings

1 lemon
1 cup cold water
1 teaspoon sugar
21 ounces veal tenderloin, cut in 8
 pieces and trimmed of fat, OR 4
 veal cutlets, cut 1 inch thick and
 trimmed of fat

Salt to taste
Pepper to taste
½ cup butter
8 Tablespoons white wine
2 Tablespoons chopped parsley

With a vegetable peeler, peel the lemon and cut peel into julienne strips. Put strips in ½ cup water, bring to a boil, drain, and refresh with cold water. Combine strips, ½ cup water and sugar. Simmer until water has evaporated. Season the veal and cook over moderate heat in ⅓ of the butter for about 5 minutes per side. Remove veal and keep hot. Pour off the butter but DO NOT WASH PAN. Add wine and deglaze the pan reducing the wine to 2 Tablespoons. Add the remaining butter and mix well. Do not boil. Add parsley and lemon strips and heat through. Arrange veal on plates and pour remaining juice into the sauce. Pour sauce over veal and garnish with lemon slices.

Marilyn Hussman Augur (Mrs. James)
Dallas, Texas

VEAL SICILIENNE

Oven: 350°
Yield: 8 servings

3 large, thin veal cutlets
¼ pound salami, thinly sliced
¼ pound bologna, thinly sliced
¼ pound cooked ham, thinly sliced
¼ cup seasoned croutons, crushed
3 cloves garlic, minced
Parsley, chopped
1 teaspoon basil

Olive oil
Salt
Pepper
4 hard-boiled eggs
5 slices bacon
3 cups tomato sauce
2 whole cloves garlic

On a chopping board, arrange veal slices side by side, overlapping slightly. Pound veal very thin, especially where veal overlaps. Place salami slices over veal, overlapping slightly. Repeat with the bologna and the cooked ham. Sprinkle with croutons, minced garlic, parsley and basil. Sprinkle with olive oil, salt and pepper. Place a row of hard-boiled eggs down the center and roll up in jellyroll fashion, making certain that the eggs stay in the center. Place roll in baking dish and top with bacon. Combine tomato sauce with garlic and pour over roll. Bake at 350° for 1 hour. Serve with remaining sauce.

Sue Gaskin (Mrs. William J.)

VEAL MADEIRA

Yield: 4 servings

1 pound veal scallops
½ cup flour
¼ cup butter, melted
2 Tablespoons butter
⅓ cup chopped onion
¾ pound mushrooms, sliced
½ cup Madeira wine

½ cup whipping cream
Paprika to taste
Salt to taste
Pepper to taste
½ cup whipping cream, lightly
    whipped
Parsley, chopped

Sauté floured veal in ¼ cup melted butter for 5 minutes, browning on both sides. Remove veal to serving dish and keep warm. Add 2 Tablespoons butter to skillet and sauté onions and mushrooms for 4 to 5 minutes. Add wine and continue cooking until liquid is reduced to 2 Tablespoons. Add whipping cream and seasonings. Cook until mixture is thickened. Fold in whipped cream. Pour sauce over veal and garnish with parsley.

Jo Ann Drew (Mrs. Tommy, Jr.)

VEAL SALTIMBOCCA

Yield: 4 to 5 servings

10 small veal cutlets
4 Tablespoons flour
4 Tablespoons butter, melted
Mozzarella cheese, grated
Sage

10 slices Prosciutto
1½ cups chicken broth
½ cup white wine
1½ Tablespoons flour
Parsley, chopped

Dust cutlets with flour and brown on both sides in butter. Remove from pan and top with cheese. Sprinkle with sage. Place proscuitto over cheese (it will probably adhere to cheese, if not, secure with toothpicks). Return meat to pan. Mix chicken broth, wine and flour until smooth and pour over meat. Cover and simmer for 10 minutes. Sprinkle with parsley. Serve with noodles.

Ellen Golden (Mrs. Lex)

TED COLUMBO'S VEAL SCALLOPPINE

Yield: 4 servings

4 veal filets
Flour
Salt
Pepper
Olive oil
¼ cup butter

¼ pound fresh mushrooms, sliced
Dry red wine
¼ teaspoon salt
¼ teaspoon pepper
¼ teaspoon tarragon
¼ teaspoon oregano

Pound the filets with a mallet until very thin. Dust with flour which has been seasoned with salt and pepper. In a 10 inch skillet, sauté veal in olive oil for 3 minutes per side. Remove from pan. Add butter, mushrooms and enough red wine to bathe the mushrooms. Cook over medium heat, scraping the residue from the bottom of the pan until the mushrooms are cooked but still firm. Add salt, pepper, tarragon and oregano. Replace veal, heaping wine and mushrooms on top. Cook, stirring occasionally until sauce thickens.

Ted Glusman

"Strange to see how a good dinner and feasting reconciles everybody."
SAMUEL PEPYS
1633-1703

LEMON VEAL

Yield: 4 servings

2½ pounds veal pieces
1½ cups flour
1 Tablespoon salt
½ cup butter
½ cup olive oil

1¼ cups chicken broth
½ cup lemon juice
2 lemons, thinly sliced
½ cup chopped parsley

Combine flour and salt. Coat veal with flour mixture. Sauté veal in butter and olive oil over medium heat for 5 to 7 minutes, turning once. Add chicken broth and lemon juice and simmer until the liquid is reduced by half. Add sliced lemons and heat only until hot throughout. Add parsley.

Julie Fulgham (Mrs. Edward)

ESCALOPES OF VEAL WITH ORANGE

Yield: 2 servings

4 escalopes of veal
2 ounces butter
1 Tablespoon flour
Grated orange rind
Juice of 1 orange, strained

1 teaspoon brandy or 1 Tablespoon
 dry sherry
5 ounces chicken stock
Salt
Pepper
1 orange, peeled and thinly sliced

Sauté the veal quickly in butter until golden brown. Remove and set aside. Add the flour to the pan drippings and mix well. Add orange rind, orange juice, brandy or sherry and chicken stock. Bring to a boil. Replace the veal, season with salt and pepper, cover and simmer for 10 minutes. Garnish with orange slices.

Helen Sloan (Mrs. John C.)

MARINATED AND GRILLED LAMB CHOPS

(Must be prepared in advance)

Yield: 8 servings

½ cup olive oil
⅓ cup lime juice
2 teaspoons onion salt
½ teaspoon white pepper

¼ teaspoon marjoram
⅛ teaspoon garlic powder
8 lamb sirloin chops

Combine first 6 ingredients, pour over chops and marinate in refrigerator for 8 hours, turning occasionally. Grill on charcoal or gas grill for 5 to 7 minutes each side.

Carole Meyer (Mrs. Charles, III)

LAMB CURRY

Yield: 4 to 6 servings

2 cooking apples, cored, pared and sliced
1 green pepper, chopped
2 onions, sliced
1 clove garlic, crushed
2 Tablespoons olive oil
2 Tablespoons flour
1 Tablespoon curry powder
½ teaspoon salt
½ teaspoon marjoram

½ teaspoon thyme
1 cup consommé
½ cup dry red wine
Juice of 1 lemon
Grated lemon rind
½ cup seedless raisins
2 whole cloves
2 cups lamb, cooked and diced
¼ cup shredded coconut
1 Tablespoon sour cream

Sauté apples, green pepper, onions and garlic in olive oil until onions are limp. Add flour, curry powder, salt, marjoram and thyme. Mix well and cook for 5 minutes, stirring constantly. Add consommé, wine, lemon juice, lemon rind, raisins and cloves. Simmer for 20 to 30 minutes. Add lamb and coconut and heat for 15 minutes. Just before serving, add sour cream and mix thoroughly.

Anne Winans (Mrs. T. Revillon)

Serve over hot rice with your choice of condiments: Major Grey's Mango Chutney, chopped kumquats, candied ginger, chopped green onions, orange rind, coconut, chopped egg yolks, chopped egg whites, chopped crisp bacon, raisins, cashews, pine nuts or peanuts.

ROASTED LEG OF LAMB

Oven: 350°
Yield: 10 servings

1 (5 to 6 pound) leg of lamb, boned, rolled and tied
Cavender's Greek Seasoning
½ cup honey

½ cup dry white wine
4 cloves garlic, mashed
1 Tablespoon lemon juice
3 Tablespoons butter, melted

Sprinkle lamb liberally with Cavender's Greek Seasoning. Place meat thermometer in thickest part of meat and roast at 350⁰ for 1 hour. Combine the remaining ingredients and mix well. Continue cooking lamb, basting every 15 minutes with honey mixture until thermometer registers 170⁰ for medium lamb.

Jo Ann Drew (Mrs. Tommy, Jr.)

LAMB TAGINE WITH ONIONS AND RAISINS

Yield: 6 to 8 servings

2 to 2½ pounds lamb, cubed
1½ Tablespoons oil
2 medium tomatoes, peeled, seeded
   and diced
2 medium onions, diced
1 teaspoon pepper
1 teaspoon salt
½ teaspoon chopped parsley
¼ teaspoon saffron or ½ teaspoon
   tumeric

½ teaspoon cinnamon
½ cup water
1 pound onions, sliced
2 Tablespoons butter
2 teaspoons cinnamon
1 teaspoon pepper
½ to 1 cup sugar
1 cup raisins, washed

In a Dutch oven over high heat, brown meat on all sides in oil. Lower heat to simmer and add the next 8 ingredients. Cover and simmer for 2 hours, stirring occasionally until meat is tender. Sauté onion in butter until light brown. Add cinnamon, pepper, ½ cup sugar and raisins. Cook for 10 minutes or until thick. Add ½ of the juice from the stew to the raisin mixture and continue to cook adding more sugar to taste until mixture is dark brown. Add raisin mixture to the stew.

Kathy Bird (Mrs. Allen W.)

This is an authentic Moroccan dish.

CROWN OF PORK AND PLUM SAUCE

Oven: 325°
Yield: 8 to 10 servings

1 (16 to 18 rib) crown of pork roast
1 cup apple cider
Salt to taste
Pepper to taste

1 (18 ounce) jar plum jelly
1 bunch green onions, chopped
3 teaspoons prepared mustard
1 Tablespoon raisins

Place a large can in center of roast to hold its shape. Place crown in a shallow roasting pan and roast at 325° for 3 hours, basting frequently with cider and pan juices. Season with salt and pepper. For garnish you may fill center with rice or potatoes and put scooped out cherry tomatoes on each bone. Mix jelly, onions, mustard and raisins and heat. Serve with roast.

Suzanne McCord (Mrs. Larry)
Fort Smith, Arkansas

PORK ROAST WITH APPLES

Oven: 350°
Yield: 6 servings

1 (4 pound) pork loin roast
Cavender's Greek Seasoning
½ cup dry white wine
2 Tablespoons butter
½ cup apple jelly

½ cup applesauce
½ cup whipping cream
3 apples, cored and cut in half
6 Tablespoons brown sugar
½ teaspoon cinnamon

Sprinkle roast liberally with Cavender's Greek Seasoning. Roast at 350° for 2 hours. Drain fat. Heat together wine, butter, jelly, applesauce and cream until well mixed. Place apples around roast and sprinkle with brown sugar and cinnamon. Return to oven for 1 hour, basting every 15 minutes with wine mixture.

Jo Ann Drew (Mrs. Tommy, Jr.)

PORK LOIN ROAST
(Must be prepared in advance)

Oven: 325°
Yield: 6 to 8 servings

½ cup soy sauce
½ cup sherry
2 cloves garlic, minced
1 Tablespoon dry mustard
1 teaspoon ginger
1 teaspoon thyme

1 (4 to 5 pound) rolled pork loin
   roast
1 (10 ounce) jar red currant jelly
2 Tablespoons sherry
1 teaspoon soy sauce

Combine first 6 ingredients. Place roast in marinade in Brown-N-Bag for 2 to 3 hours or overnight. Remove roast from marinade, place in a shallow roasting pan and roast, uncovered, for 2½ to 3 hours at 325°. Baste with marinade during last hour. Combine last 3 ingredients in saucepan and heat thoroughly. Serve roast with currant sauce.

Nancy Hutton
Memphis, Tennessee

"Let the stoics say what they please, we do not eat for the good of living, but because the meat is savory and the appetite is keen."
RALPH WALDO EMERSON
1803-1882

SCALLOPPINE OF PORK MARSALA

Yield: 3 to 4 servings

1 pound pork tenderloin, cut into ¼
   inch slices
Flour
6 Tablespoons butter, clarified
6 large mushrooms, thinly sliced
1 shallot, minced

⅔ cup dry Marsala wine
½ cup chicken stock
2 Tablespoons unsalted butter
Salt
Freshly ground black pepper

Flatten each slice of pork between sheets of waxed paper to a thickness of ³⁄₁₆ inch. Flour pork lightly on both sides. Heat ½ of the clarified butter in a large heavy skillet over medium-high heat until hot but not brown. Add pork and sauté 2 to 3 minutes per side or until golden, adding butter as needed. Transfer to platter and keep in a 200° oven. Pour off all but 2 Tablespoons butter from skillet. Place over high heat. Add mushrooms and shallot and sauté until they begin to color. Blend in Marsala and stock. Boil over high heat, scraping up browned bits, until reduced by ⅓. Remove from heat and add remaining 2 Tablespoons butter, swirling until well blended and sauce is slightly thickened. Season to taste with salt and pepper. Pour over pork and serve immediately.

Diane A. Larrison (Mrs. James H., Jr.)

PORK RAGOUT

Yield: 6 servings

3 Tablespoons oil
2 pounds boneless pork, cut into
   1½ inch cubes
1 cup chopped onion
1 clove garlic, crushed
3 Tablespoons flour
1 (10¾ ounce) can chicken broth
1¼ cups dry white wine, divided
1 bay leaf

½ teaspoon rosemary leaves
¼ teaspoon thyme leaves
½ teaspoon salt
¼ teaspoon ground black pepper
2 cups carrots, cut in ¼ inch slices
2 Tablespoons butter
1 pound fresh mushrooms, sliced
Chopped parsley

In a large, heavy saucepan or skillet, heat oil. Brown half the pork and set aside. Add remaining pork, brown and set aside. Add onions and garlic to drippings and sauté until golden. Add flour. Cook and stir for 1 minute. Stir in chicken broth, 1 cup of wine, bay leaf, rosemary, thyme, salt and pepper. Cook and stir until mixture boils and thickens. Stir in browned pork, cover and simmer for 1 hour, stirring once or twice. Stir in carrots, cover and simmer 30 minutes longer, adding water if needed. Meanwhile, in a large skillet, melt butter and sauté mushrooms until golden. Add mushrooms and ¼ cup of wine to stew, stir gently, cover and simmer for 3 minutes longer. Sprinkle with chopped parsley.

Dee Dowell Wright (Mrs. Richard L.)
Texarkana, Arkansas

PORK TENDERLOIN WITH MUSTARD SAUCE
(Must be prepared in advance)

Oven: 325°
Yield: 6 servings

¼ cup soy sauce
¼ cup bourbon
2 Tablespoons brown sugar
3 pounds of pork tenderloin
1 Tablespoon dry mustard

1½ teaspoons vinegar
⅓ cup sour cream
⅓ cup mayonnaise
1 Tablespoon chopped green onions
Salt to taste

Combine first 3 ingredients for marinade mixture. Marinate the pork for several hours, turning occasionally. Remove meat from marinade and roast at 325⁰ for 45 minutes to 1 hour, basting frequently. Dissolve mustard in vinegar and mix with sour cream and mayonnaise. Fold in green onions and salt. Carve meat and serve with mustard sauce.

Mrs. Robert M. Eubanks, Jr.

JÄGERSCHNITZEL

Yield: 4 to 6 servings

4 to 6 pork or veal chops
Flour seasoned to taste with salt,
   pepper and paprika
1 egg, lightly beaten with 1
   Tablespoon water
Bread crumbs
½ cup vegetable oil
½ onion, chopped
1 Tablespoon butter

1 (4 ounce) can sliced mushrooms,
   drained
1 Tablespoon lemon juice
1 (8 ounce) carton sour cream
1 Tablespoon water
Salt to taste
Pepper to taste
Paprika to taste
1 lemon, cut into 6 slices

Cut excess fat from chops and pound slightly with meat mallet. Dredge in flour, dip in egg mixture, and then dip in bread crumbs. Fry in oil in a 10 inch skillet until done. Remove to a warm platter. In a separate skillet, sauté onion in butter. Add mushrooms and lemon juice. Before serving, add sour cream, water, salt, pepper and paprika. Pour over chops and garnish with lemon slices.

Marilyn Owen (Mrs. William)

Authentic German dish which is good served with red cabbage, cottage fries and a cucumber salad.

MARINATED BARBECUED PORK CHOPS

(Must be prepared 1 day in advance)

Yield: 6 to 8 servings

½ cup vegetable oil
¼ cup dry white wine
¼ cup lemon juice
¼ teaspoon garlic powder
1 Tablespoon salt

1 teaspoon paprika
½ teaspoon pepper
6 bay leaves, halved
6 to 8 (1 inch thick) pork chops

Combine all ingredients except pork chops in a 9 x 13 baking dish, mixing well. Add meat to marinade. Cover and marinate overnight in refrigerator, turning occasionally. Remove chops from marinade and place about 4 to 5 inches above medium coals. Grill for 30 to 45 minutes or until chops are no longer pink, turning and basting occasionally.

Robyn Brown

SWEET AND SOUR PORK

(Must be prepared 1 day in advance)

Yield: 6 to 8 servings

1 teaspoon salt
1 teaspoon Accent
1 teaspoon sherry
1 Tablespoon soy sauce
1 clove garlic, minced
3 slices ginger root
1 pound pork butt or loin, cut in 1
    inch pieces
½ cup cornstarch
½ cup flour
½ cup water
Oil
1 egg, beaten

2 carrots, diagonally cut
1 small onion, sliced
1 bell pepper, cut in strips
1 (8 ounce) can pineapple chunks,
    drained
¾ cup sugar
½ cup ketchup
2 Tablespoons cornstarch
¼ teaspoon salt
2 Tablespoons red wine vinegar
4 drops red food coloring
Cooked rice

Combine first 6 ingredients. Add meat and marinate for several hours. Remove meat from marinade. Combine cornstarch, flour, water, 1 teaspoon oil and egg. Mix well and thoroughly coat pork cubes. Deep fry pork in oil until meat turns white. Drain on paper towels and place in warm oven. In 1 Tablespoon of oil, stir-fry carrots, onion and bell pepper over medium to high heat for 1 minute. Add pineapple and set aside. Mix last 6 ingredients and cook over medium heat until thick, stirring continuously. Add vegetable mixture and pork. Serve over rice.

Barbara V. Noland

PORK CHOPS ARDENNAISE

Yield: 3 to 4 servings

12 slices thick bacon, cut into strips
   or small squares
6 ounces white wine
3 green onions, finely chopped
4 to 5 loin pork chops
Salt

Freshly ground pepper
2 Tablespoons flour
2 ounces butter
½ cup whipping cream
1 teaspoon Dijon mustard
1 Tablespoon chopped parsley

Place bacon in a bowl and cover with wine and onions. Let stand for 30 minutes. Drain and reserve wine. Lightly season pork chops and dredge in flour. Heat butter and fry chops over moderate heat for 6 or 7 minutes per side. Add bacon and onions. Continue cooking for 2 or 3 minutes. Add the cream and the reserved wine and simmer for 10 to 12 minutes. Remove chops to a warm serving platter. Slightly reduce the sauce, add mustard and parsley. Adjust seasonings and spoon sauce over chops.

Helen Sloan (Mrs. John C.)

HAM LOAF

Oven: 325°
Yield: 8 servings

1 pound ground lean pork
2 pounds ground smoked ham
1 cup bread crumbs
2 eggs
1 cup milk

1 Tablespoon minced onion
1½ cups brown sugar
½ cup water
½ cup vinegar
1 teaspoon prepared mustard

Mix pork and ham. Add bread crumbs, eggs, milk and onion. Mix thoroughly. Form into a loaf. To make sauce, blend brown sugar, water, vinegar and mustard. Bake ham loaf at 325° for 2 hours, basting frequently with sauce. Serve with remaining sauce.

Linda Burrow VanHook (Mrs. Fred F.)

GLAZED HAM

Oven: 250°

1 cup brown sugar
¼ cup lemon juice
⅓ cup prepared horseradish

1 Cure 81 Hormel Ham, thinly
   sliced and tied with string

Combine brown sugar, lemon juice and horseradish in a small saucepan. Simmer until brown sugar is dissolved. Pour over ham and bake at 250° for 1½ hours, basting occasionally.

Pat Cook

SAUCES & ACCOMPANIMENTS

To be known by your admirers as a sorceress, a source of tantalizing hints, for a fraction of the cost of fine perfume. . .

HENRY BAIN SAUCE

Yield: 6 to 7 cups

1 (14 ounce) bottle ketchup
1 (11 ounce) bottle A-1 sauce
1 (10 ounce) bottle Worcestershire
  sauce

1 (12 ounce) bottle chili sauce
1 (17 ounce) jar good chutney
Tabasco or red hot sauce to taste,
  about ½ bottle (Optional)

Mix all together. Chop up large pieces of chutney (use blender or food processor). Taste until right. Serve with beef tenderloin, steak or ham.

Helene Zukof (Mrs. Wally)
Louisville, Kentucky

This recipe originated at the Pendennis Club in Louisville, Kentucky. Henry Bain was the man who put it together. The sauce is also good on Kentucky bibb lettuce when thinned with oil and vinegar.

BAR-B-Q SAUCE

Yield: 3 quarts

4 cups ketchup
4 cups vinegar
4 cups water
6 Tablespoons chili powder

6 Tablespoons salt
6 Tablespoons sugar
6 Tablespoons black pepper
1 large onion, finely chopped

Put ingredients in a large pot and simmer until thick, about 6 to 8 hours.

Julie Allen (Mrs. Wally)

DELICIOUS BARBECUE SAUCE

Yield: 6 to 8 servings

1 cup ketchup
1 cup water
¼ cup Worcestershire sauce
¼ cup vinegar
¼ cup brown sugar, firmly packed

1 teaspoon celery salt
1 teaspoon chili powder
1 teaspoon salt
4 drops Tabasco

Combine sauce ingredients in a 2 quart pan. Bring to a simmer. DO NOT LET BOIL. Remove from heat and pour over beef or pork tender, butterflied leg of lamb, or chicken. Marinate overnight in refrigerator.

Helen Sloan (Mrs. John C.)

BÉARNAISE SAUCE

Yield: approximately 2 cups

2 teaspoons dried tarragon
2 Tablespoons vinegar
¼ teaspoon dry mustard
3 green onions, chopped
3 eggs
3 Tablespoons lemon juice

1 teaspoon salt
2 or 3 dashes red pepper
½ teaspoon Worcestershire sauce
1½ cups melted butter (DO NOT SUBSTITUTE)
½ cup Wesson oil

Mix tarragon and vinegar and let stand for 5 minutes. Add mustard and green onions. Blend eggs, lemon juice, salt, red pepper and Worcestershire sauce in blender on low speed. Combine melted butter and Wesson oil. Turn blender on high and add butter and Wesson oil mixture in a slow, steady stream. Add tarragon mixture and blend thoroughly. May be reheated in microwave oven.

Jo Ann Drew (Mrs. Tommy, Jr.)

WONDERFUL HAM SAUCE

Yield: 1½ cups

1 cup brown sugar
¼ cup lemon juice

⅓ cup horseradish

Bring the ingredients to a boil, then remove from heat. May be used to pour over ham while baking, or cooking in a crockpot, or served on the side at mealtime.

Sissy McGuire

Very easy and will make an ordinary meal a little special.

HOLLANDAISE SAUCE

Yield: 1 cup

1 stick butter
3 egg yolks
2 Tablespoons lemon juice

Dash of salt
Dash of cayenne pepper
¼ cup boiling water

Melt butter. Put egg yolks in blender. Alternately pour lemon juice and butter while blending the egg yolks. Sprinkle a little salt and cayenne into blender and add ¼ cup boiling water. Blend a few seconds. Put sauce in a double boiler over hot water (not boiling) and stir for 5 minutes until thick.

Anne Hickman (Mrs. Robert C.)

HORSERADISH CREAM

Yield: 2 cups

½ pint whipping cream
3 Tablespoons horseradish

2 Tablespoons Dijon mustard
Salt to taste

Whip cream until it holds stiff peaks. Fold in horseradish and mustard. Add salt to taste.

Anne Fryer

This is wonderful with roast beef, corned beef or vegetables.

HOT MUSTARD SAUCE

Yield: 2 cups

1 cup brown sugar
3 Tablespoons flour
½ cup dry mustard

1 cup consommé or beef bouillon
½ cup vinegar
3 eggs, beaten

Blend dry ingredients. Add liquids. Cook slowly until thick, stirring constantly.

Melinda Morse

MARCHAND DE VIN SAUCE

Yield: 1½ cups

1 cup finely sliced mushrooms
2 Tablespoons butter
½ cup hot beef stock

1 cup brown sauce (below)
½ cup dry red wine
Pinch of thyme

Brown Sauce
2 Tablespoons butter
2 Tablespoons flour
1 cup beef bouillon

Salt to taste
Pepper to taste

Sauté mushrooms in butter. Add beef stock and simmer for 10 minutes. Make brown sauce by melting butter and blending in flour over medium heat. Stir in bouillon and bring to boiling point, stirring constantly. Season to taste with salt and pepper. Add the mushroom mixture and wine to the brown sauce. Simmer for 20 minutes. Add thyme before serving. Wonderful served over Beef Wellington.

Marti Thomas (Mrs. A. Henry)

PLUM SAUCE

Yield: 1¾ cups

1½ cups red plum jam
1½ Tablespoons prepared mustard

1½ Tablespoons horseradish
1½ Tablespoons lemon juice

Combine all ingredients in a small saucepan, mixing well. Place over low heat until just warm, stirring constantly. DO NOT BOIL.

Sunny Hawk (Mrs. Boyce)

BOURBON MARINADE FOR CHICKEN

Yield: 1 to 1½ cups

½ cup bourbon
¼ cup soy sauce
¼ cup brown sugar
1 large onion, chopped

3 Tablespoons Dijon mustard
1 teaspoon Worcestershire sauce
Juice of 1 lemon

Combine all ingredients. Marinate chicken for a few hours or overnight in dish. Cook chicken on grill and baste with sauce.

Melinda Morse

Also use for beef and pork. Very easy and different.

CHICKEN OR BEEF MARINADE

Yield: 3 cups

1½ cups pineapple juice
½ cup red wine
⅜ cup soy sauce

½ cup vinegar
½ cup sugar
½ teaspoon garlic powder

Mix all ingredients. Marinate chicken breasts or beef kabobs in liquid overnight. Cook outside on the grill. Onions, bell peppers and mushrooms are especially good marinated for the kabobs.

Julie Allen (Mrs. Wally)

Try using diet sweetener instead of sugar for fewer calories.

CHICKEN AND PORK CHOP SAUCE

Yield: approximately ½ cup

¼ pound margarine
Juice of 3 lemons
½ of (5 ounce) bottle
  Worcestershire sauce

1 Tablespoon vinegar
1 to 2 Tablespoons brown sugar
1 to 2 Tablespoons ketchup
Dash of celery seed

Simmer all ingredients together. Use to baste chicken or pork chops while grilling.

Leslie Lipke (Mrs. Jay M.)

ORIENTAL MARINADE

Yield: ¾ cup

¼ cup Hoisin
3 Tablespoons sherry
2 Tablespoons soy sauce
2 green onions, finely chopped
2 garlic cloves, minced

1 teaspoon ginger root, peeled and
  chopped
1 teaspoon sugar
½ teaspoon salt

Combine all ingredients. Pour over chicken, beef or pork. Let marinate overnight. Use sauce to baste while meat is grilled.

John Currie Sloan

SEASONING FOR SMOKED CHICKEN

*Yield: Seasoning for 2
to 3 chickens*

2 Tablespoons celery salt
2 Tablespoons garlic salt
2 Tablespoons onion salt
1½ teaspoons paprika

1½ teaspoons chili powder
½ teaspoon black pepper
⅛ teaspoon cayenne pepper

Mix spices well. Cover chicken well and cook by instructions of your smoker.

Debby Bransford Coates (Mrs. Wayne)

*"To feed were best at home;
From thence the sauce to meat is ceremony;
Meeting were bare without it."*
WILLIAM SHAKESPEARE
*Macbeth
1564-1616*

RELISH FOR BLACK-EYED PEAS

Yield: 1 cup

1 tomato, seeded and chopped
1 medium onion, chopped
1 medium cucumber, seeded and
   chopped

¼ cup tomato ketchup
½ cup vinegar

Over the chopped vegetables, pour the ketchup and vinegar. Let this marinate overnight in refrigerator. Keep in covered jar. Serve over steaming hot black-eyed peas.

Margaret Anderson Hipp

SWEET AND SOUR PEPPERS

Yield: 6 servings

3 large green peppers, seeded and
   cut into bite-sized pieces
2 Tablespoons butter
1 (8 ounce) can pineapple slices,
   drained and cut into chunks

⅓ cup brown sugar
⅓ cup vinegar
1 Tablespoon soy sauce
1 Tablespoon cornstarch

Sauté green peppers in butter. Add pineapple, brown sugar, vinegar and soy sauce. Simmer for 15 to 20 minutes. Add cornstarch and cook until sauce thickens.

Tap Horner

PICKLED OKRA

Yield: 5 pints

Okra (enough to fill 5 pint-sized
   jars)
3 cups water
2 cups white vinegar

¼ cup salt
Garlic cloves
Dill weed
Hot peppers

Wash and pack okra in sterile jars. Add garlic clove, 1 head of dill and 1 hot pepper to each jar. Bring water, vinegar and salt to a boil. Pour over okra. Seal. Let stand 2 weeks before serving.

Linda Burrow VanHook (Mrs. Fred F.)

ZUCCHINI RELISH
(Must be prepared 1 day in advance)

Yield: 3 quarts

8 medium to large zucchini
4 large onions
5 large ribs celery
½ cup pickling salt
3 cups sugar

3 cups cider vinegar
2 teaspoons celery seed
2 teaspoons mustard seed
2 teaspoons tumeric

Put vegetables, one by one, through food processor using shredding disc, or slice vegetables into ¼ inch pieces. Add ½ cup pickling salt to vegetables and let stand overnight. The next day, drain in colander and rinse under cold water. Combine sugar, vinegar, celery and mustard seeds, and tumeric in a large pan. Bring liquid to a boil and simmer 2 minutes. Add vegetables, remove from heat, and let stand 2 hours. Return to boil. Simmer mixture 5 minutes. Spoon into jars and seal.

Carol Cole Herget

PEACH CHUTNEY

Yield: 8 pints

3 cups white vinegar
8 cups sugar
1 teaspoon ginger
1 teaspoon allspice
½ teaspoon ground cloves
3½ pounds peaches

6 medium apples
1 large Bermuda onion
4 sweet red bell peppers
1 cup white raisins
1 cup currants

Boil vinegar, sugar and spices for 15 minutes. Peel and chop the peaches and apples. Add to syrup and cook 10 minutes. Grate onion and chop peppers. Add to syrup and cook 35 minutes more. Stir often. Add raisins and currants and cook 5 minutes more. Put in sterilized glasses and remove air bubbles with a knife. Seal at once.

Jane Teed (Mrs. David D.)

Try adding a little curry and use as a spread over cream cheese! Especially good with game.

"Condiments are like old friends - highly thought of, but often taken for granted."

MARILYN KAYTOR

COINTREAU FRUIT

Yield: 8 servings

3 apples, peeled and chopped
3 pears, peeled and chopped
Orange sections of 2 oranges,
   mandarin or navel
1 cup chopped dates
1 cup raisins

½ cup white wine
¼ cup sugar
Juice of ½ lemon
2 Tablespoons Cointreau liqueur
Bananas, sliced (Optional)

Chop and peel all fruit. Combine wine, sugar and lemon juice and pour over fruit. Add 2 Tablespoons Cointreau liqueur. Let stand for several hours or overnight. Delicious accompaniment to any dish, especially chicken. Serve in compotes or ramekins.

Susan K. Schallhorn (Mrs. Tom)

CRANBERRY RELISH

Yield: 1 quart

4 cups whole fresh cranberries
2 whole oranges and rind

2 cups sugar

Put cranberries in food processor and grind to a coarse consistency. Quarter oranges and grind in food processor. Mix and add sugar. Let sit at room temperature until well blended. Pour into pint jars. Refrigerate or freeze.

Gwyn Wood (Mrs. James T.)

Variations might include adding 3 chopped apples or 1 (15 ounce) can drained crushed pineapple.

CURRIED PEACHES

Oven: 325°
Yield: 6 to 8 servings

2 (16 ounce) cans peach halves,
   drained
2 Tablespoons butter

4 Tablespoons brown sugar
¼ cup raisins
1 or 2 teaspoons curry powder

Drain and dry peaches thoroughly. Melt butter and add other ingredients, mixing well. Place peaches, cut side down, in a large baking pan. Spoon sauce over peaches. Bake in a 325⁰ oven for 45 minutes, uncovered, basting 2 or 3 times.

Ellen Golden (Mrs. Lex)

Serve with ham or duck.

BAKED PINEAPPLE

Oven: 350°
Yield: 6 to 8 servings

1 (16 ounce) can crushed pineapple,
    drained
3 eggs
½ cup sugar

1 Tablespoon flour
¼ pound butter
6 slices of bread, cubed

Mix pineapple, eggs, sugar and flour together and pour into a 1 quart casserole. Melt butter and stir in bread cubes gently to coat. Put buttered cubes on top of casserole and bake, uncovered, at 350⁰ for 30 minutes.

Loris Mayersohn

CRÈME FRAÎCHE

1½ cups whipping cream

4 Tablespoons buttermilk

Combine cream and buttermilk in a jar with tight fitting lid. Shake well for 2 or 3 minutes. Let stand at room temperature for at least 8 hours. Refrigerate until ready to use.

Use as a dessert topping. Very good added to vinegar and oil dressings. Delicious over fresh fruit and berries.

LEMON MINT BUTTER

Yield: 1 cup

1 cup softened butter
1 teaspoon grated lemon peel

2 Tablespoons chopped fresh mint
    leaves

Beat butter with lemon peel and mint leaves. Serve with banana nut bread or similar cakes.

Ellen La Cour

ALMOST MAPLE SYRUP

Yield: ¾ cup

1 cup brown sugar
⅓ cup water

⅛ teaspoon salt
¼ teaspoon vanilla extract

In saucepan dissolve sugar in water. Add salt and boil for 1 minute. Add vanilla and mix well. Serve warm.

Ellon Cockrill (Mrs. Rogers)

As good as bottled pancake syrup and very easy to make.

MATEUS SORBET

Yield: Approximately 1 quart

½ quart water
1 cup sugar

12 ounces Mateus wine

Boil water and sugar until dissolved. Add wine. Pour into a deep pan. Cool, then freeze. Just before serving, scrape with scoop and serve in a compote or in glasses with sugared rims.

Carrie Dickinson (Mrs. Tyndall)

You may substitute homemade muscadine or berry wines. So good at a formal meal, either before or with meat course.

STRAWBERRY SORBET

Yield: 8 to 10 servings

3 pints fresh strawberries or frozen
   berries
⅔ to 1 cup sugar (reduce sugar if
   using frozen berries that are
   sweetened)

Juice of 3 oranges
Juice of 3 lemons
⅓ cup Grand Marnier
Freshly grated nutmeg (Optional)

Wash, hull and drain berries. Combine with sugar, orange and lemon juice. Blend mixture in an electric blender or processor until smooth. Add Grand Marnier and pour into freezer trays. Freeze until sherbet is partially frozen. Transfer to a large bowl and beat until slushy. Return to trays and freeze until firm. Serve in dessert glasses or hollowed out orange shells. Sprinkle with nutmeg, if desired, or serve with a sprig of fresh mint. May be made in an ice cream freezer, if preferred.

Eva Rand (Mrs. Benjamin A.)

Serve as a dessert or between courses to cleanse the palate.

FROSTED FRUIT

Fruit
Egg whites, beaten

Sugar

Dip fruit in beaten egg white, then sprinkle with sugar. Let dry before arranging. Grapes are beautiful done this way and draped from a candelabra.

Helen Sloan (Mrs. John C.)

This is beautiful used as a decoration, but guests may help themselves to the fruit for dessert.

DESSERTS

...When such a merry tune is played upon the palate that the mind dances a little jig.

FRESH APPLE CAKE WITH HOT BUTTERED RUM SAUCE

Oven: 325°
Yield: 12 to 15 servings

Cake

½ cup butter
2 cups sugar
2 eggs
2 cups sifted all-purpose flour
1 teaspoon baking powder
¾ teaspoon baking soda

½ teaspoon salt
½ teaspoon nutmeg
½ teaspoon cinnamon
3 Washington Delicious apples, pared, cored and chopped
1½ cups chopped nuts

Sauce

1 cup sugar
½ cup butter

½ cup Half and Half
3 teaspoons rum extract

Whipped cream

Cream butter, gradually add sugar and beat until light and fluffy. Beat in eggs, 1 at a time. Sift together flour, baking powder, soda, salt, nutmeg and cinnamon. Gradually add to egg mixture. Dough will be fairly stiff. Stir in apples and nuts. Turn into buttered 9 x 13 pan. Bake at 325° for 55 to 70 minutes. For sauce, combine sugar, butter and cream. Warm over low heat, stirring occasionally, until hot. Stir in rum extract. Serve over cake and top with whipped cream.

Nancy Mitcham (Mrs. Robert)

Very rich and special.

BLUEBERRY POUND CAKE

Oven: 350°
Yield: 10 to 12 servings

1 (18½ ounce) box yellow cake mix
1 (8 ounce) package cream cheese, softened
½ cup salad oil

3 large eggs
1 (15 ounce) can whole blueberries, drained
2 teaspoons vanilla

Mix all ingredients together in mixer for 3 minutes. Pour into a buttered bundt pan. Bake for 45 minutes at 350°.

Tish Nisbet (Mrs. Wyck)

BLACK WALNUT CAKE

Oven: 350°
Yield: 3 layer cake

½ cup butter, softened
½ cup shortening
2 cups sugar
5 eggs, separated
1 cup buttermilk
1 teaspoon soda

2 cups flour
1 teaspoon vanilla
1½ cups chopped black walnuts
1 (3½ ounce) can flaked coconut
½ teaspoon cream of tartar

Cream Cheese Frosting
½ cup butter
1 (8 ounce) package cream cheese

1 (1 pound) box powdered sugar
1 teaspoon vanilla

Cream butter and shortening. Gradually add sugar, beating until light and fluffy and sugar is dissolved. Add egg yolks, beating well. Combine buttermilk and soda. Stir until soda dissolves. Add flour to creamed mixture alternately with buttermilk mixture, beginning and ending with flour. Stir in vanilla. Add 1 cup walnuts and coconut, stirring well. Beat egg whites with cream of tartar until stiff peaks form. Fold into batter. Pour into 3 greased and floured 9 inch round pans. Bake for 30 minutes at 350°. Cool 10 minutes, remove from pans. Cool completely before icing. Frost cake with cream cheese frosting. Sprinkle with remaining walnuts.
Frosting: Cream butter and cream cheese. Gradually add sugar, beating until light and fluffy. Stir in vanilla.

Mrs. H. L. Wilkinson
Stamps, Arkansas

MOTHER'S ENGLISH PECAN CAKE

Oven: 275°
Yield: 4 small loaves

1½ pounds white raisins
1 cup bourbon
¾ pound butter or margarine
2 cups sugar
6 eggs

4 cups flour
1 teaspoon baking powder
1 teaspoon nutmeg
1 quart chopped pecans

Soak raisins in bourbon overnight. Cream butter and sugar. Add eggs, 1 at a time. Sift flour, measure, then sift again with baking powder and nutmeg. Add to butter/sugar mixture. Add raisins and pecans. Pour into 4 (7½ x 3½ x 2¼) greased and floured loaf pans. Bake at 275° for 1½ hours. Test with a toothpick in center of loaves. Cool on a cake rack.

Sharon Bowman (Mrs. Lee)

A traditional Christmas recipe that has been handed down for generations.

CAKE 'N ALE

Oven: 350°
Yield: 10 to 12 servings

Cake

2 cups light brown sugar, firmly
  packed
1 cup shortening
2 eggs
3 cups all-purpose flour
2 teaspoons soda
½ teaspoon salt

1 Tablespoon cinnamon
½ teaspoon allspice
½ teaspoon cloves
2 cups beer
1 cup chopped pecans or walnuts
2 cups chopped dates

Caramel Frosting

½ cup butter, melted
1 cup dark brown sugar, firmly
  packed
¼ cup milk

¼ teaspoon salt
1 teaspoon vanilla
2 cups powdered sugar

Cake: Cream brown sugar and shortening until smooth. Add eggs, blending well. Sift dry ingredients in a separate bowl. Add dry ingredients to creamed mixture alternately with beer, beating well after each addition. Stir in nuts and dates. Spoon batter into a well-greased and floured 10 inch tube pan. Bake at 350⁰ for 1 hour and 15 minutes. Cool. Frost with caramel frosting, if desired.

Frosting: Combine butter and brown sugar. Cook over low heat, stirring constantly, until sugar dissolves. Add milk and bring to a boil. Remove from heat and cool slightly. Add salt, vanilla and powdered sugar. Beat to spreading consistency. Makes about 3 cups.

Tandy Cobb (Mrs. William, Jr.)

CREAM CHEESE POUND CAKE

Oven: 250°
Yield: 15 to 20 servings

¾ pound butter
1 (8 ounce) package cream cheese
3 cups sugar

6 eggs
3 cups flour
1 teaspoon vanilla

Cream butter, cheese and sugar. Add eggs, 1 at a time, beating thoroughly after each addition. Mix in flour a little at a time, blending well after each addition. Add vanilla. Pour batter into a greased and floured bundt pan. Bake at 250⁰ for 2 hours and 15 minutes or until toothpick inserted in center comes out clean. May be frozen.

Marybert Prather
Anniston, Alabama

BEST EVER CARROT CAKE
(Must be prepared 1 day in advance)

Oven: 350°
Yield: 12 to 18 servings

Cake
1¼ cups corn oil
2 cups sugar
2 cups less 2 Tablespoons flour
2 teaspoons cinnamon
2 teaspoons baking powder
1 teaspoon baking soda

1 teaspoon salt
4 eggs
4 cups grated carrots
1 cup raisins
1 cup chopped pecans

Filling
2 cups sugar
6 Tablespoons flour
1 teaspoon salt
2 cups whipping cream

½ pound butter
1 Tablespoon vanilla
1½ cups chopped pecans

Icing
½ pound cream cheese
½ pound butter
1 pound powdered sugar

1 teaspoon vanilla
4 ounces coconut, shredded

Cake: Whisk together corn oil and sugar. In a separate bowl mix flour, cinnamon, baking powder, soda and salt. Sift ½ of this mixture into the sugar/oil. Add the rest alternately with the 4 eggs. Add the carrots, raisins and pecans. Bake in a greased and floured 10 inch tube pan at 350⁰ for 70 minutes. Cool, invert and split in 3 layers.
Filling: Heat sugar, flour and salt. Stir in cream. Work in butter. Stir and simmer ½ hour until golden. Cool. Add vanilla and pecans. Cool overnight.
Icing: Cream cheese and butter. Sift in powdered sugar. Mix in vanilla and chill.

Spread the filling between the 3 layers. Frost the top and sides with the icing. Pat the coconut on the sides. Decorate the top, if desired.

Patricia Shelton

"My mother keeps in two big books
The secrets of the things she cooks.
If I could ever learn to bake,
I'd send my brother Bill a cake
But Mother says it's hard to learn
How to bake cakes that never burn."
MOTHER GOOSE RHYME

GIDGE'S CHOCOLATE TORTE

Yield: 12 servings

1 Angel Food cake
1 cup butter
2 cups powdered sugar
1 egg

1 teaspoon vanilla
2 squares unsweetened chocolate,
   melted
1 cup chopped nuts, toasted

Icing
½ cup powdered sugar
6 Tablespoons cocoa

⅛ teaspoon salt
2 cups whipping cream

Slice cake into 3 layers. Cream together the butter, powdered sugar and egg. Beat until light and fluffy. Add vanilla, chocolate and nuts. Spread between layers of cake. Sift together the powdered sugar, cocoa and salt. Add to the whipping cream and chill 2 hours. Whip and ice cake with this.

Ruth McAdams
Jonesboro, Arkansas

FRESH FIG CAKE WITH BUTTER PECAN FROSTING

Oven: 350°
Yield: 16 to 18 servings

1 pound butter
2 cups sugar
4 eggs, separated
2 teaspoons vanilla
2 cups flour
2 teaspoons baking powder

1 teaspoon salt
1 cup milk
1 cup wheat germ
3 to 4 cups figs
2 teaspoons cinnamon
½ teaspoon allspice

Butter Pecan Frosting
6 Tablespoons butter, softened
4 cups powdered sugar
4 Tablespoons milk

1 teaspoon vanilla
1 cup chopped pecans

Cream butter and sugar. Add egg yolks and vanilla. Mix together flour, baking powder and salt. Stir into batter alternately with milk. Beat egg whites until stiff and fold into flour mixture. Add wheat germ. Chop figs in blender or food processor and add to batter. Stir in spices. Pour into 2 (9 inch) greased and floured cake pans. Bake at 350° for 45 minutes or until center springs back. Cool and frost. For frosting, beat together first 4 ingredients until smooth and creamy. Add pecans.

Lindy Mitchell (Mrs. Maurice, Jr.)

Rich and outstanding!

FAVORITE CHEESECAKE WITH BLUEBERRY TOPPING

Oven: 375°
Yield: 12 servings

Crust

2 cups graham cracker crumbs
1 cup (2 sticks) butter, melted
½ cup sugar

½ teaspoon cinnamon
¼ teaspoon nutmeg

Filling

6 eggs
2 cups sugar

**1 (21 ounce) can blueberry pie
  filling**

**2 (8 ounce) packages cream cheese,
  softened**

Mix together all ingredients for crust and pat into the bottom of a springform pan. Set aside. Have eggs at room temperature. Beat eggs and slowly add sugar. Blend in cream cheese. Pour over crust and bake at 375° for 30 to 35 minutes or until lightly browned. Cool. Top with blueberry pie filling and refrigerate.

Cindy Miller (Mrs. Patrick)

May use other fruits for topping.

LITTLE ROCK CHEESECAKE

Oven: 300°
Yield: 24 servings

2 Tablespoons sugar
**1½ cups graham cracker crumbs (1
  package of graham crackers -
  may be crumbled in food
  processor)**
¾ stick butter, melted
1 teaspoon cinnamon (Optional)
**3 (8 ounce) packages Philadelphia
  cream cheese, softened**

1 cup sour cream
**1 (14 ounce) can Eagle Brand
  condensed milk**
4 egg yolks
½ teaspoon salt
1 Tablespoon lemon juice
1 teaspoon vanilla
4 egg whites
3 Tablespoons sugar

Butter sides and bottom of a 10 inch spring form pan. Combine 2 Tablespoons sugar, crumbs, butter and cinnamon and cover the pan with this mixture. Beat cream cheese, sour cream and milk until creamy. Slowly add egg yolks, salt, lemon juice and vanilla while continuing to beat. Beat egg whites and 3 Tablespoons sugar until stiff peaks are formed. Fold this into the cake batter. Place a pan of water on the bottom rack of oven. Bake cake at 300° for 1 hour. Turn off oven and open door. Leave cake in oven 1 more hour. Refrigerate for 4 hours before serving. Better the second day.

Mandy Dillard (Mrs. William, II)

CHOCOLATE AMARETTO CHEESECAKE
(Must be prepared 1 day in advance)

Oven: 375°
Yield: 16 to 18 servings

1½ cups finely crumbled chocolate wafer cookies
1 cup chopped almonds, lightly toasted
⅓ cup sugar
6 Tablespoons butter, softened
3 (8 ounce) packages cream cheese, softened
1 cup sugar

4 eggs
⅓ cup whipping cream
¼ cup Amaretto
1 teaspoon vanilla
2 cups sour cream
1 Tablespoon sugar
1 teaspoon vanilla
Slivered or sliced almonds

Combine the first 4 ingredients. Pat into the bottom and sides of a greased 9½ inch springform pan. Cream together the cream cheese and 1 cup sugar. Add the eggs, 1 at a time, beating well after each addition. Add the cream, Amaretto and 1 teaspoon vanilla and beat until light. Pour into the crust and place in the middle of a 375° oven. Bake for 30 minutes. Cool on a rack for 5 minutes. (Cake will not be set). Mix sour cream, 1 Tablespoon sugar and 1 teaspoon vanilla. Spread evenly on cake and bake for 5 more minutes. Let cool, then chill overnight, lightly covered. Remove the sides of the pan and decorate with almonds.

Ben Hussman (Mrs. Walter, Jr.)

TOFFEE CAKE

Oven: 350°
Yield: 12 to 14 servings

½ cup margarine
½ cup sugar
1 cup brown sugar
2 cups sifted flour
1 teaspoon baking soda
½ teaspoon salt

1 cup buttermilk
1 egg
1 teaspoon vanilla
6 Heath bars, frozen and crushed
½ cup chopped nuts

Cream margarine with sugars. Sift dry ingredients together and add to creamed margarine. Put aside ½ cup of this mixture for topping. To remainder, add buttermilk, egg and vanilla. Pour batter into greased and floured 9 x 13 pan. To the ½ cup reserved topping, add crushed Heath bars and nuts. Spread over top of batter. Bake at 350° for 30 minutes.

Tish Nisbet (Mrs. Wyck)

COCONUT CAKE

Oven: 325°
Yield: 16 servings

Cake

1 (18½ ounce) package butter
   yellow cake mix
1 cup sour cream
½ cup Wesson oil

5 eggs
½ cup white Karo syrup
1 teaspoon vanilla

Icing

2 cups sugar
4 egg whites, room temperature
6 Tablespoons cold water
2 Tablespoons white Karo syrup
¼ teaspoon cream of tartar

1 teaspoon vanilla
Freshly grated coconut or 1
   package flaked coconut
   (Optional)

Preheat oven to 325°. Mix cake mix, sour cream, oil, eggs, Karo and vanilla with electric mixer for 3 to 4 minutes. Pour into a greased 9 x 13 cake pan. Bake 45 minutes to 1 hour. Cooking time may vary according to oven. Test for doneness by inserting toothpick into center of cake. When toothpick comes out dry, cake is done, but cake will be very soft in the center. To prepare icing, combine sugar, egg whites, water, Karo and cream of tartar. Cook over boiling water, beating constantly with electric mixer until icing stands in soft peaks. Remove from heat, add vanilla and beat 1 minute more. Spread over cake and sprinkle coconut over top, if desired.

Barbara Moore (Mrs. J. Malcolm, Jr.)

FABULOUS FUDGECAKE

Oven: 300°
Yield: 20 to 24 servings

1 cup margarine
2 cups sugar
4 eggs
½ cup cocoa

1 cup self-rising flour
1 teaspoon vanilla
1 cup chopped pecans

Icing

1 (1 pound) box powdered sugar
5 Tablespoons cocoa

½ cup hot water and 2 teaspoons
   instant coffee OR ½ cup strong
   prepared coffee
4 Tablespoons margarine, softened

Soften margarine to room temperature and cream in sugar. Add eggs and blend. Add cocoa, flour and vanilla and blend well. Stir in pecans and pour into a greased 9 x 13 baking dish. Bake at 300° for 45 to 55 minutes. Cool 5 minutes. Pat sides down even with the middle. For icing, mix ingredients and spread on cake in pan. Let sit at least 4 hours before serving. Freezes well, thaw and serve.

Lisa Foster (Mrs. Vincent, Jr.)

CHOCOLATE DEADLY DELIGHTS

Oven: 350°
Yield: 48 servings

3 (1 ounce) squares unsweetened
chocolate
1 cup butter
2 cups sugar
1⅓ cups unsifted flour

2 teaspoons vanilla
4 eggs, beaten
2 cups chopped pecans
48 (2½ inch) paper baking cups

Icing
4 Tablespoons butter
2 (1 ounce) squares unsweetened
chocolate

4 cups powdered sugar
½ cup cold prepared coffee

Melt chocolate and butter in double boiler over low heat. Mix in sugar, flour, vanilla and eggs. Add nuts and stir. Fill paper baking cups ½ full. Bake in a muffin tin or on a cookie sheet for 12 to 15 minutes at 350⁰. While deadlies are cooking, melt butter and chocolate. Add sugar and enough coffee to make a smooth mixture. Ice while hot.

Mrs. A. T. Mulligan

Great for large informal buffets. May easily be frozen in plastic bags.

BAKED FUDGE WITH RUM SAUCE

Oven: 300°
Yield: 8 servings

2¼ cups sugar
⅔ cup flour
⅔ cup cocoa
5 eggs, well beaten

1 cup plus 2 Tablespoons butter
2 teaspoons vanilla
1 cup coarsely chopped pecans

Sauce
1 egg yolk
½ cup powdered sugar

2 to 3 Tablespoons light rum
1 cup whipping cream, whipped

Mix sugar, flour and cocoa. Add to beaten eggs and blend thoroughly. Melt butter and add vanilla. Thoroughly combine butter and cocoa mixtures. Add nuts. Bake in individual custard cups in a pan of hot water for 45 minutes to 1 hour at 300⁰. Should be firm, like custard. For sauce, mix together egg yolk, sugar and rum. Fold this mixture into stiffly whipped cream. Serve on top of slightly warm baked fudge.

Sally Sanderson

HOT FUDGE SUNDAE CAKE

Oven: 350°
Yield: 18 to 20 servings

1 (6 ounce) package semi-sweet
   chocolate chips
1 cup margarine
2 cups sugar
4 eggs
1 cup buttermilk

2½ cups flour
¼ teaspoon baking soda
⅔ cup Hershey syrup
2 teaspoons vanilla
⅛ teaspoon salt
1 cup chopped pecans

Optional
Bananas
Whipped topping
Maraschino cherries

Ice cream
Hot fudge topping
Glaze

Do NOT preheat oven. Place chocolate chips in a double boiler. While they are melting, cream margarine and sugar together. Add eggs, beating well. Add melted chocolate, buttermilk, flour and soda (sifted together), Hershey syrup, vanilla and salt. Shake pecans in flour and add to mixture. Bake in greased and floured tube or bundt pan. Start in a cold oven and bake at 350° for 1½ hours. Serving suggestions: Serve 2 thin slices with sliced bananas sandwiched in between. Top each serving with whipped topping and a cherry. Or sandwich ice cream between slices and top with bananas and hot fudge sauce. Also good iced with your favorite glaze.

Judy Hupfer (Mrs. James)

MARGUERITES
(Small Cakes)

Oven: 350°
Yield: 18 to 20 cakes

Cakes
2 eggs, slightly beaten
1 cup light brown sugar
½ cup flour

⅓ teaspoon salt
¼ teaspoon baking powder
1 cup chopped pecans

Frosting
6 Tablespoons butter
2 Tablespoons milk
3 cups powdered sugar

1 teaspoon vanilla
Pinch of salt

Mix cake ingredients in order given. Fill small buttered muffin tins ⅔ full of mixture and bake for 8 to 15 minutes at 350°. Take cakes out of tin while hot and let cool on a rack. Frost when cool. Grease pan before using again.

Lucy Jackson (Mrs. Dorsey)

SURPRISE CUPCAKES

Oven: 350°
Yield: 2½ dozen

Filling
1 (8 ounce) package cream cheese,
   softened
1 egg
⅓ cup sugar

½ teaspoon salt
1 (6 ounce) package semi-sweet
   chocolate chips

Cupcake
3 cups flour
2 cups sugar
½ cup cocoa
1 teaspoon salt
2 teaspoons baking soda

⅔ cup salad oil
2 cups water
2 Tablespoons vinegar
2 teaspoons vanilla

Icing
½ box powdered sugar
½ stick butter

2 squares unsweetened chocolate
1 teaspoon vanilla

Filling: Beat together all ingredients, except chocolate chips, until smooth. Stir in chips.
Cupcakes: Sift dry ingredients together into a large bowl. Add all liquids. Mix until smooth. Fill cupcake pans ⅔ full. Top with heaping teaspoon of filling. Bake at 350⁰ for 25 minutes.
Icing: Sift powdered sugar into a large bowl. Melt ½ stick butter and chocolate over low heat. Add chocolate mix to sugar. Add vanilla. Stir. Add milk, if needed, to improve consistency. Ice cupcakes when cool.

Sally Carter (Mrs. William)

Rich but irresistable!

COBBLER, QUICHE OR PIE CRUST

Yield: 2 pie crusts plus

2 cups flour
1 Tablespoon sugar
1 teaspoon salt
¾ cup white vegetable shortening

1 egg yolk
¼ cup milk
1 Tablespoon lemon juice (or 1
   Tablespoon wine)

Mix all ingredients together (may be done in food processor). Place in refrigerator until COLD. Divide into 2 parts and roll thin on a well-floured surface for pies. Roll thicker for cobblers. Substitute 1 Tablespoon wine for the lemon juice when using for quiches.

Lucy Jackson (Mrs. Dorsey)

Use a pastry cloth to cover pastry - it makes working with it easier.

PASTRY PERFECTED

Yield: 2 (9 inch) pie crusts

1 cup Crisco shortening
2¾ cups flour
1½ teaspoons salt

1 egg
Water

Cut shortening into flour and salt mixture with 2 knives. Beat egg in a measuring cup, then add water to measure ½ cup. Add egg and water mixture to flour mixture. Do not overmix. Place dough in refrigerator for 1 hour before rolling crust.

Mandy Dillard (Mrs. William, II)

BLACK BOTTOM PIE

Oven: 350°
Yield: 9 servings

Crust
1½ cups crushed cookies, by hand
    or in food processor (chocolate
    wafers, graham crackers or
    gingersnaps)

6 Tablespoons butter, melted

Filling
2 cups milk
4 eggs, separated
½ cup sugar
2 Tablespoons cornstarch
2 teaspoons vanilla
1½ squares unsweetened chocolate,
    melted

1 Tablespoon gelatin
4 Tablespoons cold water
½ cup sugar
¼ teaspoon cream of tartar
2 Tablespoons rum

1 cup whipping cream, whipped
2 Tablespoons powdered sugar

Grated chocolate

To prepare crust, mix cookie crumbs with butter and pat in bottom of an 8 inch square pan. Bake crust for 15 minutes at 350°. To prepare filling, heat milk in double boiler. Combine egg yolks, ½ cup sugar and cornstarch. Add to hot milk. Cook 20 minutes. Add vanilla. Remove 1 cup cooked custard, adding melted chocolate to it and cool. Pour into baked crust. To rest of custard add gelatin dissolved in cold water. Let cool but don't let thicken. Beat egg whites until frothy. Continue beating until stiff peaks form while adding ½ cup sugar, cream of tartar and rum. Add to custard. Pour over chocolate layer and chill until set. Cover with whipped cream sweetened with powdered sugar. Sprinkle chocolate on top. Chill several hours.

Diane Larrison (Mrs. James H., Jr.)

QUICK COCONUT CREAM PIE
(Adapted for Microwave)

Oven: Microwave - high
Yield: 8 to 10 servings

2 cups whole milk
¾ cup sugar
¼ cup cornstarch
Dash of salt
3 large eggs, separated
1 teaspoon vanilla
½ teaspoon lemon extract

2 Tablespoons butter, melted
¾ cup grated coconut, fresh or
    canned flake
1 (10 inch) pie shell, baked
1 cup whipping cream, whipped
3 Tablespoons grated coconut,
    toasted

Pour milk in a 4 cup pyrex measuring cup which contains a wooden spatula. Cook on full power for 2 minutes. Add sugar, cornstarch and salt to beaten egg yolks. Add a little scalded milk to yolk mixture, stir well and place all in measuring cup. Stir with wooden spatula and cook 1 minute at a time, stirring after each cooking to mix well, until the custard is very thick. Add flavorings, butter and coconut. Cool. Fold in stiffly beaten egg whites. Turn into pie shell and top with whipped cream and toasted coconut. Chill.

Nancy Wood (Mrs. Craig S.)

May also be made in a double boiler, stirring custard until thick (approximately 20 minutes).

OLD FASHIONED CHOCOLATE PIE

Oven: 350°
Yield: 6 to 8 servings

Filling
1¼ cups sugar
4 Tablespoons cornstarch
3 Tablespoons cocoa
¼ teaspoon salt

1 (9 inch) pie shell

2½ cups milk
3 egg yolks, beaten
1 teaspoon vanilla
1 Tablespoon butter

Meringue
3 egg whites
3 Tablespoons sugar

Pinch of cream of tartar

Mix together first 4 ingredients in a double boiler. Add milk and egg yolks and cook over medium heat until thick, stirring constantly. Stir in butter and vanilla. Pour into baked pie shell. Chill. Beat egg whites until stiff, gradually adding sugar and pinch of cream of tartar. Spread over cooled chocolate filling and bake at 350° until lightly browned.

Monette McSpadden (Mrs. Ray)

CHOCOLATE CHESS PIE

Oven: 350°
Yield: 6 to 8 servings

1½ cups sugar
⅓ cup cocoa
2 Tablespoons flour
1 cup evaporated milk
5⅓ Tablespoons butter

2 eggs, slightly beaten
2 teaspoons vanilla
1 (9 inch) pie shell, unbaked
1 cup pecan halves (Optional)

Mix dry ingredients and set aside. Heat milk and butter until melted. Add eggs and vanilla to milk mixture. Stir. Combine liquids with dry ingredients, mixing well. Pour into pie shell. Sprinkle with pecans, if desired. Bake at 350° for 45 minutes. Allow to cool before cutting.

Linda Burrow VanHook (Mrs. Fred F.)

OUR TRADITIONAL APPLE PIE

Oven: 450°
Yield: 8 servings

Pastry
½ cup shortening
2 cups flour
¾ teaspoon salt

1 cup shredded Cheddar cheese
6 to 8 Tablespoons cold water
Melted shortening

Filling
6 large tart apples
Juice of ½ lemon
1 stick butter, separated
½ cup sugar

2 Tablespoons flour
¼ teaspoon nutmeg
2 teaspoons cinnamon

Pastry: Work shortening into sifted flour and salt until mixture resembles small peas in size. Lightly stir in cheese. Add water until it holds the mixture together. Roll out to form bottom and top crusts for a 9 inch pie pan. Place bottom crust in pan and brush with melted shortening.
Filling: Pare, core and slice apples. Place enough apples over crust to almost fill pan. Squeeze lemon juice over apples. Cut ½ stick butter into small pieces and scatter over apples. Mix dry ingredients and sprinkle over apples.
Cover with crust, flute the edge and make cutouts for steam to escape during baking. Dot with remaining ½ stick butter cut into small pieces. Bake at 450° until edges brown. Reduce oven to 350° and bake about 30 minutes.

"The best of all physicians
Is Apple-pie and cheese."
EUGENE FIELD
1850-1895

MUD PIE

Yield: 1 (9 inch) pie

21 Oreo cookies
6 Tablespoons butter, melted
1 quart chocolate ice cream
2 Tablespoons ground coffee
   granules (Optional)

2 Tablespoons instant Sanka
½ pint whipping cream, whipped
2 Tablespoons brandy
2 Tablespoons Kahlua
1 (12 ounce) jar Kraft fudge topping

Crush cookies very fine and mix with butter. Press into a 9 inch pie pan. Freeze. Whip together ice cream, coffees, 4 tablespoons whipped cream, brandy and Kahlua. Pour into frozen pie shell. Freeze until very *hard*, spread fudge over pie with a knife dipped into hot water. Return to freezer. Serve with remaining whipped cream.

Cathy Buford (Mrs. Douglas)

CHESS PIE

Oven: 300°
Yield: 2 pies

1 cup butter
2 cups sugar
½ cup milk
3 Tablespoons whipping cream

1 teaspoon vanilla
10 egg yolks
2 (8 or 9 inch) pie crusts, unbaked

Cream butter and sugar. Add milk, cream and vanilla. Beat in egg yolks by hand with a wooden spoon. Pour into pie crusts. Bake 1 hour at 300º. Pierce tops with toothpicks at intervals to keep from rising.

Debby Bransford Coates (Mrs. Wayne)

A holiday favorite.

RUM CREAM PIE

Yield: 6 to 8 servings

6 egg yolks
1 cup sugar
1 Tablespoon gelatin
¼ cup cold water

1 pint whipping cream
2 Tablespoons rum extract
1 (9 inch) graham cracker crust
Bitter chocolate, grated

Beat eggs and sugar together until light. Dissolve gelatin in water and bring to a boil over low heat. Pour into egg mixture, beating briskly. Let cool. Beat cream until stiff and fold into egg mixture. Add rum extract and pour into crust. Place in refrigerator to set. Grate chocolate on top.

Barbi Rushing (Mrs. Nolan, Jr.)

LEMON MERINGUE PIE

Oven: 375°
Yield: 6 to 8 servings

1⅔ cups crushed graham crackers
¼ cup sugar
½ cup butter, softened
½ cup freshly squeezed lemon juice
1 teaspoon freshly grated lemon rind

1 (14 ounce) can Eagle Brand condensed milk
2 eggs, separated
¼ teaspoon cream of tartar
4 Tablespoons sugar

Mix graham cracker crumbs and sugar with a fork. Blend in butter. Press into bottom and sides of a 9 inch glass pie pan. Bake at 375° for 8 minutes. Chill. Combine lemon juice and rind in a small mixing bowl. Gradually add milk. Add egg yolks and beat on medium speed until well blended. Pour into chilled crust. Combine egg whites with cream of tartar and beat until almost holds peak. Add sugar, 1 Tablespoon at a time, beating until stiff but not dry. Spread meringue on filling and bake at 325° until lightly browned (about 15 minutes). Cool. Refrigerate until ready to serve.

Carol Hodges (Mrs. Thomas L.)

SOUR CREAM LEMON PIE

Yield: 8 servings

¼ cup butter
2 Tablespoons cornstarch
1 cup sugar
¼ cup fresh lemon juice
1½ Tablespoons grated lemon peel

3 egg yolks
1 cup sour cream
1 (9 inch) pie shell, baked
Whipped cream

Combine butter, cornstarch, sugar, lemon juice, 1 Tablespoon lemon peel and egg yolks. Stir constantly over medium heat until thick. Cool in refrigerator for 30 to 45 minutes, being careful not to let harden. Add sour cream and blend well. Pour into pie shell and refrigerate until firm (best if overnight). Top with whipped cream. Sprinkle remaining lemon peel on top.

A Very Special Tearoom

To make a perfect meringue: Separate the yolks from the whites when the eggs are cold and then let the whites come to room temperature in a covered bowl. Even a trace of yolk in the whites will prevent them from reaching full volume when beaten.

BLUEBERRY CREAM PIE

Oven: 400°
Yield: 6 to 8 servings

1 cup sour cream
2 Tablespoons flour
¾ cup sugar
1 teaspoon vanilla
¼ teaspoon salt

1 egg, beaten
2½ to 3 cups fresh blueberries
1 (9 inch) pie shell, unbaked
4 Tablespoons flour
4 Tablespoons butter, softened
4 Tablespoons chopped pecans

Combine first 6 ingredients and beat 5 minutes at medium speed or until smooth. Fold in blueberries. Pour into pie shell and bake at 400° for 25 minutes. Combine remaining ingredients, stirring well. Sprinkle over top of pie. Bake an additional 10 minutes. Chill well before serving.

Susan Gregory (Mrs. H. Watt)

OLD FASHIONED PEACH COBBLER

Oven: 350°
Yield: 8 servings

Peach Filling
12 fresh peaches (may substitute
    frozen)
1 stick butter or margarine
1½ Tablespoons flour

1 cup sugar
⅛ teaspoon nutmeg
¼ teaspoon ground cloves
Juice of ½ lemon

Pastry
1 cup flour
2 Tablespoons sugar
¼ teaspoon salt

⅛ teaspoon nutmeg
4 Tablespoons shortening
4 Tablespoons ice water

Peach Filling: Peel peaches and dice into ¼ inch cubes. Melt butter, add flour and stir until smooth. Add sugar, nutmeg, cloves, lemon juice and peaches. Mix well and set aside.
Pastry: Mix flour, sugar, salt and nutmeg. Add shortening. Work mixture until it has the texture of coarse meal. Add ice water and stir with a spoon, using as few strokes as possible.
Cobbler: Roll out dough on floured surface. Prepare 4 pastry shells to fit any deep sided baking dish (9 x 5 or 8 inch square). Bake 2 of the shells at 350° until golden brown. Cool. Place 1 unbaked shell in bottom of dish. Add layer of peach filling. Place a baked shell on top of the peaches and top with more filling. Add a second baked shell and cover with remaining peach filling. Top with final unbaked pastry to cover the dish. Bake at 350° for 45 minutes or until golden brown.

Willie Braxton

PEANUT BUTTER PIE

Oven: 325°
Yield: 6 to 8 servings

1 (9 inch) pie crust
1 cup powdered sugar
½ cup crunchy peanut butter
¼ cup cornstarch
⅔ cup sugar
¼ teaspoon salt

2 cups scalded milk
3 egg yolks, beaten
2 Tablespoons butter or margarine
¼ teaspoon vanilla
3 egg whites
Pinch of cream of tartar

Bake pie crust. Cool. Combine powdered sugar and peanut butter. Blend until the appearance of bisquick mix. Spread half of this mixture on pie crust. Combine cornstarch, sugar and salt. Add scalded milk and mix well. Pour small amount over beaten egg yolks, mix well, then return to milk mixture. Cook in top of double boiler until mixture thickens. Add butter and vanilla. Pour into pie crust. Beat egg whites with cream of tartar until stiff. Spread over pie. Sprinkle the remainder of peanut butter mixture over meringue. Bake at 325° until the meringue is brown. Refrigerate until ready to serve.

Alpha B. Ambort

PRALINE CRUNCH PIE

Oven 400°
Yield: 1 (10 inch) pie

Pie
1¼ cups graham cracker crumbs
¼ cup sugar
⅓ cup butter, melted

½ gallon vanilla ice cream,
  softened
1 (7 ounce) bag Bits of Brickle

Sauce
1⅓ cups sugar
1 cup evaporated milk
¼ cup butter

⅓ cup light corn syrup
Dash of salt

Mix crumbs, sugar and butter and pat into 10 inch pie pan. Bake at 400° for 8 to 10 minutes. Spoon ½ of the ice cream into the pie crust. Sprinkle ½ of the Bits of Brickle over ice cream. Cover with just enough of the remaining ice cream to fill pie crust. Freeze. Make sauce by combining sugar, milk, butter, syrup and salt. Boil over low heat for 1 minute. Remove from heat and stir in remaining Brickle. Cool and stir. Store sauce in refrigerator. Spoon over pie pieces when serving.

Carrie Dickinson (Mrs. Tyndall)

FROZEN PUMPKIN PIE

Yield: 6 to 8 servings

1 cup canned pumpkin
1 quart vanilla ice cream
½ cup brown sugar
¼ teaspoon salt
¼ teaspoon ginger

¼ teaspoon nutmeg
½ teaspoon cinnamon
1 (9 inch) graham cracker crust
Whipping cream, whipped
  (Optional)

Sauce
1½ cups brown sugar
⅔ cup dark Karo syrup
½ cup water

⅔ cup evaporated milk
2 Tablespoons sherry
½ cup chopped nuts

Mix first 7 ingredients. Pour into pie shell. Freeze until ready to serve. Remove from freezer and top with whipped cream, if desired. To make sauce, mix sugar, Karo and water. Bring to a boil and stir constantly for 5 minutes. Remove from heat and cool 5 minutes. Stir in evaporated milk, sherry and nuts. Pour sauce over pie and serve. May be served hot or cold.

Lydia Penick Miles (Mrs. Joe)
Newport, Arkansas

RAISIN NUT PIE

Oven: 450°
Yield: 2 pies

4 eggs, separated
2 cups sugar
3 teaspoons butter
3 Tablespoons vinegar
1 teaspoon nutmeg
1 teaspoon ground cloves

1 teaspoon cinnamon
1 cup chopped pecans
1 cup chopped raisins
Pastry for pie crust
Whipped cream

Beat egg yolks slightly. Add sugar and butter, then vinegar and spices. Beat egg whites until stiff. Add these to mixture. Fold in nuts and raisins. Pour into unbaked pie shells and form a lattice crust on top. Bake at 450° for 10 minutes, then at 350° for about 30 minutes until browned and puffy. Serve with a dollop of whipped cream.

Cherry Harkey (Mrs. W.M.)
Batesville, Arkansas

Especially good at Thanksgiving.

"What calls back the past, like the rich pumpkin pie?"
JOHN GREENLEAF WHITTIER
1807-1892

HOT CHOCOLATE SOUFFLÉ

Oven: 375°
Yield: 6 servings

3 squares unsweetened chocolate
1 cup sugar, divided
4 eggs, separated
¼ teaspoon salt

2 teaspoons vanilla
½ cup broken pecans
Whipping cream, whipped

Melt chocolate in top of double boiler or in microwave. Stir in ⅓ cup sugar. Beat egg whites and salt. Continue beating and add ⅓ cup sugar. Combine yolks and whites. Fold in chocolate. Add vanilla and nuts. Turn into a well-buttered 1 quart casserole. Set casserole in pan of hot water. Bake for 30 to 40 minutes at 375⁰. Serve with whipped cream.

Julie Allen (Mrs. Wally)

GRAND MARNIER SOUFFLÉ

Oven: 400°
Yield: 2 generous servings

Butter and sugar for preparing
    bowls
¼ cup cornstarch
¼ cup sugar
Pinch of salt
1½ Tablespoons butter
5 ounces milk

¾ Tablespoon finely grated orange
    rind
3 egg yolks
1½ Tablespoons Grand Marnier
4 egg whites
Pinch of cream of tartar
2 Tablespoons sugar

Place rack in middle of oven and preheat oven to 400⁰. Butter well the sides and bottom of 2 (12 ounce) soufflé bowls. Sprinkle them with sugar, dumping out the excess sugar. Measure and mix together the cornstarch, ¼ cup sugar and salt. Place the butter and milk in a heavy saucepan and while still cold, stir in the above dry ingredients and the grated orange rind. Cook the mixture over medium heat, stirring constantly with a wire whip until the mixture thickens. Remove from heat and thoroughly stir in the egg yolks and the Grand Marnier. Beat the egg whites with the cream of tartar until limp. Add 2 Tablespoons sugar and continue beating at high speed to develop a good meringue. Take half of the beaten egg whites and, using a rubber spatula, stir them into the sauce to lighten it. Give the remaining egg whites several good whips and then fold them into the lightened sauce. Do not overfold as you will deflate the mixture. Divide the mixture between the prepared bowls. (At this point, you may delay baking the soufflés for up to 30 minutes). Place the soufflés in the preheated oven and cook for 15 minutes. Serve immediately.

Paul Bash
Restaurant Jacques and Suzanne

If desired, accompany the soufflés with sweetened, Grand Marnier flavored whipped cream. A glass of champagne adds the crowning touch!

HOT LEMON SOUFFLÉ

Oven: 375°
Yield: 6 servings

3 eggs, separated
¾ cup sugar, divided
3 Tablespoons flour
1 cup milk

4 Tablespoons butter, melted
Juice of 3 lemons
3 lemon rinds, grated
Whipped cream

Beat yolks with ½ cup of sugar until very light. Add flour, milk and butter. Mix well. Beat egg whites until stiff. Beat in ¼ cup of sugar. Add lemon juice and rind to egg whites. Fold into custard. Turn into well-buttered 1 quart casserole. Set in pan of hot water and bake for 30 minutes at 375⁰. Remove from water and return to oven to brown, about 5 minutes. Serve warm with whipped cream.

Julie Allen (Mrs. Wally)

COLD LEMON SOUFFLÉ WITH WINE SAUCE

Yield: 8 to 10 servings

1 envelope unflavored gelatin
¼ cup cold water
5 eggs, separated
¾ cup fresh lemon juice

2 teaspoons grated lemon rind
1½ cups sugar
1 cup whipping cream

Wine Sauce
½ cup sugar
3 teaspoons cornstarch
½ cup water
3 Tablespoons fresh lemon juice

1 teaspoon grated lemon rind
2 Tablespoons butter or margarine
½ cup dry white wine

Sprinkle gelatin over cold water to soften. Mix egg yolks with lemon juice, rind and ¾ cup sugar. Place in double boiler over boiling water and cook, stirring constantly, until lemon mixture is slightly thickened (about 8 minutes). Remove from heat and stir in gelatin until dissolved. Chill 30 to 40 minutes or until mixture mounds slightly when dropped from spoon. Beat egg whites until they begin to hold their shape. Gradually add remaining ¾ cup sugar. Beat until stiff. Beat cream until stiff. Fold egg whites and cream into yolk mixture until no white streaks remain. Pour into a 2 quart soufflé dish and chill 4 or more hours. Serve with wine sauce.

Wine sauce: In a small saucepan, mix together sugar and cornstarch. Stir in water, lemon juice and rind until smooth. Add butter. Bring to a boil, lower heat and cook until thickened (about 3 minutes). Remove from heat and stir in wine. Chill, stirring occasionally.

Barbara Mills (Mrs. Dennis)

COLD ORANGE SOUFFLÉ

Yield: 8 to 10 servings

1 cup cold water
2 envelopes unflavored gelatin
8 eggs, separated
½ teaspoon salt

2 (6 ounce) cans frozen orange
  juice, thawed
1 cup sugar
1 cup whipping cream, whipped
Orange sections (Optional)

Place water in the top of a double boiler and sprinkle the gelatin over the surface to soften. Beat egg yolks lightly and add them with the salt to the gelatin. Mix well. Place over boiling water and cook, stirring constantly, until gelatin dissolves and the mixture thickens some, about 4 minutes. Remove from heat and stir in orange concentrate. Chill until mixture drops from a spoon into soft mounds. Beat egg whites until stiff but not dry. Gradually beat in the sugar and continue beating until the egg whites are stiff. Fold the whites into the orange mixture. Fold in the whipped cream. Arrange a collar of doubled waxed paper around a 2½ quart soufflé dish, 2 inches above the top of the dish. Fasten with tape. Pour mixture into dish and chill until firm. Remove collar and decorate with orange sections.

A great summer dessert.

BUTTERSCOTCH SAUCE

Yield: 2½ cups

1½ cups light brown sugar
½ cup white corn syrup
4 Tablespoons butter

½ cup whipping cream
1 teaspoon vanilla
Toasted pecans (Optional)

Mix sugar, syrup and butter in saucepan. Bring to a boil over low heat. Remove from heat and stir in cream and vanilla. If desired, add toasted pecans to sauce immediately before serving. May be reheated in microwave.

Shannon Fewell

CHOCOLATE BUTTERNUT SAUCE

Yield: 8 to 10 servings

1 cup butter
1 (12 ounce) package semi-sweet
  chocolate chips

1 cup coarsely chopped walnuts or
  pecans, toasted

Combine butter and chocolate chips in top of double boiler over simmering water. Heat until melted. Stir in nuts. Serve slightly warm over peppermint ice cream. (The chocolate sauce will harden slightly on the ice cream.) May be reheated in microwave.

Gloria Allen (Mrs. Charles A.)

CHOCOLATE SAUCE

Yield: approximately 2 cups

3 (1 ounce) squares unsweetened
   chocolate
1 cup sugar
½ cup light Karo syrup

¼ cup water
1 cup evaporated milk
1 teaspoon vanilla

Melt chocolate over hot water in double boiler. Add sugar and syrup and blend thoroughly. Add water and mix. Cook to a soft ball stage (235⁰). Remove from heat and add milk and vanilla. Stir. Will keep in closed jar in refrigerator indefinitely. Heat to serve.

Linda Burrow VanHook (Mrs. Fred F.)

EASY CHOCOLATE SAUCE

Yield: approximately 2 cups

½ cup butter
2 cups sugar
¼ teaspoon cream of tartar
1 (5.3 ounce) can evaporated milk
4 (1 ounce) squares semi-sweet
   chocolate

1 teaspoon vanilla
18 large marshmallows
Pinch of salt
Chopped pecans

Melt all ingredients except nuts in double boiler. Let cool. Stir in nuts and serve over ice cream.

Ann Warrick (Mrs. Alan)
Pine Bluff, Arkansas

GERMAN CHOCOLATE SAUCE

Yield: 8 servings

1 Tablespoon butter
1 (4 ounce) bar German sweet
   chocolate
¼ cup prepared coffee

1 cup powdered sugar
Dash of salt
½ teaspoon vanilla

Melt butter and chocolate in coffee over low heat. Add sugar, salt and vanilla. Beat with a mixer until well blended.

Nancy Bishop (Mrs. William E.)

Serve over pound cake or ice cream.

GRAND MARNIER SAUCE

Yield: 8 servings

5 egg yolks
½ cup sugar

½ cup Grand Marnier
1 cup whipping cream, whipped

Whip yolks and sugar. Cook over low heat until thick and creamy, stirring constantly. Chill over ice water. Add Grand Marnier. Whip cream (not too dry). Blend cream and Grand Marnier mixture. Chill. Serve over strawberries or raspberries.

Susan Freeling Carr (Mrs. Phil)
Washington, D.C.

KAHLUA MOCHA SAUCE

Yield: 1¼ cups

3 ounces sweet chocolate
½ ounce unsweetened chocolate
2 teaspoons instant coffee granules

¼ cup whipping cream
3 Tablespoons Kahlua
⅓ cup whipping cream

Melt chocolates together in double boiler. Set aside. Combine instant coffee with ¼ cup cream. Stir until coffee dissolves. Combine coffee mixture with chocolates. Add Kahlua. In a chilled bowl beat ⅓ cup cream until fluffy. Fold into chocolate mixture. Serve immediately over coffee, butter pecan or vanilla ice cream.

If refrigerated, may be served as a mousse or pie filling.

ZABAGLIONE

Yield: 4 servings

4 egg yolks
3 ounces Marsala wine
3 Tablespoons sugar

Fresh berries
Ice Cream

Place egg yolks, wine and sugar in a copper rounded pan or double boiler and whisk until mixture has a whipped creamy texture (about 5 to 15 minutes). Pour over ice cream and strawberries or raspberries in large wine glasses.

Lex Golden

BANANA NUT ICE CREAM

Yield: 1 gallon

5 to 6 ripe bananas
1¾ cups sugar
½ teaspoon salt
1 teaspoon vanilla
1 pint whipping cream

1 quart Half and Half
1 (13 ounce) can evaporated milk
¾ cup chopped nuts
Milk

Mash bananas. Mix with sugar, salt and vanilla. Add cream, Half and Half, evaporated milk and nuts. Pour into ice cream freezer. Fill to line with milk. Freeze according to freezer directions.

Mrs. Jim Robason

Absolutely delicious!

BUTTER PECAN ICE CREAM

Yield: 1 gallon

4 eggs, beaten
2¼ cups sugar
5 cups milk
4 cups whipping cream
4½ teaspoons vanilla

½ teaspoon salt
¼ cup butter
2 cups chopped pecans
¼ cup brown sugar

In a large mixing bowl, gradually add sugar to eggs, beating until stiff. Add milk, cream, vanilla and salt and mix well. Refrigerate. Melt butter and sauté pecans. Add brown sugar and stir until melted. Cool well. Add to ice cream mixture and freeze in ice cream freezer.

Debbie R. Nolan

OUR HOMEMADE ICE CREAM

Yield: 8 to 10 servings

6 eggs
1 cup sugar
1 (14 ounce) can Eagle Brand condensed milk

1 pint Half and Half
2 teaspoons vanilla
Milk

Beat eggs until fluffy, adding sugar gradually. Fold in Eagle Brand. Add Half and Half and vanilla and pour into ice cream freezer (6 quart size). Fill to 3 inches from top with milk. Variation: add chocolate chips or any fruit that has been sweetened with sugar.

Ellen Golden (Mrs. Lex)

SNOW ICE CREAM

Yield: 2 servings

1 egg
½ pint whipping cream
½ cup sugar

2 teaspoons vanilla
Snow

Combine all ingredients except snow. When well mixed, fold in enough snow to make mixture thick. Eat at once!

Stephanie Jane Haught

A fun recipe for children to make if and when it snows!

FROZEN STRAWBERRY CREAM

Yield: 9 to 10 servings

1 (24 ounce) carton sour cream
1 (8 ounce) package cream cheese, softened
1 cup sugar (up to ⅓ cup more if strawberries are not sweet)

½ cup Drambuie
1 quart fresh strawberries, cleaned and hulled
Extra strawberries for garnish

Mix all ingredients together in food processor or blender until smooth. (May have to mix in 2 batches.) Pour into stemmed parfait or wine glasses. Freeze about 4 hours. (Freezing longer makes dessert too hard.) Let thaw about 20 minutes before serving. Garnish with fresh strawberries, if desired.

Robyn Dickey

FROZEN CHOCOLATE AND PEANUT DESSERT

Yield: 12 servings

¾ cup butter
2 cups vanilla wafer crumbs
2 cups unsifted powdered sugar
3 eggs

1 (6 ounce) package semi-sweet chocolate chips, melted
1½ cups salted peanuts
½ gallon ice cream, softened
Additional peanuts for topping

Melt ¼ cup butter. Mix with crumbs and press into a 9 x 13 pan. Beat together ½ cup butter and sugar until creamy. Beat eggs, 1 at a time, then beat in chocolate. Fold in peanuts. Mix sugar mixture and chocolate mixture together and spread over crust. Freeze. Spread ice cream over chocolate and sprinkle with peanuts. Freeze. Serve with your favorite chocolate sauce.

Mrs. Bob McCarley
West Memphis, Arkansas

ICE CREAM ROLL AND CARAMEL SAUCE

Oven: 375°
Yield: 10 to 12 servings

Cake Roll
4 eggs, separated
¾ cup sugar
1 teaspoon vanilla

¾ cup sifted flour
¾ teaspoon baking powder

½ gallon vanilla ice cream, softened

Caramel Sauce
⅔ cup brown sugar
⅔ cup sugar
⅔ cup white Karo syrup

4 Tablespoons butter
1 cup whipping cream

Whip egg whites until stiff. Set aside. Beat egg yolks until light. Add sugar gradually. Beat until creamy. Add vanilla. Resift flour with baking powder. Add flour gradually to the egg mixture. Beat until smooth. Fold egg whites lightly into the batter. Pour onto a greased 10½ x 15½ cookie sheet. Bake at 375 degrees for 12 minutes. To roll, loosen the edges as soon as the cake comes from the oven. Reverse the pan onto a clean towel that has been dusted with powdered sugar. Roll cake with towel while hot, then let cool. Carefully unroll and fill center with generous portion of softened ice cream. Reroll & place in freezer. To serve, slice and pour warm caramel sauce over each slice. For caramel sauce, boil sugars, syrup and butter until syrup makes threads when dropped in cold water. Add cream. Boil 3 minutes or until thick.

Lucy Jackson (Mrs. Dorsey)

BANANA FRITTERS

Yield: 6 servings

½ cup flour
¾ Tablespoons baking powder
¼ teaspoon salt
1 Tablespoon sugar
1 egg yolk
⅓ cup milk

6 bananas
Oil for frying
Powdered sugar
¾ cup whipping cream, sweetened
 if desired

Sift flour, baking powder, salt and sugar together. Beat egg yolk slightly. Add milk. Combine with dry ingredients and beat until smooth. Slice bananas in half lengthwise. Dip in batter and fry in oil until crisp and golden brown. Sprinkle with sugar and top with whipped cream.

MARY'S ICE CREAM DELIGHT

Yield: 12 to 14 servings

½ to ¾ box Famous Nabisco
   Chocolate Wafers
½ stick butter, melted

5 Heath bars
½ gallon vanilla ice cream,
   softened

Sauce

1 (12 ounce) package semi-sweet
   chocolate chips
½ cup butter

2 cups powdered sugar
1 (13 ounce) can Pet Milk
2 teaspoons vanilla (Optional)

Make crumbs of wafers (easily done in food processor). Mix crumbs with butter and pat on bottom of 9 x 13 pan. Refrigerate. Place candy bars in refrigerator until cold. Soften ice cream. Crush candy bars and stir into ice cream. Spread on top of wafer crust and freeze. Cut into squares and serve with hot chocolate sauce.
Sauce: melt chocolate and butter together in pan. Gradually stir in powdered sugar, milk and vanilla, if desired. Cook over low heat, stirring constantly, for about 10 minutes or until thick.

Nancy Couch Lee (Mrs. James M., Jr.)

APPLE CRUNCH

Oven: 350°
Yield: 8 servings

6 to 8 tart apples
½ cup light brown sugar

½ cup sugar

Crust

1 cup flour
1 cup light brown sugar
1 cup oatmeal

½ pound butter
½ teaspoon cinnamon
¼ teaspoon nutmeg

Whipped cream or vanilla ice
   cream

Core, pare and thinly slice apples. Blend crust ingredients. Arrange apples in the bottom of a 9 inch square glass baking dish. Sprinkle apples with the 2 sugars and top with a layer of the crust. Repeat layers, ending with a heavy ¼ inch crust. Press layers gently. Bake 50 to 60 minutes. Serve with whipped cream or vanilla ice cream.

Nancy Droege

BLENDER CHOCOLATE BAVARIAN

Yield: 8 to 10 servings

2 envelopes unflavored gelatin
½ cup cold milk
1 (12 ounce) package semi-sweet
  chocolate pieces
1 cup hot milk
1 cup whipping cream

2 eggs
⅓ cup sugar
2 Tablespoons light rum
1 cup ice cubes or crushed ice
Whipped cream

Sprinkle gelatin over cold milk in 5 cup blender. Let stand until gelatin granules are moistened. Add chocolate (reserve some for garnish, if desired) and hot milk. Cover and whirl at low speed until chocolate melts and gelatin dissolves, about 2 minutes. Stop blender. Add cream, eggs, sugar and rum. Cover and whirl at high speed until well mixed. With blender still running, remove center cap of lid and add ice cubes 1 at a time. Whirl until ice melts. Pour at once into individual dessert dishes. Chill until set, about 30 minutes. Garnish with dollops of whipped cream and reserved chocolate.

Marion Glatter (Mrs. Rick)

If made ahead, reduce gelatin to 1 envelope. Will take about 3 hours to set.

FLAN

Oven: 350°
Yield: 8 servings

1 cup sugar
6 eggs
½ cup sugar

2½ cups milk
1 teaspoon vanilla

Melt 1 cup sugar in a heavy skillet until browned but not hard (watch carefully to prevent burning). Spoon melted sugar into individual cups that have been greased with butter. Beat eggs. Add sugar, milk and vanilla. Mix thoroughly. Spoon custard mixture into cups. Place cups into a large baking pan that is filled with 1 inch of water. Bake for 1 hour at 350° or until silver knife comes out clean. Cool in refrigerator. Unmold just before serving.

Janie Headstream (Mrs. James W.)

"Better some of the pudding than none of the pie."
ENGLISH PROVERB

CHOCOLATE MOUSSE

Yield: 12 to 14 servings

Mousse

1 pound 4 ounces semi-sweet chocolate

3 eggs

5 egg yolks

1 teaspoon vanilla

2½ cups whipping cream

8 Tablespoons powdered sugar

5 egg whites

Topping

2 cups whipping cream, whipped

6 Tablespoons powdered sugar

Crust (Optional)

1½ boxes chocolate wafer cookies, crumbled

¾ to 1 cup butter, melted

1 Tablespoon sugar

Melt chocolate in top of double boiler over warm, not boiling, water. Let cool to lukewarm. Add whole eggs and egg yolks. Mix until well blended. Add vanilla. Whip cream and powdered sugar until soft peaks form. Beat egg whites until stiff. Stir in a little cream and egg whites into chocolate mixture. Then fold in remaining cream and egg whites, making sure it is all well blended. Refrigerate at least 8 hours. Serve in deep wine glasses or champagne glasses. Whip cream and sugar for topping. Note: This chocolate mousse may also be made in a 10 inch springform pan with a crust. Prepare a crust of cookie crumbs, butter and sugar and line the bottom and side of pan. Pour chocolate mixture into crust (may be frozen at this point). When ready to use, thaw in the refrigerator overnight. If not frozen, refrigerate for at least 8 hours. When ready to serve, top with sweetened whipped cream.

Georgea McKinley Greaves (Mrs. Thomas G.)
Greenville, South Carolina

MOCHA MARSHMALLOW MOUSSE

Yield: 6 to 8 servings

2 (3.5 ounce) milk chocolate bars, broken

20 large white marshmallows

⅓ cup milk

2 teaspoons instant coffee granules

2 egg whites, beaten

1 cup whipping cream, whipped

Almonds, sliced and unsalted

Additional whipped cream (Optional)

Heat chocolate bars, marshmallows, milk and coffee in a double boiler until melted, stirring occasionally. Remove from heat and cool. Fold in beaten egg whites and whipped cream. Pour into a 5 cup mold or individual cups. Refrigerate or freeze, good served either way. When serving, sprinkle with sliced almonds, or whipped cream, if desired.

Jenny Boshears (Mrs. Barry)

MAPLE MOUSSE

Yield: 8 to 10 servings

2 Tablespoons gelatin
½ cup cold water
1 cup pure maple syrup
4 egg yolks

½ cup light brown sugar
4 egg whites
2 cups whipping cream
Additional whipped cream for garnish
Pecans, chopped and toasted

Soften gelatin in water and heat until dissolved. Combine with syrup. Beat egg yolks and add to syrup mixture. Cook over moderate heat until slightly thickened and coats spoon. Add brown sugar and stir to dissolve. Set aside to cool. Beat egg whites until stiff. Whip cream to firm peaks. Fold whipped cream into mixture, then fold in egg whites. Pour into individual dishes. Chill until firm. Serve with whipped cream and sprinkle with toasted pecans.

A Very Special Tearoom

PRALINE CREPES

Yield: 15 to 20 crepes

Basic Dessert Crepe Batter
4 eggs
1 cup flour
2 Tablespoons sugar

1 cup milk
¼ cup water
1 Tablespoon butter, melted

Praline Sauce
¼ cup butter or margarine
½ cup powdered sugar
2 Tablespoons maple syrup

¼ cup water
½ cup finely chopped pecans

1 quart Pralines and Cream ice
   cream

For crepe batter, beat eggs in a medium mixing bowl. Gradually add flour and sugar alternately with milk and water, beating with electric mixer or whisk until smooth. Beat in butter. Refrigerate batter at least 1 hour. Cook on upside-down crepe griddle or in traditional pan.
Make praline sauce. In a saucepan, heat butter until light brown. Cool slightly. Gradually mix in sugar. Stir in syrup and water. Bring to a boil. Simmer for 1 minute. Add nuts. Serve warm. Makes 1 cup sauce. Scoop ice cream into crepe, fold over, and top with sauce.

Annis Hill (Mrs. Charles W.)

PEARS WITH RED WINE SAUCE

Oven: 350°
Yield: 6 servings

5 ounces sugar
½ cup water
½ cup Claret or Burgundy wine
Strip of lemon rind
1 cinnamon stick
6 small ripe pears

1 teaspoon arrowroot
1 Tablespoon water
½ pint whipping cream, whipped
2 ounces sliced or slivered almonds,
toasted

Place sugar in a pan large enough to hold the pears. Add water, wine, lemon rind and cinnamon. Dissolve slowly over low heat. Increase the heat and boil for 1 minute. Peel the pears, leaving the stalks on but removing the "eye" from the bottom. Place at once in the prepared syrup. Cover the pan and poach the pears in a 350° oven for 30 minutes or until tender. Remove the pears and strain the syrup. Mix the arrowroot with 1 Tablespoon water, add to syrup, and stir until boiling. Cook until clear. Place pears in individual dessert bowls and spoon over syrup. Refrigerate until ready to serve. When serving, pass a bowl of whipped cream and toasted almonds. May be prepared in the morning before serving.

Helen Sloan (Mrs. John C.)

CHOCOLATE STEAMED PUDDING

Yield: 6-8 servings

Pudding
2 squares unsweetened chocolate
2 Tablespoons butter
1 cup flour, sifted
1½ teaspoons baking powder
½ teaspoon salt

1 egg, beaten
½ cup sugar
1 teaspoon vanilla
½ cup milk

Topping
½ pint whipping cream, whipped
2 Tablespoons sugar

1 teaspoon vanilla

Melt chocolate and butter together. Cool. Sift flour, baking powder and salt together. Beat egg, sugar and vanilla. Add dry ingredients alternately with milk to egg mixture, beating after each addition. Add chocolate mixture last. Pour batter into a greased 1 pound coffee can and cover with a cloth. Place can in a covered kettle of water (about 3 inches). Cook 1 to 1½ hours. Begin at high heat. As steam escapes, reduce to low heat for remainder of time. Beat topping ingredients together. Serve over pudding. Top with slivered almonds or chocolate shavings, if desired.

Lucy Jackson (Mrs. Dorsey)

STRAWBERRY PARTY DESSERT

Oven: 275°
Yield: 8 servings

4 egg whites, room temperature
½ teaspoon cream of tartar
¼ teaspoon salt
1 teaspoon vanilla, divided
1 cup sugar
2 cups sifted powdered sugar
½ cup butter or margarine

3 egg yolks
1 Tablespoon lemon juice
1 teaspoon grated lemon peel
1 pint fresh strawberries
½ cup whipping cream
2 Tablespoons powdered sugar

Combine first 3 ingredients with ½ teaspoon vanilla in a large bowl. Beat until partially stiff. Add sugar gradually, beating until stiff. Spread meringue about 1 inch thick over buttered 9 inch pie pan, building a high, fluffy border. Bake at 275° for 1 hour or until meringue is cream colored and feels dry and firm. Meringue shell will crack while baking. Let cool in pan. Cream powdered sugar, butter, and egg yolks until light and fluffy. Beat in lemon juice and peel. Spread over meringue shell. Wash, drain and hull berries, reserving several berries for garnish. Arrange berries over creamy layer, pressing down lightly. Whip cream, powdered sugar and remaining vanilla until stiff. Spread over berries. Chill several hours. Garnish with berries.

Mary Sue Jacobs (Mrs. John)

A light summer dessert.

CINNAMON MERINGUE TARTS

Oven: 275°
Yield: 4 to 6 servings

3 egg whites, at room temperature
¼ teaspoon salt
¼ teaspoon cream of tartar

½ teaspoon cinnamon
¾ cup sugar

Beat egg whites until frothy with cream of tartar and salt. Add sugar and cinnamon and beat until very stiff. Shape into tarts on a cookie sheet that has been covered with foil. Bake at 275° for 1 hour. Turn oven off and let cool in oven for another hour. May be stored in a tin for weeks.

A Very Special Tearoom

Serve with a scoop of ice cream topped with Grand Marnier sauce or chocolate sauce.

TART TATIN

Oven: 400°
Yield: 6 to 8 servings

Pastry

1¼ cups flour
½ cup unsalted butter, slightly
  softened

1 egg
Pinch of salt
½ cup water (or as needed)

Filling

1 cup sugar
5 apples, thinly sliced and peeled

Cinnamon
½ cup unsalted butter

Whipped cream (Optional)

Ice cream (Optional)

Mix pastry ingredients. Chill before rolling out. Sprinkle ½ cup sugar in bottom of glass or metal tart pan (with fixed bottom). Arrange apple slices in a circle around the pan on top of sugar. Continue pinwheel fashion to center of pan. Sprinkle ½ cup sugar mixed with cinnamon on top of the apples. Cut butter into small pieces and arrange over apples. Roll out dough and place over apples. Make vent holes. Bake at 400° for 40 to 50 minutes. Invert tart on serving plate and serve with whipped cream or ice cream.

Libby Strawn (Mrs. Jim)

MELT IN YOUR MOUTH BROWNIES

Oven: 350°
Yield: 12 servings

Brownie

½ cup butter
2 squares unsweetened chocolate
1 cup sugar
2 eggs

½ cup flour
1 cup chopped pecans
½ teaspoon vanilla (Optional)

Frosting

1 cup sugar
¼ cup butter

¼ cup milk
¼ cup cocoa

Preheat oven to 350°. Melt butter and chocolate in a double boiler. When melted, remove from fire and add sugar and beat well. Add eggs, one at a time, beating after each addition. Add flour, nuts and vanilla. Mix well. Pour into a greased and floured 9 x 9 pan. Bake for 20 to 25 minutes. (Do not overbake. These are supposed to be moist.) To make frosting, mix together all ingredients and bring to a full boil over low heat, stirring constantly. Cook exactly 1 minute - NO LONGER. Remove from heat, cool, stir and frost. Let frosting harden before cutting brownies.

Mero McCreery (Mrs. David G.)

BARGAIN BARN CARAMEL CHEWS

Oven: 350°
Yield: 24 to 28 squares

½ pound margarine
2 eggs, slightly beaten
1 (16 ounce) package brown sugar

1¾ cups flour
1 teaspoon vanilla
¾ cup chopped pecans

Preheat oven to 350⁰. Melt margarine. Add remaining ingredients and mix well. Mixture will be thick. Pour into a 9 x 13 baking pan. Bake for 25 to 30 minutes. Check for doneness after 25 minutes. DO NOT OVERBAKE. These freeze nicely.

Jane Faust (Mrs. Norman)

These are a traditional favorite of JLLR volunteers during the week of our Bargain Barn sale.

DOUBLE FROSTED BOURBON BROWNIES

Oven: 325°
Yield: 15 brownies

¾ cup sifted flour
¼ teaspoon soda
¼ teaspoon salt
⅓ cup shortening
½ cup sugar
2 Tablespoons water

1 (6 ounce) package semi-sweet
  chocolate chips
1 teaspoon vanilla
2 eggs, slightly beaten
1½ cups chopped walnuts
¼ cup bourbon

White Frosting
½ cup margarine
2 cups powdered sugar

1 teaspoon vanilla

Chocolate Glaze
1 (6 ounce) package semi-sweet
  chocolate chips

1 Tablespoon butter

Preheat oven to 325⁰. Sift together flour, soda and salt. Heat shortening with sugar and water until sugar is dissolved. Stir in vanilla, add chocolate chips and continue to stir over heat until chocolate is melted. Add slightly beaten eggs. Gradually add this mixture to the flour mixture. Blend well. Add walnuts. Spread into a greased 9 x 9 pan. Bake for 25 to 30 minutes. Pour bourbon over brownies evenly. Cool to room temperature. Frost with white frosting. Chill. Spread chocolate glaze over white frosting. Cool before cutting into squares. To make white frosting, cream butter and powdered sugar. Add vanilla. For chocolate glaze, heat chocolate chips and butter together over low heat. DO NOT let this mixture overheat.

Betty Biggadike Scroggin (Mrs. Carroll)
Palos Verdes, California

CHOCOLATE BUTTER GOOEY

Oven: 350°
Yield: 24 squares

1¼ sticks butter, melted
1 (18½ ounce) box Butter Recipe
   Chocolate cake mix
1 egg, slightly beaten

1 (1 pound) box powdered sugar
1 (8 ounce) package cream cheese
2 eggs
½ cup chocolate chips

Preheat oven to 350⁰. Mix butter, cake mix and 1 slightly beaten egg until well blended. Press into a greased and floured 9 x 13 pan. Cream the sugar and cream cheese and add eggs and chocolate chips. Pour this mixture over the bottom layer. Bake for 30 to 40 minutes or until lightly browned.

Lindy Mitchell (Mrs. Maurice, Jr.)

For vanilla butter gooey use 1 (18½ ounce) box yellow cake mix instead of the chocolate and omit the chocolate chips.

CHOCOLATE SHERRY SQUARES

Oven: 350°
Yield: 36 squares

1st Layer
4 ounces Baker's semi-sweet
   chocolate
1 cup butter
4 eggs, beaten

2 cups sugar
1 cup flour
½ teaspoon vanilla

2nd Layer
½ cup butter
4 cups powdered sugar
¼ cup Half and Half

¼ cup cream sherry
1 cup chopped nuts

3rd Layer
1 (6 ounce) package chocolate chips
2 Tablespoons water

3 Tablespoons butter

Preheat oven to 350⁰.
1st Layer. Melt chocolate and butter in a double boiler. Add beaten eggs and gradually beat in sugar, flour and vanilla. Beat 1 minute. Pour into a large shallow cookie sheet that has been greased and floured. Bake for 25 minutes. Cool.
2nd Layer. Cream butter, sugar and Half and Half. Add sherry and beat until light and fluffy. Fold in nuts. Spread on cool cake and refrigerate.
3rd Layer. Melt chocolate chips, water and butter over hot water. Dribble over top of cake. Refrigerate. Cut into squares.

Dianne T. Tucker (Mrs. Robert W.)

BUTTERSCOTCH BROWNIES WITH CARAMEL ICING

Oven: 350°
Yield: 12 brownies

Brownie

4 Tablespoons butter, melted
1 cup dark brown sugar
1 egg
¾ cup flour

1 teaspoon baking powder
½ teaspoon vanilla
½ teaspoon salt
½ cup chopped nuts

Caramel Icing

½ cup butter
½ cup dark brown sugar
¼ cup Half and Half or milk

1¾ cups to 2 cups powdered sugar
1 teaspoon vanilla
Pinch of salt

Preheat oven to 350°. Mix all brownie ingredients and spread in a buttered 8 x 8 pan. Bake for 25 minutes. Cool in pan and spread with caramel icing. Cut into squares. To make icing, melt butter and cook until brown. Add brown sugar and continue cooking, stirring until sugar is completely melted. Pour in Half and Half (or milk) and stir. Cool. Add powdered sugar, vanilla and salt. Beat until thick enough to spread.

Marilyn Hussman Augur (Mrs. James)
Dallas, Texas

GERMAN CHOCOLATE CARAMEL BARS

Oven: 350°
Yield: 20 bars

20 ounces (or 70) light caramels
½ cup evaporated milk
1 (18½ ounce) box German
   chocolate cake mix
¼ cup butter, melted

⅓ cup evaporated milk
1 cup chopped walnuts
1 cup semi-sweet or milk chocolate
   pieces

Preheat oven to 350°. Combine caramels and ½ cup milk and melt in a double boiler. Set aside. Grease and flour a 9 x 13 pan. In a large bowl combine cake mix, melted butter, ⅓ cup milk and nuts. Press half of this mixture into bottom of pan. Bake for 8 minutes. Remove from oven. Immediately sprinkle chocolate pieces on top. Next, spread caramel mixture over chocolate pieces. Crumble remaining cake mixture over caramel layer. Return to oven and bake for 20 minutes. Cool slightly and refrigerate for 1 hour. Cut into bars. These may be frozen.

Mrs. Charles H. Atkins
Camden, Arkansas

TRADITIONAL HOLIDAY COOKIES

Oven: 350°
Yield: 4 dozen cookies

1 cup butter
½ cup sugar
1 egg, beaten
2 teaspoons vanilla

3 cups flour
½ teaspoon baking powder
½ teaspoon salt

Icing
2 cups powdered sugar
2 Tablespoons water
  (approximately)

Food coloring

Preheat oven to 350⁰. Cream sugar and butter until fluffy. Add the beaten egg and vanilla. Sift together flour, baking powder and salt. Stir into creamed mixture gradually. (You may use food processor for both steps.) Place mixture in refrigerator for at least 1 hour. Roll out and cut with your favorite cookie cutters. Bake for 10 minutes. Ice and decorate when cool. To make icing, mix together sugar and water. Divide into several small bowls and use different colors of food coloring.

Marguerite Golden (Mrs. Peyton)
Batesville, Arkansas

JUST THE BEST COOKIES

Oven: 325°
Yield: 8 dozen

1 cup butter
1 cup sugar
1 cup brown sugar
1 egg
1 cup salad oil
1 cup rolled oats
1 cup crushed cornflakes

½ cup flaked coconut
1 cup chopped pecans
3½ cups flour
1 teaspoon soda
1 teaspoon salt
1 teaspoon vanilla
Powdered sugar

Preheat oven to 325⁰. Cream butter and sugars until light and fluffy. Add egg and blend. Add salad oil, stirring until oil is well blended. Add oats, cornflakes, coconut and nuts. Stir until mixed. Add flour, soda, salt and vanilla and mix well. Form into balls about the size of a walnut. Place on an ungreased cookie sheet and flatten with a fork dipped in water. Bake for 12 minutes. Allow to cool a few minutes before removing. Sprinkle with powdered sugar.

Frank Spawr
El Dorado, Arkansas

LEMON CRUMB SQUARES

Oven: 350°
Yield: 2 dozen

1 (15 ounce) can sweetened
  condensed milk
½ cup lemon juice
1 teaspoon grated lemon rind
1½ cups sifted flour
1 teaspoon baking powder

½ teaspoon salt
⅔ cup butter
1 cup dark brown sugar, firmly
  packed
1 cup oatmeal, uncooked

Preheat oven to 350⁰. Blend together milk, juice and rind of lemon and set aside. Sift together flour, baking powder and salt. Cream butter and blend in sugar. Add oatmeal and flour mixture and mix until crumbly. Spread half the mixture in an 8 x 12 buttered baking pan and pat down. Spread condensed milk mixture over the top and cover with the remaining crumb mixture. Bake for 20 to 25 minutes or until edges are browned. Cool in pan at room temperature for 15 minutes. Cut into 2 inch squares and chill in pan until firm.

Nancy Couch Lee (Mrs. James M., Jr.)

MELTING MOMENTS

Oven: 300°
Yield: 3 dozen

½ cup powdered sugar
1 cup butter

1 cup flour
¾ cup cornstarch

Frosting
1 cup powdered sugar
2 Tablespoons butter, melted

Whipping Cream

Preheat oven to 300⁰. Mix sugar, butter, flour, and cornstarch until well blended. Form into small balls and bake on an ungreased cookie sheet for 20 minutes. Cookies should be slightly brown when done. Frost cookies when cool. Blend butter and powdered sugar. Add whipping cream to make desired consistency.

Mrs. Ardyce Blume
Denver, Colorado

Food coloring may be added to frosting. These freeze beautifully!

MINT SURPRISE COOKIES

Oven: 350°
Yield: 8 dozen

1 cup butter	3 cups flour
1 cup sugar	1 teaspoon soda
½ cup brown sugar	½ teaspoon salt
2 eggs	16 ounces chocolate mint *wafers*
1 Tablespoon water	(NOT filled mints)
1 teaspoon vanilla	Nut halves (Optional)

Preheat oven to 350⁰. Cream butter, add sugars, eggs, water and vanilla. Sift flour with soda and salt. Add to creamed mixture a little at a time, beating on low. Chill dough. Wrap 2 mints in dough to cover. Put walnut or pecan half on top. Bake for 10 to 12 minutes or until golden brown.

Lea Turner (Mrs. Finley)
Fort Smith, Arkansas

This is a traditional Christmas cookie in the Turner family.

MOUND BARS

Oven: 350°
Yield: 24 squares

½ cup butter	7 ounces coconut, flaked
3 eggs, beaten	1 (14 ounce) can sweetened
1 cup chopped nuts	condensed milk
1¼ cups sugar	1 (12 ounce) package chocolate
1 cup flour	chips, melted
1 Tablespoon cocoa (Optional)	

Preheat oven to 350⁰. Mix butter, eggs, nuts, sugar, flour and cocoa together. Pour ingredients into a 9 x 13 pyrex pan and bake for 25 minutes. Combine coconut and milk and spread over first layer. Bake again for 10 minutes. Spread melted chocolate chips over bars and bake for 5 minutes. Chill before cutting.

Mrs. Samuel L. Davis

OATMEAL LACE COOKIES

Oven: 350°
Yield: 4 dozen

2¼ cups quick oats, uncooked
2¼ cups dark brown sugar
3 Tablespoons flour
1 teaspoon salt

1 cup butter or margarine, melted
1 egg, slightly beaten
1 teaspoon vanilla

Preheat oven to 350°. Combine oats, sugar, flour, salt and melted butter. Add slightly beaten egg and the vanilla. Mix well. Drop dough by teaspoons on to a well greased Teflon pan. Leave plenty of space on cookie sheet as these spread out to give the lacey appearance. Bake for 5 to 7 minutes. Remove from cookie sheet while still hot.

Lucy Jackson (Mrs. Dorsey)

If the cookies get cool before removing, reheat until warm and they will come up without crumbling.

PEANUT BUTTER KISSES

Oven: 350°
Yield: 4 to 5 dozen cookies

1 cup butter
1 cup extra crunchy peanut butter
1 cup granulated sugar
1 cup brown sugar, firmly packed
2 large eggs
1 teaspoon vanilla

2½ cups sifted flour
1 teaspoon baking powder
1 teaspoon baking soda
1 teaspoon salt
1 (9 ounce) package chocolate kisses

Preheat oven to 350°. Beat first 6 ingredients at medium speed until fluffy. Sift the next 4 ingredients and add to above mixture. Mix thoroughly at low speed. Shape into 1 inch balls and roll in granulated sugar. Place 2 inches apart on ungreased cookie sheets. Bake for 12 to 15 minutes or until lightly browned. Immediately press candy kisses into cookies. Cool on racks.

Nancy Droege

Make this a "Tradition" with your little ones. They can unwrap kisses, help make cookie balls, roll in sugar, and even help push kisses into cookies.

PEANUT BUTTER COOKIES

Oven: 325°
Yield: 1½ dozen

1 cup smooth peanut butter
1 cup granulated sugar or ½ cup
   granulated and ½ cup brown

1 egg
1 teaspoon vanilla
Dash of salt

Preheat oven to 325°. Mix all ingredients until well blended. Roll into small balls. Place on an ungreased cookie sheet, 1 inch apart. Press lightly with a fork to flatten. Bake for 15 to 20 minutes.

Mary M. Jennings (Mrs. Warren)
DeWitt, Arkansas

PECAN CUPS

Oven: 350°
Yield: 3 dozen cups

2⅔ cups graham cracker crumbs
1 (13 ounce) can evaporated milk
½ cup butter
1 cup dark brown sugar

1 (12 ounce) package semi-sweet
   chocolate chips
2 cups chopped pecans

Preheat oven to 350°. Soften butter to room temperature. Mix all ingredients together. Fill miniature muffin tins to top. Bake for 10 to 13 minutes. Can be frozen.

Julie Byars

PECAN PIE SURPRISE BARS

Oven: 350°
Yield: 2 dozen bars

1 (18½ ounce) box yellow cake mix
½ cup butter or margarine
1 egg
½ cup brown sugar
¾ cup light corn syryp

¾ cup dark corn syrup
3 eggs
1 teaspoon vanilla
1 cup chopped pecans

Preheat oven to 350°. Grease bottom and sides of a 9 x 13 baking pan. Reserve ⅔ cup of dry cake mix for filling. In a large mixing bowl, combine remaining mix, butter or margarine, and egg. Bake for 15 to 20 minutes until light golden brown. Meanwhile, prepare filling. Combine reserved cake mix, brown sugar, light and dark corn syrup, 3 eggs and vanilla. Add pecans and pour over crust. Bake for 30 to 35 minutes until filling is set.

PUMPKIN BARS

Oven: 350°
Yield: 3 dozen

⅓ cup sugar
⅓ cup oil
3 eggs
1 (16 ounce) can pumpkin
1 (18½ ounce) box Butter Recipe
  cake mix

2 teaspoons cinnamon
½ teaspoon ginger
½ teaspoon ground cloves
½ teaspoon ground nutmeg
⅛ teaspoon cayenne pepper

Icing

1 (8 ounce) package cream cheese
3 cups brown sugar
3 cups powdered sugar

2 Tablespoons milk
2½ teaspoons vanilla

Preheat oven to 350⁰. Combine sugar, oil, eggs and pumpkin in a mixer on high for 1 minute. Add cake mix, cinnamon, ginger, cloves, nutmeg and cayenne. Beat on high for 2 minutes. Pour mixture into a greased and floured 10 x 15 jellyroll pan. Bake for 25 to 30 minutes. Cool. Combine cream cheese and brown sugar until creamy. Add powdered sugar, milk and vanilla. Beat until smooth. Spread on cake and refrigerate. Cut into bars to serve.

Alice Lynn Overbey (Mrs. Thomas L.)

SCOTCH SHORTBREAD

Oven: 300°
Yield: 18 squares

½ pound butter
½ cup sugar

2 cups flour

Preheat oven to 300⁰. Cream ingredients together. Work dough with hands for a few minutes. Pat into a buttered 9 x 9 pan. Smooth dough with a glass or small rolling pin. Bake for about 1 hour until golden brown. Cut into bars while still hot, but leave in pan to cool.

Mrs. Ardyce Blume
Denver, Colorado

For dusting a greased cake pan, keep a new powder puff in your flour canister.

MYSTERY BRICKLE BARS

Oven: 350°
Yield: 4 dozen

48 soda crackers or saltines
1½ cups butter (no substitute)
1½ cups brown sugar

18 ounces chocolate chips
1 cup chopped pecans or walnuts

Line a large cookie sheet with foil and spray with Pam. Line crackers on pan. Bring butter and sugar to a boil over medium heat and continue to boil for 3 minutes. Pour this mixture over crackers. Bake at 350° for 5 minutes or until mixture boils and crackers float. Remove from oven and sprinkle with chocolate chips. Spread to cover. Sprinkle with nuts. Cut when cool.

Nancy Mitcham (Mrs. Robert)
Michele Koberlein
Meredith John Brown

BLACK FOREST SQUARES
(Must be prepared 1 day in advance)

Oven: 350°
Yield: 12 servings

1 package (single layer-sized)
  chocolate cake mix
1 (8 ounce) carton sour cream
1 (3¼ ounce) package instant
  chocolate pudding mix
1 cup milk
¼ cup crème de cassis

1 (16 ounce) can pitted dark, sweet
  cherries
2 Tablespoons sugar
1 Tablespoon cornstarch
½ cup whipping cream
¼ cup sliced almonds, toasted

Preheat oven to 350°. Prepare cake mix according to package directions. Pour batter into a greased and floured 9 x 13 baking pan. Bake for 10 to 12 minutes. Cool completely. In a large mixing bowl, beat sour cream, dry pudding mix, ⅓ cup of milk and crème de cassis until mixture is fluffy. Gradually add remaining milk, beating until smooth, Pour over cooled chocolate cake. Cover and chill. Drain cherries, reserving ¾ cup of syrup. In a saucepan, combine sugar and cornstarch. Gradually stir in reserved syrup. Cook and stir over medium heat until thick and bubbly. Cook 1 minute more. Add drained cherries and cool. Spread over chilled pudding mixture. Cover and chill overnight. Before serving, whip cream to soft peaks. Pipe over in a lattice design. Sprinkle with nuts. Cut into squares to serve.

Sheffield Owings (Mrs. William Adolph)

This is a nice dessert for luncheons.

CARAMELITAS

Oven: 350°
Yield: 2 dozen

1 cup all-purpose flour
1 cup quick oats, uncooked
¾ cup brown sugar, firmly packed
½ teaspoon baking soda
¼ teaspoon salt

¾ cup margarine, melted
1 (6 ounce) package chocolate chips
1 cup chopped nuts
1 (12.25 ounce) jar caramel topping
3 Tablespoons flour

Preheat oven to 350º. Combine flour, oats, brown sugar, soda, salt and margarine. Beat on low speed of mixer until well blended. Pat mixture evenly into an ungreased 9 x 13 pan. Bake for 10 minutes and remove from oven. Sprinkle with chocolate chips and nuts. Combine caramel topping and 3 Tablespoons flour. Drizzle this mixture on top. Return to oven for 20 minutes. Cool completely before cutting.

Lynn Benham (Mrs. Paul, III)

SWEET WON TON

Yield: 50

1 cup chopped pecans
1 cup flaked coconut
1 cup brown sugar
1 cup granulated sugar

1 package won ton wrappers (about 60 to a package)
1 egg, beaten
Oil
Powdered sugar

Mix nuts, coconut, brown sugar and granulated sugar. Place one teaspoon of this mixture in the center of each won ton square. Fold into a triangle. Moisten edges with beaten egg to seal. Deep fry in hot oil until golden brown, turning once. Shake in a bag of powdered sugar. Cool. Store in an air-tight container.

Ann Warrick (Mrs. Alan F.)
Pine Bluff, Arkansas

MY MOTHER'S COCOONS

Oven: 350°
Yield: 4 dozen

1 cup butter (no substitute)
5 Tablespoons sugar
2 cups sifted flour
2 Tablespoons water

1 cup finely chopped nuts
1 teaspoon vanilla
Powdered sugar

Preheat oven to 350º. Cream butter and sugar well. Add flour, water, nuts and vanilla. Put in the refrigerator until cold (may leave overnight). Roll dough into small cocoon shapes and place on an ungreased cookie sheet. Bake for 20 minutes or until slightly browned. Remove from pan and roll in powdered sugar while hot.

Marcia Johnston (Mrs. Richard S.)

BUCKEYES

Yield: 14 dozen large or
20 dozen small

2 pounds creamy peanut butter,
  room temperature
2 cups butter, room temperature
3 pounds powdered sugar

2 (12 ounce) packages chocolate
  chips
½ bar paraffin

Mix peanut butter, butter and sugar together until a smooth texture develops. Form balls the size of "buckeyes." Refrigerate balls. Slowly melt chips and parafin together in a double boiler. Using toothpicks, dip cold buckeyes into chocolate mixture until ⅔ covered. Dry on waxed paper.

Ellon Cockrill (Mrs. Rogers)

Can be frozen. Makes a great gift.

MISS RUTH'S KARO CARAMELS

Yield: 2½ pounds

2 cups sugar
1¾ cups light Karo syrup
½ cup butter

2 cups whipping cream
1 cup chopped pecans, toasted

In a medium-sized saucepan, combine sugar, syrup, butter and 1 cup of cream. Bring to a boil. While boiling, add second cup of cream. Cook to soft ball stage. Beat by hand for 3 minutes. Add pecans. Pour onto a buttered platter. Cut when cool.

Carmen McHaney (Mrs. James M., Jr.)

QUICK CHOCOLATE FUDGE

Yield: 20 pieces

¼ cup margarine
3 (1 ounce) squares unsweetened
  chocolate
½ cup light corn syrup
1 Tablespoon water

1 teaspoon vanilla
1 (16 ounce) package powdered
  sugar
1 cup chopped nuts

Grease an 8 x 8 pyrex pan. In a 2 quart saucepan, melt margarine and chocolate. Stir in corn syrup, water and vanilla. Remove from heat. Add sugar and nuts. Stir until smooth. Pour into pan, cool, and cut into squares.

Mrs. Mike White
Bono, Arkansas

GOLDEN FUDGE

Yield: 24 squares

2 cups sugar
1 cup milk
2 Tablespoons butter

2 Tablespoons light Karo syrup
Pinch of salt
½ to ¾ cup peanut butter

Mix milk and sugar until dissolved. Over medium heat bring to low boil. Add butter, Karo syrup and salt and boil 3 minutes. Add peanut butter and mix thoroughly. Cook, stirring constantly, until mixture reaches soft ball stage (15 to 20 minutes). Remove from heat and beat until it hardens. Pour onto a buttered platter or pan and slice.

Peyton Golden
Batesville, Arkansas

MICROWAVE FUDGE

1 pound powdered sugar
⅓ cup cocoa
¼ cup milk
½ cup margarine

Pinch of salt
1 teaspoon vanilla
½ cup chopped nuts

Mix sugar, cocoa, milk, salt and margarine in a 2 quart glass bowl. Microwave on high for 2 to 2½ minutes or until margarine is melted. Stir in vanilla and nuts. Mix well. Pour into a greased 8 x 8 pan. Chill for 1 hour in refrigerator. Cut into squares.

Carol Lord (Mrs. Robert C.)

HOMEMADE HEATH BARS

Yield: 25 pieces

2 cups sugar
2 cups butter (no substitute)
6 teaspoons water

1 (2 ounce) package sliced almonds
1 (6 ounce) package chocolate chips

Combine sugar, butter and water in a large saucepan. Melt slowly and stir frequently. When sugar is melted, raise temperature to medium and cook to hard crack stage. Stir in almonds. Pour onto buttered 12 x 18 cookie sheet. Let this cool. Melt chocolate chips over *low* heat and spread over candy. Let chocolate set. Break into bite-sized pieces. Store in tightly covered container.

Becky Powell Jacobs
Wynne, Arkansas

Great and so easy! Keeps indefinitely.

CREAM CHEESE MINTS

Yield: 200 mints

1 (8 ounce) package cream cheese, room temperature
2 pounds powdered sugar

8 drops flavoring (spearmint, peppermint, lemon or butter rum)
8 drops food coloring

Knead sugar and cream cheese to form ball. Divide dough into fourths. Work with ¼ at a time. Wrap remaining dough in foil to pervent drying. Add 2 drops flavoring and 2 drops coloring to the portion you are working with. Press into molds or use a super shooter. Let mints set while mixing and molding remaining fourths. Store in a tightly covered tin, separating the layers with wax paper. These will keep indefinitely.

Kathy Palazzi (Mrs. Robert)

Easy and wonderful.

AFTER DINNER MINTS
(Use microwave and food processor)

Yield: 60 to 70 small mints

¼ pound butter
1 ounce unsweetened chocolate
¼ cup sugar
1 teaspoon vanilla
1 egg, beaten

1 cup graham cracker crumbs
1 cup oatmeal, uncooked
1 cup grated coconut
½ cup chopped pecans

Filling
4 Tablespoons butter
2 cups powdered sugar

3 teaspoons Grand Marnier
1 Tablespoon milk

Topping
4 ounces unsweetened chocolate, melted

In microwave, melt butter and chocolate for 2 minutes on high. Using the steel blade in food processor, blend together the sugar, vanilla, egg, graham cracker crumbs, oatmeal, coconut and nuts. Add the chocolate and butter. Blend until dough forms a ball. Press into a 9 x 13 pan. Refrigerate while making filling. In food processor, using steel blade, mix butter, sugar, liqueur and milk. Spread over chocolate crumb mixture. Refrigerate. Melt 4 squares of chocolate in a glass container in microwave for 3 to 5 minutes on high. Spread over filling. Chill. Cut into squares before topping gets hard. These store in the refrigerator indefinitely.

Martha H. Carle (Mrs. Kenneth)
Stuttgart, Arkansas

PEANUT BUTTER BARS

Yield: 16 squares

1 cup butter
1 pound powdered sugar
1½ cups crunchy peanut butter

1½ cups graham cracker crumbs
2 (8 ounce) milk chocolate bars

Beat butter and sugar until smooth. Add peanut butter and graham cracker crumbs. Mix well. Pat into a 9 x 9 pan. Melt chocolate in a double boiler over hot water (do not let water come to a boil). Ice peanut butter mixture with melted chocolate. Cool. Cut into small bars.

Susan Brainard (Mrs. Jay)
Lisa Chapman (Mrs. Richard W., Jr.)

MICROWAVE PRALINES

Yield: 2 dozen

1 pound light brown sugar
1 cup whipping cream

1 cup pecan halves
2 Tablespoons margarine

Combine sugar and cream in a 3 quart glass bowl. Cook on high in microwave for 13 minutes. Stir in margarine and pecans. Drop by spoonfuls onto foil. Cool. Store in tightly covered tin.

Linda Burrow VanHook (Mrs. Fred F.)

OVEN CARAMEL POPCORN

Oven: 250°
Yield: 8 to 9 quarts

Popcorn (to equal 8 to 9 quarts popped)
2 cups brown sugar
1 cup margarine

1 teaspoon salt
½ cup light corn syrup
1 teaspoon vanilla
½ teaspoon soda

Preheat oven to 250°. Pop popcorn to equal 8 to 9 quarts. Bring brown sugar, margarine, salt, syrup and vanilla to a boil. Continue to boil for 5 minutes. Add baking soda, stir and quickly pour over the popped corn, coating well. Bake on two cookie sheets for 1 hour, stirring 3 times. Store in tightly closed tins.

Mary Thomas (Mrs. Lindsay M.)

Nuts may be added to the popcorn mixture.

FRIED WALNUTS

Yield: 4 cups

6 cups water
4 cups walnut halves
½ cup sugar

Vegetable oil
Seasoned salt

Boil water in a 4 quart saucepan. Add walnuts. Return water to a boil and cook 1 minute. Rinse nuts with hot water in a course sieve. Pour warm nuts into a large bowl and gently stir in sugar until all of the sugar is dissolved. Heat 2 inches of oil in a skillet to 300°. Add nuts and fry until golden brown. Stir often. Drain in a course sieve. Add salt and cool on a paper towel. If nuts are not crisp, place in a 250° oven for 1 minute.

Katherine Anne Stewart (Mrs. George)
St. Paul, Minnesota

SPICED PECANS

Oven: 325°
Yield: 4 cups

1 egg white
1 Tablespoon cold water
¼ teaspoon salt

1 pound pecan halves
½ cup sugar
½ teaspoon cinnamon

Preheat oven to 325°. Beat egg white with water and salt until frothy. Add pecan halves and mix, coating well. Mix sugar and cinnamon in a bowl. Add pecans and stir, coating each piece. Spread pecans on buttered cookie sheet. Bake at 325° for 30 to 35 minutes or until brown and toasted. Stir often.

Barbara Moore (Mrs. J. Malcolm, Jr.)

MY MOTHER'S SOUR CREAM SUGARED NUTS

Yield: 4 cups

½ cup sour cream
1½ cups sugar

1½ teaspoons vanilla
4 cups pecan or walnut halves

Mix sour cream and sugar in a medium-sized saucepan. Heat to 223° on candy thermometer. Stir constantly. Add vanilla and nuts. Stir until nuts are well coated. Pour onto an ungreased cookie sheet and spread out. When cool, break nuts apart.

Marcia Johnston (Mrs. Richard S.)
Linda Muldrow (Mrs. Lee)

These are wonderful for coffees, teas, Christmas gifts, etc.

ON THE LIGHT SIDE

It is beyond this book to tell you why you will choose a particular set of guests to be served a thinning meal.

LOW-CALORIE DIP FOR ARTICHOKES

Calories: 6 per Tablespoon   *Yield: 3 cups*

½ cup finely chopped cucumber
2 cups low-fat plain yogurt
1 teaspoon dill weed

½ teaspoon salt
½ teaspoon garlic powder
¼ teaspoon paprika

Mix all ingredients except paprika. Sprinkle mixture with paprika. Chill. Serve with hot or cold cooked artichokes.

DIET CURRY DIP

Calories: 50 per Tablespoon   *Yield: 1 cup*

1 cup imitation mayonnaise
1 teaspoon dry mustard
1 teaspoon tarragon vinegar

2 teaspoons finely chopped onion
1 teaspoon garlic salt
1 Tablespoon curry powder

Mix all ingredients and chill for at least 2 hours. Serve with fresh vegetables.
Sandy Ledbetter (Mrs. Joel Y., Jr.)

JUDY GOSS' RELISH DIP

Calories: 100 to 75 per serving   *Yield: 6 to 8 servings*

2 (4 ounce) cans chopped chilies,
    undrained
2 (4 ounce) cans chopped black
    olives, undrained
5 green onions (tops too), chopped
4 tomatoes, chopped

2 Tablespoons red wine vinegar
1 Tablespoon salad oil
Salt to taste
Pepper to taste
Garlic salt to taste

Combine all ingredients and marinate at least 1 hour in refrigerator. Serve as dip with chips.

Liz Powell (Mrs. David)

"Now learn what and how great benefits a temperate diet will bring along with it. In the first place you will enjoy good health."

HORACE
65-8 B.C.

BRUSSELS SPROUTS

Calories: 33 per serving   *Yield: 6 servings*

**2 (10 ounce) packages frozen
Brussels sprouts**

Large jar dill or sour pickle juice

Cook Brussels sprouts according to package directions. Drain. Pack the sprouts into a jar of pickle juice leftover from dill or sour pickles. Let marinate for 4 to 5 days. Serve cold as hors d'oeuvres.

Tiny round beets may be fixed the same way.

LOW-CALORIE VICHYSSOISE

Calories: 107 per serving   *Yield: 8 servings*

2 Tablespoons oil
**1 bunch leeks, white part only,
thinly sliced**
4 cups chicken broth
**2 large potatoes, peeled and thinly
sliced**

**2 cups low-fat cottage cheese or
Ricotta cheese**
1 cup skim milk
**Chopped chives or chopped onions
(for garnish)**

Heat oil in heavy 4 quart saucepan over medium-high heat. Add leeks and sauté until softened and clear, but do not brown. Stir in chicken broth and potatoes, reduce heat, cover and simmer until vegetables are tender (about 20 minutes). Remove from heat and allow to cool slightly. While soup is cooling, combine cheese and milk in blender and blend until smooth. Place cheese-milk mixture in a large mixing bowl. Gently stir in potato-broth mixture, 2 cups at a time, stirring constantly until smooth and well blended. Return mixture to another saucepan and heat thoroughly or cover and refrigerate to serve chilled. Garnish with chopped chives or chopped onion.

Ellon Cockrill (Mrs. Rogers)

LOW-CALORIE SALAD DRESSING

Calories: 33 per Tablespoon   *Yield: 1 cup*

¼ cup vinegar
¼ cup oil
½ cup chicken consommé or broth
1 teaspoon salt

¼ teaspoon paprika
⅛ teaspoon curry powder
⅛ teaspoon mustard powder
⅛ teaspoon garlic powder

Combine all ingredients. Shake well before using.

Mary Eskridge

Will keep for 4 to 6 weeks in the refrigerator.

FRESH ZUCCHINI SOUP

Calories: 56 to 37 per serving   *Yield: 4 to 6 servings*

1½ pounds (3 cups) zucchini
2 slices bacon, cooked and
   crumbled
1 small onion, chopped
⅔ cup condensed consommé
1⅓ cup water
½ teaspoon basil

1 small clove garlic
2 Tablespoons chopped parsley
½ teaspoon salt
⅛ teaspoon pepper
½ teaspoon seasoned salt
Parmesan cheese (23 calories per
   Tablespoon)

Wash zucchini and trim off stem and blossom ends. Cut zucchini into 1 inch chunks. Place in a 2 or 3 quart glass casserole with remaining ingredients, except cheese. Cover and cook in microwave oven for 15 minutes, or until zucchini is just tender. Stir every 5 minutes. Cool slightly. Blend mixture in blender, about 2 cups at a time, until smooth. Return to casserole and reheat to serving temperature in microwave, if necessary. May be heated in individual servings. Sprinkle Parmesan cheese over each serving.

Kim Eubanks (Mrs. Robert, III)

DILLED CUCUMBER SALAD

Calories: 14 per serving   *Yield: 8 servings*

2 cups diced cucumber
2 Tablespoons sliced radishes
½ cup plain low-fat yogurt

2 Tablespoons tarragon vinegar
¼ teaspoon ground cardamon
¼ teaspoon dill

Place cucumber and radishes in a bowl. In another bowl combine yogurt, vinegar, cardamon and dill. Mix well and pour over vegetables. Refrigerate at least 1 hour before serving.

DIET HOLLANDAISE SAUCE

Calories: 74 per Tablespoon   *Yield: 1½ cups*

3 egg yolks
2 Tablespoons lemon juice (fresh is
   best)
½ teaspoon cayenne pepper (more
   or less to taste)

1 (8 ounce) tub Diet Parkay
   margarine (MUST use Diet
   Parkay or sauce will not be
   thick)

In blender, combine egg yolks, lemon juice and cayenne pepper. Mix on high until blended. Melt Diet Parkay (in microwave if available) and add to other ingredients in blender. Blend for a few seconds until thick.

Cindy Miller (Mrs. Patrick)

Great served with hot or cold artichokes.

VEAL WITH PASTA SALAD

Calories: 260 per serving   *Yield: 4 servings*

**20 small, thin slices of cold roast
    veal**
4 small tomatoes, thinly sliced
16 raw asparagus tips

**1 cup green pasta shells or green
    noodles, cooked, drained and
    chilled**

Dressing
1 cup plain yogurt
½ cup Ricotta cheese
2 Tablespoons Parmesan cheese
**2 teaspoons fresh basil leaves or ⅓
    teaspoon dried basil**

**2 Tablespoons finely chopped
    celery leaves**
Salt to taste

Combine veal, tomatoes, asparagus and chilled pasta. Chill. Mix all dressing ingredients together. Salt to taste. Chill. To serve, divide salad into 4 bowls and top with dressing.

Beverly Moore (Mrs. Richard N., Jr.)

YOGURT DRESSING FOR FRUIT

Calories: 11 per Tablespoon   *Yield: 2½ cups*

1 cup low calorie cottage cheese
1 cup plain low-fat yogurt
2 Tablespoons honey

2 Tablespoons fresh lemon juice
**1 Tablespoon pineapple juice
    (Optional)**

Place all ingredients in blender container and blend until smooth. Serve over fruit platter or fruit salad.

Jan Johnson (Mrs. Kelley)

BAKED ASPARAGUS

Oven: 425°
Calories: 38 per serving   *Yield: 6 servings*

2 pounds fresh asparagus   **Salt**

Break off and discard the tough ends of the asparagus. Peel the stalks. Rinse the asparagus, drain it well, and wrap it in a large sheet of foil, crimping the edges tightly to seal the package. Bake in a preheated hot oven (425º) for 25 to 30 minutes or until done to taste. Season to taste with salt.

Ben Hussman (Mrs. Walter, Jr.)

ORANGE BROCCOLI

Calories: 80 per serving   *Yield: 6 servings*

**1 bunch broccoli (about 1½
    pounds), separated into spears**
Water
2 Tablespoons margarine

1 Tablespoon flour
1 Tablespoon grated orange peel
½ cup orange juice

Cook or steam broccoli until tender. Meanwhile, melt margarine, stir in flour and orange peel. Gradually stir in orange juice. Cook over medium heat until thickened. Serve over broccoli.

Kathy Moore

SESAME BROCCOLI

Calories: 80 per serving   *Yield: 5 servings*

1 Tablespoon sesame seeds, toasted
1 pound fresh broccoli
Salt
1 Tablespoon salad oil

1 Tablespoon vinegar
1 Tablespoon soy sauce
4 teaspoons sugar

Toast sesame seeds on a cookie sheet. Cook broccoli spears in salted boiling water until tender. Drain. In saucepan, combine salad oil, vinegar, soy sauce, sugar and sesame seeds. Heat to boiling. Pour over broccoli. Turn spears to coat.

Anne Winans (Mrs. T. Revillon)

CITRUS CARROTS

Calories: 80 to 64 per serving   *Yield: 8 to 10 servings*

2 pounds carrots, sliced
1 cup water
1 teaspoon salt

**1 teaspoon brown sugar flavored
    Sweet & Low**
2 Tablespoons margarine
Zest of 1 lemon and 1 orange

Bring water, salt and Sweet & Low to a boil. Add carrots. Cook, covered, until tender. Melt margarine and stir in fruit zest. Stir carrots and drain. Toss melted margarine and zest with carrots.

Helene Zukof (Mrs. Wally)
Louisville, Kentucky

EGGPLANT "CAVIAR"

Oven: 400°

Calories: 96 per serving

Yield: 4 servings

2 eggplants, about 1 pound each
¼ cup finely minced onion
¼ cup finely minced scallions
1 teaspoon finely minced garlic
¼ cup finely chopped green pepper
1 cup cored, peeled and diced tomatoes

¼ cup olive oil
1 teaspoon sugar or equivalent sugar substitute
1 Tablespoon lemon juice
Freshly ground black pepper to taste

Preheat oven to 400°. Place the eggplant on a sheet of heavy-duty aluminum foil and bake for 1 hour, or until eggplant "collapses." Let cool. Remove the pulp. (Should be about 3 cups.) Add the onion, scallions, garlic, green pepper, tomatoes, olive oil, sugar, lemon juice and pepper. May be served on toast or crackers.

Maureen Williams Bowen
Fort Smith, Arkansas

STUFFED SUMMER SQUASH

Oven: 350°

Calories: 75 per serving

Yield: 6 servings

14 small yellow summer squash
1 teaspoon diet margarine
3 Tablespoons chicken broth
½ cup finely chopped onion
1 cup finely chopped mushrooms

⅓ cup finely chopped fresh parsley
½ cup high-fiber bread crumbs
1 Tablespoon chopped pimiento
Pepper
Salt, if desired

Cook unpeeled squash until just barely tender. Drain and cool. Cut a lengthwise slice from top of squash and with a teaspoon dig out center being careful not to break the squash as they are delicate. Sauté onions in chicken broth, add mushrooms, parsley and margarine. Take 2 whole squash and chop pulp, seeds and all, to make 1 cup. Mix with bread crumbs, onions, parsley, mushrooms and fill cavities of squash. Arrange in pyrex dish and bake at 350° for 15 or 20 minutes.

Marjorie Thalheimer (Mrs. Bruce)

" 'How long does getting thin take?' Pooh asked anxiously."
A.A. MILNE
Winnie the Pooh
1882-1956

ZUCCHINI ROMA

Oven: 350°

Calories: 60 to 40 per serving   *Yield: 4 to 6 servings*

2 medium zucchini
½ medium onion, chopped
1 (16 ounce) can stewed tomatoes,
   undrained

½ teaspoon basil
½ teaspoon oregano
2 Tablespoons grated Parmesan
   cheese

Scrub zucchini and slice crosswise in thin slices. Combine onion and zucchini and cook in a small amount of salted water for 5 minutes or until tender crisp. Drain well. Add tomatoes, basil and oregano. Put in a 1½ quart casserole and sprinkle the top with Parmesan cheese. Bake at 350⁰ for 30 minutes.

Barbara H. Amsler (Mrs. Guy)

DIET COQUILLES ST. JACQUES

Oven: 450°

Calories: 340 per serving   *Yield: 4 servings*

1 pound small fresh scallops
2 cups dry white wine
1 Tablespoon dried onion flakes
1 teaspoon chopped parsley
2 Tablespoons diet margarine
3 Tablespoons cornstarch or
   arrowroot
1 egg yolk (may be omitted)

½ cup skim milk
1 (4 ounce) can mushroom pieces,
   drained
Salt
White pepper
Ground nutmeg
½ cup grated Gruyère or Monterey
   Jack cheese

Combine scallops, wine, onion flakes and parsley in a pan. Poach gently in the wine mixture for 5 minutes. Remove scallops with a slotted spoon to 4 baking shells making sure all juice is drained. Boil wine and reduce to 1 cup. Set aside. Melt margarine in non-stick skillet over low heat and slowly add cornstarch, then the wine to make a thick cream sauce. Then add milk with beaten egg yolk. Last of all, add the mushrooms. Cook slowly until thick. Add salt, pepper and nutmeg. Spoon over scallops and top with cheese. Bake at 450⁰ for 10 to 12 minutes or until bubbly.

Marjorie Thalheimer (Mrs. Bruce)

"Eat, drink and be merry, for tomorrow ye diet."
LEWIS C. HENRY

SOLE STUFFED WITH SHRIMP AND MUSHROOMS

Oven: 350°

Calories: 150 per serving *Yield: 4 servings*

½ cup finely chopped mushrooms
1 clove garlic, crushed
1 bunch green onions (white part only), chopped
¼ cup minced green pepper

12 cooked shrimp
1 Tablespoon parsley
½ teaspoon salt
⅛ teaspoon pepper
4 filets of sole to make 8 ounces

Put mushrooms, onion and garlic in pan with small amount of water. Cook until barely wilted. Add green pepper and cook until crispness disappears. Dice the shrimp and add to the pan together with the parsley, salt and pepper. Place about 2 Tablespoons of shrimp mixture on each filet, roll and place on cookie sheet, rolled side down. When all have been rolled, tuck any leftover stuffing in the ends of the rolls. Refrigerate at least 10 minutes. To cook, place rolled, stuffed filets in a non-stick baking pan, sprinkle with lemon juice and a dash of paprika. Cover with foil and bake at 350⁰ for 25 to 30 minutes or until barely flaky.

Louisa Barker
Tina Poe

MARGARET'S DIET BARBECUE CHICKEN

Oven: 350°

Calories: 328 per serving *Yield: 8 servings*

2 large fryers, split in half or cut up, skinned

1 medium onion, sliced

Sauce
¾ cup tomato juice
⅛ teaspoon cayenne pepper
1 teaspoon salt
⅛ teaspoon pepper
⅛ teaspoon dry mustard
2¼ teaspoons Worcestershire sauce

1 bay leaf
½ teaspoon sugar
¼ cup cider vinegar
¼ teaspoon garlic powder
1¼ Tablespoons margarine

Cut fryers in half and arrange in a single layer, meat side up, in a large roasting pan. Sprinkle with salt and pepper. Pour enough hot water to just cover the bottom of the roasting pan. Slice one medium onion over the fryers. Bake, covered, at 350⁰ for 30 minutes. While chicken is cooking, make a sauce using the remaining ingredients beginning with the tomato juice. Simmer sauce for 10 minutes. When fryers have baked 1 hour (30 minutes on each side), pour off all but ½ cup of liquid in bottom of pan. Turn fryers skin side up and pour barbecue sauce over all. Put fryers back in oven and bake another hour, covered. Baste frequently.

Patrick D. Miller

CHICKEN CACCIATORE

Calories: 139 per serving   *Yield: 4 servings*

¾ **cup fresh sliced mushrooms**
1 **(8 ounce) can tomatoes, cut up**
½ **cup sliced or coarsely chopped**
   green pepper
½ **cup chopped onion**
3 **Tablespoons dry red wine**
1 **clove garlic, minced**
½ **teaspoon dried oregano, crushed**

½ **teaspoon salt**
¼ **teaspoon pepper**
2 **whole chicken breasts, boned,**
   skinned, and halved lengthwise
Paprika
2 **teaspoons cornstarch**
2 **Tablespoons cold water**
Fresh mushroom crowns

In medium skillet, combine sliced mushrooms, tomatoes, green pepper, onion, wine, garlic, oregano, salt and pepper. Place chicken breasts on top. Sprinkle lightly with additional salt. Bring to a boil, then reduce heat. Cover and simmer for 25 minutes or until chicken is done. Remove chicken to warm platter. Sprinkle with paprika. Combine cornstarch and water. Stir into skillet mixture. Cook and stir until thickened and bubbly. Cook 1 minute more. Spoon sauce over chicken breasts. Garnish with fluted mushroom crowns.

Nancy Mitcham (Mrs. Robert)

Delicious served with rice pilaf.

CHINESE CHICKEN WITH VEGETABLES

Calories: 145 per serving   *Yield: 6 servings*
   82 per ½ cup rice
   124 per ½ cup noodles

2 **cups water**
2 **Tablespoons chicken flavored**
   instant bouillon
2 **Tablespoons cornstarch**
1 **Tablespoon soy sauce**
1 **Tablespoon sugar**
2 **cups cooked chicken (white meat),**
   skinned and chopped

1 **medium green pepper, thinly**
   sliced
1 **medium onion, thinly sliced**
1 **cup diagonally sliced celery**
½ **pound fresh mushrooms, thinly**
   sliced
½ **cup thinly sliced water chestnuts**
Cooked rice or chow mein noodles

In a large skillet, combine water, instant bouillon, cornstarch, soy sauce and sugar. Cook over medium heat until bouillon dissolves and sauce slightly thickens. Add chicken, green pepper, onion, celery, mushrooms and water chestnuts. Simmer, uncovered, until vegetables are tender. Serve over rice or chow mein noodles.

Kathy Moore

HERBAL CHICKEN

Oven: 350°

Calories: 405 per serving

Yield: 4 servings

4 chicken breast halves
Lemon juice
Parsley
½ cup oil
2 Tablespoons lemon juice
1 Tablespoon chopped parsley
1 Tablespoon chopped watercress
1 Tablespoon chopped green onion
1 teaspoon savory

1 teaspoon dill weed
1 teaspoon tarragon
1 teaspoon chervil
**Artificial sugar to equal ¼
   teaspoon**
1½ teaspoon salt
Freshly ground black pepper
2 hard-boiled eggs, chopped

Place each chicken breast on a layer of foil. Moisten with lemon juice and a sprig of parsley. Seal and bake at 350⁰ for 20 minutes or until done. Cool. Beat together oil and lemon juice. Stir in all herbs and seasonings. Fold in chopped eggs. Pour the sauce over the cold chicken.

Louisa Barker
Tina Poe

LOW-CAL CHICKEN

Oven: 350°

Calories 146 per serving

Yield: 4 servings

**2 chicken breasts, halved and
   skinned**
3 Tablespoons lemon juice
¼ teaspoon pepper
½ teaspoon poultry seasoning
2 teaspoons paprika

2 Tablespoons Worcestershire sauce
10 drops Tabasco
¼ cup water
4 artichoke hearts
Parmesan cheese
Paprika

Place chicken breasts, meat side up, in a 9 inch square pan. Mix these ingredients and pour over chicken: lemon juice, pepper, poultry seasoning, paprika, Worcestershire, Tabasco and water. Cut artichoke hearts in half and place 2 halves on each breast. Coat well with Parmesan cheese. Sprinkle a light coating of paprika on chicken. Bake at 350⁰ for 45 minutes to 1 hour, uncovered.

Julie Allen (Mrs. Wally)

Quick and easy to prepare.

CHICKEN ROSEMARY

Oven: 325° to 350°

Calories: 185 to 245 per serving

Yield: 8 servings

1 (3 to 4 pound) fryer
Rosemary to taste
½ small onion, quartered

Celery leaves
Salt to taste
Pepper to taste

In a large pan, place washed chicken. Sprinkle cavity and outside generously with dry rosemary, salt and pepper. Add onion and celery leaves to cavity. Bake at 325° to 350° for 1¾ hours until done.

Liz Burks (Mrs. Larry W.)

FRENCH CHICKEN "SCALLOPS"

Calories: 185 per serving

Yield: 4 servings

1 pound chicken breasts, boned and
** skinned**
2 Tablespoons sherry
2 Tablespoons margarine

Onion salt
Pepper
Paprika

Cut the chicken into 1 inch cubes. Arrange in a single layer in a shallow flameproof dish. Pour sherry over chicken. Dot with margarine. Sprinkle with seasonings. Broil for about 10 minutes, turning once. Baste with pan juices several times while broiling.
Variations:
Lemon broiled - Follow preceding recipe, substituting lemon juice for sherry. Sprinkle with oregano. (178 calories)
Scallops and Mushrooms - same as above. Add 1 cup small mushroom caps with the chicken. (185 calories)
Potatoes and Scallops - Add one can of new potatoes, sliced or whole. Allow to brown slightly. (207 calories)
You may also add artichoke hearts. (189 calories)

Julie Truemper (Mrs. John J., Jr.)

AVGOLEMONO SAUCE

Calories: 9 per Tablespoon

Yield: 2 cups

3 eggs
¼ cup lemon juice

1 cup warm chicken stock or
** bouillon**

Beat eggs in top of a double boiler. Gradually blend in juice and stock. Cook over hot water until thickened. Beat until foamy. Serve hot over vegetables.

TIPSY CHICKEN

Calories: 162 per serving   *Yield: 6 servings*

1 (2½ to 3 pound) fryer, cut up
Salt
Pepper

Cream sherry, bourbon, soy sauce,
or Worcestershire sauce, or any
combination of the above

Place chicken in a large pot or Dutch oven. Salt and pepper the chicken, then add liquid ingredients. Total liquid should not amount to more than ½ cup. Cover, cook over high heat until liquid is boiling. Then cook *slowly* for at least 1 hour, preferably 2 hours. Serve over rice - it makes its own gravy.

Ted Glusman

Frozen chicken may be used.

HAMBURGER SKILLET NAPOLI

Calories: 220 per serving   *Yield: 4 servings*

1 pound ground round
2 cups tomato juice
2 Tablespoons dry red wine
1 large onion, chopped
2 to 3 zucchini, thinly sliced
1 teaspoon oregano

½ teaspoon fennel seed
Garlic salt
Freshly ground pepper
2 Tablespoons grated Parmesan
   cheese

Brown meat in a non-stick skillet. Drain off any fat. Add remaining ingredients, except cheese. Cover and cook for 5 minutes. Uncover and cook until all liquid has evaporated leaving a thick tomato sauce. Sprinkle with cheese.

Julie Truemper (Mrs. John J., Jr.)

LONDON BROIL

Calories: 220 per serving   *Yield: 6 servings*

1½ pounds top-quality beef flank
   steak
¾ cup low calorie Italian salad
   dressing

2 Tablespoons soy sauce
⅛ teaspoon onion juice
⅛ teaspoon lemon pepper
Salt

Score steak on both sides. Place in a shallow pan. Blend salad dressing, soy sauce, onion juice and lemon pepper. Pour over steak. Cover. Let stand at room temperature for 2 to 3 hours; turn several times. Place steak on rack of broiler pan. Broil 3 inches from heat for 5 minutes. Season with salt. Carve broiled steak in very thin slices diagonally across grain.

Anne Winans (Mrs. T. Revillon)

MEAT LOAF

Calories: 120 per serving

Oven: 350°
Yield: 4 (4 ounce) servings

1 pound lean ground beef

2 slices white bread, crumbs

Place in blender

4 ounces onion, finely chopped
2 Tablespoons chopped parsley
1 teaspoon seasoned salt
½ teaspoon oregano
2 Tablespoons ketchup

1 Tablespoon Worcestershire sauce
1 Tablespoon brown sugar
** replacement**
1 to 2 Tablespoons water (use as
** needed for desired consistency)**

Combine all ingredients. Place in baking dish in meat loaf form. Bake, uncovered, at 350° for 45 minutes to 1 hour. For variation, an indentation may be made down the middle of the loaf and ketchup poured into it. Cover with cornflake crumbs prior to baking.

Kay Anderson

LOW-CALORIE SPAGHETTI AND MEAT BALLS

(Microwave)

Calories: Approximately 290 per serving

Yield: 5 servings

Tomato sauce

¼ cup chopped onion
1 (16 ounce) can whole tomatoes,
** undrained**
2 teaspoons instant chicken bouillon

½ cup canned mushrooms, drained
¼ teaspoon oregano
Salt
Pepper

Meat Balls

1 pound lean ground beef
¼ cup chopped onion
1 clove garlic, chopped
½ cup soft whole wheat bread
** crumbs**

2 Tablespoons chopped parsley
½ teaspoon salt
½ teaspoon pepper
1 (16 ounce) package spaghetti,
** cooked**

Place onion in 1½ quart casserole. Cover with plastic wrap or glass lid. Cook in microwave oven, covered, on FULL POWER for 2 to 3 minutes, or until onion is tender. Add remaining ingredients. Season with salt and pepper, as desired. Set aside. Combine all ingredients for meat balls. Make meat balls about 1 inch in diameter. Place in a 1½ quart casserole dish. Cover with plastic wrap. Cook in microwave, covered, on FULL POWER for 5 to 6 minutes, or until meat is not longer pink. Turn meat balls over halfway through cooking time. Drain. Pour tomato sauce over meat balls. Cook, covered, on FULL POWER, for 4 to 5 minutes, or until heated through. Serve over cooked spaghetti.

Gloria Allen (Mrs. Charles A.)

FRESH FRUIT AND YOGURT DELIGHT

Fresh Fruit (blueberries, peaches, strawberries, raspberries)

Yogurt (low-fat, plain)
Diet Sugar Twin brown sugar

Put fruit in bottom of large round wine glass or compote. Spoon low-fat yogurt over fruit. Sprinkle brown sugar over the top.

Melinda Morse

EGGLESS SPICE CAKE

Oven: 350°

Calories: 309 per serving　　　　　　　　　　　*Yield: 18 servings*

1½ sticks butter
1½ cups sugar
3 cups sifted cake flour
1 teaspoon cinnamon
1 teaspoon allspice
1 teaspoon cloves

1½ cups buttermilk, at room temperature
1½ teaspoons baking soda
1½ cups chopped pecans
1½ cups raisins

Grease a 9 x 13 pan or 3 (8 inch) pans. Preheat oven to 350⁰. Cream butter and sugar together. Sift flour with spices. Add soda and dissolve in buttermilk. (Do not do this too early as the buttermilk expands.) Alternately add the buttermilk mixture and flour mixture to creamed butter, mixing well as you go. Add pecans and raisins. Bake at 350⁰ for 25 minutes. Serve with Penuche Frosting.

Kenan Keyes (Mrs. Griff)

PENUCHE FROSTING

Calories: 130 per serving　　　　　　　　*Yield: Frosting for 1 cake*

1 cup brown sugar
¼ cup milk
3 Tablespoons shortening
1 Tablespoon butter

¼ teaspoon salt
1½ cups powdered sugar, sifted
1 teaspoon vanilla

Combine brown sugar, milk, shortening, butter and salt in saucepan and cook for 3 minutes. Cool mixture and add powdered sugar and vanilla. Frost cake immediately.

Kenan Keyes (Mrs. Griff)

INDEX

The Junior League of Little Rock, Incorporated
P.O. Box 7453
Little Rock, Arkansas 72217
(501) 666-0658 • FAX (501) 666-0589

Order Information

Individual Cookbooks

_____ copies of *Apron Strings* @ $24.95 each $ _____

_____ copies of *Traditions* @ $18.95 each $ _____

_____ copies of *Little Rock Cooks* @ $18.95 each $ _____

Case Orders (*Case contains six books. Shipping included in case price.*)

_____ cases of *Apron Strings* @ $130 each $ _____

_____ cases of *Traditions* @ $99 each $ _____

_____ cases of *Little Rock Cooks* @ $99 each $ _____

Subtotal Books $ _____

Shipping/Gift Wrap

Shipping ($4 – first book, $2 – each additional book) $ _____

Gift wrap charge ($1 per book) $ _____

Subtotal Shipping/Gift Wrap $ _____

Order Total $ _____

Payment Information

[   ] I have enclosed a check payable to *Junior League of Little Rock Publications,* or

[   ] Please charge my: [   ] VISA   [   ] MasterCard   [   ] American Express

_____

Account Number   Exp. Date

_____

Name on Card (Please print)

_____

Signature

Customer Information

_____

Name

_____

Street Address

_____

City   State   Zip Code

(   )
_____

Telephone   e-mail

Photocopies accepted.